D0908719

Development Administration

Development Administration

Concepts, Goals, Methods

George F. Gant

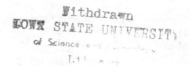
THE UNIVERSITY OF WISCONSIN PRESS

Published 1979

The University of Wisconsin Press
114 North Murray Street
Madison, Wisconsin 53715

The University of Wisconsin Press, Ltd.
1 Gower Street
London WC1E 6HA, England

First printing

Printed in the United States of America

For LC CIP information see the colophon

ISBN 0-299-07980-5

Publication of this book has been made possible in part
by a grant from the Center for Development, University of Wisconsin–Madison

To Jeannette C. Gant

Contents

Preface

This book is a product of my experience and observation in the Tennessee Valley Authority, the Ford Foundation, and the University of Wisconsin. In TVA, from 1935 to 1951, I served in a number of capacities including Chief of Training and Education, Director of Personnel and Assistant General Manager for Management, and General Manager. The TVA was concerned with the integrated development of the Tennessee Valley in cooperation with the people of the valley. During this period I developed the concept of, and coined the term, "external administration" to indicate the processes involved in forging cooperative relationships with other agencies and groups when such relationships are needed in the achievement of common goals.

At the Ford Foundation, from 1955 to 1971, I was successively Representative in Pakistan, Director of the Asia Program, and Special Representative in Southeast Asia. The Foundation's purpose was to cooperate with developing countries as they strengthened their institutional and personnel capabilities in development planning, public administration, education, agricultural production, rural development, and population policy. Egbert de Vries, a prominent Dutch economist, and I learned in discussions with each other that each of us had started to use the term "development administration" in 1955 or 1956. I used it to conceptualize the nature of the administrative research and training program contemplated for the Academy of Rural Development established subsequently at Comilla in East Pakistan (now Bangladesh) and for the academy at Peshawar in West Pakistan, to which the Ford Foundation, which I represented in Pakistan at that time, gave assistance.

At the University of Wisconsin–Madison since 1971, as Visiting Professor of Political Science, I have been absorbed with the university's Center for Development, whose program for civil servants on leave from their planning and other government posts in Asia, Africa, and Latin America involves the deepening of our understanding of development planning and administration. During this period I visited both East and West Africa as well as the Middle East to review trends in administration for development. I thank Edwin Young and William Young for their encouragement and the University of Wisconsin for the time it gave me to write this book.

Development administration is a large subject. In this book I have written about its concepts, its expression in organization and in management systems, its applications in selected sectors, and its involvement in international relations. The book does not, however, include more than passing reference to other important factors in development administration such as taxation and financial policy and administration, industrial production, trade and investment, transfer of technology, and labor organization. Such omissions are due partly to limits of space and partly to the limits of my own experience and observation.

I have written *Development Administration* to share my views of that difficult subject in various of its expressions with students and fellow teachers, with the planners and administrators of development in developing countries, and with those who give and those who receive assistance for development.

George F. Gant

Madison, Wisconsin
January 1979

Development Administration

1

The Concept of
Development Administration

The Demands of Independence upon Public Administration

The term "development administration" came into use in the 1950s to represent those aspects of public administration and those changes in public administration which are needed to carry out policies, projects, and programs to improve social and economic conditions. During a period of fifteen years following the end of World War II, in 1945, colony after colony threw off the imperial yoke. Country after country achieved independence and political autonomy. This new status gave promise of freedom and liberty and self-determination in political systems of representative democracy. It gave hope of greater individual freedom and equality of treatment in the society. And independence created hopes of higher national and per capita income, a rapid rise in standards of living, and an increase in individual opportunity. Even in countries which had not been colonies but had been administered by some other form of authoritarian government, this was a generation of rising and insistent expectations pressing for rapid political, social, and economic change. New governments and their bureaucracies, their administrative agencies and processes, were expected to give reality to these anticipated fruits of independence and liberty. These new functions, these demands upon the administration system, were not only enormous in size and weight, they were novel and complex in character.

An urgent and perhaps the first task of a new country was to establish its identity as a unified and integrated nation-state and to create a new system for deciding policy and for making decisions. This political development involved building a valid and recognized hegemony internally and achieving recognition externally by establishing effective communications and relationships with other countries and the international community. The task of building a national polity required the accommodation of diverse and even disparate social, tribal, and ethnic groups in the population. A foreign policy to achieve international recognition and amity involved the creation of a foreign service. At the same time, numerous and demanding specific needs had to be met by each new country at independence and by its new, inexperienced government and ill-equipped bureaucracy. Taxes had to be assessed and arrangements made for their collection. Courts and the continuity of justice had to be assured.

Perhaps even more important and more difficult than establishing its identity was the task of a new country to devise a system to translate the aspirations and demands of its population into viable policies and programs, a responsive process for making decisions on major matters. Most new countries have set up, or tried to set up, some system of representative democracy, with its accompanying institutions and processes including legislatures and assemblies, elected executives, political parties, the conduct of elections, and the control of the public bureaucracy. Perhaps there was no higher priority among the aspirations and expectations of the peoples of new and recently liberalized countries than an effective process of self-determination and self-government. Such new concepts and methods of decision-making are a governmental perplexity; in their execution they represent a new and pressing demand on the administrative system.

Another immediate though less tangible demand upon the governments of new countries, and recently democratized ones, is the correction of inequalities and injustices in the society. Such inequities are sometimes found in caste systems such as those in India, which subjugate certain members and limit their freedom of choice and opportunity. Other inequities are illustrated by land tenure systems such as those in Pakistan and the Philippines, by which a small and favored segment of the population is assured of prosperity at the expense of the opportunities of other, larger segments. An even more aggravated problem of justice and comparative equality of treatment is sometimes found in the status and relationships of different racial groups, as in Malaysia. The status of women is often a major and pressing issue. The pressures upon government to solve these problems are usually very heavy. The solutions are usually not readily apparent, however, and in terms of administration the application of solutions is often the most difficult and burdensome aspect of the situation.

High in the expectations of the peoples of newly independent countries, if not first in the priorities of self-determination, is the increase in their standards of living and the widening of their individual opportunities for personal expression and advancement. The additional burdens upon government and its administrative apparatus to bring about this social and economic development are enormous. The components of development—natural resources, capital, technology, and manpower—must be brought into focus for the purpose. The government must provide an environment of safety and stability which at least permits and even encourages development. To put all of these elements together in a productive process which provides benefits equitably and rapidly enough to be acceptable is an enormous and a complex burden on any system of administration. It is a burden which was of unaccustomed and difficult dimensions and characteristics.

These problems of economic policy and development with which governments and their bureaucracies must cope are even more staggering when considered in their specificity. Many new countries, such as Korea, have natural resources which are inadequate in quantity or quality or accessibility to yield satisfying products even with advanced technology. Or the technology is not available, or the capital. In countries like Pakistan and Ethiopia the resources are, or were, controlled by a few powerful families. Professional and skilled manpower does not exist in sufficient number, nor do the institutions to produce it. Savings in significant amounts have not been accumulated for capital investment. The orientation of colonial economies to the production of raw materials and their export was not usually the best basis or starting point for the most promising economic growth of the new country. The shift of the focus of economic systems and the institutions which support and depend upon them from the imperial orbit to the national interest is slow and hard, even when the targets and methods become known.

Another factor in the economic condition of a recently freed colony, and also in a recently democratized country, is the weakness of the private sector. If private enterprise were strong in a new country, with a generous endowment of entrepreneurship and adequate funds for investment, the administrative burdens on the government would be less severe and not so urgent. In most countries, however, such private enterprise as existed was oriented toward and had vested interests in the older extractive economy and was not necessarily interested in new economic ventures. Such enterprise, also, was usually foreign owned and controlled. Under such circumstances it is inevitably incumbent upon a new country which wishes to accomplish the aspirations of its people to give governmental attention and support to economic development.

Even when a private enterprise sector of respectable proportions is active or capable of becoming active in the economic life of a country, there may be reasons why a government feels obliged to intrude its administrative presence. One such reason is to assure that the nation's resources are developed in the interest of the people as a whole and not only of a select group. Another is to assure that an underprivileged region of the country or class in the population has a fair opportunity to share in the country's growing economic prosperity. Or it might be desirable for the government to undertake an economic enterprise in a field neglected by the private sector though necessary to the growth of the economy as a whole. One or more of these considerations has led many countries to extend their administrative apparatus to economic endeavors of a number of kinds. Governments and their administrative agencies become involved in economic development by encouraging and controlling the private sector, or by engaging in business directly or through new public enterprises, or both. Under any of these alternatives, however, new and enlarged and more complex administrative agencies, systems, and processes are required. The functions of public administration are increased by these undertakings and the demands of development upon the administrative apparatus are enlarged.

Administration in newly independent countries was sadly wanting in its capacity to meet these demands of independence. Bureaucracies, faced with new, staggering, and unfamiliar tasks they were not set up to perform, were further weakened by the overly rapid replacement of experienced expatriate personnel with inexperienced recruits and by inexperienced and often inept leadership. In almost every such country the immediate consequence of independence was the lessening of administrative efficiency and bureaucratic effectiveness. Administration for development was required to evolve from that point.

The Meaning of Development

The words "developed," "undeveloped," "underdeveloped," and "less developed" are often used to denote the social and economic condition of the people in a given country or region. The concept of development is elusive; it is perceived not only as a condition of life but also as a goal to be attained, and as the capacity to grow and change and develop. These three ideas of development are bound together in efforts to understand and deal with the phenomenon of development. The evidences of the condition of underdevelopment are frequently given in terms of poverty. The starkest evidence of underdeveloped populations is found and expressed in terms of hunger and starvation, the scantiest of housing, the barest of clothing, and the poorest of health. According to the World Bank, "About 40 percent of the population of developing countries, 800 million people, are still living in absolute poverty."* They are hungry and are not sheltered adequately from hostile weather. They suffer ill health and those who survive childhood die early. These people are illiterate, insecure, and experience only unhappy leisure. Words such as "destitution," "privation," "want," and even "suffering" are used to describe their condition, certainly a condition of underdevelopment.

The comparative size of the national per capita income is frequently used to distinguish the developed from the underdeveloped countries. Low per capita income conceals even greater poverty in regions or classes because of an unequal distribution of the national product. The eradication of this poverty—that is, the achievement of a sustenance level of survival—is the first target of development. Increases in incomes as shown in per capita income statistics can be used thereafter as an evidence of progress and of relative well being, at least in gross terms, in comparison with other countries. Such data also help to identify the relatively underdeveloped and relatively developed countries.

It is not possible, however, to state when the essential needs of a poverty-stricken people have been met nor when their basic wants have been satisfied. Definitions of "essential" and "basic" are fluid; they change, and the measures of minimum standards of sustenance fluctuate as knowledge of adequacy grows and as feasibilities and expectations expand. Scientific findings reveal new nutritional requirements for good health, productive lives, and longevity, so that what was previously considered adequate diet is no longer believed to be sufficient. As sanitary toilets, clean water, screens, electricity, and other contributions to better housing become more available and more desired, to that extent they come to be expected and included within the categories of "essential needs" and "basic wants." Development, then, is not an absolute condition. There is not a fixed point at which a people, region, or country passes from a state of undevelopment to a state of development. The relative condition of development, rather, is comparative and ever changing—it fluctuates according to what is needed, what is possible, and what is desired. Development is relative also in terms of the possible; it fluctuates according to what is feasible at any particular time. A country which utilizes its resources effectively is considered to be more developed than a country which does not. This utilization potential increases with the growth and application of scientific knowledge and technology.

* World Bank, *World Development Report, 1978* (New York: Oxford University Press, 1978), p. 7.

A country which is not satisfying the expectations of its population is to that extent not developed; the goal of development has not been reached. Development is relative to the aspirations of the people—how the aspirations are defined and how firmly they are expressed. These expectations increase as the information about feasibilities becomes known. Because development is comparative in terms of scientific knowledge, feasibilities, and desires, it is also comparative in terms of time because what is known, possible, and desired all change as time goes on. People's desires and expectations are heavily influenced by comparisons of their own conditions with conditions in other regions, or countries or classes. There are examples of economically depressed regions in countries whose populations, aware of their less affluent condition, press for ameliorative development programs—such as the Appalachian region of the United States or the northeastern region of Thailand. There are examples of depressed racial or caste populations in countries whose members demand special measures of relief, such as the rural Malay population in Malaysia or the untouchables of India. Most such comparisons, however, are made between countries. The categorization of nations into developed and underdeveloped countries in accordance with per capita incomes of five hundred dollars more or less, or other arbitrary measures, is useful for purposes of analysis and treatment, perhaps, but it does not describe a state of "development" beyond which no improvement of the human condition can be achieved or will be sought.

To define development as the goal of a people or a country is thus as elusive as to define it as a condition, and for many of the same reasons of feasibility and aspiration. There are two levels at which development as an objective can be considered. The first is the eradication of poverty. Destitution need no longer be the fate of most human beings. The world's knowledge and processes for development, if applied, should make it possible to meet essential needs and satisfy basic wants, even under changing conditions and ever higher standards of what the minimum requirements are. Even though droughts still bring crop failures and starvation, and even though swollen populations make the task greater, the job can be done. Certainly the first and highest goal of any legitimate development program is to accomplish this purpose—the elimination of poverty.

The potentials of development are not limited by the world's resources or by man's ingenuity to the elimination of poverty. Nor has man proved to be satisfied with a subsistence level of existence. It is not enough, therefore, to fix the target of development at this level, though it might be the first priority in many situations. Nor is it sufficient to state the purpose of development merely in terms of physical standards, or even income, because these increase with new opportunities and desires and hence are not static, to be achieved for once and for all. Certainly a concern of development is the quality of life beyond mere sustenance as assured by respect for the rights of human dignity and liberty. This is the second, higher purpose of development.

One way of stating the purpose of development at the higher level is that it is to increase progressively the choices, the opportunities, that individuals have in planning and leading their lives according to their personal ideas of happiness and fulfillment. This purpose extends to all of the individuals in a population or a country, and not merely to some of them. Such choices depend upon the freedom of people to move about, their mobility, and upon their voice in the social, political, and economic decisions which affect them. It is assumed that if they are given the choice and the opportunity, human beings are likely to make their optimum contribution to society and to express their individual geniuses most readily. The purpose of development is to advance that happy condition.

The capacity for development is the third conceptualization of development, along with development as a condition and development as a goal. This capacity, in the private and the public sector, consists of the methods and systems and activities by which development policies, projects, and programs are carried out to accomplish the specific goals of development, goals which are articulated for a particular period of time and place. The capacity for development involves the organizations and agencies and institutions, both private and public, to sustain and support the several processes of development. The capacity for development also includes the will of the people, and their preparedness as individuals— through or in spite of their social institutions—to engage in risk-taking and other adventures which promise change for the better while threatening change for the worse. Development, then, and the promise thereof, can be measured in terms of the comparative excellence of the relevant processes—that is, the delivery systems—and the capacity that exists in the social, economic, and political institutions. Processes and capacity which are effective and responsive should take people where they choose to go. The people of a country are the center of the development interest.

The Role of People in Development

Development can be considered as the interaction of people with the natural resources available to them—that is, people's utlization of their resources. The involvement of people in this interaction has many interrelated and seemingly contradictory aspects, all of which must be taken into account and accommodated in a fully effective process of development. It is instructive to examine the several roles of people in the development process.

First of all, people are the target of the development process; their well-being is the purpose of development. Political units such as nations and states may also gain strength from systematic development, and it is desirable that they do so, but such strength is legitimately used to improve the welfare of the population as a whole, rather than to aggrandize some elite portion of the population, whether military, political, religious, or caste—or the state itself. It has been argued by some that a strong state is necessary to and will assure a happier and more prosperous population. This is true if the state is considered to be an instrument of that felicitous process and not its goal. In the latter case portions of the population will benefit at the cost of other portions, or the population as a whole will suffer lesser benefits from development than otherwise possible in terms of food or housing or social security, for example, because of the diversions of resources to the military or outer space or other excursions considered by the state to be important if not necessary to its own status.

At the same time that people are the target of development they are the instruments of development. In this respect people are a human resource and, from that point of view, in a category not unlike other resources such as soil and water. It is not particularly appealing to be thought of as a resource, to be managed and used, but the concept is useful as an aid to understanding the development process. Techniques and programs of manpower analysis and planning are based on this concept of people as resources, resources necessary in relevant numbers and skills to an effective program of development. These human resources are physical labor and they are also technical and professional skills of a variety of kinds and levels. Considered in this perspective, people are labor in the classical categorization of "labor and capital" as the prime factors in economic development. Their number and skills are of significance, in this context, only in terms of what is required for the optimum utilization of physical resources and efficient and effective planning and implementation of development policies and programs.

Fortunately or unfortunately, the number of people required as human resources to serve the development programs of a country is seldom the same as the population. The people are usually too few or too many—usually too many. They are too old or too young and possibly living in the wrong places to be efficient human resources. Therefore, while legitimate targets and beneficiaries of the development program and instruments of its conduct, populations are often a problem and a burden. Populations must therefore be dealt with, planned for, not only as people to benefit from development and as human resources to contribute to development but as a major complication both in fixing development targets and development methods. Populations, human resources, unhappily from this point of view, do not lie dormant like coal, not eating or talking. Their demands are vocal and insistent.

Hence, like manpower planning for human resources, there is population planning for the consuming and articulate public. Many countries are striving to find the biologically and philosophically correct population policy—without too much success. India clearly has too many people to feed and encourages family planning and birth control. Israel wants a larger Jewish population and encourages both immigration and larger families. Other countries, with less dramatically extreme population situations, are less clear on the appropriate course. The questions are practical—can the population be fed, can families give satisfactory upbringing to numerous children? And the questions are philosophical—is it necessary, or even desirable, that every adult have gainful employment? If every adult must work and development needs and opportunities do not require so much in human resources, how long should he work and at what? Should all adult members of the family be required to work? Only some? And if adults do not work, or cannot work, will the economy support them? How? Very few, if any, nations have resolved these and many other questions about their populations, considered from this point of view. Studies and policies on employment and public works and welfare and social security are in this area, and clearly related, but they do not encompass population policy as a whole.

People, then, are to be considered as populations to be supported, human resources to be utilized, and the public to be cherished as the beneficiaries of the development process. There are additional roles which people play, not the least of which is that of manager-entrepreneur in development agencies and undertakings. It is not enough to have the ingredients for development. Those ingredients have to be related to one another and made productive in a myriad of ways at local, national, and intermediate levels and in public, semi-public, and private sectors. It is the function of this manager-entrepreneur class to see and act upon the development opportunities in any particular environment or framework.

It is not enough for development and change to be merely possible. Development must also be attractive, powerfully attractive, to the participants and desired by them. The availability of resources and even of the knowledge and technology to utilize those resources will not assure their utilization if the people do not choose to change their ways. Even a literate population, and a healthy one, will not, merely because of its literacy and health, undertake development activities. It is true that resources and technology and literacy and health are also factors in development, but in themselves they are not sufficient. Development must also be attractive if people are to be motivated to make the changes in their lives, often drastic, to bring it about.

A major, perhaps the major, motivation to engagement in development activity is improved material well-being. More money and goods are, of course, interpreted in terms of better standards of living and wider opportunities of choice in work and leisure for present and especially future generations. If interest in material well-being or at least the improvement of material well-being is lacking, interest in development will also be lacking. The first requisite is that the concerned people know what the alternative feasibilities and choices for change and development may be. As long as they remain ignorant of the possibilities they cannot judge the desirabilities.

To the extent to which the benefits of growth are not shared with the people or are shared unevenly and unjustly by the population, to that extent does the environment discourage investment and participation in the process. Injustice, in this perspective, can take several different forms. One form of perceived social injustice which is not only theoretical but also real occurs when the state, the government, insists that the earnings of increased growth be reinvested in development so fully and for so many years that the population not only does not enjoy current fruits but cannot foresee future benefits. There is a real dilemma here, because so much of a country's current earnings and even capital could be distributed for consumption or social welfare that the whole development process would grind to a halt and become stagnant. Difficult judgments must be made, and accepted by the participating public, on the optimum balance between consumption and investment with consideration for both present enjoyment and future development. Some countries such as Singapore have found that investments in higher wage rates and pension systems and investments in education facilities commensurate with increased productivity are ways of sharing the benefits of development with the people while contributing further to the development process.

These are chiefly matters of choice which developing countries and their populations face all of the time. There are starker kinds of situations involving the comparative attractiveness of development to the people as a whole. One such situation is that characterized by economic domination by a small group or number of families to such an extent that the profits and benefits of development accrue to them rather than to the people, though the people may be providing much of the labor and professional and even managerial skill. Such vested and controlling interests might even oppose and resist and prevent change if it threatens their position. It is unlikely, however, as demonstrated even in China, that people will be attracted to new and risky economic activities and will work harder if they do not share in the profits sufficiently to be so motivated. This problem is illustrated by slow progress in extending multiple cropping systems under which the farmers grow two or three crops where one grew before, but when the landlords and not the farmers reap the rewards. The problem is illustrated more classically by land tenure systems which seem to limit the farm worker to a low level of sustenance, even when improved technology permits much higher yields and returns. The development process fails unless the people are motivated by shares in the fruits.

In almost all countries the target of development is the people. The purpose of development is to improve their lot, first by assuring a level of sustenance acceptable to them and second by increasing the choices they have for living their own lives up to their optimum expression. Only the people can decide as individuals and communities what standards of living and choices in life are acceptable. The people, one way or another, must be involved in setting the goals of any development program for any particular place and for any particular time. Beyond the general goals of development, this participation should extend for its effectiveness to the policies and the methods of development, to the several projects and perhaps above all to the timing. Many of the issues of present well-being and pleasure versus future security and benefits arise over questions of the speed and sequence with which development projects and programs are undertaken. The decisions depend upon the choice of the people.

The Role of Institutions

Institutions are the forms in which people organize their affairs in relationship with each other. An institution is a system of action. Systems of action comprehend the structures and mechanisms which provide the capacity and support for action in the form of agencies or organizations. Bureaus or departments are institutions of this kind, as are schools, prisons, hospitals, and banks. Systems of action also comprehend processes and delivery instruments by which specified tasks are executed or by which categories of functions are supported or controlled. Accounting and budgeting systems are institutions in this sense, as are arrangements to deliver credit to entrepreneurs and fertilizer or seed or water to farmers. Accepted patterns of economic and social behavior are also embraced by the term "institution."

An institution as a system of action possesses certain indispensable qualities. First of all the institution, the system, must have the capability to produce or deliver the product or perform the function for which it was created; the institution must be effective in accomplishing its purpose. Second, the institution, whether as agency or process or convention, must be accepted in the society and environment of its location. The institution must represent the way in which people, as individuals and in groups, wish to be served and to work with or relate to one another. The institution must therefore have value and meaning for those people if it is to serve in a fully effective and productive way. And in the third place the institution must be able to survive because it is adequately supported with the necessary financial, personnel, and political capacity and because it has the capability to adapt itself and its program to changing and evolving conditions and situations, including the ability to learn from its own experience and to correct its mistakes. If the institution is lacking with respect to any one of these three qualities of capability, public acceptance, and survival capacity, it fails as an institution.

Institutionalization thus is the process by which systems of action acquire capability and competence, public acceptance, operating resources and the stability of a standard way of doing things. The term should also embody the concept of expendability if and as relevance and competence and acceptability decline. Unfortunately the term "institutional behavior" has come to mean tenacity in the adherence to routinized ways of doing things which, although perhaps good ways when introduced, become outmoded. This tenacity may result from the creation of vested interests in the institution itself, or in some of its processes, or in the establishment of vested interests in minority portions of the clientele public served by the institution. The tendency to rigid adherence to the policies and procedures initially adopted to serve competence and achieve stability thus threatens to produce a condition of routinization and even ossification and stultification of the institution's operation. The problem is to find ways to establish effective institutions which are responsive and to keep them viable in terms both of function and of public purpose and acceptability.

Institutions are created and grow in a number of ways. Most institutions, and especially the traditional ones, are born out of custom or habit and evolve slowly and gradually. Revolution can bring about the need for new institutions, or make it possible to establish the kinds of institutions desired by the revolutionaries, but revolutions do not in themselves create institutions. Institutions can be established or changed by a central authority. Reform movements are an important and continuing influence in institution building and in the institutionalization process, an influence which seeks to correct those aspects of the institutionalization process which tend to ossification, or regimentation, or abuse by agency officeholders.

Still another way in which institutions are created or renovated is by plan, by a calculated program to produce agency capability and the capacity and effectiveness of relevant systems to implement designated parts of a development program. This method of creating new agencies and systems or of modernizing old ones has come to be known as "institution building." The logic of including institution building in a country's system of development planning and implementation is clear, considering the importance of planning and arranging for the ways of accomplishing the purposes and projects of the plan, as well as merely specifying its targets and activities. Fortunately, although tardily, planning agencies are giving increasing attention to the institution-building aspects of their responsibility. Their attention, to be most effective, requires knowledge of the nature of institutions—that is, their components, the environment needed to support and sustain them, and the processes involved in producing them.

Certain of the component parts of an institution are obvious and readily apparent. To take as illustration an institution in the form of an agency, it must have a capital plant fully adequate to the effective performance of its assigned functions. Such plant would include buildings and sometimes special facilities such as laboratories, libraries, a computer center—and even on occasion staff housing and cafeteria and other service facilities. The physical plant should be located in the place or places most appropriate to its work and it should be designed to meet the unique requirements and characteristics of the agency to be accommodated.

The competent agency must be well staffed with adequately trained personnel. The assurance of such staff depends of course upon the quality of personnel administration, including the adequacy of supporting educational agencies, provisions for compensation and security, and consideration for status and public esteem. The staff of the new institution must have the specialized qualifications to perform the work of the organization competently and with understanding and enthusiasm. It is unlikely that such staff is readily available in sufficient numbers in many developing countries to undertake novel and unfamiliar programs of social and economic and technological development. At the same time the institution is often expected and even required to go into operation before it has time to arrange for the technical and professional training of staff. Under such circumstances a less than fully qualified and committed staff is obliged to begin operations in a traditional way and tends to establish job rights in the patterns of an older system.

When men and women trained abroad return—and usually they are young people with little seniority in the older system—they have great difficulty in practicing their newly acquired skills in the older system which persists. Many give up and quit under such circumstances. The remedy, short of correcting outmoded personnel systems which do not adapt readily to the requirements of merit and specialized qualification, and short of postponing the operational aspects of new institutional programs until fully trained staff is available, is to train enough able persons, large numbers of them, so that when employed they can have the weight and influence of mass on program and management decisions. The availability and full utilization of highly trained and motivated staff is the crucial factor of success in a new institution and the first point of concern in the institution-building process.

Of prime importance to the institution is the quality of the administrative leadership and direction of the agency. The administrative qualities of this leadership should include those of outstanding competence in administration. The leadership of an institution in the process of its creation can fail if it does not have status and influence in the controlling power structure, if it does not have the respect and confidence of staff, or if it does not have sympathetic understanding of the novel purposes and functions and methods of the program or service to be accomplished. To find an administrator who possesses all three of these sterling qualities is difficult indeed. A senior official who has status and influence in the bureaucracy would not naturally, in the course of things, have great enthusiasm for a new development program of uncertain status and future, nor would he have compatible familiarity with the new technology involved. He and his staff would not be in easy accord, either, unless the staff also were on easy terms with the work of the new institutions.

The components of an institution also include a clear definition of purpose, policy, program activity, and method. They include the legal authority and the requisite delegation of administrative powers to be able to operate effectively as desired. An unambiguous assignment of agency purpose and program is important to the government and the development plan and the bureaucracy so that the agency's relative place in development administration is understood and so that there is an objective and fair basis for its reporting and for the evaluation of its performance. This component of purpose and program extends to policy and method, also, because the effects of program activity as governed by policy and the impact of projects as facilitated and cushioned by work methodology can be as significant in impeding or advancing the cause of development as the work program itself. The understanding and acceptance of purpose, program, policy, and methodology by agency staff is directly important to agency effectiveness. Ignorance of purpose and policy and program method or, if not ignorance, disagreement with these on the part of the responsible personnel could result in less than full agency effectiveness and even lead to program failure.

The institution of course needs the authority to act upon its designated purposes and to carry out its assigned program functions according to the policies and methods most appropriate to them. This authority and these powers are of both a legal and an administrative nature. A clear status in law, with foresighted statement of purpose and policy and function, contributes not only to clarity and understanding of program. Such legal status also provides the basis of stability and the assurance of continuity that most institutions need for their growth to maturity, a process which takes much time. Legal authority alone is not usually sufficient in itself to empower the agency to go ahead with its work. Required in addition are delegations of such administrative authority as will vest in the agency the capacity to operate efficiently and responsibly—delegations for personnel actions, for example, and for reasonable financial discretion and for procurement.

There are two remaining and essential components of an institution. One of these is assurance of financial resources for continuing operation, either from appropriations or from revenues or from borrowings or from combinations of these as are appropriate. The last component on the list is that of agency administration itself, not only the division of labor as represented in an organization chart and the erection of a work structure suitable to the job, but also a system of decision-making in happy consonance with agency staff on the one hand and concerned external agencies and communities on the other. This process of decision-making is not only for the purpose of agreeing on what projects and activities should be undertaken but also, and equally, on the policies and the methods of doing that work.

Agreement on policy and method, especially, as well as agreement on projects, is involved in the concept of coordination, which has the function of synthesizing all of the component parts of the institution into an effective instrument for program accomplishment—the components of physical plant, staff and leadership, assigned purpose and program, financial resources for continuing operation, and sound organization structure. All of these components must be present in an institution if it is to be viable and, more than that, the components must be synthesized into an efficient instrument for the prosecution of the assigned development task.

It is not only the adequacy of an institution's component parts and their articulation in a successful synthesis that determines its capability and its effectiveness. The environment in which the institution is expected to work is also important. Individual institutions do not exist in isolation; rather, they function in a complex of relationships and a network of interactions which, if friendly and supportive, enhance their effective performance and which, if hostile and uncooperative, can impede the intended operations and thwart the accomplishment of institutional purpose. The key elements in this environment include the enabling and controlling authorities, the agencies and systems of supply and service, the related sister or complementary institutions, the competing and potentially hostile institutions, the institutional and public consumers of the subject institution's product or the intended beneficiaries of its work, and the overall public and institutional perception of the role of the agency or the system in the bureaucratic and social environment.

Institutions, agencies, and systems have an essential and a complementary relationship with other institutions in a larger system which embraces them all. An institution is invariably responsible for providing a product or a service upon which another institution or other institutions are dependent. In turn, an institution is invariably dependent upon the work of other institutions for its own program success. Thus a series of complementary and interacting institutions in an effective association of relationships, a kind of network, is involved in the accomplishment of a program. The agency charged with the construction of an irrigation system and the agency charged with the engagement of farmers in the use of the system complement one another in an inseparable way. Too often this complementarity is not recognized adequately in program coordination or expressed effectively in project timing and execution so that program objectives are not met or are delayed or are not achieved to their full expectation. Complete institutional success depends on an environment of well-coordinated and thus effective relationships among sister institutions, complementing each other to their mutual advantage as they progress toward a common program purpose.

The Meaning of Development Administration

Traditional systems and institutions of public administration were not designed to respond to demands for social and economic development, whether in colonies such as Indonesia and Nigeria or in kingdoms such as Thailand and Ethiopia. They were not expected to be responsive to legislatures or other representatives of the people. They did not recognize the function of rectifying inequities in the social system. They were not as much concerned with the encouragement or support of economic growth or the distribution of the benefits of that growth as with the allocation of resources to assure continuing profits and revenues to government or, rather, to those who controlled the government. These traditional administrative systems were established to perform other functions. Those functions included the maintenance of law and order so as to assure a reasonable degree of security and of stability in the community. They included the provision of certain public services considered to be essential at the time, such as roads, and they included mechanisms for settling disputes.

Traditional governments and their bureaucracies were highly centralized. Authority was focused in the capital city and comparatively few decisions could be made by officials in outlying districts. Even at the center, authority was not well dispersed for expeditious and well-informed expression. The top officials could not or did not share the power of office with colleagues or with subordinates or even with other officials in the same office. They were not supported by specialist staffs which could give informed advice based upon sound analysis. They were not supplied with an adequate number of middle-level personnel trained to handle the routines and details of office management. This personnel situation and the limited and narrow concept of the exercise of authority were aggravated by ponderous procedures of administration. The failure to delegate decision-making powers to field officers in the outlying districts and the dilatory pace of action at the center had the effect of impeding and not expediting action.

The major supportive systems of these traditional bureaucracies, notably the fiscal and the personnel systems, also represented barriers to development processes no matter how relevant they seemed to be to the processes of security and stability and status quo which they had been designed to support. Budgets in this environment tended to be more restrictive than energizing both in their form and in the limited authority they granted for expenditure. The personnel, the civil servants who manned these systems, were the instruments of throne and empire and not of nations and particularly not of the people of nations. These civil servants were on the whole honest and efficient and effective in preserving order and maintaining stability and in assuring the revenues. They were governors, in that sense, and were not involved in the realization of popular aspirations.

The term "development administration" was coined in 1955 or 1956. It seemed to be a simple and clarifying way to distinguish the focus of administration on the support and management of development as distinguished from the administration of law and order. In some respects it is the counterpart of the term "development economics," which came into renewed and heightened usage with the growing impact of economic planning in newly independent countries after World War II. The term and concept of development administration is now found in the titles and programs of many agencies and institutions, such as the Institute of Development Administration in Thailand and the Development Administration Unit in the prime minister's office in Malaysia. The U.S. Agency for International Development changed the name of its public administration unit to development administration in the mid-sixties. The United Nations' regional center for training and research in administration in Asia has the title Asian and Pacific Development Administration Center. Many universities have introduced courses in development administration.

The five-year plans and the reports of the administrative reform commissions of many countries in Africa and Asia as well as Latin America call for the strengthening of administration to assure acceptable levels of implementation of national plans of social and economic development. These include, for example, India and Pakistan, Indonesia and Malaysia, Nigeria and Ghana, Kenya and Tanzania. There are many others, reflecting the fact that administration for development is the concern and the responsibility of each of the developing countries.

"Development administration" is the term used to denote the complex of agencies, management systems, and processes a government establishes to achieve its development goals. It is the public mechanism set up to relate the several components of development in order to articulate and accomplish national social and economic objectives. It is the adjustment of the bureaucracy to the vastly increased number, variety, and complexity of governmental functions required to respond to public demands for development. Development administration is the administration of policies, programs, and projects to serve development purposes.

Development administration is characterized by its purposes, its loyalties, and its attitudes. The purposes of development administration are to stimulate and facilitate defined programs of social and economic progress. They are purposes of change and innovation and movement as contrasted with purposes of maintaining the status quo. They are to make change attractive and possible. These purposes are to apply policies and to conduct programs of development specified by the people as a whole through evolving political systems of democratic decision-making. This definition of purpose makes the bureaucracy for development administration accountable to the public, through its representatives. Bureaucratic loyalty in development administration must thus be to the people and not to its own vested institutional interests nor to a non-public sovereign such as king or empire. The attitudes of development administration are positive rather than negative, persuasive rather than restrictive. Development administration encourages innovation and change where desirable or necessary to accomplish development purposes and discourages adherence to traditional norms and forms for their own sake. The attitude of development administration is outward reaching and not inward looking.

Development administration is distinguished from, although not independent of, other aspects and concerns of public administration. Certainly the maintenance of law and order is a prime function of government and is basic to development, although it precedes and is not usually encompassed within the definition of development administration. Similarly the provision of such essential services as roads and other communication systems and health and school facilities as well as water supply and other utility systems and the organization for tax collection are distinguished from development administration because they have been a responsibility of government traditionally. The comprehensiveness and effectiveness of these services support and strengthen the environment for development, however, and their provision in adequate measure is necessary to development.

Distinctions should also be made between administration for development and other systems of administration such as those for the police and the military, the judicial, and for foreign representation. Each of these other systems has its own unique requirements, attitudes, and methods. Again, each system, depending upon its operation, has an impact upon development administration, and therefore development administration and the government as a whole must be aware of and accommodating of the consequences of these impacts and interrelationships. The police and military systems could be repressive toward the people, for example, and inhibit the kinds of freedom of movement concomitant with the development process. Or they could be so intertwined with district administration as to inhibit the conduct of development activities. On the other hand, enlightened police and military systems can, through their own or the regularly constituted agencies, encourage and support educational, health, social welfare, and even public works programs so as to enhance markedly the overall programs of development. These separate systems thus become a concern of development administration.

The quality of the administration of justice, similarly, is related to attitudes toward development administration by giving evidence to the people of the government's intentions of achieving equality of treatment and opportunity regardless of wealth, class, or race. The administration of foreign representation can have a direct bearing on development, not only by facilitating the good general relationships conducive to business associations but even more by providing for economic experts in the embassies who can work directly to realize fruitful trade and investment connections.

The methods of administration in these diverse systems vary, and vary quite appropriately, because of the distinctive purposes of the several systems. The methods of law and order, for example, are those of restraint and punishment. Law and order administrators, and also those who collect the taxes, must by nature be objective, aloof, and even distant in their relationships with the public. The primary interest of public administrators who provide public services is efficiency in the performance of their specified functions. Efficiency—that is, the achievement of economies in time, personnel, and materials in the accomplishment of purpose—is an important aspect of public administration. These aspects of administration might be called "internal administration" as distinguished from the primary methodological concerns of development administrators, which might be called "external administration." Internal administration is defined here to mean the management of an organization, an agency. It involves the systems and processes and methods by which needed resources of personnel, materials, and technology are used to perform prescribed functions.

External administration, on the other hand, refers to the activities and processes of administration which are needed to establish and to activate relationships with agencies and groups outside the administrative control of an agency, relationships which are essential to the achievement of that agency's purposes. These relationships are required to implement a policy or program or to carry out a project because such implementation would be impossible without the participation and contribution of these external entities. External administration thus involves patterns of interagency collaboration and of client participation above and beyond the regular patterns and systems of coordination and supervision.

Forms of interagency collaboration range from informal, unstructured relationships expressed in meetings, conferences, and the exchange of information to more formal associations expressed in contracts or agreements calling for systematic methods of cooperation. Patterns of client participation are needed to involve the people served by and also those engaged in the execution of a collaborative effort—people in their private capacity either as individuals or, more usually, through their autonomous private organizations. Such groups include agency sponsored or encouraged committees or councils for advisory purposes; cooperatives and farmers' organizations; special districts for conservation, education, and sanitation; trade associations; unions; and professional organizations. Patterns of client participation also range from the informal to the formal, the unstructured to the structured. A program which illustrates external administration is a major irrigation project involving the collaboration of a central agency such as the public works department, a state or local agency such as the department of agricultural extension, and the farmers as individuals and through their private organizations. Development administration is outward looking; it is basically external.

Efficiency is by no means inconsistent with development administration, or out of place in its conduct. Quite the contrary; the application of technology to the performance of management functions and the improvement of management skills, particularly at the middle levels of management service, have their own important contribution to make to the effectiveness of administration for development. In spite of this dependency on competent administration, however, the term "development administration" is usually not employed to refer to scientific management or administrative efficiency as such. For the purposes of understanding development administration, and discussing it, emphasis is placed upon its distinctive features. If all of its interdependencies were included in the definition, "development administration" would be but another term for public administration and too broad therefore to permit the particularized consideration it deserves and requires as a phenomenon in the development process.

Another aspect of this consideration of efficiency in public administration calls for attention in this context. A part of the concept of development administration is that its function is to achieve specifically defined development purposes; its effectiveness should be measured and judged in these terms. If the purposes of administration are accomplished, it is considered good; if the purposes are poorly or inadequately accomplished, administration from this development point of view is considered bad. This approach to the design of administrative systems is quite different from approaches based on some generalized concept of what is considered to be "good administration." Development administration is designed to achieve specified results and is good or bad in terms of its delivery of results. This approach to administration does not exclude efficiency or considerations of time and money and honesty, but it begins with a definition of the target and proceeds with the formulation of administrative methodology suited to its achievement, rather than with an abstract conception of efficient administration as such. Merely efficient administration could in fact thwart development if it were its purpose to do so.

To use the development approach to administration, sometimes called "sectoral administration," is to design management systems needed to carry out defined and agreed-upon policies, programs, or projects. This approach is quite different from that usually expressed in the term "administrative reform." The targets of administrative reform are typically the central management system and, predominantly, the civil service. The function of development administration is to assure that an appropriately congenial environment and effective administration support are provided for delivery of capital, materials, and services where needed in the productive process—whether in public, private, or mixed economies.

The Applications of Development Administration

The manifestations of development administration, its unique purposes, loyalties, and attitudes, are found in new and reoriented agencies and in new management systems and processes. These agencies include planning boards to facilitate decisions about development policies and the allocation of resources toward the accomplishment of those policies, and reconstituted "nation-building" departments such as those for agriculture, industry, education, and health. An essential aspect of the competence of these agencies is their ability to judge the management as well as the technical and financial and economic feasibilities of development projects and programs and, when such feasibilities are suspect, to take the leadership in assuring the adequacy of such programs and projects from the management point of view. The essence of development administration is its concern with the "how" of accomplishing the "what" of the development plan and its constituent programs and projects. New kinds of agencies are often needed for development. Public enterprises and also stronger private enterprise management systems are called for. In the field, cooperative organizations, community development programs and a variety of farmers' organizations are evidence of requirements for new agencies to support development.

The major expression of development administration in the field is decentralization, the unclogging of business at the center by delegating authority to a larger number of agencies and to a larger number of places in the countryside. New management systems, as well as management agencies, must be devised to make such decentralization possible—new budget and fiscal as well as planning systems, information and reporting systems, personnel systems, and systems of coordination. Development administration, therefore, is not only the administration of development; it is the development of administration. Development administration encompasses the innovations which strengthen the capacity of the bureaucracy to stimulate and facilitate development. For these purposes development administration needs its own supporting institutions, chiefly in the form of training, research, and consulting agencies, but also in the form of an articulate and informed public expectation of good administrative behavior and performance.

The reorientation and strengthening of each of the nation-building departments or ministries to accommodate the development dimension of its responsibility requires first of all an overhaul of its organization to assure a structure suitable to the ministry's function. This reorganization should concern itself with the adequacy of the subdivisions of departments and bureaus in terms of the specializations needed to do the work and the need to share the work load. It should concern itself with the clarification of delegations and lines of communication so that both the powers for acting and the accountability for actions are assigned sufficiently to permit effective and expeditious decision and performance. The distinctive capacities needed by nation-building departments to discharge their development responsibilities are planning competence, staff analysis capability, expert specialized personnel, management skill, field organization, and effective coordination.

The introduction of competent planning in the central ministries and departments is a key factor in reorienting and strengthening the nation-building departments upon whom the heavy and diverse burdens of development fall most heavily. With the assignment of development duties, these central departments and ministries can no longer satisfy the requirement of their existence by merely presiding over mechanisms to manage comparatively modest operations. They are now obliged to arrange for and to carry out urgent and much larger programs of road building and other construction of utilities and infrastructure, a much larger system of schools and training institutions, nationwide systems of family health clinics, and, most prominently, complex programs to increase agricultural productivity and investment in industry and trade. These programs and projects must be formulated, their several feasibilities tested, and they must be integrated in the national as well as in the appropriate sectoral plan. For these purposes a planning capability and process is needed in each nation-building department.

These central ministries in their traditional form did not have the capacity for staff analysis, for setting up and operating or monitoring delivery and support systems, or effective mechanisms in the provinces and districts to express their program and project interests throughout the country. Staff analysis involves the application of objective and scientific skills to the data and the problem. At an earlier time, in the days of traditional administration, the public establishment was on the whole small and the functions comparatively simple rather than complex in nature. The conduct of the public business did not seem to require much specialized professional analysis. The burdens and complexities of development, however, and the larger and unfamiliar programs to be carried out compel the utilization of expert and specialized staff services. Staff services of this kind depend upon information and data systems, including systematic appraisal of project and program progress, which provide material accurate and complete enough to permit operable conclusions. These staff services include personnel, budget, and operations and management research as well as planning analysis.

A nation-building department needs professionally trained personnel in the field or several fields of its substantive interest, and it needs the services of staff analysts. The applications of technology to development opportunities depend upon the capability of the relevant ministry to give the specialized support and leadership which only such experts can provide. This personnel requirement means the introduction of specialists into the civil service not only in much larger numbers, but also at higher levels of influence and decision-making in relation to the generalists in the administrative services. The dedication of these specialists to the application of their professional skills and their sympathy with the problems and opportunities of the public community are additional attributes of the personnel complement of the effective nation-building department.

Ministries reconstituted for development administration must have the management skill and capacity to establish or to arrange for the establishment and competent operation through private or other public agencies of management systems to carry out or support development programs. To use a familiar example, the increase of any consequence in grain production usually involves the introduction of a new variety of seed, which is fruitful only if it is supported with adequate amounts of fertilizer, water, insecticides, herbicides, and cultivating implements available at the right times and places. The introduction of the new seed depends upon systems which will assure the production of the support items and their delivery to the farmers. These are in addition to, but related to and interdependent with, price policies which will motivate the farmer, credit facilities which will finance the farmer, and extension services which will advise the farmer. A plan that contemplates the increase of grain production with the use of new seeds is obviously not viable unless it also contemplates and provides for the essential support systems. Those systems could be in the private sector, or could be provided by cooperatives or other public or semi-public enterprises, or could be undertaken by the regular government departments.

Nation-building departments need to be retooled in their capacity to apply their plans, programs, and projects for development throughout the country. This capacity depends in part upon the evolution of competent agencies and mechanisms in the field and in part upon the devising of methods by which the central ministry can relate its guidance and support to the field agencies. In traditional administration the bureaucracy in the field was preoccupied with keeping the peace and collecting the taxes. Central ministries sometimes had their own agents there also, agents who performed somewhat vague, desultory, and procedural duties. A very few countries at independence, such as India and Nigeria, set up state governments and bureaucracies with their own authority for planning and carrying out development programs. Most did not, however, but sought to strengthen their field organizations by assigning more comprehensive duties, including those of development, to the district commissioner or other head civil servant in the district or province. In some countries the specialists of the central ministries were made a part of a newly integrated field bureaucracy, but in most cases these specialists continued to report back to the center with only uncertain coordinating relationships in the district. There is movement now to increase the size and competence and also the powers of the administrative establishment in the field. This process of decentralization is necessary to speed up decisions relating to program and project matters peculiar to the field or to a particular location in the field, and to make the decisions more realistically and accurately because of the likelihood of fuller knowledge and understanding of the requirements of the local situation.

Thus development administration involves the establishment of new agencies and the reorientation of existing agencies in order to discharge the enormous responsibilities and to perform the multifarious and complex functions of social and economic development. Institutions involved in the development process are not limited to those of government but include also the agencies and systems of the private sector. They include the relationships of individuals and private and public agencies and programs in such evolving and complex social and economic systems as those for agricultural production.

Note on Sources

The conceptualization of development administration owes a great debt to the Comparative Administration Group (CAG). Organized in 1960–61 under the aegis of the American Society for Public Administration, it focused its efforts on development administration. The CAG was put together by a small group of political scientists and students of public administration who had been frustrated and disappointed with efforts at technical assistance for public administration in developing countries. The CAG, with financial support from the Ford Foundation, sponsored fruitful research and seminars and issued, in mimeograph form, the CAG "Occasional Papers." These were widely distributed. Many of them have been revised, related to one another, and published in book form. The most prominent of them are the following:

Ralph Braibanti, ed., *Political and Administrative Development* (Durham, N.C.: Duke University Press, 1969). Ralph Braibanti was also general editor of the whole CAG series.

Bertram M. Gross, ed., *Action under Planning: The Guidance of Economic Development* (New York: McGraw-Hill, 1967).

James P. Heaphey, ed., *Spatial Dimensions of Development Administration* (Durham, N.C.: Duke University Press, 1970).

Allan Kornberg and Lloyd D. Musolf, eds., *Legislatures in Development Perspective* (Durham, N.C.: Duke University Press, 1970).

J. D. Montgomery and W. L. Siffin, eds., *Approaches to Development: Politics, Administration and Change* (New York: McGraw-Hill, 1966).

Fred W. Riggs, ed., *Frontiers of Development Administration* (Durham, N.C.: Duke University Press, 1970).

Clarence E. Thurber and Lawrence S. Graham, eds., *Development Administration in Latin America* (Durham, N.C.: Duke University Press, 1973).

Dwight Waldo, ed., *Temporal Dimensions of Development Administration* (Durham, N.C.: Duke University Press, 1970).

Edward W. Weidner, ed., *Development Administration in Asia* (Durham, N.C.: Duke University Press, 1970). Edward Weidner also wrote the interesting article "Development Administration: Origin, Concept, and Diffusion," *Korean Journal of Public Administration* 6, no. 1 (1968): 237–43.

Fred W. Riggs was the prime mover of CAG's interest in and devotion to the new field of development administration, and he was the long-time chairman of the group. His own earlier books, still of great value in development administration, set much of the tone, the framework, for CAG's subsequent studies. Among them are two pioneering works: *The Ecology of Public Administration* (London: Asia Publishing House, 1961), and *Administration in Developing Countries: The Theory of the Prismatic Society* (Boston: Houghton Mifflin, 1964).

Other books contributed to the understanding of development administration; although not sponsored by CAG, several were written or edited by scholars active in CAG:

Joseph La Palombara, ed., *Bureaucracy and Political Development* (Princeton: Princeton University Press, 1963).

Irving Swerdlow, ed., *Development Administration: Concepts and Problems* (Syracuse, N.Y.: Syracuse University Press, 1963).

Edward W. Weidner, *Technical Assistance in Public Administration Overseas: The Case for Development Administration* (Chicago: Public Administration Service, 1964).

C. Y. Wu, *Development Administration: Current Approaches and Trends in Public Administration for National Development,* Sales No. E. 76. II. H. 1 (New York: United Nations, 1976).

Bibliographies have been published from time to time. These are three of the most recent:

Milton J. Esman and John D. Montgomery, "Systems Approaches to Technical Cooperation: The Role of Development Administration," *Public Administration Review* 29, no. 5 (Sept./Oct. 1969): 507–39.

Richard W. Gable, *Development Administration: Background, Terms, Concepts, Theories and a New Approach,* American Society for Public Administration, Section on International and Comparative Administration, Occasional Papers, Series No. 7 (Washington, D.C.: American Society for Public Administration, 1976).

Garth N. Jones et al., *Planning, Development and Change: A Bibliography on Development Administration* (Honolulu: East-West Center Press, 1970).

An effort closely allied to that of the Comparative Administration Group and involving many of the same people was the Inter-University Research Program on Institution Building composed by Indiana and Michigan State universities and by the University of Pittsburgh, under the leadership of Milton J. Esman. The productive and stimulating work of this group was used by the U.S. Agency for International Development (AID) and some of its cooperating land grant universities as an aid to planning and evaluating technical assistance projects in agriculture. The emphasis is continued in the AID-financed activities of PASITAM—the Program of Advanced Studies in Institution Building and Technical Assistance Methodology. PASITAM is a program of MUCIA—the Midwest Universities Consortium for International Activities, whose members are the universities of Illinois, Iowa, Minnesota, and Wisconsin, and Indiana, Michigan State, and Ohio State universities. The sections in this chapter on institution building rest heavily upon the literature produced by this group, especially:

Melvin G. Blase, *Institution Building: A Source Book* (Beverly Hills, Calif.: Sage Publications, 1972).

Milton J. Esman, "The Institution Building Concepts—An Interim Appraisal," mimeographed, produced as part of the Inter-University Program in Institution Building (Pittsburgh: University of Pittsburgh, 1967).

Milton J. Esman, "Building Institutions for Management Development," in *Interregional Seminar on the Use of Modern Management Techniques in the Public Administration of Developing Countries,* Vol. 2, Add. 3, Sales No. E/F/S. 71. II. H. 8 (New York: United Nations, 1971).

George F. Gant, "The Institution Building Project," *International Review of Administrative Science* 32, no. 3 (1966): 1-8.

Hiram S. Phillips, *Guide for Development: Institution Building and Reform* (New York: Praeger, 1969).

D. Woods Thomas et al., eds., *Institution Building: A Model for Applied Social Change* (Cambridge, Mass.: Schenkman Publishing Co., 1972).

There is a wealth of literature relevant to the economic and social components of the development process. The World Bank's *World Development Report, 1978* (New York: Oxford University Press, 1978) is a review of the progress and current status of developing countries with a very useful annex of "World Development Indicators." Everett E. Hagen's studies are among the best. They include *On the Theory of Social Change: How Economic Growth Begins* (Homewood, Ill.: Dorsey, 1962) and *The Economics of Development* (Homewood, Ill.: Richard D. Irwin, 1975). On the importance of human factors, reference may be made to Irma Adelman and Cynthia Taft Morris, *Economic Growth and Social Equity in Developing Countries* (Stanford, Calif.: Stanford University Press, 1973), and Gunnar Myrdal's monumental *Asian Drama: An Inquiry into the Poverty of Nations,* 3 vols. (New York: Pantheon, 1968); see also his *Challenge of World Poverty* (New York: Vintage Books, 1970).

With respect to traditional administrative systems, and political systems as well, the following are particularly helpful:

A. L. Adu, *The Civil Service in New African States* (New York: Praeger, 1965).

Harold Alderfer, *Public Administration in Newer Nations* (New York: Praeger, 1967).

Gabriel A. Almond and James S. Coleman, eds., *The Politics of Developing Areas* (Princeton: Princeton University Press, 1962).

Ralph J. Braibanti, ed., *Asian Bureaucratic Systems Emergent from the British Imperial Tradition* (Durham, N.C.: Duke University Press, 1966).

Ferrel Heady, *Public Administration: A Comparative Perspective* (Englewood Cliffs, N.J.: Prentice-Hall, 1966).

Popular Participation in Decision Making for Development, Sales No. E. 75. IV. 10 (New York: United Nations, 1975).

Lucian W. Pye, *Aspects of Political Development* (Boston: Little, Brown, 1966).

The requirements of nation-building departments in order to meet the obligations of administration for development are referred to in the works listed below:

Appraising Administrative Capability for Development, Sales No. E. 69. II. H. 2 (New York: United Nations, 1969).

George F. Gant, "A Note on Applications of Development Administration," *Public Policy* 15 (1966): 199–211.

Kenneth J. Rothwell, *Administrative Issues in Developing Economies* (Lexington, Mass.: Heath, 1972).

Albert Waterston, *Development Planning: Lessons of Experience* (Baltimore: Johns Hopkins University Press, 1969).

2

Administration for Agricultural Production

The Role of Agriculture in Development

The focus of development administration is the execution of defined programs and specified projects planned to achieve identified targets of social and economic development. These development programs and projects are found for the most part in the functional areas of economic and social activity—programs and projects in the fields of agriculture, industry and commerce, health and population, education and manpower. Programs and projects in these fields are often called "sectoral," to distinguish them from regional activities characterized by geographical location. Development administration comprehends the overall national, state, and local systems of public administration in those many respects in which they support social and economic development. Efforts to reform the public administration establishment as a whole are made too often without sufficient regard for the requirements of the functional areas to be served, of the substantive sectors of development whose particular administrative needs deserve special attention. When consideration is given to the administrative organizations and systems required to assure the successful achievement of a development program or project, the questions of ways and means are clearer, their answers more easily found.

Agriculture is a sector of the economy—of the world's economy and of the economies of developing countries—which needs and which can benefit directly and enormously from administrative support. Moreover, increased agricultural productivity has high priority both in its key role in the development programs of most countries and in its strategic influence upon the comity and the stability of the world community. The needs for greatly increased agricultural production are great and they are urgent. Vastly greater amounts of food are required by growing populations and by populations increasingly able to eat more and better food. More food and fibers are desired by most countries to support their growing economies and to provide their populations with healthier and happier lives. Greater agricultural productivity is relied upon to support in- dustrial growth in most developing countries by earning capital for investment, by supplying labor and raw materials, and by supplying a market for consumer and production goods. The agricultural sector is expected also to contribute to the welfare of the rural population. Agricultural productivity is a major target for development almost everywhere.

The world's growing demand for food is staggering, increasing as it is at the rate of about twenty-five million tons of food grains a year. This increase is at the rate of 2.5 percent per annum, of which 2.0 percent is for the growing population and 0.5 percent for an increasing per capita consumption supported by larger incomes. There is no doubt of the need for larger consumption by the existing population, given the conserva- tive estimate that five hundred million people are hungry and un- dernourished. In addition there are those millions actually starving because of acute famine conditions. The normal food requirement for adults in the West is 3000 calories a day, whereas it is 2500 a day for the smaller peoples in Asia, at least until better diets make them larger and increase their caloric requirements. But the average per capita con- sumption in Asia and other developing countries is at the present time only 2000 calories per day, a deficit of 500 calories. These measurements are in terms of food grains, the cheapest and most economical form for calories. Because every calorie of animal foodstuffs requires five to eight primary calories for its production, the West's consumption of calories requires the production of as much as three times the basic calories— 9000 per day. As the people of developing countries are able to produce or buy and eat more food—and more meat as their affluence increases— the demands for higher agricultural production will rise still further.

It is not only the quantity of food which is of concern but also its quality as it affects people's health, productivity, and happiness. Too little food is itself a cause of malnutrition. Adequate quantities, however, if of deficient composition, do not protect against malnutrition. The lack of protein—which is to be found in meat, fish, beans, cheese, milk, eggs, and peanuts—in the diet is the cause of serious nutritional deficiencies. Protein shortages in the diets of babies and young children can impede or even impair the development of the brain and central nervous system. Deficiencies in iron and vitamin A are also common and create serious nutritional problems that cause malnutrition. Malnutrition can and does lead to anemia, apathy, and stunted growth of both mind and body. It makes its sufferers more subject to infection and disease and death. Malnutrition reduces the hours per day a person can work and even his efficiency through lassitude and lethargy during those hours—and this low productivity has the circular effect of reducing still further his ability to buy more and better food. The educational programs being undertaken to improve eating habits and the food enrichment programs such as those to add iron to salt and amino acids to plant proteins will increasingly, though slowly, reduce malnutrition. They will at the same time, however, increase still further the demand for more and better food.

The need is great. The Food and Agriculture Organization (FAO) reported in its *World Food Survey* in 1978 that about 40 percent of the women in developing countries are anemic, because of malnourishment, and that up to 100,000 children go blind each year. The countries having the most serious problem of inadequate food intake were reported to be Bangladesh, Brazil, Burma, Colombia, Ethiopia, India, Indonesia, Nigeria, Pakistan, Philippines, Sudan, Tanzania, and Zaire. Classified as having extreme nutritional problems were Bolivia, Chad, El Salvador, Maldives, Mali, Mauritania, Niger, Somalia, and Upper Volta.

Each developing country faces this problem of food and nutrition. Each developing country must also be concerned with the desire of its people to live happier as well as healthier lives, a desire which is met at least basically by the assurance of larger and better meals. And each developing country must be concerned not only with its capacity for growing food but also fibers in the form of trees or grasses or cotton or hemp or sheep in the support of clothing, housing, and even export as these are needed and desired in connection with its development program. Food and fiber for development are the direct targets of increased agricultural productivity.

The agricultural sector has a major contribution to make, in addition, to a country's industrial development and to its economic development as a whole. As the agricultural community emerges from its traditional and largely subsistence form and begins to produce for the commercial market, its earnings and its savings are a major source of investment funds. Agricultural revenues for investment are sometimes tapped by the government through taxes or are channeled into other sectors of the economy by the agriculturalists, either directly or through their banks. In addition to capital and raw materials, the agricultural sector makes labor available for industrial employment by releasing manpower when technology and mechanization reduce its own requirements for labor. Finally, and of exceeding importance in the development process, the agricultural sector provides the industrial sector with a market for both consumer and producer goods. Modern agriculture depends heavily upon industry for energy, machines, fertilizers, pesticides, and food processing, and it supports industry by providing a growing market for these products and services of industry.

The agricultural sector is also expected to make a major contribution to the welfare of the rural population. There is usually not a direct one-to-one relationship between a rise in the profits of farming and the economic or other happiness of all the residents of the farm community. On the contrary, the adjustments to modern agriculture which make profits possible are bound to be the cause of maladjustments in the lives of the populace, maladjustments which might or might not be brought into happy balance in time. And the transition to modernization in agriculture frequently displaces a large proportion of the rural population which must be accommodated in some other way in a restructured rural economy or, most usually, in towns and cities. Nevertheless the growing productivity of agriculture is generally expected to play a prominent part in improving the condition of the rural population as a whole. In these several crucial ways—for food, for industrial development, for rural development, and for economic growth generally—agriculture has a key role in development.

Agricultural Production Can Be Increased

One way to make the existing food supply go further is to make better use of it. As much as 10 percent of the food grains produced, grains such as wheat and rice, is lost through spoilage and wastage while being transported from place to place and stored. Another 10 percent or so is lost to rats and other pests and to vagabond cattle and other animals. Substantial amounts of food are involved in these categories, and the comparatively moderate efforts devoted to reducing these losses might well be intensified. It is not consoling to contemplate that the rat and insect populations are increasing even more rapidly than our own. There has also been a profligate waste of food on the part of those who eat more than they need, and some concerned observers deplore the large quantities of food consumed by pets. Perhaps those views are somewhat strained. On the other hand, the quality and distribution of such food as is available could certainly be improved so that it would reach more people and in more nutritious forms. The science and technology of nutrition, now receiving increased attention, are producing important new knowledge being translated into education and food programs which promise to be rewarding in terms of human health.

The growing requirements for food are so great, however, that the fundamental need is to grow more of it. This increase can be achieved by opening up new lands to farming, by increasing the yields of crops on lands now being farmed, by increasing the number of crops grown per year on lands now being farmed, or by combinations of two or more of these three ways. There are in the world large areas which could and no doubt will be opened to and developed for farming, particularly in Africa and South America, depending upon the availability of water and the interest of farmers in moving to new places. As large as these new areas may be, they are small in comparison with the farm lands under cultivation. It is to these existing areas of cultivation which the world must look for more food. Where good soil, adequate water, and beneficent climate permit, as they do in many parts of the world, including many developing countries, three or even four crops a year might be grown, under systems called multi-cropping or inter-cropping, where only one or two crops were grown before. When high-yielding varieties of plants are available to replace less productive plants, and particularly varieties which mature quickly so as to permit multi-cropping, and where the technologies and infrastructures are established to support the use of such varieties, the yield of each crop can be increased.

The happy fact is that the technology exists to increase agricultural production with high-yielding varieties of food grains, chiefly rice and wheat, which mature in relatively short growing seasons and permit multiple cropping. This technological breakthrough is sometimes called the "Green Revolution." The Green Revolution was sparked by the successful research on wheat and corn at the International Maize and Wheat Improvement Center (CIMMYT) in Mexico (preceded by a cooperative Mexican-Rockefeller research program) and the International Rice Research Institute (IRRI) in the Philippines. Dynamic leadership was provided by officials of the Rockefeller and Ford foundations, including Norman Borlaug (a winner of the Nobel Peace Prize), Robert Chandler, George Harrar, and Forrest Hill. The new varieties of high-yielding dwarf rices and dwarf wheats produce up to double as much grain per crop as the traditional varieties. Because of their short stature they are more resistant to wind and rain. These new varieties require, however, the application of specified amounts of fertilizer and water or they are not productive. The lush growth of the new varieties often supports disease or attracts insect pests which must be combatted with pesticides. The preparation of the soil and the treatment and harvesting of the heavier yields, in shorter seasons, involves the use of more tools and machines in a process of mechanization which in turn depends upon fuel and oil. When pumps are needed for water in an irrigation system, as they often are, they require electricity for their operation.

Each high-yielding rice or wheat plant in effect becomes a factory in which the ingredients of soil and water and fertilizer and the protection of pesticides are combined to produce a product in the form of food grains. Each of these inputs must be available to the farmers in adequate quantities and at the right times and places. The technology of the Green Revolution requires that the inputs be produced by seed multiplication farms, irrigation systems, fertilizer and pesticide plants, electric and fuel plants, and farm machinery manufacture, and it requires that the inputs be supplied by reliable delivery systems. The farmers have to have the knowledge and the skill to manage and conduct the whole agricultural operation to its high-yielding conclusion.

It is not only the production and the delivery of the inputs for modern agricultural production and the skill of the farmer but also the supporting infrastructure which must be provided to complete the system and make possible the result of greatly increased productivity. This infrastructure of support assumes first of all the stability assured by the maintenance of law and order and the provision of essential public services. More specifically required by the agricultural operation are storage facilities for the harvest and practicable systems to protect, preserve, and subsequently process and market the harvested grains. Roads and vehicles adequate to the purpose of transporting farm produce most be provided. Maintenance, service, and repair facilities are needed for the buildings, roads, and machines involved in the agricultural enterprise. These massive inputs, their production and delivery, and the supporting infrastructure, must all be available and in place in reasonably effective relationship to make possible the increase in agricultural productivity which has such high priority in world and national economies and which is so basic to human health and welfare.

Increased agricultural production depends not only upon its technological feasibility but also upon its attractiveness to the farmer, the agricultural entrepreneur. Agricultural modernization must be not only possible—it must also be attractive. This attractiveness, if sufficient to motivate the farmer to modernize his operation, depends upon the degree of its profitability and upon its feasibility, its practicability. The farmer will certainly not under normal circumstances make extensive changes in his agricultural practices if such changes would mean a loss, or even if they would bring only a modest profit, especially considering the heavy investment required of him in comparison with the method of traditional farming and the consequent increase in the risks of a crop failure. Experience and observation have shown that farmers, generally, in all parts of the world, will adopt the new technologies of agriculture if the profits are in the neighborhood of twice the profits of their earlier operations. This experience applies of course in those situations in which the farmer has the choice to make.

The farmer's choice, however, depends upon the practicability of his change to a new system, that is, whether he can adopt the new system even if he wants to. The practicability of the change and the incentive for making it are closely related. The importance of the inputs and of the infrastructure has already been emphasized; the farmer must also be able to rely upon their availability. The size and form of the farmer's landholding might not be suitable to the requirements of modern agricultural practice; it might be too small, or divided into too many separate parts, or inaccessible. He and his neighbors might therefore be dependent upon a form of land reform which relates land systems to the land use patterns imposed by the technology of maximum agricultural productivity. Another question for the farmer, if he gets more land and changes his farming methods, is whether he has access to the labor supply he will need for his operations.

Before investing in the land and equipment and in the more expensive inputs of the annual crop or crops, the farmer needs assurance that there is a demand for his production and a fair and reliable market, domestic or international, through which to sell it at an attractive price. He must be concerned with his government's supervision of the market and its policies and practices with respect to price floors which would reduce the risks of his heavy investment. The government's taxes are relevant to a farmer's choice because they can inhibit agricultural modernization or they can encourage it by their form and their weight.

Even with assured prices which are attractive, the farmer must have access to credit at reasonable rates and in reasonable forms to finance the large investment he must make. The size of his investment might be larger or smaller, depending upon his government's subsidies for certain inputs such as fertilizer. The availability of crop insurance at reasonable rates to protect against the risk of crop failure is an important question related to the feasibility of change. Finally, the farmer will wish to be assured of access to professional and technical advice and assistance because the technologies of modern agriculture are complex, not simple, and because new problems can arise, such as a new and threatening plant disease, with which the farmer cannot deal without specialized help.

Agricultural production can be increased, but not easily, because of its requirements of a new technology with the concomitant inputs and support systems, and because of its requirements of new economic policies and systems to motivate and sustain the agricultural entrepreneur. Development administration for agricultural productivity has the task of dealing with this complexity.

The Impact of Agricultural Modernization

Modern agriculture and its vastly increased productivity is accomplished by advances in technology and the application of that technology by farmers who master the necessary skills. The application of the new technology depends upon supplies such as seed and fertilizer and machines from outside the community; it must be motivated and supported by markets and usually financed from outside the community. Traditional agriculture without the benefit of new knowledge, without the support of supplies and services from external sources, and without the inducement of external markets was just about as productive as it could be. Additional investment and labor, given the land and the level of scientific knowledge about agriculture, would not have increased the farm output measurably. The rice and wheat and other food grains grown were borne by plants which were slow to mature and which gave a comparatively low yield. Those plants were less reliant upon and responsive to the application of fertilizers and pesticides and thus the farm community was relatively independent of supplies and services from external sources. Investments in farm machinery were not substantial, nor were the cash outlays for the annual crop very heavy. Similarly, much traditional agriculture was subsistence in nature and was not dependent upon external markets or for extensive support from an accompanying infrastructure of storage and preservation systems and roads and transport.

The transition from traditional agriculture to modern agriculture, for the purpose of securing greater productivity and profit, changes all of that. The modern farm community is interdependent with the outside world for services and supplies on the one hand and for markets on the other. The individual farm operation involves much larger investments on plots of land large enough to justify the investments and in much more complex farming systems. Thus the introduction of modern agriculture through the Green Revolution and in other manifestations has disturbed pre-existing social and economic balances in the rural community. Farmers on good land are better able to benefit from up-to-date agricultural methods than those on poor lands. Rich farmers can more easily finance the large investments required by modern farming than can poor farmers. Farmers with large holdings feel more justified in buying the equipment of intensive farming than farmers on small holdings. The benefits of the Green Revolution have thus accrued more generously to large landholders and to the wealthy in countries like Pakistan, Mexico, and the Philippines than to small farmers on small farms in poorer areas. The Green Revolution in this way underlined and increased inequalities of income between regions and classes, although it did not create them. The Green Revolution did not make the poor any poorer, but it did make the rich richer still.

The Green Revolution does not necessarily reduce the number of jobs but in many local situations it has created unemployment. Cultivation with new varieties of seeds can actually require more labor because of the repetitive attention required for irrigating, fertilizing, weeding, and replanting. Many new jobs are created in the fertilizer and pesticide plants and in the food processing and marketing enterprises associated with the Green Revolution. With larger farm units and mechanization, however, modern agriculture makes it possible to grow much more food and fiber with fewer people. The difference in the proportion of rural residents in an underdeveloped and in a developed country illustrates this point—85 percent and 15 percent of the total population respectively. The change from traditional to modern agriculture is an unsettling, indeed a disruptive, process.

Programs to increase agricultural productivity and programs to improve the condition of the rural population, programs of rural development, are not necessarily the same and they are often in conflict. If there were a nice balance between the number of farmers and the land and capital requirements of modern agriculture, or if that balance could be reached by moving surplus farm labor to towns and cities, the targets of agriculture and of rural development could be the same or at least consistent because rural development includes the totality of the interests of the population in the countryside including health, education, and social protection. But there is often not a nice balance of population with the agricultural enterprise. Quite the contrary, the interests of the two may be in conflict, as in Bangladesh and Java in Indonesia, and this conflict creates a serious dilemma of policy and of program for governments. If too much priority is given to productivity there are social and political problems; and if too much consideration is given to the current welfare of the rural people, productivity will not increase as desired and the food supply will continue to be short. Given the terrible consequences of malnutrition and starvation in a world with an inadequate food supply, and given the urgent need for a profitable agriculture to finance and support national development in the long run, most countries are inclined to give preference to the requirements of increased agricultural productivity and to make efforts in other directions to ameliorate the impact of the revolution in agriculture and to meet the needs of the rural population.

Although the Green Revolution disrupted the balance in land operations, that earlier balance was not necessarily a happy one; more frequently than not, it was unhappy. The independence achieved by so many developing countries in the forties and fifties and early sixties brought with it demands for reform in systems of land tenure, systems characterized by the control of large and often absent landlords whose terms of tenancy for the farmers on their land or whose wage scales for landless laborers were so poor and in such form as to keep them in virtual bondage. These people quite naturally and vocally demanded their freedom, most usually in the form of claims on the land they worked but at least in terms which would give them more secure tenure and a larger and fair share of the profits of the farm enterprise. The Green Revolution and its increased profits added to the pressure of these demands but it by no means created the pressure in the first place; that pressure was there already. The more successful tenure reforms in response to this pressure are those which increase the security and the wage or other return of the farmer without necessarily giving him the land except where the landlord's holding is so large or so remote in terms of absentee residence as to make it relatively inefficient.

The political motive for such distribution is often strong not only because of the demands of the rural people but also because of the desire in many countries to redistribute political as well as economic power in the interest of the status and opportunities of the populace as a whole. Reform efforts which have blindly expropriated large holdings and distributed them to the tenants or the landless laborers have encountered enormous difficulty, such as those in East Bengal (now Bangladesh) in the 1950s. The systems, such as they were, for credit and supplies as maintained by the landlords collapsed before new systems were in place. Many of the new owners did not have the knowledge or skill or resources to manage productive operations, particularly the operations of an expensive modern agriculture, and those not selected were of course more unhappy even than before. The number of those demanding land often exceeded by a substantial amount the parcels of land which could be made available. The problem of employment for the rural population remained, while the base for agricultural productivity, at least for the time being, was in such cases badly damaged.

Partly to accommodate the landless farm tenants and laborers, partly to displace the wealthy and politically influential landlords, and partly to form large enough management units to justify investments in equipment and supplies, collective farms of one kind or another have been attempted in a number of countries, some with satisfying success and some with disappointment. One such is the cooperative farm or the farm managed along with others by cooperative management and organization, as in Egypt and Sudan. In this form the owners retain title to their portion of the land under cultivation but they pool it for operation, to which they might or might not contribute labor or other services. Another form of land operation is the commune, as in China, which is the organization of a collective governing body of the farm community in which the members share both directing and working responsibilities as well as ownership. Finally there is the state farm, found in Russia, which is controlled and managed by the state and which is manned by the farmers of the district with such security of wage and tenure as the state provides. All of these systems are an effort to organize the agricultural enterprise on a scale and in a way which is effectively and efficiently productive while satisfying, as far as possible, the legitimate desires of those who do the farm work for tenure and a fair share of the proceeds.

When a balance cannot be struck between the decreasing labor requirements of the modern agricultural sector with its supporting industrial segments and a labor supply which is increasing in most countries, it is incumbent upon governments to find ways to give employment to surplus rural manpower and to utilize it in the country's social and economic development. One channel for this labor supply is to the cities and industries there. This flow is an important factor in the development process but it is often uneven and without adequate preparation for the severe cultural adjustment involved. Programs of rural development sometimes attempt to cope with this problem by providing vocational training to migrants or prospective migrants to the city. Another channel of surplus population from overmanned rural areas is to rural areas being opened to agriculture for the first time. When programs of transmigration and land settlement are well planned and managed they can help solve the two problems of unemployment and agricultural productivity through the same transaction, as has been attempted in Malaysia, Indonesia, Sudan, and elsewhere. Migrants attracted by such opportunities are often ill suited to their new enterprise, however, because they are frequently the least successful farmers of the community of their origin. At the same time the task of conquering a new frontier of jungle and bush and of establishing the whole complex structure of government and economy and society to support and sustain the pioneers is staggering and requires such expert administration as is too seldom available to it.

The more typical situation therefore is the rural community where there is a population which is surplus to the needs of the new agricultural economy and its related enterprises and which is not wanted or needed soon enough or rapidly enough in other areas, urban or rural. Under these circumstances the first effort is often to encourage and even to insist upon the use of systems and methods of farming which are labor intensive rather than systems and methods which are capital intensive. This approach would give preference to human rather than to machine or even animal labor in working the land and planting, cultivating, and harvesting the crop. It would use hand labor rather than chemicals to get rid of the weeds. It would use human labor rather than machines in many of the operations involved in processing the harvest for storage, transport, and sale. Such policies of labor-intensive farming are eminently sensible insofar as they do not limit the productivity of the agricultural operation or make it so expensive, so burdensome with overemployment, as to negate much of its advantage. Human labor has advantages, too, over machines, in that the capital costs, both recurring and nonrecurring, can be reduced. As a general proposition, however, labor-intensive methods when adopted ease only a fraction of the unemployment load and are in opposition to the mainstream of efficient production methodology.

Programs of rural development therefore very often and quite appropriately call for the provision of public works programs which engage surplus and unemployed labor in projects of economic and social value to the community. India and Bangladesh are among the countries moving in this direction. There are many projects suitable for public works, including the construction, repair, and maintenance of local roads, of dikes, canals, and drains for irrigation, of school and community buildings, of parks and playing fields. Other kinds of projects extend to conservation and resource development in the form of reforestation and forest fire protection and the salvage of badly eroded farming areas. Still other kinds of projects are to be found in the area of service in community programs of health and sanitation. The contributions of carefully selected and well-planned and executed public works projects to rural and national development can be very great while giving gainful employment to surplus labor. This course of government policy and action would seem wiser than the alternative of burdening the agricultural production sector with inefficient and uneconomic employment practices which inhibit its potential to grow more food and fiber and to earn money for development.

Issues in Organization for Agricultural Production

Clearly there has been a breakthrough in the technology of agriculture which makes it possible to increase significantly the production of such food crops as rice and wheat. There are similar technological advances in the production of corn and sorghum and of cotton, rubber, palm oil, and other commercial crops. Technology is fundamental, but in itself it is not enough to assure the desired increases in any significant volume. Such increases depend upon the supplies and support which make the application of the new technology possible and they depend upon the profits from the application of the new technology which make it attractive. Organizing for agricultural production involves the identification of the several functions needed to make it possible and to make it attractive, and it involves the effective and reliable performance of these functions.

Six of these functions are readily named. They include (1) research, not only to achieve further technological advances but to solve problems of local adaptation of known scientific systems; (2) educational and informational services to help farmers introduce new farming methods; (3) the production and supply of such inputs as seeds, fertilizers, water, and insecticides; (4) the assurance of markets in appropriate balance with the assurance of price and credit support; (5) the provision of the whole of the agrobusiness complement, including not only utility and communication facilities but, more specifically, storage, preservation, processing, and transportation systems; and (6) educational programs both to produce the trained manpower needed in the agriculture sector and to serve the functional literacy needs of the rural population at the desired levels.

The first issue of organization for agricultural production is whether additional functions and responsibilities should be charged to the agency or agencies accountable for the first six functions which are related directly to the productivity of the land. One group of functions not inconsistent with those of agricultural productivity and frequently assigned to the agriculture department or ministry of agriculture is the development and use of livestock, forestry, and fisheries resources. These activities are often and desirably related to the activities of farmers and of farming and for that reason are appropriately located with the functions of agricultural production for the purposes of agency assignment. It is not so clear that natural resources such as those of oil and minerals and water should be added to those of lands and forests for protection and development by the agriculture agency. While there is not essentially a conflict in the functions and while the functions are or should be performed in mutually beneficial ways, the additional burdens would call for an agency so large and for an industrial and consumer population so large as to diffuse too much the focused attention needed by each. Concerns for natural resources other than land and forests should be and usually are assigned to another agency.

Other functions which bear upon agricultural practice might or might not be supportive of productivity as such and therefore raise issues of conflict of interest or threaten to divert the agricultural productivity agency in some degree from its main purpose. Functions of this kind are those of land, forest, and wildlife conservation and the protection of the environment generally, which, in the degree to which they inhibit intensive agriculture, limit productivity. From this point of view, conservation and agricultural functions should not be joined in the same agency. From the point of view of a viable system of public administration, however, it is preferable that a single agency be responsible not only for agricultural productivity but also for productivity within the limits of policy and practice which preserve the integrity and the productivity of the land on a continuously renewable and therefore inexhaustible basis. The unified context for decisions about land use and agricultural practice avoids the partisan and sometimes irresponsible confrontations of developers and protectionists when one agency is charged only with increasing production and another only with conservation or environment. Unfortunately, however, the few countries which are up to now formulating environmental policies and creating agencies to monitor them, such as the Philippines, do so in a way which tends to create parallel but overlapping bureaucracies. Such arrangements entail much expense and delay in the decision-making process and usually involve a third agency at a higher level, which itself must act as it would have been desirable for the agricultural agency to have acted in the first place.

Another issue when organizing the agricultural agency is whether it should also be the agency for rural development. Certainly the government must be concerned with the quality of rural life as it is also concerned with the level of agricultural production. As in the case of natural resources in their entirety, the rural population and its welfare have too much breadth and scope for one department or ministry to deal with. Rural development involves not only farming and agrobusiness but also rural industries, health, education, utilities, and communications. To the extent that the nature of the agricultural program or the government's policy calls for land reform or land tenure reform, however, it would be wise to make the agriculture department responsible for such reform because of the inseparable relationship of land size and tenure to the farming enterprise. Programs of rural public works for the employment of surplus labor, on the other hand, although they can contribute to the strength of the infrastructure for agriculture, such as market roads and local irrigation facilities, are not very close to the central interests or capabilities of an agricultural agency and are better administered by public works departments. A good basic rule is for the agricultural agency to focus on productivity and to take on additional functions only if they are inseparably and centrally related to that focus and if they are easily and naturally within its personnel and organizational capabilities. Most countries, however, do not follow this rule but continue the combination of agricultural production and rural welfare in the same ministry. Malaysia, which has a ministry for each function, is an exception.

In some countries, as is the case in India, Malaysia, and Nigeria, agriculture is considered to be, or is in their constitutions provided to be, a "state subject," that is, a function reserved to the jurisdiction of the state rather than to the central government. Otherwise, and most commonly, as is the case in Thailand and Tanzania, the several functions to support agricultural productivity are lodged in the central ministry or department. In those countries where the state governments do exercise some autonomous authority over agriculture, an issue inevitably arises over the relationship of the state to the central bodies, and central governments invariably have central agencies of agriculture even when agriculture is a so-called state subject. In these cases the central ministry is in a position to, and does, influence state agricultural policy and program because it almost always has financial resources to use for bargaining, whereas the state is usually too short of funds to enjoy unhampered autonomy. The central ministry usually has good reason to exert pressure on state agricultural practice, too, in addition to the expected purposes of improving efficiency and effectiveness in production. If there is foreign trade in agricultural produce—as in Malaysia and Ghana, for example—which is almost always the case in the form of either export or import or both, the central government must be concerned not only as the agent or the agent supervisor but also because of the financial consequences of deficits or surpluses. The central government is also concerned with the level of productivity either to increase trade advantages or to reduce food shortages. Especially in times of severe food shortages do the individual states tend to raise restrictive and harmful barriers, a tendency which compels the central government to intercede.

Each of the several functions involved in agricultural productivity poses its own problem of organizational accommodation. Questions must be asked and answered even with respect to the function of agricultural research. Most would agree, although some would not, that the research assignment should include qualitative considerations, such as nutritive value, as well as quantitative goals, and should include the argobusiness aspects of the total agricultural industry as well as the soils and agronomic aspects. There are more frequent differences of opinion about the organization of research, whether it should be by function or by discipline or by commodity. A form of research organization of growing and proven practice is to combine all of the several research interests in one research department organized by professional specialization but with provision for interdisciplinary commodity task forces and for multipurpose field stations—although occasionally a field station might need to focus on one crop, such as rubber, or one problem, such as rats. This kind of organization avoids the unnecessary duplication and competition entailed in parallel research organizations for each of a number of commodities.

Most agricultural research programs in developing countries are located in the central agriculture ministry, although a few are found in a separate ministry of science or research, or in state departments, or in agricultural universities, or in government research corporations, or in combinations and mixtures of these. Malaysia has set up a government corporation for agricultural research—the Malaysian Agricultural Research Development Institute (MARDI). There are vigorous proponents and strong arguments in favor of each of these alternative homes. The government agency gives the advantage of direct support and immediate influence; the university gives the advantage of academic freedom and of support from other disciplines; the government corporation gives the advantage of administrative latitude and flexibility as well as autonomy in the conduct of research. No one organizational format for agricultural research would prove to be the best for all countries because the environmental opportunities for its best expression vary according to other institutional conditions. The most important considerations therefore are that the arrangements for its conduct should be rational and advantageous in terms of the local situation, that they be clear, and that they have strong support.

A prerequisite to the introduction of the "Green Revolution" or other new technology for significantly increased agricultural production is the availability to the farmer of the essential inputs—the new seeds, the water and fertilizer upon which they must thrive, the pesticides to protect the young plants, the machines and implements of modern agriculture and the electricity and other fuels necessary to them. These inputs must be produced or imported and they must be delivered—delivered to the right place at the right time. The farmer or the farm operator must be willing to buy the supplies and materials and equipment he needs because their cost to him is reasonable in terms of his risk and his prospective profit and he must be able to buy them because he has the necessary cash or because he has access to credit on acceptable terms. It is incumbent upon the government and its central agricultural agency to see to it that those conditions of production or procurement, delivery, and terms of sale are in the interests of the increased yields possible with the application of modern agricultural technology.

It is unlikely that the central agricultural agency will attempt to perform all of those service functions itself. It would be prudent for it to engage in as few operations as possible in order to conserve its energies for the discharge of its central responsibility, which is to anticipate the several requirements of supply for the agricultural sector and to arrange that they be met. The ministry of commerce, for example, might be immediately responsible for marketing products abroad, as in Thailand, and for the import of fertilizer or other supplies; the ministry of industries would ordinarily be in charge of the development of the fertilizer, pesticide, and other production industries upon which agriculture must rely; the ministry of public works or its equivalent is almost always responsible for planning and developing the country's irrigation and electricity and road systems. The administrative problem here, an organizational issue of coordination, is how to establish by committee and by planning and budgeting processes a viable method of agreeing, in this interministerial environment, upon production priorities and delivery systems for the agricultural sector.

From the point of view of meeting the farmer's needs, the primary function is to give assurance of procurement and delivery of the requisite materials. Selection of the instrument for production or procurement and delivery is secondary, although important. Private enterprise can be encouraged and assisted to meet these production and delivery and service and banking requirements under the government's surveillance. Cooperatives, a form of private enterprise, are often organized to perform procurement and supply functions at the local level and even on occasion to go into production. Public enterprises, corporations, and companies of a variety of kinds are frequently created by governments to engage in the production, delivery, and credit activities so important to agriculture. These public enterprises are found in the form of agricultural development authorities, as in Pakistan, or fertilizer companies, as in India, or commodity produce boards, as in Kenya, or agricultural credit associations, as in Thailand.

Governments occasionally, through their ministries, engage in some of these support activities directly, and most often in seed multiplication and distribution, in irrigation, in electric supply, and in road construction and maintenance. In the mixed economies which characterize most developing countries there are varying combinations of these several kinds of agencies and institutions to serve agriculture. This circumstance emphasizes and makes even more compelling the crucial role of the central agricultural agency in planning and coordinating the provision of supplies and services to the farmers to assure that those supplies and services are adequate to the national purpose.

Remaining Issues in
Organizing the Central Agricultural Agency

The central agricultural agency must initiate and monitor the policies and practices of government which motivate and justify the farmer in using the materials of modern agriculture. For this reason the prices of fertilizer, pesticides, pumps, tractors, and other materials need to be supervised; quite often governments elect to subsidize agriculture by arranging for fertilizer and other materials to be sold at a reduced rate. Such practice, found quite effective in its operation, does however involve reimbursement to the producers or suppliers of the subsidized material. Farmers in many countries are not accustomed to paying for irrigation water, and the agriculture department is obliged to find ways either to repay the irrigation investment in some other way or to induce the farmers to adopt a new practice. The terms of credit, particularly private credit, invariably require regulation in both cost and time and often in method of repayment, whether in cash or kind. All of these several issues of financial policy in development administration for agriculture call for the leadership of the central agricultural agency, which, however, is dependent upon the helpful cooperation of other central agencies of government—such as the central bank, the treasury, the planning and budget agencies, and the ministry of industries—for the fixing of the policies and for their application.

Similarly, the central agricultural agency must become heavily involved in the marketing of agricultural products. This function includes such aspects of agribusiness as storage, preservation, and processing. It includes very prominently the policy issue as to whether the farmer will be guaranteed a floor price for his production, a practice accepted more

and more for the purpose of encouraging increased agricultural production. The issue of a guaranteed price, however, is complicated by the
demands of domestic urban consumers for lower prices and by the competition of the international market.

The central agricultural agency is again confronted with issues of
economic and administrative policy which involve the responsibilities of
other government agencies, such as commerce and treasury. Closely
related issues are those of tax policy, as they encourage or inhibit
agricultural production and trade in agricultural commodities, and those
of marketing agencies, whether they be public or private. A number of
countries, including Kenya and Nigeria, have set up marketing boards in
the form of public enterprises to buy and sell the total production of a
specified crop such as coffee or rice or cocoa—with mixed results. The
governments of others have intervened only at the level of international
trade agreements and the allocation of limited domestic supply. These
are issues of broad national economic purpose and policy requiring for
their resolution the participation of planning, treasury, and commerce as
well as agricultural agency officials. It is the special responsibility of the
agricultural agency, however, to initiate the consideration of those issues
and to monitor the policy decisions which emanate from such consideration as they pertain to agricultural productivity.

Education for agricultural development is another issue of policy and
organization involving not only the agricultural agency but other central
agencies as well, including in this case the educational as well as the
planning authorities. Modern agriculture is dependent upon the scientists
and professional specialists and technicians who support and apply its
technology. Modern agriculture is dependent upon the managers and
entrepreneurs of small business and, perhaps above all, it is dependent
upon a farming population which is both literate and thus accessible to
effective communication and also open and alert to opportunities for
agricultural advancement and development. Even though agencies and
institutions of education are established to serve agriculture as well as
other sectors in these several respects—universities, technical institutes,
secondary and primary schools—it remains an obligation of the
agricultural agency to analyze the manpower and educational requirements of the agricultural sector and to represent them persuasively to the planning and educational agencies. Such analysis should
include not only a forecast of the specialized personnel requirements of
the public and private sector components of the agricultural sector, but
also an identification of the particularized contributions of primary and
secondary education to the farming enterprise.

It is by no means sufficient for a government, through its agricultural agency and associated agencies, to do the research, provide for production and supply of materials, arrange for the infrastructure of agribusiness, assure profitable markets, and develop a sound base of educational and manpower support, although each of these is essential. It remains for the agricultural agency to serve the thousands of individual farmers themselves with educational, informational, and advisory services so that they may adopt new agricultural practices with confidence and success. This is the function commonly known as "agricultural extension." The key role of extension is to serve as an effective two-way liaison between the research and other specialized branches of the agricultural establishment and the farmers, transmitting new information to the farmers and conveying intelligence about the farmers' problems to the establishment. This role is indispensable because local and regional differences in farming can be very great, requiring particularized attention. The quality of the extension service is the measure of the agricultural agency that gives priority to the use, and not only the development, of helpful agricultural technology.

There are temptations in the use of an extension service which if yielded to are almost certain to weaken its effectiveness. One of these is to burden the extension workers with regulatory functions of one kind or another, such as the administration of crop quotas, tenure laws, or even assessments for taxation. Another is to make the extension service responsible for one or more of the delivery systems for farm supplies. These additional functions, although they are important and must be performed by somebody, inevitably distract the extension agent from his primary responsibility and change his relationship with the farmers from one of technical assistance to one of supervision and control. There are other pitfalls in organizing the extension function, such as the tendency in some countries, as in Thailand, to create parallel extension services for each of several special purposes, such as rice and corn and livestock, thus burdening the single farmer with multiple contacts and sometimes with pressures to join more than one farmer organization. It is usually sounder for the extension service to be organized in a single unit but with the capacity to enlist the service of specialists in the various aspects of agriculture when needed.

From the foregoing it is seen that much, even a preponderance, of the support for increased agricultural productivity is not provided directly by the ministry of agriculture or other central agricultural agency. It is clear, then, that the central and by all odds the most important functions of the ministry of agriculture are those of planning and of coordination. These are the very points, however, at which the agricultural agencies of most countries are weak. The strong ministry of agriculture is the one which encourages others to do the operating work in support of agriculture and focuses its attention upon its planning competence and upon its coordinating skill.

The planning function in agriculture is to comprehend and analyze the potential for increased productivity and the disposition of that productivity and to coordinate or formulate and monitor those policies, programs, and projects necessary or desirable to act upon that potential. Such planning depends heavily upon reliable and up-to-date statistical data and reports on the condition of agriculture, information which is important also to operating programs, be they in the agricultural or some other agency. Such planning should be characterized by its emphasis on the management aspects of policy, program, and project feasibility; that is, on the ways to accomplish program goals in administrative terms. The coordination function in agriculture is to engage the several central ministries and agencies—industries, commerce, education, public works, treasury, budget, and planning—in effective bilateral and multilateral associations for the purpose of collaborating on policy formulation and agreeing on programs and projects for agriculture and clarifying administrative responsibility for the execution of those programs and projects. In those countries where there are strong state agencies for agriculture, they also should be enlisted in this planning-coordinating process. Representatives of the private sector and of the farmers themselves should be involved.

The first three organizational units to be identified in the agricultural agency therefore are those for planning; for data collection, reporting, and statistical analysis; and for coordination. These units should be the chief staff arms of the minister or top executive officer in the agency. Other staff offices would normally be those for budget and personnel.

The operating units or divisions of the agricultural agency would then be those for the conduct of those programs assigned to the agency—units for research and extension, for example. There need be no such units for functions and programs assigned to others; the agency's interests should be expressed through the staff units for planning and coordination unless there are substantial activities needed to support others. For example, the central government might wish to subsidize the agricultural research or agricultural extension conducted by universities and states, and to take some leadership in guiding and coordinating these activities through the agricultural agency. The extent of this kind of activity might warrant the creation of a unit or units for research and extension. Similarly, there might be gaps in the production and supply of agricultural inputs which would call for action by the central agricultural agency, such as in seed multiplication and distribution, or in support of major irrigation works.

In such cases organizational units suitable to the defined tasks should be set up.

Marketing, with its correlative functions of storage, preservation, processing, and transportation, is still another area where the agricultural agency might have to organize units to the extent that other agencies do not do the whole job. One area where it is crucial for the agricultural agency to have great strength and organizational capacity in almost all circumstances is that of financial policy as that policy affects farmers and influences their performance for agricultural productivity—policy relating to price supports, controls of and subsidies for the costs of fertilizers and other inputs, taxes, and the terms and supply of credit. This area of agricultural production incentives is too large to be subsumed under the planning function. Finally, to the extent that additional functions are assigned to the agricultural agency, organizational units would have to be set up to accommodate them—functions such as forestry, livestock, fisheries, new land development, soil conservation, and land and land tenure reform.

The significance of development administration as it is applied to the agricultural sector is that it focuses upon the unique needs of that sector to be served by especially designed administrative arrangements, and it is concerned with support to operators—farmers—external to the public agency. This characteristic of external administration is illustrated also by the agricultural agency's reliance upon the cooperation of other agencies. It is recognition of this principle of external administration which should induce the agricultural agency to decentralize its service and other operations in support of farmers throughout the country. A part of this decentralization, a large part, can be achieved by reliance upon the private sector and upon other agencies—very often state agencies—for the performance of coordinated functions. Another and significant achievement in decentralization can be brought about by the field offices of the central agency. Such offices should be given wide discretion to support both public and private efforts organized by farming communities at the local level and to raise the level of the services required. Organization for agricultural production should involve all the agencies and resources which can be engaged to contribute to it at all levels, and not merely the central agricultural agency alone.

Note on Sources

The literature on agriculture in economic development, on the components of agricultural production, and on the Green Revolution is voluminous. It is comparatively meager in the area of organization and administration. My conclusions about the issues in organization for agricultural production come primarily from my own observations and experiences in a number of countries.

Among the books about agriculture in economic development, I would like to mention the following:

Carl Eicher and Lawrence Witt, eds., *Agriculture in Economic Development* (New York: McGraw-Hill, 1964).

Yuijro Hayami and Vernon W. Ruttan, *Agricultural Development: An International Perspective* (Baltimore: Johns Hopkins University Press, 1971).

Nural Islam, ed., *Agricultural Policy in Developing Countries* (New York: Wiley, 1974).

Andrew W. Kamarck, *The Tropics and Economic Development* (Baltimore: Johns Hopkins University Press, 1976).

John W. Mellor, *The Economics of Agricultural Development* (Ithaca, N.Y.: Cornell University Press, 1974).

John W. Mellor, *The New Economics of Growth: A Strategy for India and the Developing World* (Ithaca, N.Y.: Cornell University Press, 1976).

Theodore Schultz, *Transforming Traditional Agriculture* (New Haven, Conn.: Yale University Press, 1964).

For the components of agricultural production, the following analytical reviews are particularly good:

David Hapgood, ed., *Policies for Promoting Agricultural Development: Report of a Conference on Productivity and Innovation in the Underdeveloped Countries* (Cambridge, Mass.: MIT Center for International Studies, 1965).

Max E. Millikan and David Hapgood, *No Easy Harvest: The Dilemma of Agriculture in Underdeveloped Countries* (Boston: Little, Brown, 1967).

Arthur T. Mosher, *Getting Agriculture Moving: Essentials for Development and Modernization* (New York: Praeger, 1966).

The Green Revolution and its contradictory aspects are treated in several works:

Lester R. Brown, *Seeds of Change: The Green Revolution and Development* (New York: Praeger, 1970).

Thomas T. Coleman and Donald K. Freebairn, eds., *Food, Population and Employment: The Impact of the Green Revolution* (New York: Praeger, 1973).

Francine R. Frankel, *India's Green Revolution: Economic Gains and Political Costs* (Princeton: Princeton University Press, 1971).

International Rice Research Institute, *Changes in Rice Farming in Selected Areas of Asia* (Los Banos, Philippines: International Rice Research Institute, 1976).

Stanley Johnson, *The Green Revolution* (New York: Harper and Row, 1972).

A useful book on nutrition and development is that edited by Alan Berg, Nevin S. Scrimshaw, and David L. Call: *Nutrition, National Development and Planning* (Cambridge, Mass.: MIT Press, 1973).

To check my own views on organization for agricultural development, I used three books in particular:

Willard W. Cochrane, *Agricultural Development Planning: Economic Concepts, Administrative Procedures, and Political Process* (New York: Praeger, 1974).

Arthur T. Mosher, *To Create a Modern Agriculture* (New York: Agricultural Development Council, 1971).

Arthur T. Mosher, *Serving Agriculture as an Administrator* (New York: Agricultural Development Council, 1975).

3

Population Policy and
Administration for Development

The Weight of Population in the Development Equation

The world's population is about four billion. In 1950, just after World War II, it was 2.5 billion; and in 1900, at the turn of the twentieth century, it was about 1.5 billion. Even with some reduction in the speed of its growth, the world's population will reach 6.5 billion in the year 2000, at the turn of the twenty-first century, and 13 billion in 2075. This exceedingly rapid increase of geometric proportions in the size of the population is due to a decrease in the rate of mortality—that is, to a marked reduction in child deaths and an extension of longevity—while birthrates have remained high. Mortality has declined, chiefly since World War II, because of safer water supplies and better sanitation, the extension of public health services and their improved resources of antibiotics, insecticides, and inoculations, and the control and even eradication of such major hazards to health as malaria. Longer life is also attributable in part to better nutrition.

Larger populations can be sustained, however, only so long as the food supply is adequate to nourish them. Widespread famine both in Africa's Sahel and on the subcontinent of India only a few years ago is evidence enough that an imbalance between populations and the food resources to sustain them has reached serious and even disastrous proportions. It is probable that the world can produce enough food to feed even a population of 13 billion if sufficient areas of new lands are cultivated and if scientifically modern agriculture is applied more generally. Recent crises were due not so much to lack of food supplies as to lack of international reserve and distribution systems to make them available to hungry peoples at the right time and place. The lesson should be clear that populations and the resources to support them must be in happy or at least adequate balance, which is the function of development, and that the grim realities of famine will control populations if more rational and humane systems of control are not adopted.

It is not only the large and rapidly increasing size of the population which is a factor in the resource-development equation, but also its distribution and its composition. As a group, developing countries have a much more serious problem of population-resource imbalance than the more developed countries. Their rate of population increase is 2.4 percent per year, which will take them to 11.5 billion by 2075, whereas the developed countries, with an increase of 0.88 percent per year, will reach only 1.5 billion by that time. While it is true that some developing countries do not at present have a population which is too large in proportion to the resources available to a satisfactory standard of living, many countries do have that problem and almost all of them in any case have populations which are increasing so rapidly that the population factor becomes significant in the development equation. The larger the population and the more rapid its increase, the smaller the per capita income because the national product has to be divided among a larger number of people. This equation means that about two-thirds of a developing country's total investment is required to maintain income at its same level, and only one-third is available for increases in the standard of living.

The larger the population the larger the requirement for consumer goods and the consequent reduction of funds for investment in development. Given the objectives of development, which are to improve the general welfare of the population as a whole and to raise its standard of living, the size of the population in each country and the rate of its growth have too much weight on their side of the development balance. Countries with an annual population increase of 2 percent will double in size in thirty-five years; those with an increase of 3 percent will double in population in only twenty-five years. Algeria, for example, has a 3 percent annual increase. Unless curbed, its 15 million population will rise to 285 million in one hundred years.

The trends in population growth also govern its composition by age groups, and this composition has direct and significant consequences for the definition of development needs and for the satisfaction of those needs. The rapidly growing populations which characterize developing countries tend to be quite a bit younger than the more stable populations of developed countries. In the developing countries, 42 percent of the population is under fifteen years of age and 11 percent is fifty years and over, whereas in the developed countries only 25 percent is under fifteen but 24 percent is fifty and over. Life expectancy in the developed countries is seventy-one, but it is only fifty-four in the developing countries.

Interestingly, the dependency populations and the working populations of the developing and of the developed countries are in about the same proportion. Nevertheless, even though the developed countries have larger proportionate burdens of old age benefits, the developing countries have greater problems with the costs of education. Moreover, the developing countries must anticipate and prepare for an increase in the number of fertile couples, for an increase in the labor supply and its demands for employment, and for even greater pressure on the land and the size of farms. The composition of a population, therefore, and the nature of its dependency ratios are factors in the development equation, both on the consumption and on the investment sides of the balance. The costs of the consequences of rapid population growth are a significant aspect of development.

The cost and consequences of a rapidly growing population are measurable even more readily in terms of the several sectoral requirements of development than in overall national terms of consumption versus investment and of dependency versus productivity. The annual increases needed in housing, food, clothing, and each of the other components of the standard of living to match increases in population are direct and obvious. Increases in the school population place immediate and large burdens on the countries least able to afford them. Burdens of proportionate weight appear in the field of medicine and health. As the growing population matures and gets older, other consequences of its size appear, including the pressure on the land, problems of employment and wages, and the costs of old age retirement. All of these phenomena of the behavior of populations and their needs and demands insist upon accommodation in development planning and administration as a whole and in the treatment of the several sectors of development.

The size of populations is determined by the size of families. The comparative consequences of large or small numbers of children on the health, well-being, and happiness of those families and their members are also to be considered when weighing the merit of alternative programs and policies of development. Too many children, for example, closely spaced, can put an economic burden on a family which it is not able to handle adequately. School might be out of the question, especially after the elementary years, not only because of its costs but because of the need for the children's labor. Satisfactory health care is less likely to be available, and yet nutrition is likely to be insufficient, thus increasing susceptibility to disease and the probability of poor health. The health of the mother is often broken by too frequent and too many childbirths. From the point of view of family and individual health alone, therefore, population practices become directly relevant.

The social and economic status of the woman is to be considered in this context of family size too, as well as from the point of view of her health. If the woman's opportunities for political, cultural, and economic expression are to be opened up and extended, to that extent must she be freed from the burdens of childbearing and housekeeping which restrict her to those occupations alone. The ways in which women's rights and opportunities are perceived, recognized, and expressed are still another dimension of the development process as it is tempered by population policy and practice.

For all of these several reasons of inextricable interrelationships between populations, resources, and development, planning and administration for development should have the benefit of reliable vital statistics of births, deaths, and migrations and of expert demographic analysis of population size, growth rate, composition, and location, and of the projection of these aspects of population which are necessary to an understanding of its relevance and significance. This understanding of a country's population is an integral part of planning and administration for economic growth and social change.

Over a long period of time the rate of population growth and its distribution are determined by economic conditions, educational levels, and social status; and it can be expected that over long periods population growth will decrease and become stable under favorable circumstances of economic and social progress. From this point of view, and in terms of time spans of long duration, problems of population size and composition solve themselves if there is a reasonable degree of development progress—and especially if the development plan and program are designed to solve the population equation. This slow and evolutionary approach to the problem of population imbalance, however, overlooks the possibility and even probability of disaster in some countries unless it is supplemented, and effectively, by measures designed to operate directly and immediately on the variables of population size, composition, and location. Since the determinants of these variables are fertility, mortality, and movement or migration, these are the three factors which are usually considered the immediate targets of a country's policies and programs to mold its population from the quantitative point of view.

Movements and migrations of the population and employment and development programs designed to influence those movements are usually dealt with in a country's plans for rural, industrial, and urban development or in special regional projects. Death or mortality rates are a matter of nutrition and health, protection from accident and disease, and longevity. These are public concerns traditionally assigned as responsibilities to health departments or ministries. Other agencies often play a part, such as agriculture ministries for aspects of nutrition and education departments for instruction in hygiene and health. No one seriously proposes that mortality rates be increased to reduce populations or their rate of growth, which means that decreases in births must be the target.

Issues in Reducing the Birthrate

Birthrates, if they are to be reduced, require special and intensive attention. Programs designed to hit this target are called birth control or, more popularly, family planning. The first major question in birth control, or contraception, is whether the technical means are easily and readily available. Conception can be avoided by abstaining from sexual intercourse, by withdrawing before ejaculation, or by limiting intercourse to the sterile periods of the woman's monthly menstrual cycle—the rhythm method. These so-called natural methods of preventing conception and childbirth have not proved to be successful in reducing a country's birthrate in any significant degree. It is not natural to abstain or to withdraw, and there are too many temptations and accidents to make reliance on these methods a responsible system of family planning. The rhythm method is more promising as a system of birth control, but women's individually irregular rhythm cycles, the failure of calendar systems to measure the safe periods in the cycle reliably, and the errors people are prone to make in keeping the calendars have so far made it imprudent for a country to rely on it as the basis for its family planning programs. More violent methods of birth control are infanticide, which is rarely practiced anymore and which no one would seriously advocate, and abortion. Abortion is increasingly accessible to women by law, cost, and surgical safety, and some countries, notably Japan since World War II, have succeeded in reducing the birthrate by the widespread practice of abortion. Abortion, however, does physical violence to the mother, and if conception can be avoided rather than aborted that is clearly the preferred practice.

Unfortunately the perfect contraceptive device has not yet been discovered. Such a device should be harmless and painless yet fully effective, and it should be cheap, readily available, and easy to use. Sheaths, that is the condom for men and the vaginal diaphragm for women, are relatively expensive and inconvenient, and the woman must be fitted for the diaphragm by a doctor. Spermicides in jellies, creams, and foams are expensive and not yet very reliable as contraceptive agents. Progestin pills and vaginal inserts have as yet unresolved side effects and require personal medical attention, as do implants, although these methods are promising, particularly the long-term skin implant. Intrauterine devices of a number of kinds are still being tested, and one of them may yet prove to be the perfect contraceptive device, but involuntary ejection of the device by some women and bleeding and other harmful or frightening side effects suffered by others have reduced the earlier widespread reliance on them in many countries. Another contraceptive method is sterilization of either men or women, vasectomy in the case of the one and tubal ligation in the case of the other. Sterilization is fully and completely effective and is pushed as a major birth control system in some countries, such as India, for parents of two or three children. Sterilization is not reliably reversible, however, and it requires a surgical exercise by medical, or specially trained paramedical, personnel.

Hence the perfect contraceptive device for worldwide mass use in reducing birthrates is not yet available. Those which are available are either unreliable or expensive or require clinical attention either for initial application or for observation and follow-up or both. Clearly the additional research in contraceptive technology now being widely supported has the highest priority of any aspect of birth control and family planning.

The parents who really want to exercise birth control and thus limit and space the number of their children can do so if they have access to the requisite information, supplies, and services. The question here, and a major issue in family planning, is whether individual families really want to practice birth control. Information is not enough; there must be personal motivation as well. In this connection there is economic consideration—that is, will there be enough surviving children to help carry the family's labor load and to care for the parents in old age? Assurance of reduced child death rates, public old age security benefits, and changes in employment which reduce the importance of the family as a productive unit are all factors related to this economic consideration. There are also cultural considerations—that is, does religious belief consider birth control, at least in some of its forms, to be sinful, and do community mores give status to the parents of sons and many children? In many cases, although not all, progressive religious leadership has endorsed family planning and overridden the parochial understandings of local priests and mullahs. As education and employment opportunity expands for those children and young people able to grasp it, it becomes clearer that the children of smaller families have an advantage over children of larger families and thus increase family status. Also, as the political, economic, and social status of women improves, including the relative position of wives and mothers, so does the tendency increase to reduce the years of women's lives given over to childbearing and raising children. Nevertheless, the economic and cultural (including religious) barriers to the practice of birth control are very high.

The third major issue in family planning and in reducing birth rates is the attitude of a country's government and its policy and practice—whether it creates an environment which is indifferent to family planning, or one which encourages it, or one which rejects it as a policy and a program. Most countries these days recognize the right of the families in their populations to have the information they need about birth control and the relative merits of small and large numbers of children so as to make their own choices and to be able to act on those choices because contraceptive supplies and services are made available. Government policies limited to this area of individual right and family health avoid the resolution of issues of national political significance. This avoidance of issues might be due to the desire to avoid confrontation with a religious leadership which considers certain forms of birth control to be sinful. Or the government might wish to avoid conflict with a civil leadership which may worry about the deterioration of the standards of the population's moral behavior with respect to sex, with a military leadership which worries about manpower resources for defense, or with a communal leadership which is concerned lest one racial or religious group gain numerical and thus political ascendancy over another.

It is even more likely that a country's failure to take a firm position on population problems is because family planning as such seldom has its own politically influential constituency. It is only when the grim facts of the consequences of population imbalance in the development equation, as reflected in food shortages for example, or when women's rights movements become powerful, or when international agencies and organizations become effective with their urging, that governments are inclined to act. And when they do act, they do not always react in the same way. Some countries like Laos continue to encourage larger rather than smaller families and populations. Most countries, however, are gradually moving from positions of mere neutrality about the rights of parents to know about birth control to positions of greater support of family planning programs designed to reduce the birthrate.

Once a country advances to the point where it accepts responsibility for providing family planning information, supplies, and services to the population, usually accompanied by legalization if necessary of birth control supplies and practices, even abortion, the issues it faces are whether to encourage birth control practices and, if so, how and in what degree. One set of practices to provide incentives for family planning is a system or systems of fees and bonuses—to those for example who agree to sterilization or some less drastic form of birth control and to the "finders" of such acceptors, or to the doctors, nurses, and midwives who provide birth control services. Occasionally such bonus incentives are arranged on a community basis, as in the form of pumps or tractors for a village which has successfully reduced its communal birth rate.

Another and weightier set of practices to influence family planning and reduce births is through a system of negative and positive tax and benefit allowances. Income taxes might provide for deductions for no more than three children, for example, maternity leave given only twice, hospital and medical costs of confinement paid for two or three children only, and a ceiling placed on family allowances. Some countries go so far as to make payments, into savings accounts and otherwise, as "no-birth" bonuses for controlling periods of time. Such limits remove at least some of the inducement to produce large families and give economic encouragement to smaller families. Care must be exercised, however, to ensure that the penalties for large families, if any, do not fall upon innocent children. Finally, a country has the option of advancing the age of marriage, by law, and even requiring evidence of a couple's ability to support a family reasonably before authorizing the union.

Even these more vigorous interventions into private child-producing practices are held to be consistent with the ideal of free and voluntary individual choice. Nevertheless, most countries now do put a minimum age requirement on marriage, traditionally to stop child marriages, and it is but a short step to raise that requirement to higher ages for population control purposes. This practice moves a country nearer to systems of birth control and family planning which are mandatory rather than voluntary. If voluntary programs supported by education and economic and social pressure are not sufficiently successful in getting results, some stricter forms of mandatory inhibition on individual child-producing irresponsibility may well be justified to escape population control through starvation and other forms of suffering and violence.

Small countries such as Singapore, Korea, and Taiwan have for several years achieved dramatic reductions in birthrates and population growth by pursuing family planning programs very vigorously, with heavy reliance upon powerful negative and positive incentives. Singapore, especially, has instituted strong measures to reduce or increase medical and social welfare benefits and employment opportunities in proportion to adherence to national policy on family size. India conducted a massive campaign of sterilization with the full force of both the central and state governments in 1976. Preferential treatment was given for jobs to those who were sterilized, and penalties were levied against those families with three or more children in which one spouse was not sterilized—in the form of limiting access to government housing, loans, education, and even employment. West Bengal considered the imposition of fines or imprisonment as punishment for failure to be sterilized after three children. The rigor of this campaign produced seven million sterilizations in one year, mostly vasectomies for men. And still, by September 1976 only 18 percent of India's couples of reproductive age were protected against conception—12 percent by sterilization and the rest by intrauterine or other birth control devices. India's vigorous campaign resulted in riots in opposition to government pressure, particularly in rural areas. A factor in Prime Minister Indira Gandhi's defeat in the 1977 elections was opposition to her mass sterilization program. The successor government has made family planning and birth control entirely voluntary. The resistance to family planning is great.

Issues in the Administration of Family Planning

Organizing and administering a program of family planning is particularly difficult. Family planning is a comparatively new field; its technology is less than satisfactory; social, economic, and political obstacles to it are great; and government policy is often vague and uncertain. Opinions and experience vary with respect to the best way to go about it. One logical location for the family planning program in a government's structure is the child and family health division of the ministry of health. The assignment of responsibility to that division for conducting birth control and family planning activities gives certain obvious and immediate advantages. The child and family health division is the agency through which the government's concern with the health and physical well-being of mother and child has been expressed traditionally, and it is so identified in the public mind. Placing responsibility there emphasizes the generally acceptable motivation of health and the basis of voluntary choice which first encourages countries to undertake family planning programs and gives them justification for doing so.

A child and family health division, separately or in conjunction with other divisions of the health ministry, usually has a network of field hospitals, clinics, and other facilities, staffed by medical and paramedical personnel, which can be organized to serve or to begin to serve family health needs with comparative ease. Sometimes these networks are impressively complete and their range of services very effective in meeting public health needs. In other cases the field organizations are not so well developed, but there are almost always plans to perfect them and an understandable reluctance to dilute or delay such plans in order to set up a parallel organization for the birth control aspects of child and family health. Finally, in their contacts with mothers, the doctors and other personnel of field hospitals and clinics are in a particularly advantageous position to give pertinent information, advice, and birth control services—especially, for example, at the time of confinement, in postpartum programs, which have been proved to be widely effective.

Yet several of the functions involved in the successful conduct of a family planning program are not natural to the traditional child and family health agency. For this reason it is not uncommon to find family planning set up in a new and separate division or other unit of the health ministry. A new family planning unit, if put in effective association with other divisions of the ministry, has the advantage of several and related facilities and specialist contributions in an appropriate form of coordinated effort. A review of the several functions of family planning will emphasize this point. They include (1) the effective dissemination of information about the comparative advantages of family planning and its methods through schools, mass media, and special campaigns; (2) the establishment and operation of delivery systems to assure the distribution and availability of birth control supplies; (3) the provision of advisory and clinical services to prospective mothers and fathers involved in the program; (4) the administration of both direct and indirect incentive systems to encourage the practices of birth control; (5) the conduct of research—both biomedical and social science—to advance the methodology of birth control and its acceptance by the population; and (6) the introduction of data reporting and evaluation systems as a basis for improving program planning and execution. Whether set up in the child and family health division or elsewhere, each of these functions is importantly relevant to a successful program of family planning and must be performed.

There is another body of opinion, with some experience to back it up, as in Pakistan and Malaysia, that a national family planning program is better assured of success if it is organized outside the health bureaucracy.

This view acknowledges the inevitable and desirable involvement of such components of the health organization as district hospitals, field clinics, and central research and training facilities, but considers that the health ministry already has so many prior claims on its resources—including demands for the eradication of malaria, the control of venereal disease, vaccination for smallpox, and the assurance of safe water supply—that family planning as such would not and could not receive the competitively preferential attention required for the level of success needed and desired. Other reasons given for supporting the establishment of a separate organization for family planning are the fears that rigid bureaucratic practices and conservative views in the medical profession and its branches would provide less than enthusiastic and effective support for family planning and birth control. Lack of confidence in the bureaucratic adaptability of traditional ministries or major divisions of the public establishment has inhibited the assignment of family planning to other existing agencies—even to community development, because of its already demonstrated weaknesses of overload.

These same kinds of consideration influence governments in deciding whether family planning should be a national subject or a state subject of concern. Where family planning is considered to be a part of the health function it would normally fall to state initiative because health is commonly considered a state subject, although that initiative might be stimulated to a larger or smaller degree by the central government according to the extent of the national interest. In general, the countries deeply concerned with their population situation, those which see its size and rate of growth as threats to development and national welfare and increases in standards of living, are the countries most inclined to set up new agencies to conduct vigorous family planning programs rather than to rely exclusively on existing ministerial and state organizations to do so. Countries which have been aroused only moderately to the dimension of the population problem, such as to the point of permitting the dissemination of information and supplies, are more likely to authorize existing organizations to carry out these permissive activities than to create a new agency and a new system. Thailand is one of these.

Still another reason for establishing a new and strong agency for family planning and for locating it at a strategically high level in the bureaucracy is that all of the requisite functions cannot in any case be carried out by that new agency and, even if that were theoretically possible, the wisest course is to enlist the interest and support of all of the several ministries and agencies which are in a position to advance the family planning effort. The dissemination of information about family planning and birth control, for example, should involve the schools and the mass media as well as the support of special programs such as community development. The import and production and distribution of birth control supplies by the private sector should be encouraged as far as possible within the limits of medical safety. Many services basic to family planning are best and appropriately provided by hospitals, clinics, and other health centers of the central and state health ministries. Much and probably most of the medical and social and economic research bearing on methods and motivations, and much of the demographic analysis of census data and vital statistics, are better performed by existing agencies of government and by universities. The central family planning agency, under these circumstances, must clearly exercise the functions of program planning, leadership, and coordination not only competently but at such level of influence and authority in the government as to assure cooperation in the overall national endeavor.

Although a large part of the total responsibility of the family planning agency may and should in this way be discharged by enlisting the contributions of all other relevant organizations and agencies, much remains for it to do directly. The specialized demographic analysis of census data and vital statistics, for example, is a function natural and central to the family planning agency, although the conduct of the census and the collection of vital statistics are better and more appropriately done by others. The family planning agency should possess such competent specialists in biology, the social sciences, and education as to command respect in initiating and interpreting research, setting standards for birth control devices, recommending legal conditions and social benefit systems which encourage—or at least which do not inhibit—the practice of birth control, and preparing materials for education and informational campaigns. The agency will itself, through its own network of directly administered field offices, normally manage incentive schemes of fees and bonuses, conduct mass campaigns and, as much as is possible through individual contacts, persuade and assist prospective parents to turn to the practice of birth control.

These activities, both those performed directly by the staff of the family planning agency and those performed by cooperating organizations, involve very prominently in the work load of family planning administration the training and recruitment, or all too often the recruitment first and the training afterward, of the thousands of workers required in a vigorous national effort. This training assumes the several dimensions both of pre-service training, by supplementing and enriching the curricula of medical, nursing, social work, and community development education; and of in-service training—special indoctrination and orientation for those newly recruited from related fields of work. Recruitment of family planning workers is frequently impeded by the lack of civil service status, tenure, and even of competitive remuneration which so often characterizes the conditions surrounding the development of a new organization. An especially crucial aspect of the personnel problem for family planning is the selection of skilled administrators at the several levels of operation and their careful induction into the specialized competencies involved in their agency's work. Equally crucial are the complicated problems of interagency relations, medical hazards and standards, and the public's cultural and economic reaction to family planning and birth control, all of which characterize family planning programs.

These elements in the management of family planning programs are not uniquely distinctive; the management of programs in other fields can be similarly complex and difficult. Family planning programs are much more than ordinarily difficult to conduct and manage, however, because of three rather special circumstances. One is the intimately personal nature of the subjects of sex and childbirth and birth control and their vital closeness to perspectives of social status and economic well-being, not to mention religious salvation. These aspects of the subject of family planning require a high level of tact and understanding in program methodology and individual public relationships.

A second of these circumstances, and perhaps of inhibiting significance second only to the personal delicacy of the subject, is that the contraceptive devices are either too expensive to be adopted as primary methods of mass birth control efforts or they are essentially clinical—that is, they require individual attention upon the occasion of first use, not only for sterilization but also for IUD insertion and even prescription for the pill, and they require monitoring and follow-up to guard against and ameliorate harmful or frightening physical side effects. As long as contraceptive devices are in this respect insufficient and unsatisfactory and demand individual clinical attention for their use in any great degree, the mass impact of family planning programs and the wide adoption of birth control will be greatly limited and long delayed.

In the third place, and finally, there is a predilection on the part of family planners to overload their administration and their program systems with reports. No one can deny the value of reports in measuring the results of program performance, or in judging the competence of program management, or in evaluating the enterprise as a whole. These positive attributes of reports are clearly present when conducting family planning programs because it is essential to know the numbers and proportions of the acceptors of various kinds of contraceptive devices and their faithfulness in continuing use thereafter. It is also important for the family planners to know the patterns of birth control knowledge, attitude, and practice in the communities of concern to them and, even more fundamentally, the prevailing demographic configurations and their trends.

There has been a tendency, however, and still is, for the reports and the reporting procedure to overshadow the birth control activities as such and to make them less productive than they might be otherwise. For one thing, women coming to a clinic for information, advice, and especially for service are often presented with an interview questionnaire of such length and such intimacy that it puts them off entirely and in any case consumes time that reduces the caseload measurably. Another consequence of report overloading is that the time to complete periodically required report forms subtracts disproportionately from staff time that might be spent better in family planning information or assistance or similar functions. This preoccupation with reports, almost an obsession in some cases, combines with the unhappily clinical nature of the family planning endeavor at the present time to individualize and slow down the whole enterprise and thus thwart any significant mass result. This overdocumented clinical approach also encourages the family planners in many developing countries to seek to control contraceptive supplies and to maintain detailed records of their distribution and use which impedes, of course, the mass broadside effect that would more probably be achieved by multiple private and public delivery systems and distribution to anonymous purchasers and users.

Family planning has very far to advance in its technology and in its administration, as well as in its public acceptance, before it makes more than a perceptible difference in the basic long-term trend in rates of population growth. There is the exception of a few small countries like Korea, Taiwan, and Singapore, where birth control programs of greater intensity than feasible in large countries have combined with rapid economic growth and social modernization to achieve rather dramatically successful results. Otherwise the global picture is dark. Family planning programs must be seen as merely supplementary to the longer-term—much longer-term—influences of social and economic development which in time bring about reductions in fertility. They can be seen, optimistically, as preparatory to the time when the more perfect device is available and when it can be urged upon the population without the uneasinesses of medical or economic or other reservations. In the meantime, family planning programs serve to discharge governments' responsibilities to their populations for providing them with information about family planning and with supplies of such devices as are currently available so that they are able to act on such information and to this degree exercise their freedom of individual choice.

Population Policy, Planning, and Coordination

Planning for family planning involves the design of the programs and the projects—and the methodology—needed to realize the policy of the government and to achieve its targets of population size, birthrate, and family health. These projects and programs for their effective execution invariably require the participation and the cooperation of a number of agencies—public and private, central and local—including the areas of health and medicine, education and mass communication, vital statistics, census and demography, contraceptive supply and distribution, and social welfare. This multiplicity of involvement presents a major problem in the planning process because it is necessary to assure the informed and sympathetic contribution of the several parties and agencies affected by it and to achieve the coordinated and effective formulation and conduct of the overall program.

The central planning and budget staffs should also be engaged in these considerations, for the resources allocated to family planning and the weight given to programs of birth control depend in part at least upon analyses and judgments about the costs of such programs as compared with the benefits. These costs and benefits are measured by the larger per capita income of a smaller population and by the savings of lower costs for such services as education and health which are related to the size of the population. Central planning organizations were surprisingly slow to include those considerations and demographic analyses generally in the perspective of their methodology, although they are doing so increasingly now.

Although a country's attitude and position on family planning are sometimes described and accepted as its "population policy," this limited concept of population is by no means complete or sufficient. Family planning has to do with birth control and fertility rates. The other determinants of the size, growth rate, composition, and location of a country's population are its mortality rates—influenced by at least experience and it is hoped by policy and program as well—and migration and residence patterns, which may also be modified by policy and program. Mortality rates and longevity are a product of health and of protection from disease and other hazards to life. These concerns are the preoccupation of health ministries and agencies; planning for those concerns and the consequent programs emerging from that planning are normally handled through the regular channels for planning and programming the several sectors of development, including health. Nevertheless, not only the quantitative influences of the national health program but its qualitative benefits in terms of the population's energy and vigor are also aspects of population as that subject is more completely and adequately conceived.

Similarly, countries by their restrictions or lack of them on emigration and immigration and internal movements, and even more by their practices to encourage or discourage urbanization and land resettlement, are involved advertently or inadvertently in the evolution of policies and practices modifying the structure of their populations. Most of the planning and programming which influence migration and residence, however, are done not in the name of population policy but for the purposes of sectoral development. Urbanization—movement to the towns—is primarily due to employment opportunities, or hopes for them, induced by the processes of industrialization and trade. Programs to increase agricultural productivity might encourage migration from the countryside, while programs of rural development might perpetuate the attractions of rural life somewhat longer and inhibit migration. But in most countries the development policies and programs that influence population movements are the sectoral programs for the development of agriculture, trade, and industry, and they are planned and coordinated in these development terms.

On the other hand, when plans are undertaken to develop or modify the nature of employment opportunities for populations as such, considerations of population policy become primary and considerations of development become secondary. As matters of policy, for example, a country might open up new lands and encourage settlement there, even though other methods of increasing agricultural output might be quicker and cheaper. Industry might be instructed to disperse its new plants in satellite towns, or otherwise throughout the countryside, to inhibit further growth of large metropolitan areas which have grown too fast for the economy to support. Priority in development might be given as a matter of policy to regions where the populations are depressed. Public works projects might be undertaken to ameliorate unemployment problems even though their contributions to overall economic growth might be marginal. Programs of people-oriented rural development might be given precedence over programs of agricultural productivity.

All these illustrations exemplify tendencies in greater or lesser degree to give preference on occasion or in particular areas to specialized problems of the population's well-being. These are the qualitative aspects of a population's configuration, along with its literacy and educational levels and its standards of health and vigor. Not to be left out are those policies and programs of a country designed to deal even more directly with the population's well-being—public housing, access to reasonably priced food supplies, health and medical protection, benefit allowances for the unemployed, the needy, and the aged. Population policy therefore should embrace all these fertility-mortality, quantitative-qualitative, direct and indirect aspects of development and administration which influence the number of persons in a country and their well-being.

There is a body of opinion which holds that planning for development should be in terms of people and populations rather than in the terms of resources and money and economic growth which tend to dominate the concerns and processes of planning at the present time. Advocates of this view will probably not have their way, at least fully. Central planning and sectoral planning will continue to focus on the expansion of the economy and the best allocation and use of resources in order to get an optimal result for the people as a whole. As illustrated above, however, there is more and more tendency to modify economic and managerial equations of development by emphasizing the population factor, and there is a constantly growing demand to do so. Aspects of this demand extend to considerations of equity in the development process, fairness in the sharing of its benefits among the several classes and regions of the population and also among the present and successive generations of the population. It is evident, therefore, that the several aspects of development which affect or are affected by the size, composition, quality, and location of the population should be identified and dealt with in policies and plans for development. This is the proper area of population policy and planning.

Programs and projects in this broad area of population need to be harmonized and reconciled through appropriate systems of coordination. The application of this concept of population policy, planning, and coordination does not require the reorganization of all of government nor of all of planning. It does, however, require the formulation of a population policy as a whole and not merely of a family planning policy; and it requires the incorporation into the structure and methodology of central, sectoral, and regional planning of the capacity and influence of specialist population analysts to assure the application of population policy in balance with growth policy in the development equation and program. The identifiable and distinguishable aspects of population programming would benefit, both in planning and in the coordination of plans in their implementation, from the attention of a high-level council, possibly of cabinet rank, on population policy and programs. The acceptance of the concept of population policy and its recognition in planning and administration would acknowledge the necessity of bringing populations into balance with resources and their development. It would express the expectation that economic growth and the equitable distribution of the benefits, taken in conjunction with easy access to family planning services, should produce the reduction in fertility needed to achieve this balance.

Note on Sources

The estimates and other figures in this chapter come chiefly from *Concise Report on the World Population Situation in 1970–1975,* Population Studies, No. 56, Sales No. 74. XIII. 4 (New York: United Nations, 1974); *World Bank Operations: Sectoral Programs and Policies* (Baltimore: Johns Hopkins University Press, for the International Bank for Reconstruction and Development, 1972); and Timothy King et al., *Population Policies and Economic Development: A World Bank Staff Report* (Baltimore: Johns Hopkins University Press, for the World Bank, 1974).

Because of the size and critical nature of the problems it presents, the literature on population and its several aspects is voluminous. The statistical and other studies of the Population Commission of the United Nations Economic and Social Council—which works closely with the United Nations Statistical Commission—including *The United Nations Demographic Year Book,* are of special value. One of these, for example, is Population Studies, No. 56, cited above. The single most useful volume is the 661-page first volume of the two-volume Population Studies, No. 50: *The Determinants and Consequences of Population Trends: New Summary of Findings on Interaction of Demographic, Economic and Social Factors; The Report of the United Nations World Population Conference, Bucharest, 1974,* Sales No. E. 75. XIII. 3 (New York: United Nations, 1975); and particularly, the numerous conference background papers on country and topical aspects are a mine of information. A recent and very good study is *Status of Women in Family Planning,* Sales No. E. 75. IV. 5 (New York: United Nations, 1975). The most recent United Nations document of relevance is *The Administration of National Family Planning Programs,* Sales No. E. 78. II. H. 3 (New York: United Nations, 1978).

The World Bank's analyses, and those prepared for it, complement those of the United Nations. They include the chapter titled "Population Planning," pp. 291–371 in *World Bank Operations: Sectoral Programs and Policies* (Baltimore: Johns Hopkins University Press, 1972); Timothy King et al., *Population Policies and Economic Development: A World Bank Staff Report* (Baltimore: Johns Hopkins University Press, 1974); and George C. Zaidan, *The Costs and Benefits of Family Planning Programs* (Baltimore: Johns Hopkins University Press, 1974).

The concern of the Organization for Economic Cooperation and Development (OECD) is expressed in a number of studies and reports, including these three:

Assessment of Family Planning Programs: Summary of Proceedings of the Fourth Annual Population Conference of the Development Center (Paris: OECD, 1972); Goran Ohlin, *Population Control and Economic Development* (Paris: OECD, 1967); and Theodore K. Ruprecht and Carl Wahren, *Population Programs and Economic and Social Development* (Paris: OECD, 1970).

The most prolific of the private groups is the Population Council in New York City. Two of its series, "Studies in Family Planning" and "Reports on Population and Family Planning," constitute an invaluable record of experience and analysis. Its 1975 publication edited by Warren C. Robinson, *Population and Development Planning* (New York: 1975) should be noted.

Resources for the Future, Inc., is represented by Ronald C. Ridker, ed., *Population and Development* (Baltimore: Johns Hopkins University Press, 1976), and the National Academy of Sciences by the two-volume work *Rapid Population Growth: Consequences and Policy Implications* (Baltimore: Johns Hopkins University Press, 1971). The National Academy of Sciences has also published *In Search of Population Policy, Views from the Developing World: A Report of Five Regional Seminars* (Washington, D.C.: 1974). The Eastern Regional Organization for Public Administration, in Manila, the Philippines, held its sixth General Assembly and Conference in May 1971 on the topic of "The Administrative Implications of Rapid Population Growth in Asia," reported in mimeographed form in three volumes, including conference documentation.

Four other works deserve to be noted here:

Ansley J. Coale, *Economic Factors in Population Growth* (New York: Wiley, 1976).

Ansley J. Coale and Edgar M. Hoover, *Population Growth and Economic Development in Low Income Countries* (Princeton: Princeton University Press, 1958).

Philip M. Hauser, *The Population Dilemma* (New York: Prentice-Hall, 1970).

Richard Symonds and Michael Carder, *The United Nations and the Population Question* (New York: McGraw-Hill, 1973).

4

Administration for Educational Development

The Importance of Education to Development

The quality of the human resources applied to economic development has a direct relationship to the pace and the level of that development. The quality of human resources is dependent upon education, as well as upon health and upon the supporting environment. Physical capital would be wasted to the degree that productive skills are not applied to it. The adaptations and applications of science and technology upon which development depends so heavily are not accessible to an uneducated and untrained population. Research and the further development of technology are themselves appropriate and important functions of education. With the new scientific systems which accompany them, they are directly relevant to economic progress and growth. Economic growth is reliant upon sufficient numbers of qualified professional specialists, technical experts, skilled craftsmen, managers, and entrepreneurs to develop a country's capacity for growth. The production of this skilled manpower is a function of education—education in formal schools, on the job, and in non-formal but systematic programs of information dissemination and skill improvement.

The contributions of education to economic growth extend beyond manpower training. They include a level of literacy which permits reliable and effective communication between the specialists and specialized development agencies on the one hand and the agricultural

75

and industrial workers engaged in the development process on the other. There is a positive statistical correlation between the literacy rate and the average per capita incomes of developing countries; illiteracy is an impediment to development. Other benefits to economic growth which can be attributed to significant proportions of literacy and schooling are the acquisition of attitudes which encourage and support the changes which precede and accompany development and the attitudes which assist individuals to define and solve the problems they face in their own work and lives. Education is clearly a major factor in economic production and growth.

Education contributes to a nation's civic and political development as well as to its economic development. The lessons of the schoolroom and the associations with the educational system as a whole can contribute directly and heavily to the integration and national unity of a country, and especially a newly independent country, by emphasizing its common identities of language, history, and culture. The social discipline and morality exemplified and taught in the classroom can help a community and a nation to adjust to the new forms of social behavior required in modern agriculture and modern industry. Such discipline and morality, as well as the skills of communication, are basic to an understanding of and participation in a country's government and its political systems. A schooled and literate population is more able and more likely to define and articulate its economic, social, and political values than an illiterate and unschooled population. It is better prepared to participate responsibly in its country's political processes as well as to insist that such process be available to it.

Finally, in the contribution of the educational system to development lies the opportunity to sustain, advance, and disseminate a nation's distinctive culture as expressed in its art and sculpture, its architectural and building skills, its music and dance, and its literature. These cultural aspects of a nation's development are equivalent to economic, civic, and political dimensions in the establishment of the high level of civilization and of civilized existence for its people which is the nation's reason for being. In many emerging countries there is danger, or at least fear, that ancient and indigenous art or music and dance forms might die out, or that they might be lost to and overwhelmed by the popular social forms of entertainment of other countries.

In some instances traditional forms of cultural expression are unfortunately associated with traditional forms of economic and political existence which are no longer acceptable and thus rejected. It is not as important in this respect to preserve art and other cultural forms which are dying out, although such preservation can be historically and culturally valuable, as it is to encourage and assist a people, and particularly its creative members, to express themselves in those several ways which will give the country and its populations pride and enjoyment in a distinctive culture, a distinctive civilization. The life of the mind and the spirit is also the subject of development.

Education in these ways is important to economic development, to civic and political development, and to cultural development. These benefits are contributions of education to a country as a whole and to its population as a collective entity. Education in this sense is a sector of national development in much the same way as are such other sectors as agriculture and industry. In addition, however, education is of great importance to each individual in the population and to each family because each one has or at one time might or ought to have had the opportunity to improve his relative welfare and status in life by virtue of going to school. Education can help a participating population and its members to live happier, healthier, more productive, and more politically active lives. Education is also of great value to the individual because it gives him the opportunity to earn a higher and more assured income, or to work in more congenial surroundings with higher social status. There is a correlation between the earnings and economic condition of a person and the years of his schooling, except for occasional maladjustments due to the special circumstances of time or place. This correlation is more direct when school work is in preparation for skilled technical work and for specialized professions, but it also exists for general education at primary, secondary, and higher education levels.

This correlation between earnings and schooling makes education important to national development as a general proposition because it increases the productivity of the population. The perception of the correlation is also of great importance because it creates an enormous demand on the part of the general public, great social and political pressure, for the establishment of educational institutions and an opportunity to attend them. And beyond the limited aspirations to higher income there is the overriding drive of many, if not most, human beings to get assistance from education as from other sources in the fullest possible expression of individual creative potential.

The existence of this demand, the apparently insatiable appetite for education, has great significance for a developing country in several different respects. In the first place the readiness of the population for more schooling is consistent with and contributes to the achievement of national goals of developing countries to increase the quality of human resources for economic growth, to initiate civic and political development, and to sustain indigenous forms of cultural expression—all of which are aspects of development. In the second place, the provision of educational opportunity is an excellent means of sharing the benefits of economic growth with the people in ways which are consistent with the methods of development. This dual role of education, which is symbiotic in nature, is in happy contrast to other ways of sharing benefits, such as social welfare schemes which, although desirable, deplete resources for future development by expenditures for present well-being. In the third place the location of schools and other educational institutions so as to provide educational opportunity in disadvantaged areas is a means of distributing national wealth to correct regional inequalities and inequities in the population. Planning and administering a national system of education in this way extends and expresses the government's interest in and concern for its citizens wherever they live. The demand for education, therefore, and its satisfaction, are matters of great political importance.

The satisfaction of this great popular demand for more and more education is very costly in terms both of money and of personnel—as would be the satisfaction of a country's educational requirements for development in the form of educational institutions and programs even if the public's demand were lagging. The percentage of a developing country's budget for education averages about 15 percent; it averages 4 percent of the total gross national product. The education portion of the budget of many developing countries is 20 percent and goes as high as one-third. If these percentages were doubled, and most countries have targets which would do at least that, a reduction in the proportions of other components of the development budget would be required. To improve the quality of a system by getting better teachers and paying them more than the clerical personnel with whom they are too often equated might require an increase of as much as one-third because teachers make up such a large part of the education budget. Education is a staggering burden. Administration for educational development thus becomes a matter of considerable moment because of the indispensability of education to a nation's economic, political, and cultural health, because of the popular and politically potent demand for education, and because of the great costs of serving these educational interests.

The Interrelationship of
Educational Issues and Administrative Considerations

Administration is important in planning, organizing, and managing the educational establishment as a whole and in establishing and operating the several individual schools and institutions in the system.

Administration is also directly relevant to the feasibility and comparative effectiveness of one educational program as opposed to another, of one educational policy as contrasted to an alternative, or one pedagogic or instructional method or standard selected in preference to some other. Clearly, the choices made when these issues are defined should be those which most nearly represent a country's educational goals and the best pedagogical methods and standards insofar as they can be ascertained. If the theoretically most desirable programs, policies, or methods are too costly for the country's treasury, they might have to be given up for a less desirable but more attainable alternative, or else postponed, to be undertaken gradually.

Even more frequently, the choice is not whether to give up a program or method but rather which of roughly comparable programs or methods to select. Here again the primacy of a country's fundamental goals and of the professional, pedagogic selection of methodology should prevail if at all possible. In more cases than not, however, the educational differences in results between alternatives are so comparatively slight that considerations of management feasibility can and should be taken into account as well. Such considerations may be crucial not only in selecting among alternative programs, policies, and methods to achieve educational purposes but even more crucial in assuring that the alternative selected can be carried out effectively.

An illustration of this unavoidable relationship between educational issues and the administrative considerations relevant to the choice among alternative solutions is readily seen when the length, the number of years, of schooling is set at each level—primary, secondary, and higher. Should the primary school include a kindergarten and even a nursery year or be limited to six grades, one through six? Most developing countries feel that they can postpone pre-primary programs, desirable as they may be, for lack of management resources of money, personnel, and facilities that are needed more urgently in other parts of the educational system. Should countries which have a five-year secondary-school system, such as the Philippines, add a sixth year to meet world standards as well as to enrich the high school program? Many countries have been well advised to postpone the acceptance of that additional burden, especially considering the fact that their secondary-school graduates who decide to continue their education seem to do college work acceptably.

Some countries, like Pakistan, which have a system of two-year intermediate colleges between high school and university, are tempted to abolish them or to merge them with stronger secondary schools below or with four-year colleges above. Such steps lead in many cases to administrative confusion and expensive additions to educational plant and facilities. More important, they encourage larger numbers, prematurely, to aspire to the baccalaureate degree rather than to be satisfied by the previously acceptable terminal intermediate certificate.

One of the most difficult problems in developing the educational system is the degree of specialization which will be expressed in the curriculum or syllabus at each level—primary, secondary, and higher. The greater the specialization the greater the costs in teacher preparation, textbooks, and facilities, and the more complex the task of organizing and conducting such specialized programs. At the primary level the question often arises in terms of language teaching—that is, whether the vernacular and a second language such as English will be taught, as well as the national language, and in some cases even the languages of religion and culture. In Punjab, for example, the languages sought to be accommodated are Punjabi, Urdu or Hindi, Arabic, Persian, and English. Other subjects where the question arises are art and music. At the secondary level a major issue in addition to these is often whether science should be introduced and with what coverage and intensity. Science teaching of much depth requires expensive laboratory equipment and supplies as well as specialized teachers—teachers of biology, chemistry, and physics.

Few developing countries can really provide much specialized instruction in science for want of personnel and equipment and supplies, yet most of them wish to do so. The fact is that even when such instruction is offered at the secondary level it is almost always duplicated at the intermediate and college level, and sometimes high school work in science is not even accepted for college credit. Broader introductions to science with simple but manageable demonstration kits would usually suffice and would serve even better to meet the needs of students as well as to be effectively viable from the administrative point of view. In such cases the practicability dictated by administrative common sense should take precedence over educational perfection even though the worthwhileness of such idealism must be granted. At the level of higher education, the lessons of premature overspecialization at postgraduate and professional levels are all too frequently to be learned from examples of great investment for a very small number of students who might be trained abroad better and more cheaply.

Perhaps the most controversial issue of specialization in education is whether and to what extent vocational and technical training should be offered and at what levels. The really desperate need of most developing countries for skilled manpower for industry and commerce and for modern farming encourages and supports many of them in efforts to offer such instruction in high schools and even, in rural areas and for agricultural purposes, in primary schools. These efforts are, and have often proved to be, ill-advised. In the first place, countries with scarce resources would be mistaken to divert machine tools and shop equipment and skilled workers from production in industry to schools for teaching. It is wiser to encourage and support training on the job in industry under these circumstances. Training on the job is probably sounder from the educational point of view in any case because students, given the basis of a sound general education and a broad orientation, are more suitably prepared for a changing variety of employment opportunities than are narrowly trained machine operators.

The same kind of reasoning applies to agricultural education in the rural school. The simplest and probably the best role of the teacher is to equip farm children to understand and benefit from subsequent instruction and guidance from agricultural extension agents and specialists rather than to attempt specialized training himself. It is not administratively attractive to contemplate the conversion of rural schoolteachers into agricultural specialists. On the other hand, a major branch of a country's educational system is obliged to be a network of technical institutes, most generally at the post-secondary intermediate level, for the preparation of those technicians who are specialists at the technical-supervisory level, midway between engineer and craftsman, and who are an indispensable segment of the industrial manpower pool. Such technical institutes may also be used effectively for the pre-service and in-service training of agricultural extension and community development workers and small enterprise managers.

The fewer the specializations represented in the curriculum, the fewer the teachers whose own specialized training takes time and money. The simpler and the more general the syllabus, the shorter and cheaper can be the process of teacher training. In most developing countries, and in many developed countries up to a couple of generations ago, primary-school teachers are matriculates, high school graduates, with perhaps a year or two of teacher training thereafter. This teacher training is most commonly offered in separate institutions—comparable in this and other respects to technical training institutes for industry and agriculture. As soon as possible, on the other hand, most countries seem to want their secondary-school teachers to be baccalaureates. Perhaps this aspiration, inspired primarily by the standards of other countries and international agencies, has been given too much priority considering the quite satisfactory performance of teachers prepared at the intermediate level—performance observed in times past in developed countries and currently in developing countries.

The time and cost required to produce the increasing numbers of teachers needed is such a large item in a country's development budget that these factors are an administrative consideration in deciding the pace of any increase in standard and requirement. The instructional system calling for an additional year of professional training—for primary-school teachers after high school or junior college (intermediate) and for secondary-school teachers after college—seems eminently sensible from the administrative point of view, particularly for a developing country. That system avoids the cost and other burdens of personnel and facility and management involved in setting up a separate network of teacher training colleges. Other illustrations could be given of the administrative factors that need to be given weight in resolving issues about educational programs and methods.

The really major issue, the unavoidable question requiring administrative as well as educational consideration, is who should be entitled to go to school and for how long. If it is decided that all children should go to school through the sixth year—the primary level—why was not the fourth year selected, or the fifth or seventh or eighth? The decision would be partly pedagogic and partly political, depending on the level considered to be appropriate to functional literacy and responsible citizenship. But the decision would also depend upon what the country could afford and what it could manage. Secondary but nevertheless very important questions must also be answered, such as whether education to a prescribed level should be required or optional and how education should be made available in remote areas and to poor people. These are questions beyond pedagogy; they go to issues of national policy and to administrative method. On the other hand, questions relating to dropouts and the reasons therefore, and the related question of whether primary-school children should pass to the succeeding grade automatically, involve considerations of both pedagogy and administration.

Issues of access to education extend beyond policies at the primary levels, where schooling is generally expected to be of universal applicability. Will all students who so desire be accommodated in secondary schools and even in colleges, or will there be limitations imposed by virtue of location, or of competitive examination, or of fee or tuition? In addition to consideration of manpower needs, these are policy problems rooted primarily in national outlook and purpose and administrative feasibility rather than in concepts of educational method and pedagogy. On the other hand, planning the curriculum to meet the needs and interests of the school population that the nation decides to accommodate is the primary responsibility of the educators. The interaction of educational and administrative considerations in this as in the case of other issues produces the answer for activating purposes which educational and administrative personnel working independently could not produce.

Organizational Issues
Affecting Educational Administration

Functionally, for purposes of organization and administration, the field of education is usually divided by level—that is, primary education, secondary education, and higher education. Practice varies somewhat from country to country in that primary education may be considered to extend to the seventh or eighth rather than to only the sixth year, and the intermediate or junior college years are sometimes included with secondary and sometimes with higher education. The basic divisions of primary, secondary, and higher education nevertheless predominate.

Three additional organizational divisions are not infrequently found. One of these divisions is often established for some or all aspects of vocational and technical education at the sub-university level, including at least the technical institutes at intermediate and secondary levels, usually vocational instruction in secondary schools, and even such vocational work as might be offered at the primary level. Apprenticeship and on-the-job training might or might not be considered a part of this category of technical education, although it is certainly obliged to be related to it. A second of these additional functional divisions of education is the way in which teacher training institutions are often organized separately from the other higher education institutions, either as a separate division or in conjunction with the primary or secondary schools they serve.

It is common to find in most countries a third organizational category in addition to the basic breakdown by level, a category which might comprise one or more divisions depending upon the country's program priorities. Most such programs in this category would be in the area sometimes called non-formal, such as those for functional literacy in general, or in support of a particular sector such as agriculture or health, or for adult or continuing education for cultural as distinct from vocational purposes. Sometimes also, although less frequently in developing countries, separate divisions are set up for special education of a variety of kinds, such as for the handicapped on the one hand or for some elite group on the other.

The responsibility for these several categories or divisions of education is commonly assigned at least in some degree to the central ministry or department of education at the national level. This orderly assignment to one ministry of all the divisions of the whole field of education is not usually to be found, however; on the contrary, there are almost always exceptions in the form of assignments to other ministries and other bodies. It is not unusual to find the responsibility for at least the apprenticeship and on-the-job training aspects of vocational and technical education and sometimes this whole field—and also sometimes certain aspects of child welfare—to be assigned to the ministry of labor. Functional literacy and other educational programs for adults, at least the adults of the rural population, are sometimes given to the charge of the ministry of agriculture, and the health care and education of schoolchildren is not infrequently in the hands of the ministry of health. There are countries in which the home ministry, or the ministry of the interior—the ministry which monitors the field administration of the central government—is given responsibility for primary schools; less frequently is it responsible for secondary schools. There are cases where separate ministries have been set up for higher education.

Certain categories of education can be the primary responsibility of other ministries or of other agencies external to the ministry of education. Universities, for example, may be given autonomous or semi-autonomous status with their own governing boards, as in India, sometimes coordinated by central boards and commissions and sometimes not. It is not uncommon for other bodies, in the form of government corporations, to be set up with relatively autonomous authority in their designated fields, such as the boards for textbooks, secondary education, research and development, and examinations in Pakistan. Finally, most developing countries are characterized by educational systems in which, particularly at the secondary although also at the higher and primary levels, the preponderance of schools is in the private sector—parochial or religious schools, schools set up to serve special racial or language groups, missionary schools, and commercial schools for profit. Thus the whole field of education in all its branches and aspects is seldom the sole responsibility of one ministry of education to plan, organize, and administer. Rather, education is a diverse complex of institutions, programs, and systems which requires coordination because of its importance and its cost but which is exceptionally difficult to manage.

Schools and educational programs of one kind or another are not limited to the capital city, although perhaps too high a proportion are unfortunately located there. On the contrary, the country's schools and educational programs should be set up and expressed throughout the length and breadth of the land. The issues of educational organization in the field must also be faced, as well as the problems of the functional organization and coordination of education at the center. In quite a few countries, as in India and Nigeria, education (like agriculture and health) is, by constitution or by statute, a "state subject"—that is, the primary responsibility of the state rather than of the national government. In such cases substantially the same problems of functional organization face the state as would face the national government. The added dimension in this situation would be the degree of leverage exercised by the center with the weight of its financial and personnel subsidies.

When education remains the responsibility of the national government, the problems of administration are very largely the problems of decentralization and decongestion by vesting the appropriate powers and resources in field representatives of the central ministry. Much the same kinds of problems of field administration would face states, too, when they are in charge of the educational system for their areas. Considered from the point of view of a government's overall field organization for administration, including planning and development, arrangements for the decentralization of education should parallel the system of decentralization for agriculture, health, industry, communications, and other sectoral functions. This provision for interfunctional coordination of planning and development permits the educational system and its schools and institutions to make their full contribution to the development process at each state, district, and local level. These contributions consist of manpower training, functional literacy, political identity, and individual opportunity and satisfaction.

Education and the management of the school system have significant political as well as management aspects which markedly affect educational administration. Education is rarely if ever made the constitutional responsibility of a local level of government under the state. The deep interest of people in their schools, however, and their active concern for the educational opportunity of their children, combine with forces which support the enlistment of the people's participation in their government and its development programs to make education one of the major subjects of local self-government and one of the chief aspects of the process of political development. There is a close and often conscious and certainly a desirable connection therefore between systems of educational development and systems of political development. Even when the quality of local school administration and education suffers by the transfer of responsibility to elective bodies, consideration of the long-term benefits of local self-government often prompts the authorities, and the people, to support systems of local school control, as in Tanzania. That control is of course limited and guided by superior government agencies, state and national, which with the power of their resources as well as their statutory authority set minimum standards, at least, and often control the selection of teachers as well as of curriculum and textbooks.

The governance of schools, universities, and school systems has a unique political flavor. Recognition and expression of the distinctive character of education and its control is found not only in the autonomy of universities, which have independent boards to assure a measure of academic freedom. It is found also in systems organized around special school districts, separate from the areas and organizations of other political units, which have distinctive forms of control and governance, such as appointed or elected or professional boards. These separate systems customarily have their own budgets and their own personnel systems.

This recognition of the separate identity of the school-education establishment and the efforts to express and give effect to it through systems which respect local participation and control but which insulate them from the central political mechanism is especially difficult to achieve because of the complexities of governance which plague educational institutions and systems. Not only the voters who elect the school boards or those who appoint the school boards but the parents of the schoolchildren seek to influence program and policy through their own organizations. The teachers, through their unions and otherwise, are increasingly intent on participating in the formulation of teaching as well as employment standards. The administrators, superintendents, and principals and inspectors consider that they have a stake in policy-making and program-planning. Organizations of professional groups assert accrediting jurisdictions in efforts to control segments of education, particularly at the higher and technical levels. The students themselves, even at the secondary level, are becoming more insistent on their rights to be consulted, at least, on educational decisions. The confrontations between the several conflicting groups and their distinctive sets of objectives and values in education are staggering, including as they do the views of government versus professional versus layman versus parent versus pupil-student groups. Administration for educational development is colored and conditioned by these tensions.

It is not enough to organize education at national, state, and local levels by the major dimensions alone—primary, secondary, higher, technical, non-formal, and teacher training. It is necessary also to provide for the several major specialized components of an educational institution—school or otherwise—and system. The most apparent and important of these are designing the curriculum, selecting teachers, preparing or selecting textbooks and other materials, and designing and providing school buildings and facilities. These aspects of the educational process should be subject to continuing research and development based upon evaluation of experience. Such evaluation, for reliability, depends upon professionally prepared instruments for testing and measuring pupil and teacher performance under varying conditions. Monitoring depends upon constructive and professional supervision as well as upon informative reporting and inspection. In most countries these specialized functions of organization are provided separately for both secondary and primary divisions, as well as higher and technical, because of significant differences in their respective pedagogical environments. However, aspects of professional attention common to two or more of these levels of education are sometimes combined in research and development units.

The central or state education ministry or agency would normally be responsible either for planning and conducting these several specialized functions in the operation of schools and of the educational system or for setting standards for their performance—standards giving directions to supervisors which are enforced by the control of financial and personnel resources and used as a basis for accreditation or equivalent systems of endorsement. Most countries are extending the applicability of their minimum standards to private schools as well as to the government schools. These standards are increasingly being made mandatory even when not accompanied by the grants-in-aid which in most cases were initially used as the occasion for imposing standards. Central and state ministries of education thus often have divisions to monitor private schools. Other divisions are set up from time to time to administer or to monitor and coordinate special aspects of the educational system.

Many countries continue the practice of external examinations—that is, tests on prescribed curricula content administered by examiners outside the school or college. This practice is of much significance to the system and its several syllabi, to the teachers who prepare students for the examinations, and to the students who pass or fail. The management or at least the supervision of these examinations, particularly at the secondary level, becomes a function of the education ministry or of an institution set up separately for the purpose, such as an examinations board. In countries such as India and Pakistan, where external examinations persist, universities customarily conduct them for baccalaureate candidates from affiliated colleges and often for matriculates or high school graduates aspiring to college admission. This practice involves a problem of coordination between the high school leaving exam and the college admission exam, a problem too often unsolved.

Finally, in many countries, including developing ones, a major function of the central educational agency is not only to administer grants-in-aid and other subsidies to state and local schools and school jurisdictions but to do so in such a way as to extend educational opportunity to those who would otherwise be deprived. This function of educational equalization involves the support of educational facilities in all areas and regions, including those in remote and isolated locations, the provision of fellowship or other forms of assistance to the children of the poor otherwise unable to go to school, and arrangements for supplements to the educational experience of those who otherwise, because of the poor quality of the schools available to them, would not be able to qualify for higher schooling. An additional year of high school, the "fifth form," is one means of providing this supplement, and it is a good way—better for example than lowering standards for disadvantaged students. These programs of school equalization frequently require the establishment of one or several organizational units in the central or state education ministry to provide the necessary services.

Financing Educational Development

The effectuation of programs to accomplish a country's objectives in education is dependent not only upon the organization of specialized functions but also upon the quality of the administrative policies and systems which are needed to make them operational. Organization for education involves the identification of the schools and other institutions at the several levels and of the various kinds required to conduct the whole program, the definition of the specialized functions which must be performed, and the assignment of responsibility for all of these to central, state, and local agencies within a chosen framework of governance. The activation and the implementation of these organizational mechanisms and of the several schools and educational institutions is the product of the administrative systems for planning, financing, staffing, and supervising the educational establishment.

The fastest and most economical way to make substantial progress toward a newly independent or developing country's goals is by utilizing the existing structure of institutions and facilities to the utmost by making corrections and improvements in their management. Progress achieved in this way is particularly suitable to quantitative and equalizing extensions of educational opportunity and coverage—that is, in the number and location of pupils and students who can be accommodated. Improvements in quality can also be attained by good administration, such as by lowering the ratio of pupils to qualified teachers, although substantive changes in curriculum and instructional methodology must wait for research and development. Good management is also essential to the successful introduction of innovations in education over longer periods of time.

Schools and all educational institutions are expensive. They cost a great deal to establish at the outset and they cost more and more to operate as time goes on. The money-absorbing processes of enriching the curriculum and improving the quality of instruction never end, nor does the demand for more schools and facilities for more students and higher salaries for their teachers. Developed and comparatively wealthy countries find the burden of financing education not insubstantial. Developing and poorer countries face a very difficult problem in this regard, a problem which assumes several aspects.

One of these aspects is how to finance the rapid increase in schools, particularly primary schools, throughout the country. Experience has shown that the residents of a community are usually more willing to help pay for a government service, and especially education, if it is provided visibly and adequately in their own community than if it is for some general and comparatively remote national purpose. Some countries, as in the case of the Philippines, have for this reason authorized local governments to levy taxes, usually property taxes, to support local schools. Others, like Pakistan and Indonesia, have adopted the policy and the practice of agreeing to provide teachers for elementary schools if the local community will provide the land and buildings and assume responsibility for maintenance and upkeep. These financing schemes for primary education would appear to be sound not only because they help to protect the central or state budget but also because they encourage the assumption of local responsibility for an important public function.

In many developing countries the secondary schools—the high schools—are parochial or missionary or other private schools which those countries are well advised to encourage, even with subsidy, because they represent an existing educational resource which it would cost a great deal to duplicate or replace. In rural and remote areas, however, and in urban areas to serve the poorer families, the developing country is obliged to establish and usually to pay for a network of high schools from state and federal funds. The same is true of specialized technical schools, professional colleges, and general colleges and universities. Practices vary widely with respect to such costs as transportation, housing, and textbooks.

A majority of the developing countries subsidize the students in professional colleges, such as those of medicine, education, and engineering, in return for commitments from the students to give public service for a stipulated period upon graduation. The underlying and pervasive issue, however, particularly at the higher education level, is whether students should pay a tuition toward the cost of their schooling as well as pay for room and board and even books. The forces of democracy are gradually succeeding in accomplishing the reduction and even the elimination of tuition in public institutions—certainly the high schools and the specialized institutes and colleges—and the extension of free public education through the university level. This trend increases enormously the financial burden on the public treasury. It creates other problems in addition, notably whether to increase facilities to meet all public demands, and if so, how fast; if not, how to restrict enrollments.

In any case the cost of education is very great and it is growing, not shrinking. This burden must be borne almost always and in large part by the central government and its superior sources of revenue and not alone by the state or other local districts or agencies for school administration. In those cases in which the central government does not operate the schools and colleges and universities directly, a favorite device is a grant-in-aid to the responsible administering agency. By using the grant-in-aid system the central government is in a position to insist upon nationally approved policies and standards of education and it is in a position to extend and equalize educational opportunity by subsidizing more heavily the otherwise deprived regions or classes.

The budget is the instrument by which the several components of the educational establishment are allotted funds annually and, of equal importance, it is the instrument by which are fixed the conditions under which those agencies are authorized to expend funds even after allocation. Budget offices are almost always powerful staff units in the executive branch, where decisions are made about the annual allocation of funds. Budget offices typically and traditionally judge and help decide on budgets, including those for education, with the assistance of two kinds of criteria. One criterion is a comparison with past practice and past experience—whether there is justification, in other words, for any increase in the budget, and if so on what specific grounds. This way of measuring and judging budget proposals is sometimes called the "incremental" approach. The other criterion is composed of those formulas which budget examiners are prone to collect and to apply when nothing better is offered by the proponent. In education, for example, the budget officer is almost certain to have his own ideas about acceptable teacher-student ratios, the size of school buildings and their facilities per pupil population, and other similar measures.

The typical budget office is also inclined to prefer itemized budgets to general and broad categories, partly because line items are easier to judge but largely because such budgets are thereby easier to control and to audit. It is not only the form of the budget but the conditions governing the release of funds under it which determines its character, its flexibility, and its constructive usefulness in activating education programs. If the budget even when approved is only a framework within which further detailed requests must be made before funds are actually released, it serves chiefly as a control, as a restraint—and a ponderous and centralized restraint at that. If the budget, on the other hand, is a clear-cut authorization to proceed with some vigor and imagination once it is approved, it is an altogether different kind of instrument. Unfortunately, in too many developing countries the budget system is one of control and restraint.

The so-called "development budget" is another complication in the fund allocation process because it is too frequently a capital budget insufficiently related to the budget for recurring expenditures which are needed subsequently to make that capital investment operational. Also, a capital addition—building or equipment—does not necessarily have the same priority as an innovation in educational or in administrative methods which increase the capacity or effectiveness of the existing plant and program. In some countries, including India and Indonesia, it is easier to get funds for a new school or classroom building from the development budget than to get funds for the less costly repair or renovation of the same building from the regular recurring budget. Thus the effort of the central planning agency and the chief budget office to accommodate if not to reconcile their jurisdictions through the device of the development budget often compounds rather than clarifies or simplifies the budget planning of a sector such as education.

It is therefore incumbent upon the educational authorities concerned with innovative development to be vigorous and aggressive in the budget process, first by developing criteria, formulae, and other evaluative measures of their proposals which are more valid and at least as rational as the incremental methods the budget office is otherwise obliged to fall back on; and second by coordinating and reconciling the development and the regular recurring budgets so that they are truly complementary. Even more important to fully effective educational administration is a system of program budgeting, which avoids the rigidities of itemized budgeting, and a system of budget authorization which permits discretionary expenditure within approved program budgets on a decentralized basis.

Two budget improvements alone would convert the budget system from one of inhibition, control, centralization, delay, and waste to a process which encourages and supports educational administration response to ever-changing need and opportunity when the need occurs and when the opportunity arises. The first improvement would be to give authority to education officers in the field, or school principals or superintendents, to operate promptly on the basis of their budget authorizations without going back up the bureaucratic line and down again with requests for second and third approvals. The second improvement would be to strengthen the capacity and authority of the educational establishment to act flexibly in correlating the resources of the development and regular recurring budgets.

Staffing the Educational Establishment

Similarly, the personnel system to provide the teachers, supervisors, and school and other administrators needed to man the enormous education establishment can, by its effectiveness, maximize the productivity of such investment as is available to it or can, by its ineptness, make poor use of the investment and thus thwart its purposes. First of all there must be a supply of trained personnel—teachers, supervisors, administrators, and others sufficient to fill the positions needed in the approved institutions and programs. The size of this pool of qualified persons depends upon a competitive level of salaries and other components of compensation, benefits, and status sufficient to attract people to that field and its professions. In spite of the high cost, countries which stint on teacher salaries soon learn that their educational purposes are not being served and their total investment in education is not yielding the returns expected of it because of the poor quality of the personnel.

The size of the educational manpower pool is also dependent upon a large enough number of teacher training and other preparatory preservice programs to produce the needed numbers of qualified persons. Here it is necessary for countries to make the difficult judgment of just how long and how intensive such professional training need be at any particular stage in the evolution of their educational programs. Granted that minimum levels of training are needed to assure acceptable teaching performance, some countries have been tempted to raise those levels more rapidly than might actually be required at any given time and, in so doing, to make it more difficult both in capacity and in time to institute or expand the desired training facilities. Nevertheless, the quality of the educational personnel as well as its ample quantity is a major factor in the effectiveness and the productivity of the school and university systems.

Poorly prepared teachers, and particularly those who in addition lack the supporting qualities of personal ability and general education, will not serve a country's educational purposes well or justify the heavy investment in the establishment. The additional margin of the cost of training and paying teachers well rather than poorly, although indeed great, is small in proportion to the greatly increased quality and effectiveness of the system. An important aspect of teacher education and preparation is in-service training both to orient the teaching staff to new subject matter and methods in their fields and to boost their morale not only by giving them a break in their often isolated teaching routines but also by bringing them together to express and share interests in and concern for the educational system as a whole. Such programs of in-service training, properly and carefully organized, are an excellent vehicle by which teachers can actually participate, and feel the reward of participating, in program formulation and implementation.

A serious and glaring weakness in the education personnel systems in many countries is the inadequacy of the selection and training of administrators and of administrative staff of the individual schools and institutions, and also of the operating and supervising offices, both central and field, of education ministries, departments, and governing boards. Such administrative personnel are typically selected from teaching and clerical staff who were selected and trained for duties different from those of administration. As a matter of fact, this source of recruitment is a good one because it is virtually impossible to select and train a class of administrators before they learn and experience something of the substantive profession or professions involved in the program to be administered and until they demonstrate on the job and in their relationships a sufficiently promising personal aptitude for the administrative art.

The difficulty is that selections from teaching and office staff for administrative posts are too frequently based on seniority rather than aptitude and merit and that, perhaps even more seriously, those chosen are given virtually no orientation or training for their new careers. At the very least they should be instructed in their duties, institutional policies, methods, and powers and responsibilities, and also in their coordinate relationships with not only subordinates and superiors in the environment of the system as a whole but also their counterparts in sister agencies and institutions, such as those of agriculture and health. This kind of orientation and instruction, well done, would in itself, especially if directed to persons giving promise of administrative capacity, improve quickly and markedly the quality and reliability of school and education management and come closer to the achievement of the educational purposes intended by the educational investment. A country would be well advised to organize special training courses for those selected for administrative posts after they have demonstrated their aptitude and capacity for such work on the job but before they undertake their new duties.

What is important in a competent personnel system is not only the quantity and quality of persons in the manpower pool for education, but the promptness of their selection for and thus their availability for vacant teaching and other posts. Speed in filling positions with qualified persons is the measure of a responsible personnel system. Many systems are so ponderous and even so indifferent in their operation that a position may remain vacant for weeks or even months while an inept process of selection is undertaken by a state or central ministry of education or by a state or central civil or public service commission. Procedures of advertising, testing, and individual interviewing are often required for each and every position after it is established or becomes vacant.

The consequences of delay in filling jobs are failures to do the teaching or to perform the other intended functions of the educational institution involved, and to that extent there are losses in the system's productivity. By the simple devices of establishing open registers of persons found to be qualified for specified types of positions and of allowing the responsible educational authority to make his selection from those approved lists of pre-tested and examined candidates, almost all of that delay could be avoided and the educational machinery could continue to function without interruption. Moreover, by being able to make a choice from among a number of qualified and acceptable candidates, the locally knowledgeable and responsible officer can select the one who most nearly fits the needs of the local situation.

One of the reasons for the harmful ineptitude of these selection procedures is the understandably desirable objective of open public competition for government positions on the basis of comparative merit. That there are ways to meet this objective without the encumbrance of so much delay has been illustrated above and has been demonstrated in practice. Another issue in selection is whether the personnel decision is within the jurisdiction of the local authority, or the state department, or the national ministry, tempered in each case by the possibly preemptive jurisdiction of the public service commission at the central or state level. Typically, countries have either a national or a state education personnel service, operated by the public service commission or by the education ministry or department under the aegis of that commission. These services are characterized not only by considerations of merit on the occasion of entrance but often, in addition, by considerations of race or religion, as in Malaysia, represented in quotas considered in both the selection and the promotion processes.

Educational services are often characterized by seniority in selections for promotion and by restrictions upon disciplinary action on the part of the individual school or other local jurisdiction involved. Under these circumstances, the external control of teachers and other personnel is often superior to the authority of the principal or other local administrative officer nominally in charge. The progressive administrative system is the one which will recognize the importance of increasing the local administrator's discretion and control with respect to personnel matters while continuing to protect the individual civil servant by means of equitable grievance and appeal procedures. The importance of compatibility of personnel in various locations, positions, and institutions can thus be recognized and accommodated.

The maximum effectiveness of persons in their jobs, both administrators and teachers, is the purpose of administrative systems for educational development. These systems extend not only to the availability of financial and personnel resources adequate to the defined purpose, and the authority to use those resources expeditiously as well as accountably, but also to arrangements for supervision or inspection devised to supplement and strengthen administrative and professional leadership and guidance. One of the functions of supervision, and of administration, is that of evaluation in order to know whether program purposes are being achieved and in what degree and whether methods and materials in use are effective or whether they could be improved. The supervisory system shares with the financial and personnel systems the overriding purpose of increasing the administrative capacity for effective decision and action at the locations in the field where the programs of concern are being conducted.

Problems of Planning for Educational Development

Planning is another of the administrative systems, along with finance, personnel, and supervision, by which the educational intentions and expectations of a country are defined and realized. Planning, in this case for education, is the process by which choices and decisions are made about the policies, programs, projects, and methods needed to achieve desired results in the most effective ways. Education is properly defined in comprehensive terms—that is, to include not only "formal" and institutionalized education in primary and secondary schools and in colleges and universities and in technical institutes, but also the so-called "non-formal," or out-of-school, education, as illustrated by on-the-job and in-service training, adult literacy programs, educational projects in agriculture, and other continuing education programs. For planning and development purposes, education includes not only the domain of the central ministries, departments, and boards of education, but also separately defined and administered educational programs in other ministries and agencies, such as apprentice training in the ministry of labor, for example, and functional literacy projects sometimes found in the ministry of agriculture or rural development. Educational planning should deal with schools and technical and other training in the private as well as in the public sector.

Education, and planning for it, must be relied upon to develop the human resources needed in the accomplishment of a country's development goals and programs. This obligation includes manpower planning to define and arrange for the production of the numbers and kinds of trained personnel needed for economic growth and also to increase the literacy and motivational levels of the population generally so as to permit and support full popular and productive involvement in the development process. Education, looked at from this human resource point of view, is a sector in development comparable to the sectors of agriculture and industry. Expenditures to improve education and develop it in this regard can be considered as investment and can be justified in terms of an expected economic return. At the same time, there are public demands for kinds of educational opportunity which are not needed for a country's economic development and yet, for political reasons and to serve more general social and cultural purposes, a country usually finds it necessary to oblige these demands in some degree. Expenditure for education of these kinds is considered to be consumption— that is expenditure which does not contribute to general economic growth and which reduces amounts otherwise available for investment in development. In this respect educational planning is different from agricultural or other development sector planning: it must accommodate both the economic investment in, and the popular-demand requirements upon, the education system.

Planning for educational development in this comprehensive sense is clearly needed to assure the provision of the desired schools, programs, and projects central to the accomplishment of a country's educational aspirations. The development aspect of the situation makes incremental budgeting a method inadequate to the need because that method is based on the existing rather than a projected establishment and is measured by past trends and current standards rather than by defined targets. Other aspects in the educational situation call for foresight and planning to facilitate reasonable progress toward goals, such as the need to integrate and coordinate educational programs on a national basis so as to relate effectively the several levels, kinds, and geographical expressions of the educational enterprise. A special problem of educational planning and development is the long lead time usually required to get approved programs or new schools into full operation, chiefly because of the years it takes to train the needed numbers of additional teachers or specialists.

Educational planning takes on even greater importance considering that developing countries, countries which in almost all cases are poor, simply do not have enough money to finance all of the educational development which would otherwise be desirable for economic development, let alone political purposes. Other and competing claims upon available funds for national development and other purposes make it necessary to decide, on the basis of analysis and planning, how much money should be allocated to education instead of to agriculture, industry, commerce, or other development sectors. After the difficult decision about how much is available to education, other difficult decisions have to be made about allocations to the competing levels, kinds, and regions of educational need and aspiration. The central problem of educational planning thus becomes that of who should be educated to what levels and in what subjects, and in what places in which ways.

The first set of questions to ask and answer in the attempt to solve the problem of educational planning—the problem of choices among alternatives in educational development possibilities—is quantitative. How many persons of which skills need to be trained to meet the personnel requirements of the development plan? How many children and adults need to be schooled or otherwise made literate and suitably prepared for the modernization process—and in programs of how many years and of what length? Not only the question of what is needed for economic development but what is desired to meet the demands of the public involves quantitative aspects. How many children are there and how many are there to be, and of what ages and in what locations? How many of these can be accommodated in schools and at what levels? What are the dimensions of any imbalances in educational opportunity by class and by region? What are the dimensions of imbalances which create a surfeit of educated underemployed or unemployed on the one hand, and which leave a shortage of needed specialist personnel on the other? The techniques of manpower analysis and planning are useful in counting, categorizing, and projecting the specialist and skilled personnel needs of the development plan.

Techniques of cost-benefit analysis can be used to judge the rate of return from a given additional investment in education as compared with an investment of similar size in some other sector, thereby assessing its relative merit. Cost-benefit analysis as applied to education is based upon computations of increased earnings, over time, of individuals or categories of workers by virtue of added years of education, minus the earnings forgone because of work years lost while in school. Cost-benefit techniques are also being used with moderate success in measuring the returns of such added education of individuals to the economic as well as the social well-being of the community as a whole.

These systems of cost-benefit analysis as applied to education are not so precise or reliable as to make them the exclusive and authoritatively determining measure of the relative merits of alternative investment opportunities, but they do provide analyses which are helpful, together with other judgments, in reaching a conclusion in this difficult area of public choice. The techniques of cost-benefit or other economic analysis are not applicable, however, to the problem of the relative ability of projects in educational development to satisfy social and political demand as contrasted with achievement of economic goals. A government's policy concerning equalization of educational opportunity by region, religion, race, and class, and its judgment about the pace of such equalization as is financially possible, are the controlling factors in this situation. On the other hand, in broad terms, cost-benefit analysis can give clues as to which level of education should be strengthened in comparison with other levels in economic terms—primary versus secondary versus higher—and which therefore would provide additional information useful in deciding at what level to extend educational opportunity. Cost-benefit and other contributions of economic analysis are therefore important to the solution of the quantitative problem of educational planning, but they must be matched with political and social considerations in reaching conclusions and making decisions.

The second set of questions in educational planning and development is qualitative—that is, how to improve pedagogic methodology and how to increase administrative efficiency and effectiveness. Pedagogy involves the curriculum, the methods of teaching, the quality of teachers, and the excellence of learning materials. It is the appropriate domain of the professional educators in the regular ministries and departments of education and of their research and development agencies. Of prominent interest in this area is the promise and relevance of educational technology—radio and television supported by cable and satellite, teaching machines, and programmed instruction. So far the experience with such technology has been more frustrating than rewarding. It does not replace teachers and thus fill teaching gaps, but carefully selected technology can improve the quality of teaching. It is expensive, which is an inhibition to a poor country, and it is no better than the "soft ware," that is, the materials prepared for processing through the transmitters and machines, whose appetite is voracious and endless.

From the point of view of development administration, the question of quality in the educational system is how to make the best use of it and how to get the maximum return from the investment. There is great opportunity, through improved and decentralized systems of finance, personnel, and supervision, to increase the effectiveness of schools and other educational institutions quickly and markedly. Systematic attention to the results that are possible to achieve from alternative policies concerning the years of schooling provided on the several levels, teacher-student ratios, and examinations and promotions, all measured in terms of cost and management feasibility as well as of relative pedagogic perfection, should yield more nearly optimal policy and practice. Careful assessment of the content and length of training needed to qualify personnel for technical and professional positions would reveal opportunities to save time and money in education without lowering performance standards. For example, there is no need to insist upon an engineering degree for certain types of work when the qualification of a technical diploma would serve as well. There is no need for medical doctors to be engaged in technical work which nurses or aides could do as well, or in administration which professional managers could probably do better. Computation and analysis of the costs of alternative systems and methods having approximately the same degree of effectiveness is a very useful technique to apply in these and other circumstances.

Cost-effectiveness analysis is a tool which could be used more often than it is to help ascertain the best use of such funds as are available to the educational endeavor. The fact is that the conflict between what is needed in education for economic development, what is desired in education to satisfy political, social, and individual aspirations, and what can be afforded from the planning budget for educational development creates a tension which it is the function of the planning process to ease. Add to this confrontation a further dimension—that is, what can actually be accomplished managerially even if it can be afforded—and the fundamental role of education is defined.

In most countries there is no dearth of educational planning agencies, which means that the problem is not to create them but to clarify their relationships so that there can be a reasonably satisfactory result. A logical place for the main focus on educational planning for a country as a whole is the central ministry or department of education. This unit for educational planning should be staffed with highly competent specialists in education and in economic and management analysis. It need not, or should not, be a large organization because the educational research and development activities should be undertaken in other organizations. Similarly, statistical data collection and demographic analysis are more properly done elsewhere, although both kinds of functions and their product are needed in the separate analyses required by the planning process.

Manpower planning is sometimes, and not inappropriately, included among the functions of the educational planning unit, but no violence is done if that work is performed in another agency, such as the labor ministry or even the central planning office itself. Annual budgeting should not be added to the work load of the educational planning unit, although that unit should be given a strong role in connection with budget preparation to help assure that the allocation of funds supports the projects and programs in approved plans for educational development.

The relationships with the central economic planning office are complex and more difficult to clarify. One question is whether the central office should prescribe the amount of money to be allocated within the total plan to education, or whether the educational planners should initiate and attempt to justify proposals on their merits in debate with the central office. A workable system to resolve this issue provides that the central planning office set forth policy and priority guidelines in non-monetary terms within which the educational planners, as well as the planners in other sectors, prepare their specialized plans of projects and programs for consideration in money terms.

Another major question about the central-sectoral relationship in educational planning is who makes the analyses and project decisions in the several key areas involved. Certainly the educational planning unit should have the responsibility for pedagogic analyses and for analyses and proposals about the management feasibility of the implementation plans and projects put forward. The educational planning unit should also make the economic analysis, including cost-benefit and cost-effectiveness aspects, of the comparative value of alternative educational development projects. The central planning office, however, must make analyses of the comparative value of educational projects and programs which are competitive with projects and programs in other sectors.

It remains to assess the merit and relative priority of educational projects which are proposed to satisfy popular political and social demand when such proposals do not contribute measurably to economic growth. It would be sensible for the central planning office to be equipped to deal with these political questions as well as economic questions and thus to be able to advise on the non-economic as well as the economic dimensions of a plan needed to move toward a country's political and social as well as economic targets. Within such dimensions, the educators are in the best position to make plans for the specific education projects and programs which would fit into those dimensions.

Another issue in the educational planning relationship is the reconciliation in the educational plan of educational projects proposed by ministries other than the ministry of education. Such programs and projects might include apprentice and job training in the labor ministry, health education in the health ministry, and functional literacy education in the ministry of agriculture or rural development. It is probable that the project planning in such areas as these would be done by the ministry of responsibility, with coordination and synthesis performed by the central economic planning office, but with the advice of the central educational planning unit. Occasionally an entire level of education, such as primary schools, is the charge of a ministry other than education, such as interior or home affairs. In such cases the ministry of education might do the planning, but make arrangements with the operating ministry for advice and consultation.

It is desirable for other educational jurisdictions outside the center, such as states and large district and municipal school boards, to have their own planning units. These units would have functions and relationships similar in kind to those of the central educational planning unit. The area of final responsibility of these state and local planning agencies would be limited by the amount of funds over which they have direct control. Since such funds are almost always insufficient to need and purpose, assistance is usually forthcoming from the center in the form of grants-in-aid or some other kind of subsidy and support. This dependence puts the central educational planning unit, in conjunction with the central economic planning office, in a position to prescribe guidelines for state and local educational planning. An important function of state and local educational planning remains, because it is important to assure the preparation of projects and programs which meet the tests of local acceptance and viability.

Note on Sources

With respect to educational development, as in other sectors, the publications of the international organizations are of particular value. Among the most useful of UNESCO's publications are those listed below:

J. D. Chesswas, *Methodologies of Educational Planning for Developing Countries,* 2 vols. (Paris: UNESCO, 1968).

Philip H. Coombs and Jacques Hallak, *Educational Cost Analysis in Action: Case Studies for Planners* (Paris: UNESCO, 1972).

Economic and Social Aspects of Educational Planning (Paris: UNESCO, 1964).

Educational Planning: A World Survey of Problems and Prospects (Paris: UNESCO, 1970).

"Fundamentals of Educational Planning," a continuing series of twenty-five or so excellent booklets, edited by C. E. Beeby.

Readings in the Economics of Education (Paris: UNESCO, 1968).

Maureen Woodhall, *Cost-Benefit Analysis in Educational Planning* (Paris: UNESCO, 1970).

The World Bank's activity in educational development is summarized in its sector working paper, *Education* (Washington, D.C.: World Bank, 1974).

The International Labor Organization is active in the manpower and employment fields. Among its publications is that by Mark Blaug, *Education and the Employment Problem in Developing Countries* (Geneva: ILO, 1973).

The Organization for Economic Cooperation and Development has issued a number of useful studies and reports, including the following:

Budgeting, Program Analysis and Cost-Effectiveness in Educational Planning (Paris: OECD, 1968).

Forecasting Education Needs for Economic and Social Development (Paris: OECD, 1962).

Herbert S. Parnes, *Planning Education for Economic and Social Development* (Paris: OECD, 1962).

Policy Conference on Economic Growth and Investment in Education (Paris: OECD, 1962).

Educational planning and development, the economics of education, and related topics are the subject of a fairly large body of literature. Selected books are listed below. The first list covers educational planning and development:

Don Adams, ed., *Education in National Development* (New York: David McKay, 1971).

Arnold C. Anderson and Mary Jean Bowman, *Education and Economic Development* (Chicago: Aldine, 1965).

C. E. Beeby, *The Quality of Education in Developing Countries* (Cambridge, Mass.: Harvard University Press, 1966).

Samuel Bowles, *Planning Education Systems for Economic Growth* (Cambridge, Mass.: Harvard University Press, 1969).

Hobart Burns, ed., *Education and the Development of Nations* (Syracuse, N.Y.: Syracuse University Press, 1963).

Philip H. Coombs and Manzoor Ahmed, *Education for Development: Case Studies for Planners* (New York: Praeger, 1975).

Adam Curle, *Educational Strategy for Developing Societies* (London: Tavistock Publications, 1963).

Adam Curle, *Educational Problems of Developing Countries* (New York: Praeger, 1973).

Frederick Harbison and Charles A. Myers, *Education, Manpower and Economic Growth* (New York: McGraw-Hill, 1964).

Frederick H. Harbison, *Human Resources as the Wealth of Nations* (New York: Oxford University Press, 1973).

Muhammad Shamsul Huq, *Education, Manpower and Development in South and Southeast Asia* (New York: Praeger, 1974).

Eugene Staley, *Planning Occupational Education and Training for Development* (New York: Praeger, 1971).

C. Kenneth Tanner, *Designs for Educational Planning: A Systemic Approach* (Lexington, Mass.: Heath, 1971).

M. I. Tugan, *Education, Society and Development in Underdeveloped Countries* (The Hague: Center for the Study of Education in Changing Societies, 1975).

F. Champion Ward, *Education and Development Reconsidered* (New York: Praeger, 1974).

The economics of education is the subject of the following books:

Mark Blaug, ed., *Economics of Education,* Modern Economics Series, 2 vols. (London: Penguin, 1968–69).

Mark Blaug, *An Introduction to the Economics of Education* (London: Allen Lane, 1970).

Elchanan Cohn, *The Economics of Education* (Lexington, Mass.: Heath, 1972).

Martin O. Donoghue, *Economic Dimensions in Education* (Chicago: Aldine, 1971).

Daniel C. Rogers and Hirsch S. Ruchlin, *Economics and Education: Principles and Applications* (New York: Free Press, 1971).

Theodore W. Schultz, *The Economic Value of Education* (New York: Columbia University Press, 1963).

Hans Henry Thias and Martin Carnoy, *Cost-Benefit Analysis in Education: A Case Study of Kenya* (Baltimore: Johns Hopkins University Press, 1972).

John Vaizey, *The Economics of Education* (London: Faber and Faber, 1962).

Other books of relevant interest are listed below:

James W. Armsey and Norman C. Dahl, *An Inquiry into the Uses of Instructional Technology* (New York: Ford Foundation, 1973).

Harry L. Case and Richard O. Niehoff, *Educational Alternatives in National Development: Suggestions for Policy Makers* (East Lansing: Michigan State University Institute for International Studies in Education, 1976).

Eli Ginzburg, *Manpower for Development: Perspectives on Five Continents* (New York: Praeger, 1971).

H. M. Phillips, *Educational Cooperation between Developed and Developing Countries* (New York: Praeger, 1976).

5

Management of
the Public Enterprise Sector

The Public Enterprise Phenomenon

Country after country has turned over substantial and even pre-dominant responsibility for developing and managing its economy to new kinds of public agencies. These new kinds of agencies constitute the public enterprise sector. They have been created in many countries, among them Pakistan and Indonesia, in an ad hoc manner and on a pragmatic, case-by-case basis. In other countries, as in Tanzania, India, and Egypt, they have been set up as a central system of agencies to manage the economy as a whole, or large parts of it. Public enterprises have become one of the new and key kinds of institutions for develop-ment, and together they constitute another and separate sector in the bureaucracy.

Public enterprises are government organizations established for the purpose of engaging in defined commercial or business types of economic activity, although they are on occasion established for non-business purposes to escape the shackles of the existing bureaucracy—which may be the purpose, for example, of a scientific research foun-dation or a technological institute. Primarily, however, these agencies of public enterprise represent active involvement by the government in the economic sphere. They are distinguished by their function of conducting economic activities. They represent the government's active participation in economic development beyond the provision of guidelines and the

104

creation of an environment encouraging to the private sector. Public enterprises represent and reflect a government's active intervention in the economy by engaging directly in business. Some functions of a commercial type, such as postal services, have been and are performed in regular departments of government. Most of these functions of public enterprise, however, are now conducted by distinctive types of agencies, particularly by public corporations but also by state or mixed companies.

The principal reason for the emergence of the public enterprise sector in a country is the government's decision to intervene directly and actively in the economy in order to achieve the purposes of its development plan. More frequently than not this decision follows the creation of a planning process, leading in turn to analyses and findings that show the institutional needs for development which the government believes the private sector will not meet, at least by itself. Some countries, the collectivist socialist countries, believe that substantially all of the economic functions of production and distribution should be managed in the public sector. Other countries, also for ideological reasons, believe that certain kinds of economic activity, such as the exploitation of natural resources, should be in the hands of government. Still other countries are loath to engage in any more activity than they are compelled to by some temporary weakness or shortcoming in the private sector. There are many shades of belief and policy from country to country, varying from those which conduct as much as possible of the nation's economic life in the public sector to those which do as little as possible through government and as much as possible in the private sector.

Regardless of ideology and policy, however, almost every country has found it desirable and even necessary to establish public enterprises in order to meet responsibly the requirements of its development program. Even without establishing new administrative systems, but often doing so, most countries have engaged in education, health, social welfare, banking, transportation, and communication activities for the express purpose of providing support and encouragement to economic development in the private sector. This list of supporting activities becomes longer as governments become more and more involved in providing services which are themselves basically economic in their character. These include credit and marketing institutions to bolster agriculture, water and power agencies to serve both agriculture and industry, and development banks and applied research centers to assist and encourage private industrial growth and expansion.

Countries go beyond the conduct of these supportive, infrastructure types of activities for both doctrinaire and pragmatic reasons. Intense nationalist feelings of pride and desire for self-sufficiency have led many nations, at or shortly after independence, to nationalize foreign-owned enterprises, particularly those based upon natural resources, and to assign public agencies to operate them even when the goal in the long run is to sell them to indigenous investors. Even more commonly, when the private sector has been too weak or too disinterested to undertake economic activities in a field or a region considered by the government to be important to the objectives of the development program, government agencies have undertaken to fill the gap, at least temporarily, by managing entire industries or systems of commercial services. There are still other reasons which lead governments to active engagement in the economy, such as to gain control of a monopoly economic power, or to reduce the proportion of wealth in private hands, or to capture profits for investment in the development program as a whole, or to manage foreign trade, or even to create a model or yardstick of performance for the private sector. Whatever the reasons and motivations, government intervention in some greater or lesser degree in the economy is the general practice.

Public enterprises exist primarily in order to represent the government's interventionist objectives in the economy. They exist as distinctive institutions, however, because of governments' efforts to create agencies with the management capability to conduct business activities effectively and efficiently. If the existing management systems of the public bureaucracy had been or were sufficient to the performance of new enterprise functions in accord with the expectations of the government and the operating requirements of those functions, the already established departments and bureaus and management systems could have been relied upon to so perform. Even if new departments or divisions or bureaus had to be set up to handle an increased work load, a public enterprise sector of new and different kinds of agencies would not have emerged because it would have been necessary only to extend the existing financial, personnel, and management systems of the government bureaucracy.

The public enterprise sector, therefore, is distinguished prominently and importantly by its management characteristics as well as by its economic functions. The public enterprise sector exists as an identifiable and separate segment of the public establishment because of these distinguishing management features. It is this aspect of the public enterprise sector that makes it especially significant to development administration.

The administrative systems devised to satisfy the requirements of traditional government activities are not adequate to the requirements of industrial and commercial enterprise. They were not set up to serve the needs of business for flexibility and economic efficiency, but rather to serve expectations of political responsiveness and bureaucratic conformity. Procedures for getting and spending annual appropriations are ponderous and uncertain. Accounting and pre-audit systems to prevent mistakes in government thwart the expeditious decisions about the use of money that are essential to business. Admissions to and tenure in the civil service are necessarily governed by tedious rules to satisfy public acceptance and opportunity to compete for positions as well as, and even more than, to meet the specialist performance requirements of a production operation or a trading corporation.

The political whims and dilatory practices which jeopardize appropriations and the forms of personnel sanctions in government would be fatal to the conduct of a successful economic enterprise. Neither can it be argued that the improvement of efficiency in the public administration system as a whole would meet the requirements of business management, desirable as such efficiency is, because the needs are justifiably different and deserve different and tailor-made administrative systems to serve them. The public enterprise should be able to be sued and be subject to suit, for example, in order to act responsibly in the marketplace. It cannot be dependent upon annual appropriations for the continuity or flexibility of its operations. The accounting and audit and personnel systems needed in traditional government do not satisfy the management systems of commerce.

When President Franklin D. Roosevelt recommended to Congress the creation of the Tennessee Valley Authority in 1933 he asked that it be established as "a corporation clothed with the power of government but possessed of the flexibility and initiative of a private enterprise." Around the world, public enterprises have been established separate and apart from the existing public bureaucracy so that they could be endowed with the management capabilities uniquely necessary to their success. Very few such enterprises remain in the charge of the older government departments.

The Several Kinds of Public Enterprise

There are several different kinds and forms of public enterprise. They can be classified according to the source and nature of their legal authority, according to the nature of their functions, and according to their location and position in the governmental bureaucratic structure. If we consider first the categorization of public enterprises according to their legal base, five forms can be identified: direct departmental management, government contract with a private agency, government participation in company ownership and management, public corporation, and cooperative society.

The direct departmental management of public economic enterprise is the traditional form of government intervention in the economy. It was expressed most commonly in the operation of posts and telegraphs, ports and harbors, railways, and electric and water systems. These services were and are often considered to be in the same category of essential public services as roads and schools and police and fire protection. They were administered as bureaus, integral segments of the relevant government department. Efforts to manage these services efficiently and effectively within the administrative system applicable to other government functions, however, have almost always failed. Most countries have established public corporations to manage them. The usual systems of government involving annual appropriations, pre-audits, and other restrictive financial and personnel controls did not serve the management needs of these enterprises. They could not sue or be sued, for example, or own and control property in their own name.

The government contract with a private firm or other agency is a form of public enterprise in only a technical and limited sense. The contract is usually for a construction or maintenance or operating job of either short duration, such as the erection of a building or an electric system; of a routine nature, such as the dredging of a harbor or the maintenance of a canal or road system; or for the provision of highly specialized professional services, such as those required for technological research. The contract, typically on a cost-plus basis, is the legal framework for this kind of government enterprise, and contains within its terms the standards, criteria, and other terms of work exacted by the government. Such contracts are the instruments of regular government departments or of government-managed companies or corporations.

The two major legal forms of public enterprise are the commercial company and the public corporation. The company device is frequently used. The public company is usually established under a country's regular companies act, which provides for the creation and conditions of operation of private companies. The government can acquire some or all of the shares in an existing company or it can create a new company under the companies act in which it owns some or all of the shares. The government's participation in the management of a company in which it has an ownership interest is expressed as a shareholder. Such companies are almost always commercial in character and they are expected to make a profit. Government's participation in them can be for the purpose of acquiring a controlling or other interest in an enterprise formerly controlled by foreign interests or in a field considered to be so vital as to require government intervention. On the other hand, a government might buy into a company to bolster it up, or even create a new company in a needed area with the idea of selling out when the company is established and thriving. Companies in which a majority stock is held by government are sometimes called "state companies." Companies in which stock is held both by government and by private interests, including foreign interests, are sometimes called "mixed enterprise."

The public, or government, corporation is an entity wholly owned by government and created by a specific statute which gives it authority to engage in designated activities under designated conditions. In Malaysia and a few other countries, public corporations are often called "statutory authorities"; in many African countries they are called "parastatals." Public corporations are established to avoid the restrictions of the usual management controls of government, particularly financial and personnel controls, and to exercise the management capabilities required for effective engagement in the designated activities, such as the right to sue and be sued, enter into contracts, hire and fire staff and labor, acquire and control property, and have access to sources of funds in such ways as by borrowing and by use of revenues.

Statutes which create public corporations vary widely from country to country, and even within countries, as to their provisions not only with respect to these management powers but with respect to the specificity and nature of their provisions about services to be provided, the standards of such services, and whether such services are to be provided at cost or for a profit. In every case, however, the public corporation is established to permit the conduct of a function under an administrative system outside the usual government system and is designed, at least in intention, to provide the management capabilities requisite to the designated function. The public corporation form can be used for purely industrial, commercial, and profit-making activities, but it is used most frequently to perform utility and financial and development services that involve income but where the objective of the service is often considered to be paramount over that of profit.

The cooperative or cooperative society is not, strictly speaking, a public enterprise. A cooperative is a private business which is owned and operated by its members to secure for the members, at cost, certain production, marketing, purchasing, or financial services. Cooperatives can be single-purpose or multi-purpose. They can be independent local units or they can be related to larger federations. Most countries give encouragement to cooperative societies by granting them special tax privileges and by giving them preference in the conduct of certain government-subsidized services such as the distribution and sale of electricity or fertilizer.

The point at which the cooperative-society system in a country becomes almost indistinguishable from public enterprise is when the government sponsors and uses it as a chosen instrument for the conduct of a public program, such as the supply of goods and services to farmers, as an alternative to the encouragement of competitive private enterprise or the establishment of government agencies or enterprises to assure those services. Such choice means that the cooperative society would get priority and special assistance from government. It might also mean, and often has, that the government would take such initiatives in establishing and supporting cooperatives as to organize, staff, and finance them through agricultural extension or other government agencies so that control is in fact in the hands of government and not lodged with the members of the cooperative. These cooperatives are therefore more nearly state enterprises than autonomous private societies. Even though governments declare their intention to withdraw their financial support and personnel control when the desired network of cooperatives is established, they and their civil servants are well known to be slow to do so. When a government recognizes and relies upon a system of cooperative societies to provide a public service, even though commercial in type, and extends its interest to financial and personnel intervention in cooperative management, the cooperative system becomes for all intents and purposes a public enterprise.

Egypt is a country which relies heavily upon a national network of five thousand farmer cooperatives for the management and development of agricultural production. There is one cooperative for every fifteen hundred acres and six hundred farmers, approximately. There is a federated cooperative for every ten farmer cooperatives, and these are associated in a national cooperative union. The cooperatives provide seeds, supplies, and credit to the farmer and they purchase the farmer's output for sale to government-owned export firms. The government provides an agronomist, an accountant, and a storekeeper to each cooperative at public expense. This is another large bureaucracy. Similarly, Tanzania and other developing countries operate large national bureaucracies of cooperatives.

A second way to categorize public enterprises is according to the nature of their functions. One group consists of production and trading companies, industrial and commerical enterprises which, generally speaking, are expected to operate at a profit. These companies include mines, rubber and tea estates, wholesale and retail stores, fertilizer, steel and pharmaceutical plants, and shipping companies. Another, second group of enterprises categorized according to function is composed of the public utilities and services of a utility type which constitute the supportive infrastructure for business and industry, whether public or private. These services include power, water, communications, ports, railways, irrigation systems, and similar public works and operations. These are income-producing activities whose effective conduct depends upon especially granted administrative powers. Many governments consider, however, that the first obligation of this group of enterprises is to give efficient and reliable service; only second, and as specified, is it to break even financially or to make a profit.

A third group of public enterprises described according to function is composed of those created explicitly for the purpose of development, that is, for the purpose of giving encouragement, credit assistance under special terms, and support to the production and commercial interests of other institutions, both public and private. Enterprises in this group would include industrial development authorities, and regional, state, and river-basin development agencies. This kind of activity also requires for its effective conduct the management freedom of private enterprise, and it is characterized by the expectation of revenue. Such enterprises are rarely profit-making, however, because their success is measured by the prosperity of the clients or sectors or areas which they serve rather than by their own income.

The last group of public enterprises described according to function is made up of corporations such as applied research agencies and universities, which do not have business or commercial functions. They have been given the form of public enterprises entirely for the purpose of acquiring the administrative flexibility and capability they need to perform their functions. These might be called non-commercial enterprises.

A third way to categorize public enterprises is according to their location and position in the governmental bureaucratic structure. In many countries not only the central government but states and even provinces have established more or less systematic networks of public enterprise agencies. Many times the interest boundaries of the national and state enterprises overlap and even clash. Enterprises, often in the form of authorities, are not infrequently set up to develop a particular region, or the mineral or water resources of a particular region. Such authorities are usually instruments of the central government, but their creation invariably involves complicated relationships with both the central and the state bureaucracies. Within the burgeoning world of public enterprise another kind of hierarchical relationship is emerging, such as that between holding companies which control several operating companies that are in charge of individual industrial plants or mines or importing firms. Other enterprises, such as trading companies, often have branches in districts and towns.

In one sense this review of the different kinds of public enterprise according to their grouping by legal base, function, and hierarchical location helps to explain the pattern of a new system of government expression and administration. In another sense, however, this categorization dramatizes the complexities and the dilemmas and even the confusions of this newly emerging and distinctive public enterprise bureaucracy. The characteristics of this bureaucracy as it appears to be evolving, and especially the policy and the management issues raised, are of central concern to the consideration of administration for development.

The Major Policy Issues in Public Enterprise

The success or failure of any particular public enterprise must be judged in terms of the purposes it was created to serve and the special privileges or, alternatively, the special obligations stipulated in its founding charter or by an authorized governing authority. Since a public enterprise represents an intervention in the economy, the first question usually asked about its performance is whether it is making a profit or whether it is operating at a loss, particularly in comparison with private enterprises in the same field. This question is legitimate if the market is free and competitive and if no constraints or advantages are given the public enterprise that are not also given to private enterprise. Such conditions are most often found when the government buys shares in a company and does not alter the management sufficiently to modify significantly its money-making purpose or capability.

Even in those public enterprises for which the government has no purpose other than financial success in the form of a profit, questions arise as to the size of the profit: All the market will bear? If the enterprise enjoys a monopoly, what measures of economic viability will be applied? Should prices and rates be related to the costs of investment and operation plus a larger or smaller margin, or should prices be related to the costs or hypothetical market prices of comparable imported goods? Or both? Hence, the size of the profit of a public enterprise and the form of its measurement is not a fully satisfactory basis for evaluating the success even of those public enterprises which have no other stipulated criterion than to be economically viable. A broader perspective is necessary. A marketing board, for example, or a fertilizer plant which enjoys a monopoly often makes a large profit in its dealings with farmers, and the proceeds can be used to help finance other government undertakings, especially those of development. Nigeria's marketing boards buy farm products such as cocoa from the farmers at a fixed price low enough to assure a handsome profit from sales on the international market. This practice constitutes a form of taxation on the farmers. Judgments about the performance and effects of the enterprise should be made from this wider view.

A larger number of public enterprises, probably a majority of them, have been given stipulations of purpose and method of operation which make evaluation on the basis of overall profit and loss difficult and misleading—even irrelevant. As an extreme case there is the public research foundation, which has no income or other basis for easily measuring its financial contribution or success. The more typical example is the water or electric or other utility service or transport system conceived as a public service first, and a money-making operation only second. A public bus company, for example, such as Malaysia's Mara Bus Transport Service, is required to serve routes and to operate on schedules to serve some special social or development purpose, even though it is known that the company will lose money. Irrigation water and municipal water supplies are frequently made available to consumers below cost, and sometimes free, and the costs of the services are made up by revenues from other sources, including higher taxes on those same consumers and others. Electric rates, conversely, are sometimes set high enough not only to recompense investment and operating costs but to yield enough additional return to permit a reduction of taxes.

Development authorities and development banks are another kind of public enterprise where the purposes are not those of making the highest possible profit or even a good profit in comparison with private enterprise. The development authority, for example, is often created to assist a depressed region where the opportunities for large economic return are low but where the needs to alleviate poverty are high. Development banks are created to give lower rates of interest for longer periods of time and often for higher risk investments than commercial banks—and that is the reason they are created. Such enterprises are sometimes required to serve a particular sector of the economy— agriculture for example, or a selected segment of the population, such as a particular racial group—which is important to the national purpose but is not the best investment of money from the limited view of profit and loss.

These are the policy issues of purpose which must or at least should be decided by government for each of its public enterprises and which then become the basis for evaluation. There are also important policy issues with respect to the conditions and methods of the operation of a public enterprise which influence its performance and modify the standards by which it should be judged. On the one hand the public enterprise might be given special privilege, advantages not available to comparable enterprises in the private sector. It might be given grants or loans on more favorable terms than available on the market. The depreciation rate might be made lower than customary. The public enterprise might even be exempted from the payment of some or all the customary taxes which burden private enterprise. Policy determinations about privileges of this kind affect the operations of an enterprise and are factors in judging its relative success.

On the other hand, it is typical of governments to impose special obligations upon public enterprises, to prescribe standards of operation which affect their efficiency and profitability as measured by the practice of private enterprise, although those standards are perhaps well justified in public purpose. The enterprise, for example, might be expected to serve as a model employer by providing comparatively high standards of housing, health, and educational facilities and services to employees and their families. The enterprise might be required to give preference in employment to selected groups and to follow ponderous procedures in termination of employment. It might be required to establish workers' councils with more or less weight in management and program decisions. The enterprise might be requested to use labor-intensive methods of construction and operation and to operate plants and branches at sites located for that purpose, although such location may not be the most efficient from the point of view of the production or distribution of goods. These stipulations of operating behavior to accomplish yardstick or other public purposes are not necessarily detrimental to efficiency. Well-housed employees who participate responsibly in decisions affecting them might well be more productive than ill-housed, unhappy, and surly labor. As often as not, however, efficiency and productivity in such issues are given second place to other values. In either case the special conditions imposed upon the enterprise become the standards of performance by which its efficiency should be measured and its success or failure determined.

 It is important that these major policy issues of public enterprise purpose and operating method be resolved because they are crucial to the efficiency and effectiveness of each enterprise and basic to the judgment of each enterprise's relative success. The first and the fundamental authority on these issues is appropriately the statute or ordinance or articles of incorporation or other instrument which provides for the creation of the public enterprise. It is important that this establishing instrument be clear as to the purposes of the enterprise and as to its operating privileges and conditions and its expected performance and results. Any such founding charter, however, must of necessity be relatively general in its terms so as to allow desirable flexibility in the conduct of the designated activities which permits adjustment to changing circumstances as time goes on. The question, then, is who should decide what the modified purposes and adjusted methods of operation should be and how the policy issues of program execution should be resolved.

In most countries a public enterprise looks to a designated minister to produce the answers to policy questions. Decisions at this level are necessary for fixing prices and rates, or establishing the criteria by which the enterprise would fix them, and subsidies for major new investments or program extensions, and for additional grants, appropriations, loans, or borrowings. Ministerial decisions are the typical form of the government's answers not only to express the government's supervisory responsibility but also to assure the consonance and harmony of the public enterprise's activities for those of the development plan, the acceptance of the enterprise's financial undertakings by the budget and the treasury, and the approval of its program by the parliament or other appropriate political body. These are the customary functions of coordination expected of ministries; they become somewhat more difficult in the case of public enterprises than in the case of the standard bureau or department because the enterprise is not usually subject to the regular financial systems of annual budget and appropriation review. Nevertheless, the legitimate interests of the planning agency, the budget office, the treasury, and the parliamentary or other political committee need to be assured both by the needs for consistency and balance in the country's development program and by the needs of the public enterprise for understanding and support.

At the level of decision-making under review here, major program policy issues are usually reflected either in the desire for new funds or the disposition of generous profits through dividends or reinvestment. The questions are usually clear-cut and fall naturally and easily into the normal cycle of the government's annual development budget review process, which involves the concerned central planning and control bodies as well as the ministry. In addition, through its representation on the governing boards of the enterprises, the administrative ministry is assured of knowledge of and appropriate participation in major program and operating decisions. Sometimes, and not infrequently, unfortunately, the bureaucratic and political involvement in the affairs of public enterprises is not limited to the major issues but extends to intervention in the conduct of authorized program activities under already sanctioned policy—that is, in management. For the successful conduct of public enterprise, therefore, the sound resolution of major management issues is in the same category of importance as the solution of major program policy issues.

The Major Management Issues in
Public Enterprise: Financial

The primary reason for establishing public enterprises as separate agencies outside the regular bureaucracy of government is so that they can be provided with the management capacity suited to the efficient and effective performance of their distinctive tasks. This capacity consists for the most part of three components: financial flexibility, personnel control, and insulation from bureaucratic and political interference in administration. The relative autonomy represented by their authority to make independent financial, personnel, and administrative decisions to discharge their responsibilities is thus the chief characteristic of public enterprises. This autonomy, however, although given so that the public enterprise can achieve a public purpose, immediately raises the question of accountability. Since the enterprise is established as an instrument to execute government policy and program, it must be accountable and thus subject to some kind of monitoring and some degree of control. It is the tug of war between the degree of autonomy on the one hand and accountability and the degree of control and supervision on the other that creates the major management issues respecting the public enterprise sector. The pulling and hauling in this conflict between autonomy and accountability produces a variety of solutions in the management balances achieved from country to country and from time to time.

One of the two fundamental needs of the public enterprise—the other being control of personnel, discussed below—is access to funds and freedom to expend them as they are required in operations and maintenance and, to a lesser extent, for expansion and investment. The annual appropriation procedures and the tight financial controls of the traditional bureaucracy make it virtually incapable of performing effectively in the business world. It is therefore important that public enterprises be authorized to use their revenues and to borrow money from the government, or from the market, or both. In addition, there might be a loan or a grant from government to get started.

Even for those enterprises which earn a profit, it is not unreasonable for the government to put a limit on both borrowing and the use of revenues and on the size of the debt, either by amount or by purpose or for both, so long as financial capability to discharge the enterprise's basic responsibility is preserved. For example, the government should be represented in the shareholders' meetings of companies where decisions are made about the distribution of revenues and the reinvestment of reserves and the adjustment of prices and rates. Limits can be placed on public corporations in terms of length of amortization and rate of new investment, as distinct from normal operations, maintenance, and replacement.

The limits and conditions of the public enterprise's access to money are best expressed, to assure clarity and reliability, in the founding charter. In addition, however, decisions of financial policy involving government interest are required as the enterprise evolves. This government interest is usually expressed through the minister of the administrative ministry—that is, the ministry responsible for monitoring the enterprise. This minister is commonly called upon to give formal approval to certain kinds of financial decisions, such as those involving new investments representing expansion, and the relationship between rate or price and profit and dividends. It is not appropriate for the minister to be involved in the use of funds or the borrowings needed for regular continuing operations and maintenance.

In a large number of cases the public enterprise operates at a loss, not infrequently because it is required to perform services which are uneconomic, even though in the public interest, or to sell services or products at a price below their cost. In such circumstances government subsidies are inevitable; the government must make periodic appropriations or grants to sustain the enterprise. The need for government money tends to involve the enterprise in the regular, cyclical processes of government appropriation. These processes inevitably involve the treasury and the budget and the planning agencies in the review, and therefore in a degree of control, of the policies and programs which require subsidy. The larger and more frequent the subsidy, the closer and more detailed the control by the regular bureaucratic system. This control is especially true of the treasury, which the enterprise is often required to consult, as well as of the administrative ministry, on matters of financial policy, even when a subsidy is not involved.

The budget and planning offices are usually not related directly to the operations of public enterprises, but both are quite naturally concerned with the size and justification of subsidies, if required, and the availability and use of revenues, if there are profits. These budget and planning interests are customarily served by reports from the enterprise and representations by the appropriate minister at the time the annual development program is being put together, and also when investment for program expansion is proposed even if that investment derives from revenues and profits. The planning office must also concern itself with the effectiveness of the enterprise's program results, and not only its financial aspects, since the enterprise is expected to serve the public interest as an instrument of development.

The underlying assumption of public enterprise is that it will use money effectively and efficiently to achieve stated purposes. The realization of this assumption requires the kind of accounting system that will show not only cash expenditures but also allowances for interest and depreciation and all other elements of cost assignable to each function—the kind of system often called "cost" or "management" accounting. This is not the kind of accounting system usually found in traditional bureaucracies; it is more often encountered in the world of business. Public enterprises are therefore usually exempt from the requirements of government accounting but are required to install a commercial type of system.

The excellence of management accounting is of great importance to the success of a public enterprise. In the first place it is a tool of good internal management because by an analysis of costs it shows the efficiencies and inefficiencies in the organization and the successes and failures in the program. In the second place, management accounting is the basis for accurate analysis and reporting on actual costs, so that the components of uneconomic programs or services or methods or standards imposed by government can be shown and separated from the financial success or failure of the central operation. This kind of information is crucial to the justification of subsidy. In the third place, a sound management accounting system provides the basis for reliable and informative reports to government, which provide not only evidence of the degree of the enterprise's efficiency and effectiveness but also the data upon which policy judgments can be based by the administrative ministry and other concerned agencies of government. When such reliable management accounts are not available, there is an understandable tendency on the part of monitoring agencies to supervise the enterprise and its operations closely and in detail. For lack of satisfactory reports, the supervisors are driven to become engaged in current management decisions, a practice which defeats the very purpose of separating the public enterprise agency from the bureaucratic system.

Complete reports provide the parliament and the public with information to use in their political judgments about the success and relative value of the enterprise. Such reports avoid the suspicion aroused by the mystery of secrecy and silence. More specifically, full reports provide grist for the planning mill and enable the enterprise to be properly related to the development program. Even more specifically, such reports show the costs of peripheral and uneconomic functions and conditions so that their value and justification for subsidy can be fairly assessed. Finally, and perhaps more important, such reports are one of the primary sources for the evaluation of the relative success of the enterprise's work, both its effectiveness and its efficiency. As noted earlier, there is sometimes a tendency to judge a public enterprise a success or a failure according to its overall profit and loss statement in comparison with a private enterprise. This practice is manifestly unfair and inaccurate if the public enterprise serves other and uneconomic purposes or if it enjoys competitive advantages. Good management reporting will separate out the several elements of cost and make possible meaningful comparisons.

Public enterprises are almost always exempt from the regular government audit system. Many government audits include the requirement of a pre-audit before any significant expenditure is made and, whether pre- or post-audit, such expenditure is evaluated according to criteria suited to traditional government functions and not to transactions of a commercial type. Public enterprises are therefore usually freed from government audit but are typically required to submit to a commercial type of audit: Many countries assign to the government comptroller the function of overseeing the performance of the commercial audits. Sometimes this duty is discharged by merely assuring that a reliable commercial auditor has performed the audit. In other cases a separate government agency is created to conduct such audits, as exemplified by Ghana's State Enterprise Audit Organization and Tanzania's Audit Corporation. In still other cases the comptroller's office itself might conduct the audit or prescribe whether another agency or private firm should do so. In any case the government comptroller and his office are involved in a management relationship with the public enterprise sector.

The Major Management Issues in Public Enterprise: Personnel and Governance

Control of its own personnel system is another distinguishing administrative feature of the public enterprise, along with relative financial independence, and is one of the major reasons for establishing such agencies outside the framework of customary government policy and procedure. The primary purpose for putting the public enterprise in charge of its own personnel—giving it the right to hire and fire staff and labor—is to give it the capacity to perform the functions for which it is to be held accountable. There are additional reasons for granting autonomy in personnel matters to public enterprises. One of these is to permit the establishment of salary scales and other conditions of employment competitive with the scales and amenities in private industry and higher than those usually prevailing in government service. Such considerations are particularly relevant because public enterprises typically require types of specialized personnel, industrial engineers and business managers for example, not often found in significant numbers in traditional government employment. Existing civil service systems do not, or at least until recently did not, accommodate personnel systems which would give adequate weight to specialist as opposed to generalist personnel and which would provide for job assignments and job tenure on the basis of merit and performance as judged by agency management rather than as judged by an external public service commission or personnel agency.

Comparatively few public enterprises, however, have been able to sustain their independence in personnel matters. Perhaps the main reason for this failure is their slowness to create their own distinctive systems having personnel standards and procedures which are not only sufficient to the need but which can be explained and justified to a skeptical public. Public enterprises in some countries, and especially conglomerates of enterprises, have prominently included personnel and manpower offices in their headquarters. Some countries have made efforts to establish central industrial management pools to serve the public enterprise sector.

By and large, however, and frequently in developing countries, the public enterprise sector has not acted as vigorously, imaginatively, or as effectively as it might in setting up and sustaining the personnel systems that are needed to perform the enterprises' functions and that are justifiable by public standards. Partly for this reason of delay in establishing acceptable personnel standards and viable systems, but also because of apparently inevitable bureaucratic and political pressures, poor judgment in making appointments, fixing salaries at suspiciously high levels, and supervising too permissively with respect to assignments and tenure are abuses not uncommonly found. There are outstanding and laudable exceptions. Also, as time goes on and public pressure is brought to bear, corrections are made. In general, however, delays and abuses in the personnel systems of public enterprise have brought about external intervention in their personnel policies and actions.

This external intervention and the resulting dilution of personnel autonomy and capacity in public enterprise was probably a threat from the beginning. In many countries public enterprises were created because private entrepreneurship was not serving an effective role in the development program—that is, the private sector did not have the managerial or the technological capacity to perform effectively in the target area. This situation suggested strongly that the country as a whole was deficient in the kind of personnel needed in that field. Under these circumstances it was natural for the managers of the new public enterprise agencies to be recruited from the only class of experienced personnel available—the senior civil servants of government. The civil servants were attracted by higher salaries. Many of these officers were more than usually competent and did outstanding service in novel and difficult circumstances. But as a class the only management system they knew was that of the traditional bureaucracy in which they had been trained and had grown up professionally. Most of them took leave in order to preserve the security of their tenure and were thus loath to offend colleagues in the civil service by the vigorous exercise of unaccustomed new financial and personnel authorities. Only as time went on did countries begin to require civil servants to resign their government positions in order to accept positions in the public enterprise sector.

The civil service establishments in many countries have opposed, not supported, the personnel autonomy of public enterprises. In some cases this hostility resulted from resentment because their own elite system was not extended to the new functions of development, a task for which they believed that their system was adequate. In other cases there was jealousy of higher salary scales and more generous amenities. In still other cases the issue was in the form of a power struggle between bureaucratic systems. Partly because of the essentially unfriendly attitude of the traditional civil service, but often because of abuses and failures in the public enterprise sector, it is not uncommon now to find countries setting up public enterprise service commissions, comparable to the public service commissions of the civil service, to regulate the personnel practices of the public enterprise sector and even, in some cases, to make or pass upon personnel appointments. It is not infrequent that such commissions are controlled by a majority membership of civil servants. In some countries still a third commission, also dominated by civil servants, has the function of reconciling the personnel practices of the public enterprise sector and the civil service. These trends can blunt the capacity for relevant personnel administration, which was one of the main reasons for establishing public corporations in the first place. Nigeria is a case in point. It has established a Statutory Corporation Service Commission, parallel to the traditional Civil Service Commission, plus a National Commission on Establishment to coordinate not only those two bodies but also the personnel policies of the several states.

In a few countries, particularly in those where the public enterprise sector has become quite large and complex and has begun to take on the aspects of a distinctive bureaucracy, there has been some success in finding ways and in gathering political strength to protect the personnel autonomy of public enterprises through holding companies or bureaus of public enterprise management. These new central agencies of the public enterprise bureaucracy have begun to find ways to develop the needed professional personnel staff capacity and to provide leadership in formulating distinctive and relevant personnel policies, standards, and recruitment and training services. Some such holding company personnel programs provide consultation in organization and management to their members.

When these combined efforts go so far as to intrude on the individual enterprise's freedom of action, to that extent of course they nullify its autonomy. The proper obligation of these central holding company personnel staffs for public enterprise management therefore is to evolve the methodology and the rationale for establishing, justifying, and reporting appropriate levels of compensation in comparison with similar agencies, particularly in the private sector, and to set standards and provide recruitment services for the selection of personnel who would be employed and paid at these levels. This service, reliably performed, would also help public enterprises to ward off intrusions of government which insist upon reconciliation of their personnel systems with those of the civil service. It is incumbent upon the public enterprise sector to act imaginatively but responsibly to capitalize on its needed autonomy in personnel administration.

Another kind of government intrusion into the personnel independence of its public enterprises is the imposition upon them of certain standards or conditions of employment, such as in health or housing, in the hope that such practices will be a kind of model for private enterprise or in the belief that certain doctrinaire social objectives will be served, such as the participation of workers' councils not only in hiring and firing but in other managment decisions. There is no particular reason why a government should not make such external systems an obligation of the enterprise as long as their effects are measured, reported, and taken into account in judging the enterprise. Too frequently, however, when such additional conditions of operation are imposed on an agency, some other external agency is given or assumes the responsibility for monitoring their application and thus becomes involved in and dilutes the management capability and responsibility of the enterprise of primary accountability.

The third component of the management capacity of the public enterprise, along with its financial flexibility and personnel control, is its insulation from bureaucratic and political interference in its day-to-day administration. The governing board is the body typically entrusted with the function of protecting its enterprise in these respects, as well as with the function of representing the government in the management of that enterprise. Governing boards vary widely in their ability both to preserve the integrity of the enterprise and to give administrative leadership according to the length and conditions of their appointment. Boards differ in character: their members serve sometimes full-time and sometimes part-time; they sometimes have tenure of some specified time and they sometimes have none at all, serving at will; sometimes they are policy boards and sometimes they are functional, in that their members are also assigned management tasks such as general manager, comptroller, and chief engineer; and boards are sometimes composed of political and sometimes of professionally influential persons.

There is no such thing as a perfect board; they all have their limitations. The best, perhaps, from the point of view of the enterprise itself, is the part-time policy board of members selected for professional quality and appointed for terms of some overlapping length. A board of this nature would tend to provide continuity and integrity and to stay out of operations. Even this board can be weak if its members fail to be responsive to government policy or if poorly qualified persons are appointed. The small, full-time board whose members are appointed from senior staff, such as a general manager and chief engineer, is possibly the least satisfactory. This kind of board must be immediately responsive to the appointing authority and such whims as that authority expresses, and it confuses operating with policy functions while diffusing and segmenting enterprise management.

Many boards, perhaps most of them, are appointed by the minister of the administrative ministry, and include some ex-officio members such as a representative of one or more relevant bureaus of the administrative ministry and of the treasury. Boards are typically composed of government officials, at least in the majority. Sometimes the ministers themselves are also members of the governing boards of major public enterprises, such as those which are in effect holding companies for a large number of development operations. In at least one country, Zambia, the president himself is the board chairman of the paramount public enterprise in the hierarchy of development companies, and the other board members are ministers. The cabinet, in effect, is the governing body of two separate bureaucracies.

Such arrangements as these are inconsistent with the basic conceptions of public enterprises and tend to thwart the purposes of relative autonomy for which they were separately established. A public corporation's board is not the vehicle for coordination; rather, coordination should be achieved with the assistance of an advisory committee to the board, on the one hand, and by stronger integrating capacity in the minister's office. The board's function is to support the enterprise for which it is responsible and to determine its policy within the limits of the controlling statute and guidelines from government.

The administrative or supervising ministry has responsibility for monitoring and coordinating the public enterprises attached to it. Sometimes each enterprise is treated much like another department of the ministry in its relationship to the minister. In other cases a separate office or division is set up for the several enterprises attached to the ministry with its own corps of supervisory staff. In this pattern the ministry represents the corporations and companies to the planning and budget offices, to the treasury, and also to the parliament. The ministry performs coordinating functions where necessary or desired. The ministry, and often the minister himself, expresses the government's position in program and policy issues to the corporation, and it performs the normal functions of supervision and reporting which in turn require the use of systems by which to measure performance in terms both of efficiency and of effectiveness. Sometimes this supervisory relationship is so close, as in Egypt and Indonesia, as to be hardly distinguishable from the minister's administration of bureaus which have less autonomy. In other cases the relationship is more correct in respecting the integrity of the enterprise.

The major management issues in public enterprise—those of finance, personnel, and governance—are thus fluid, never static in the sense that they are resolved once and for all. They are represented by a series of tensions at points representing the relationship of the public enterprise agency with a number of external government agencies. These include the administrative ministry, the treasury, the planning and budget offices, the public service commission and comptroller, and the parliament itself. These are the issues and the relationships which distinguish the management characteristics of the public enterprise.

The Public Enterprise Bureaucracy

The distinctive characteristics of public enterprises which set them apart from other government agencies would not have any great significance if the number of such enterprises was small. This is the case in some countries, where virtually the whole of the economy is in the hands of the private sector under conditions of more or less close governmental guidance and regulation. In a very large number of countries, however, the number of public enterprises is enormous, even in the hundreds, and the extent of their interest and influence in the economy is very great. Some countries have in effect turned over much of the whole economy to the public enterprise sector and entrusted to it responsibility for carrying out their development plans. Even in countries which wish to rely heavily and primarily on the private sector for economic development, especially in the long run, the size of the public enterprise sector can be formidable. Tanzania's National Development Corporation has fifty subsidiary companies; in addition there exists a countrywide National Trading Corporation. Zambia's Industrial Development Corporation alone has eighty subsidiary companies with a total of eighty thousand employees. Egypt has four hundred operating companies under forty holding companies. Turkey has one hundred public enterprises, and the government is represented in sixty-five others. Ghana's Industrial Holding Company has nineteen operating companies. India has almost one hundred enterprises in banking, air, shipping, oil, steel, fertilizer, drugs, and heavy industry.

Thus in many countries the public enterprise sector is very large, is exceedingly important in the economy, and is characterized by systems of management and control that distinguish it from the bureaucracy serving the more traditional government functions. In a growing number of such countries, the public enterprise sector is being shaped into hierarchical form. This development, together with its distinctive management characteristics, is converting the public enterprise sector into a third bureaucracy approaching the dimensions and importance of those of traditional public administration and the private sector.

A more or less typical hierarchical pattern is for public operating companies in a particular field to be grouped under, or even to be formed by, a central holding company. In Ghana, for example, there are separate holding companies for industrial, mining, trading, and financial enterprises respectively. In India, holding companies have been formed to control enterprises in each of the several fields of oil, shipping, fertilizer production, heavy engineering, banking, pharmaceuticals, and transport. In some countries, as in Tanzania, large public enterprises, notably trading companies, have set up operating branches to serve regions and districts. In several countries, including Tanzania and Egypt, farmers' cooperative societies created to provide supply and marketing services are organized into regional and then national bodies to assure comprehensive coverage. In these several ways, public enterprises are related horizontally and vertically in a bureaucratic hierarchy.

The organization of the public enterprise sector in Zambia illustrates what appears to be a movement of power and authority from the traditional bureaucracy to a hierarchical public enterprise bureaucracy. The Zambia Industrial and Mining Corporation (ZIMCO) is the central holding company for the country's investments in mining, commerce, industry, transport, and the financial sector. Its major subsidiaries are also holding companies in direct charge of numerous operating companies. These subsidiaries are the Finance and Development Corporation (FINDECO), the Industrial Development Corporation (INDECO), and the Mining Development Corporation (MINDECO). The governing board of the holding company of each subsidiary is composed of the relevant ministers plus the chairmen of the boards of its subordinate operating companies. ZIMCO's board, the paramount body in the hierarchy, is also composed of the relevant ministers and the chairmen of the boards of the major subsidiaries. The chairman of the ZIMCO board is the president of Zambia. Clearly this body is more important in Zambia's development and economic life than is the cabinet.

Public enterprises become a bureaucracy for still another reason and in another sense—that is, they are often treated as a separate and distinctive group for purposes of governmental surveillance. It is not uncommon to find a central bureau of public enterprises in the treasury, as in India, or in some other ministry, with an overall monitoring function. Such a bureau typically does not have control functions in the sense that it can issue orders, but it usually has the function of evaluating, reporting, and advising on public enterprise affairs and on the performance of individual enterprises. Even more commonly, one finds commissions or committees set up to coordinate aspects of enterprise administration, such as personnel systems, within the public enterprise bureaucracy as a whole and with the traditional government bureaucracy. Comptrollers sometimes issue reports on the entire public enterprise sector. Not a few countries have passed laws, such as public corporation control acts, which stipulate conditions and standards of enterprise management and which supersede the provisions of individual articles of incorporation. In these several ways governments seek to deal with and accommodate the public enterprise sector as a distinctive entity.

Finally, the public enterprise sector is taking the form of a separate bureaucracy by creating its own supporting institutions. In at least one country, India, the general managers of public enterprises have formed their own professional association, partly for the purpose of improving the quality of enterprise management, but also for mutual protection against the invasion of traditional bureaucratic systems and interests. In several countries the public enterprises in a specialized field, such as banking or development finance, have formed organizations comparable to trade associations in private enterprise to support informational and innovational systems to undergird the technological and administrative aspects of their professional charge.

The most common and perhaps the most important of the kinds of institutions needed to support reliable public enterprise management are centers for training, research, and consultation. In too many countries, one after another public enterprise has been created because of the lack of capacity of the private sector or the existing bureaucracy, or for some other reason, but in any case without regard for the fact that the public enterprise sector also lacks the capacity for the function because of a scarcity of specialized and management personnel and relevant expertise. There has been a singular oversight and failure not only to recognize the training and research preparation needed to assure the success of new public enterprises, but even more to establish and support the institutions which could contribute to this preparation. Most countries quite correctly rely upon their universities and institutes of public administration to discharge this responsibility, but these are too frequently inadequate both in their capacity and their relevance to serve even the burgeoning needs of traditional government systems, let alone the novel requirements of public enterprise management.

Faced with this situation, the more progressive enterprise leadership in some countries has taken the initiative in setting up centers and even whole systems of training and research to serve their recruitment and supervisory needs. This tendency is probably not desirable because it segments and compartmentalizes teaching and research unnecessarily and expensively—even to the detriment of professional teaching and research—as countries formulate and carry out national programs for these purposes. Nevertheless it is understandable that the public enterprise bureaucracy, or some parts of it, acts independently when the government and the existing educational institutions do not realize and act upon the enormous need of the public enterprise sector for support.

One impediment to the development of fully effective training and research and consultation in support of public enterprise management is the failure to isolate and deal with those aspects of management which are troublesomely unique to public enterprise. As seen, these aspects include personnel systems which meet enterprise needs in competition with the market while satisfying the requirements of public accountability; financial systems which provide funds and flexibility in their use while assuring consistency with national development policy; management accounting and reporting systems which serve commercial management purposes and phases of the operation to permit evaluation and policy decisions on subsidies; and monitoring systems which deal with the difficult points of tension between, on the one hand, public enterprises (individually and, as a sector bureaucracy, collectively), and, on the other hand, the budget, treasury, planning, personnel, accounting, and functional agencies which have interrelating responsibilities for national development planning and implementation. These are the difficult and complex issues of public enterprise management which would benefit, for purposes of resolution, from the special attention of education and research institutions. The regular disciplines of public and business administration have their relevance and importance also, of course, but for effective public enterprise management those aspects of administrative policy and method which are unique to it are the aspects of significant and demanding relevance.

Unfortunately there are widespread examples of inefficiency, of ineffectiveness and of corruption, in public enterprise management. Instances of inefficiency, ineffectiveness, and corruption are so numerous in many countries as to cast doubt on the continuance of the management autonomies of the public enterprises and even of the enterprises themselves. It is not surprising that inefficiency and corruption should occur in this new sector. Even when management autonomy is given, it has no meaning unless it can be exercised well and responsibly. In many countries, however, neither management systems nor managers are available to assure competent and responsible administration of public enterprises—or at least were not available to begin with. It can be expected under such circumstances that occurrences of failure in performance and of corruption in the public enterprise sector will be found. Too many countries set up government corporations without taking concurrent action to assure the support of management capabilities.

The perplexing problem of corruption is not limited to the public enterprise sector but is found in the private sector also, and in government service generally. Corruption is dramatically associated, however, with the public enterprise sector because of the new and burgeoning commercial environment in which it lives and because the traditional constraints to bribery in government and in the private sector have not been replaced with new restraints shaped to a new situation. It is unlikely that corruption in the public sector would differ in degree or in kind from corruption in the private sector once the public sector finds its place in the community—except perhaps to the extent that higher standards of behavior might be expected of the public sector. Similarly, corruption in the regular government service is a severe problem and differs from corruption in the enterprise sector chiefly because of differences in activity and opportunity and in bureaucratic maturity.

The problem of inefficiency and corruption in the public enterprise sector can be solved by abolishing the sector and assigning its operations to private enterprise; or by reinstating the traditional management controls in personnel, finance, and other areas of the traditional government bureaucracy; or by instituting the management systems distinctively needed in public enterprise and by recruiting and training the managers to operate those systems efficiently and honestly. The least attractive of these alternatives is to reinstate the traditional management systems of government bureaucracy, which are manifestly not suited to the successful accomplishment of the commercial type of purposes the government wishes to achieve. Public enterprises would exist in name only, and their program operations would not be served. Unfortunately, however, several countries have been moved by current demands for reform to elect this alternative.

Another alternative, to turn public enterprise over to the private sector, has its attractions and has been adopted by some countries. Other countries have, however, ideological objections to this course or, pragmatically, recognize that there are several forms of public enterprise which do not lend themselves to private ownership or management or which are not attractive to private investment. The third alternative, which is to devise and strengthen the distinctive management needed by public enterprise, is thus the best solution to problems of inefficiency and corruption. Its success depends, however, upon understanding on the part of the government of the administrative requisites of a successful public enterprise, and upon the government's resolve and energy in satisfying those requisites and in providing the institutions for management training, research, and consultation to undergird and support the public enterprise sector.

Note on Sources

In the works listed below, the classic study of the organization and administration of public enterprise is that of A. H. Hanson. Lloyd Musolf's monograph is useful on the one aspect of the relationship of mixed enterprise to development planning. The United Nations documents are exceptionally useful.

Financing of Public Enterprises in Developing Countries, Sales No. E. 77. II. H. 2 (New York: United Nations, 1977).

A. H. Hanson, *Public Enterprise and Economic Development,* 2nd ed. (London: Routledge and Kegan Paul, 1965).

A. H. Hanson et al., *Organization and Administration of Public Enterprises: Selected Papers,* Sales No. E. 68. II. H. 1 (New York: United Nations, 1968).

Lloyd D. Musolf, *Mixed Enterprise: A Developmental Perspective* (Lexington, Mass.: Heath, 1972).

Fouad Sherif, *Measures for Improving Performance of Public Enterprise in Developing Countries,* Sales No. E. 73. II. H. 2 (New York: United Nations, 1973).

V. V. Ramanadham, *Organization, Management and Supervision of Public Enterprises in Developing Countries,* Sales No. E. 74. II. H. 4 (New York: United Nations, 1974).

C. Y. Wu, "Public Enterprise as an Instrument of Development," in *Development Administration: Current Approaches and Trends in Public Administration for National Development,* Sales No. E. 76. II. H. 1 (New York: United Nations, 1975).

I wish also to cite the papers of two of my students: Mohamed El Haj Amara, "The Public Corporation as an Instrument for Development in the Sudan," Occasional Paper, Center for Development, University of Wisconsin–Madison, November 1976; and Rohani Binti Harun, "Problems of Public Enterprise Management in Malaysia," Occasional Paper, Center for Development, University of Wisconsin–Madison, March 1978.

6

Organization for Planning

The Place of Planning in the Bureaucracy

Effective administration for development depends upon new management systems as well as the establishment of new or the reorientation of old agencies and organizations. If the work habits and methods of the new agencies are no different from those of their predecessors, not much improvement in capability will be made. If the processes and systems by which such agencies conduct their affairs are not adapted to their new purposes, the agencies will be hampered and frustrated in their performance and accomplishment. If the reconstituted agencies are not related harmoniously and productively with their sister agencies and with their public clients—that is, if they are not well in-stitutionalized in a revitalized bureaucracy—their impact will be blunted and limited. The systems and processes as well as the agencies of development administration are of crucial importance.

The essential purpose of management systems is to give sufficient authority, staff, money, and materials to qualified and responsible officials at the most strategic locations so that they have the capability to accomplish tasks assigned to them. The whole focus of such systems is action and accomplishment by the officials who are made responsible for specified functions and given the authority to perform them. The two major management systems in this context are therefore those for budget and for personnel, which are discussed in chapters 8 and 9, below.

Planning is also a system in this sense; it is an administrative process as well as an agency and organization. As a process, operating not only in a central agency but in the ministries and in the provinces, planning is an instrument for making decisions about development goals, programs, projects, and policies which become the assigned responsibilities of designated agencies and officials within these agencies. It is the identification of these components of the development program which fixes, or at least should fix, the tasks for which qualified personnel must be assembled and for which resources must not only be allocated but made easily available.

It is now only an occasional country which does not have a planning process incorporated in the public bureaucracy. The movement to establish organizations for planning surged after World War II, when so many countries, particularly in Asia and Africa, achieved their political independence and started their search for improved economic well-being. These countries were impelled to concern themselves with economic matters because their populations and their leaders alike aspired to and expected higher standards of living, even though under circumstances which were generally not favorable to improvement. Natural resources were often lacking in availability. The infrastructure to support vigorous agricultural and industrial growth was weak. Colonial economic systems had been disrupted and new systems of indigenous private enterprise, supported by trained and experienced populations, were not strong enough to carry the whole burden of development. Funds for investment were scanty.

Given popular economic demands on the one hand and the lack of capability to meet them on the other, a logical step for a country to take was to set up a planning agency to help decide what measures should be taken, and in what sequence and relationship, because not all desirable programs, projects, and policies could be undertaken at the same time. This step was supported by multilateral and bilateral givers of foreign aid who stressed the desirability of some kind of planning as a means of choosing priorities and of giving some order to the multiple associations involved in economic and technical assistance. In the early fifties, the Colombo Plan, designed for Asian nations, expected each of its members from among the developing countries of the Commonwealth of Nations to prepare a six-year plan. Those plans, in the early days, were not much more than "shopping lists" of desirable projects and programs; they contained little reference to comparative importance or order of implementation. Today the United Nations Development Program, the World Bank, and bilateral contributors all give careful attention to the technical excellence of national plans, as well as to their political standing and the priorities for development which they represent, as a means of judging the validity of projects proposed for assistance. In terms of development administration as well as in chronological terms, planning agencies were the first of the new organizations for development in most newly independent countries. Planning symbolized the intention and expectation of social and economic development.

Development planning conceived of in terms of economic growth consists of three processes: (1) the identification and selection of goals and purposes; (2) adjustments in broad aspects of the economy which are most likely to accomplish these purposes—aspects such as savings, investment, production, consumption, and foreign trade; and (3) the selection of policies, programs, and projects in effective relationship with one another to make the best use of available resources to achieve those goals. Some countries, predominantly socialist ones, attempt central comprehensive planning of the entire economy. This kind of planning assumes sufficient availability and control of resources to make the plan realistic, and it assumes adequately complete data and information and sufficiently competent and honest planners to make it reliable. Such conditions cannot often be found.

Other countries, those with mixed economies, attempt less substantial planning efforts—efforts which are limited to plans for public sector investment and to policies to guide the private sector. Almost all countries, however, have found it desirable to intercede in the economy through planning decisions about development in order to speed up the process of growth or to encourage its expression in selected areas or places in preference to others. Some countries become involved in their economies, and planning for them, more than others. The detail, size, and complexity of their planning often grow in geometric proportion to the degree of involvement.

There are many varieties of perception and conception, of style and method, with respect to planning. There are those who oppose planning for doctrinaire reasons, retaining faith in the infallibility of *laissez-faire* and the superiority of the free market system. There are others who, in anticipation of practical obstacles and difficulties, or having experienced such barriers, resist the establishment of planning agencies and processes, preferring to rely upon traditional government systems, such as that of the budget. And it is true that the handicaps which many and probably most countries face in attempting to establish viable planning systems are numerous and severe. Data are frequently lacking in their coverage and reliability, and the specialists trained to analyze and use the data are in short supply. Government and other institutional capacity to support planning and to implement plans is, more frequently than not,

woefully inadequate. The list of deficiencies is long and such planning as
is undertaken can, in its ineptness, slow down and even in some cases
impede the development process. Certainly, planned targets are frequently not achieved.

In spite of these differing views, however, the overwhelming majority
of developing countries now have planning agencies and systems and are
determined to retain them. Their efforts are bent to improve and
strengthen planning processes and not to schedule their demise. A few
countries are attempting to merge their planning with some other
government decision-making process such as budgeting. The general
practice, however, is to maintain a distinctive planning process as well as
a budget system.

The term "planning" is sometimes used to mean the application of
professional skill to the processes of analysis and synthesis involved in
planning. This professional skill, considered to be possessed by
economists, is expected to be rational, competent, and objective. It
involves the application of mathematical economics and statistical
analysis to economic data to determine the dimensions and components
of a plan for development. It applies methods of cost-benefit and cost-
effectiveness analysis to program and project evaluation. This approach
to planning is useful even when there are deficiencies in the data and their
applicability, but it is limited. First of all, planning is at present rarely
confined to the economic aspects of development without concurrent
consideration of other aspects, such as social objectives, which involve
judgments of justice and equity and environmental effects, as in the case
of the location and the technology of a new chemical plant. These additional considerations go beyond the field of economics; they are not
treated adequately by quantitative and mathematical methodology
alone.

Second, and even more fundamental, econometric planning is
inadequate and incomplete because choices in the planning process must
frequently be made between alternative projects and programs and
policies which hurt some parts of the population and favor others. The
choices must be made because of the very shortages of resources which
necessitate planning in the first place. While econometric or other
analysis by professionals is of assistance in making choices, the choices
are almost always made on a subjective basis. The judgments are rooted
in the value systems represented in the populations. The choices thus
involve the country's political and administrative decision-making
processes and are seldom left for determination to an elite group of
professional plan-makers. The professionals can and should provide
analyses and models and, even more, alternative courses of action. They

cannot and do not, however, decide what a plan should be nor the projects, programs, and policies of which it would consist.

The assumption which underlies this perception of planning as a decision-making process is that a plan is not merely academic but that it is meant to be acted upon, to be implemented. To be carried out, a plan must be acceptable to and accepted by those who must be relied upon to carry it out—the ministries, the state and local agencies, and the people themselves. It must reflect the approval of the appropriate executive officials and legislative bodies. The plan must be feasible; that is, the government should possess or acquire the capacity to execute it, and the government should have the clear intention to execute it. Because a development plan is not separate from a country's decision-making process, the planning agency cannot be isolated from the normal operations of government. There is not one bureaucracy for government and another for planning and development; rather, planning and development should be integrated in a country's administrative system. Thus, planning can be seen and understood as an administrative, decision-making process.

The best way to proceed with social and economic planning and development is to make the functional ministries and departments a regular and systematic part of the process. For the sectors over which they have responsibility, such as agriculture, industry, health, and education, these agencies have or ought to have the best information on needs and opportunities, on problems and feasibilities. They are in the best position to know in their respective fields what policies, projects, and programs have the highest priority in productivity in the area of their expertise and the greatest promise of successful implementation. Their data systems, their knowledge of relevant resources which are available, and their acquaintance with the respective desires and demands of the people are, or at least should be, of great value in making plans. It is only sensible to strengthen and use the resources of the ministries for planning according to their own areas of responsibility and their potential. Moreover, an agency—a ministry or any other agency—is far more likely to understand, support, and carry out those plans, projects, and programs which it helps to formulate rather than those which are prepared for it by external bodies. A viable system of planning and implementation incorporates the participation of the ministries and does not separate either planning or development implementation into a parallel bureaucracy.

Similarly, state and local organizations both of government and of the bureaucracy should be drawn into and relied upon for participation in and contributions to planning as well as plan implementation and development. State and local organizations, as in the case of central functional ministries, possess distinctive information about the development needs and opportunities of their respective regions and localities and the availability of resources and capabilities to support proposed projects. Of equal importance to the planning process is the special advantage that field organizations have in learning about the feelings of the residents in their areas, their aspirations and demands, and their comparative likelihood to support proposed development projects. It is not necessary for a new and separate planning agency to attempt to duplicate these sources of information, judgment, and plan support, but rather to utilize the services and to draw the energies of local bodies into the planning effort. Local and state governments and agencies are a ready-made system by which to engage the public's participation in the national planning effort as well as in local development projects.

Certainly the planning process and the planning agency cannot exist without systematic working relationships with the agencies which control budgets, monetary and fiscal policy, personnel, and other support indispensable to any substantial activation of social and economic plans. It is highly unlikely that any country would attempt a system of plan preparation without some method by which these implementing associations were involved—not for very long, anyway. The planning agency itself, therefore, is only one of many agencies involved in the planning process—agencies which include ministries, state and local agencies, and such central control agencies as those for budget and personnel. A plan is properly a product which emerges from a network of linkages of all of these agencies in the bureaucracy. Even this product is not a plan for activation until it secures the approval of the chief executive, the president or prime minister and his cabinet, and also of the legislative body, when one exists. These additional associations and linkages in the process are often represented by councils and committees, such as a national economic council.

Two important characteristics of the national planning agency become clear in the light of this review of the place of planning in the bureaucracy. First, the national planning organization is a staff and not a line agency. It does not make planning decisions or give orders concerning development plans; rather, it gives information and advice and makes recommendations about development policies, projects, and programs. The planning choices and decisions are made at other points in the bureaucratic and political systems. In the second place, the national planning agency is only one of several, even quite a few, agencies engaged in the planning exercise as a whole. These several agencies are appropriately related and linked in systematic ways for the purpose of producing plans and the several projects and programs provided in them. The national planning agency is properly at the center of this network; its own functions are performed best in the context of the many associations involved.

Because of these characteristics of the planning agency's functions and relationships, it is located best in the office of the chief executive, as in the case of the Economic Planning Unit in Malaysia. This connection makes it clear that planning is a decision-making process in the direct line of executive responsibility and puts the planning agency in a position to benefit from the full coordinating powers of that office. The planning agency becomes a part of the central office of administration, at the apex of government. This position is much more favorable to the planning process than that of a separate ministry on a par with other ministries, as in India, and thus of status and capacity insufficient for leading and guiding effectively. Incorporation in another ministry, such as finance or economic affairs, as in Korea, makes this disadvantage even more severe. Location in the prime minister's office is also more favorable than is status as an independent board or commission which, while seeming to give objectivity and to protect rationality, tends to remove the agency from the full effect of the bureaucratic process. Planning should be an integral part of the bureaucratic process. It should be a powerful instrument of the chief executive and of his administration.

The Functions of the Planning Agency

The central interest of a national planning agency is plans for social and economic development. They might include plans for each major sector, such as agriculture and industry; for each state and local government or other regions selected for development; and for the nation as a whole, involving a synthesis of the subordinate plans. Such plans are usually for a period of five or six years but they are almost always reflected in annual development budgets and are frequently put in the perspective of a much longer planning period, such as twenty or even thirty years. The preparation of these plans is not a single, one-time, ad hoc exercise resulting in a blueprint. Rather, planning for implementation by the bureaucracy is a continuing, never-ending process of administration so as to accommodate changes in need, feasibility, experience, and circumstance.

Plans and planning are not the exclusive province of the national planning agency. They involve the coordinated participation of the central ministries and their divisions and of the state, local, and regional governments and administration throughout the country. The major function of the national planning agency is to orchestrate the participation of these many agencies, to give leadership and guidance to their planning work in the name of the chief executive. The several plans emerging from those integrated activities are then the subject of approval, modification, or rejection by the chief executive and by the supreme legislative body.

The long-term and short-term goals intended to be reached by carrying out such plans are identified and defined in much the same way as the plans themselves are prepared. If targets and purposes to be served by plans have not been stated clearly by the chief executive and the legislative, it is a function appropriate to the national planning agency, with contributions solicited from the other participating agencies, to propose such purposes and goals for consideration. These recommendations might well be accompanied by alternative choices and analyses of the probable consequences of the selection of one alternative as against another. The chief executive and the legislative then decide on the goals to be sought, the purposes to be achieved.

A first major function of the national planning agency is thus to lead and coordinate the planning work of the several central and field organizations and to synthesize it into a consistent and feasible whole. A second major function is to make broad assessments of the country's social and economic condition as a basis for recommending, in connection with the national plan and its goals, correspondingly broad policies and programs in such areas as investment, production, trade, fiscal and monetary practice, population, and social welfare. This function is basic to informed and rational adjustments in major trends in the economy and in the society to accomplish the public purpose; and it is basic to competent synthesis of sectoral and regional plans in a consistent and viable program. Although assistance can be drawn for the performance of this function from such authoritative centers as the ministry of finance and the state bank, the planning agency itself must have the organizational and staff capacity to make its own analyses, judgments, and recommendations in terms of development goals, policies, and programs.

A major component, perhaps the major component, of a development plan is the several specific programs and projects to achieve its purposes through the best use of available resources. It should be assumed that most of these programs and projects will be formulated in the appropriate ministries, states, and localities together with their sectoral and regional plans and that they will be analyzed there for their comparative effectiveness, for the purposes they have, and as against available alternatives. The national planning agency should not aspire to perform this function. It should of course assure itself that the programs and projects are soundly conceived and competently analyzed and assessed; for that work it must have its own capability for cost-benefit and other types of analysis. And it certainly has the function of articulating the projects and programs of the several sectors and localities into an effectively interrelated overall plan. But the planning agency should itself do no more sectoral or regional program planning or project formulation than absolutely necessary. Nor should it undertake the research which so frequently precedes, and should precede, the planning of a program or project—fertilizer research in agriculture, for example, or attitude surveys in family planning, or reasons for dropouts from school. The planning agency has the function of encouraging research of this kind and judging its competence and reliability when used to support development plans, but it should not undertake that kind of research itself.

Unfortunately, in many developing countries, especially when planning is first introduced as a process in the bureaucracy, the several ministries, states, and localities have very little if any capacity for planning or program and project formulation. The research function may be weak, also. In these circumstances the national planning agency itself frequently undertakes sectoral and regional program and project planning functions. This move is understandable and justifiable because, if not taken, there might be no development plan at all for that sector or that place. However, there is often a tendency for the planning agency, once it is organized to do the planning and project work for education or agriculture or some other sector or for this or that state or region, to continue to do so rather than to encourage and assist the proper ministry or local jurisdiction to develop its own capacity and competence for the work.

There are those who advocate a continuation of a larger rather than a lesser role for the national agency in sectoral and regional planning and project formulation and evaluation. This position is wrong and is self-defeating, however, because of the long-range psychological and functional advantages of sharing planning functions throughout the bureaucracy. It is wrong also because the larger the operating workload undertaken by the planning agency, the greater the tendency to give lesser attention to its staff leadership role in the prime minister's office and its role in enlisting and harmonizing the planning efforts of the many agencies involved. The planning agency in such a case weakens its capacity to perform its major functions in order to perform comparatively subordinate functions. Its proper role is to encourage and help the agencies to undertake more and more rather than less and less of the planning operation.

The planning agency should keep itself as small as possible so as to reserve its energy and talents to the central planning and coordinating function and to avoid as far as possible the assumption of operating functions which, although closely related, can be undertaken by others as well or better, at least in time. If it attempts to do all of this work itself, either it must fail because the work load is too large and too divergent or because it would unnecessarily duplicate in staff size and competence large portions of the staff competence of ministries and other agencies, thus creating such jealousies and confusions as well as demands on inadequate professional resources as to defeat the effort.

It is not the function of the national planning agency to implement the plan or to supervise the execution of programs and projects incorporated in the plan. Implementation is the function of the existing bureaucracy, although that bureaucracy might need to be reoriented, renovated, and even expanded for the purpose. It is not practicable to set up a second agency in the form of the planning agency or to create a separate set of executing agencies in the form of a second bureaucracy to administer development. Nor is it practicable to make the planning agency a separate coordinating office for the purposes of development alongside the existing coordinating center of government, which is usually the office of the president or the prime minister, the chief executive. Development is best served by reshaping the existing structure of public administration to the purpose. Development is poorly served by efforts to relieve the regular bureaucracy of that responsibility by creating alternative and parallel systems.

Nevertheless, the national planning agency should be involved heavily in the process of plan implementation. It should participate with the budget office, through the development budget and in other ways as might be desirable, to assure the consistency of proposed projects and programs with the approved development plan. Systems to record, measure, and report progress, or lack of it, under approved plans for authorized programs and projects are needed so that adjustments can be made from time to time and corrective measures taken to assure reasonable balance and continuity in the development program as a whole. Various parts of the program must progress at speeds and ways which support other parts interdependent with them. It is the responsibility of each agency involved in a development project or program to record, measure, and report on its own performance and relative progress and to evaluate its experience. It is a proper function of the planning agency to analyze all such reports in relationship to each other so as to advise the chief executive of the actions to correct or to ameliorate shortfalls in the plan. The planning agency should itself make periodic evaluations of progress and experience under the plan as a whole, and for the economy and society as a whole, for the purpose of helping the government to adjust ongoing development programs or to formulate new ones. Most countries have the advantage of such evaluations, including India and Pakistan, Malaysia and Indonesia, and Ghana and Nigeria.

The processes for such evaluations and adjustments are very similar to and even identical with the processes of preparing plans in the first place. The planning agency relies heavily upon other units in the bureaucracy for their analysis, judgments, and recommendations, although it makes its own distinctive technical and synthesizing contributions. These processes of recording, measuring, evaluating, and reporting relative progress and the reasons therefore are essential to those aspects of implementation known variously as "monitoring" or "progressing." They are the sources of information upon which, after analysis, coordinating and administrative decisions are made. In the implementation of development programs, the planning agency should be responsible for analysis, and the chief executive should be responsible for administrative decisions and coordinating action.

There is a second very important aspect of reporting, and that is to inform the public of accomplishments and disappointments in the conduct of government programs. A major way for a public agency or the government as a whole to discharge its burden of accountability to the public is through the medium of both periodic and special reports. These reports should take care to measure accomplishments, or short- falls, in terms of the purposes, goals, policies, and methods explicitly understood and expressed in advance in plan, budget, statute, or other ways. A more positive purpose of a vigorous program of reporting is to involve the public more fully in understanding and support of the development program as a whole or of selected ones of its parts. This public reporting function, with respect to development, is appropriately assigned to the national planning agency.

Administrative Considerations in Planning

Planning for development involves not only the identification of the policies, programs, and projects proposed to accomplish the desired purposes. It also involves the identification of the agents or agencies which will carry out those policies, programs, and projects and a prescription for their being carried out. A development plan is more than a description of what it is hoped will be done to achieve established goals. The plan, if it is to be operational, if it is to be realistic as a guide to policy and action, must also include a finding that the proposed policies, programs, and projects are feasible and that they will be implemented by specified agencies in specified ways. Development policies, projects, and programs should pass the test of management feasibility.

These policies, projects, and programs must also pass other tests of feasibility if they are to be reasonably undertaken and assured of accomplishment—tests of technical feasibility, economic and financial feasibility, and political feasibility. Traditionally, planning agencies have focused their analyses on technical and financial feasibility. Failures to give sufficient regard to popular expectations about the distribution of the benefits of development have forced planning agencies to consider the political feasibilities of proposed courses of action. More recently, shortfalls and failures in plan implementation have led planning agencies to give more systematic attention to the ways of accomplishing the desired policies, programs, and projects. If a particular project or activity is found to be administratively impracticable, either an alternative activity or course of action will have to be substituted for it or, preferably, measures can be devised to make it feasible to undertake the desired activity with some assurance that it will be successful. The planning process is thus not limited to the managerial capacity as it exists and to screening proposed projects only in those terms. Planning extends to ways of increasing managerial capacity and competence so that the policies, projects, and programs necessary to social and economic development can be executed.

There are four different tests of management feasibility, any one of which, if found to be negative, requires corrective or ameliorative attention if the desired activity—policy, program, or project—is to be included in the development plan and carried out. The first of these tests is whether the supporting environment in the area of the activity's proposed expression will sustain the activity. The road and rail system, for example, might be so inadequate as to make impracticable the exploitation of mineral resources in a remote range, or as to prevent the introduction of a new commercial crop in a distant area because of lack of transport. A new industry to be based on promising natural resources might fail if it were dependent upon electric power, water, and skilled manpower which were not yet available in the area. The provisions to maintain law and order might not be sufficient to assure enough protection of persons or property to make investment safe. Or the monetary and banking institutions might not be adequate in their service to a particular place or to a particular kind of economic activity to make it possible to invest in the desired project of economic development. These are weaknesses in the general infrastructure of public services.

The second kind of management feasibility question is whether an existing agency or group of agencies, either public or private, has demonstrated by its past performance that it is sufficiently competent and reliable to be counted upon to carry out the desired policy, program, or project in the plan, or whether it could be strengthened to do so. If an agency of the desired description does not exist, the question is whether a new agency or series of agencies needs to be created if the activity is to be undertaken. In the case of private enterprise, feasibility might depend upon tax policies, investment inducements, import licensing barriers, or other conditions coloring the attractiveness of the environment for private business. In the public sector the choice among the methods for achieving administrative feasibility often rests between reforming an established traditional institution and infusing it with the will and competence to conduct a novel development activity, or creating a new agency to accomplish the desired purposes of the plan. Such new agencies might be at the center or in the field or both. They might be additions to the traditional bureaucracy or they might be in the form of public enterprises of one of several varieties. Whether the agencies chosen to perform the tasks of the development plan are new or old, there must be assurance that they already have or will acquire the competence in the form of specialized personnel, sound organization, imaginative administrative leadership, and relevant delivery systems so that they can do the desired job if given the requisite authority and money.

Very often there might be an agency to which it would appear natural and logical, and under some political circumstances even necessary, to assign the responsibility to carry out a given policy, or program, or project. The assigned activity to be carried out, however, might require the setting up of a new delivery system. The existence and reliability of a management delivery system to serve a development policy, program, or project is therefore the third question about the feasibility of the development proposal under consideration. A program to increase crop yields by introducing a new variety of seed is feasible to the extent that the new seeds, with the supporting water, fertilizer, and pesticides essential to their successful use, are actually delivered to the farmer at the right time and place at the prices he can and will pay. The development plan must therefore include specific assurance that the ministry of agriculture, the farmer cooperatives, the private sector, or some new public enterprise will singly or together meet the delivery requirements.

The fourth kind of management feasibility test is whether all of the several policies, programs, and projects desired to be in the development plan can be carried out during the five-year or other prescribed time period, even though each of them is found to be viable. Is the skilled manpower pool, for example, large enough to serve all of the programs and projects concurrently or in the contemplated sequence? Can each of the projects and programs rely upon the others for necessary support, and does each one make its complementary contribution? Does the pre-existing economy and its administrative structure provide the overall environment needed by the whole package of plan activities? A development plan is capable of execution only to the extent that these questions can be answered with reasonably positive assurance.

Policies, projects, and programs which are incorporated in development plans should therefore show not only what is to be done, but also how they are to be done, how they are to be implemented. Plans should be based on evidence that implementation is possible, that the policies, projects, and programs are individually and collectively feasible. The responsibility for planning the management as well as the technical and financial aspects of projects and programs, and giving assurance of their practicability, rests with those who prepare and evaluate them in the first place, usually the appropriate ministries and the state or other regional planning offices. The national planning agency must also check the adequacy of judgments of project feasibility, but even more particularly and importantly, at that central level, the planning agency must be sure that the several policies, projects, and programs constituting the development plan are feasible in their collective entirety and that they support each other in their execution from the management point of view in addition to being consistent with each other from the point of view of the development plan. This synthesizing function in plan preparation is the unique contribution of the national agency.

Another aspect of the question concerning administrative capability is who should make plans for public administration as it relates to development—that is, plans for improving development administration in general. Traditional administrative systems do not lend themselves readily to the conduct of development programs. Arrangements for the administration of specified and particular development policies, projects, and programs have to be tailored to fit the needs of each. Several countries at one time or another have launched ad hoc administrative reform commissions charged with the responsibility of assessing the management aspects and requirements of the government's administrative functions and recommending reforms in the existing systems to improve the responsiveness and effectiveness of the bureaucracy in a new political environment. Most such commissions were preoccupied with the civil service system and gave less, even though perhaps some, attention to other major areas of public management crying for reform, including budget and fiscal systems, central-field relationships, and public enterprise management. This special attention to the civil service in developing countries, most of them newly independent, is understandable because of the importance of the capabilities and loyalties of the newly nationalized personnel of the bureaucracy. It is also understandable because most reform commissions were influenced heavily, if not actually dominated, by the civil service elite, whose members quite naturally were concerned about their status as well as their duties.

In general, the recommendations of administrative reform commissions, although many of them were quite well drawn, are noted more for their academic interest than for their adoption and implementation. It is probable that the failure of this reform approach to administration is because it was considered primarily in terms of what is "good" or "bad" administration. Such considerations involve value judgments, judgments bordering on the philosophical and certainly obsessed with the methodological because the focus of interest is on administration as such rather than on the management requirement of the programs and projects, which are or at least should be the objects of administration. The comparative merit of alternative systems of administration in the abstract can be debated indefinitely because many systems have merit and because the reasons of urgency or relevance in selecting one instead of another are not prominent. The object of reform is to correct what is wrong, corrupt, or unsatisfactory in the administrative system. The environment for administrative reform is usually hostile because there are at least two views of what is wrong or right, good or bad, in the world of administration as such. This climate of consideration is therefore subjective and political and is limited by its tendency to treat administration as a system disembodied from the purposes which it exists to serve.

A sounder approach to administrative reform is to analyze the management requirements of the programs and projects to be served and to adjust or establish the organizational and methodological arrangements to meet those requirements. In this context the debate about the merits of alternative administration systems is based on the comparative effectiveness of those systems in achieving program results which themselves are not in debate. Evidence of the influence of these program considerations in determining changes in administrative style is found in the growth of public enterprises and in new agency systems for rural and community development. For the most part, unfortunately, these new administrative forms emerge on an ad hoc basis and too frequently in an environment of transient pressure.

What is needed in many countries is a small but highly competent staff unit which can give continuing attention to the changing administrative requirements in the discharge of governmental development and other responsibilities. Such a unit might also give leadership or at least assistance to both staff and line agencies in strengthening their own competence to improve their management systems and performance and in solving the administration problems posed by new projects and programs. Such a unit might or might not be called upon to appraise the adequacy of the performance of established agencies and systems. Prototypes of this kind of organization are found in Malaysia's Development Administration Unit and in Ghana's Management Service Division, both in the prime minister's office. Embryonic expressions of this staff service are found in the treasuries of some countries, or in the personnel office, sometimes in the form of O&M (organization and management) units, although these typically work at a comparatively middle level of management systems and technology.

It would not be inappropriate for this function of planning for development administration to be assigned to the central planning agency, where it would complement very productively the planning for social and economic projects and programs—planning activities for which good administration should be available. An administrative planning unit in the central agency could also give leadership and support to the performance of management feasibility analysis. It would be inconsistent with the role of the planning agency, however, to burden it with the function of monitoring or appraising the administrative performance of ministries and agencies in the bureaucracy. This task of evaluation would inevitably prejudice and inhibit the agency in its primary purpose of advancing the planning process. It would no doubt be preferable for this reason for the planning staff for development administration to be a separate component in the group of direct staff services in the chief executive's office, the others most prominently being those for planning, budget, and personnel.

The process of planning for social and economic development must in any case include planning for the implementation as well as the prescription of development projects and programs in particular and the administration of the development program as a whole. The planning process is thus an administrative process. This perception of planning shows it in the context of governmental action, political and administrative, although it also benefits from the staff contributions of professional planning experts.

Correlative Functions: Statistics and Foreign Aid

There are two other major functions which must be performed effectively if the national planning agency and the planning process as a whole are to succeed in producing realistic plans which it is feasible to carry out. These are the functions of collecting and analyzing statistical data and of coordinating the foreign economic aid and technical assistance received by a developing country. Practice varies from country to country, and expert opinion differs with respect to the assignment of these correlative functions to the national planning agency. Certainly, in any case, they are functions essential to successful planning and must be performed in such a way as to serve and support the planning process.

An enormous volume of data is needed to prepare development plans, as well as the projects and programs which are suitable to their purpose, and to measure and evaluate their effect. Such data are also needed in many operations of government, including budgeting for example, and the administration of the many sectoral programs and other functions of government. These data are demographic, including population size, composition, distribution, and growth rate, and the nature and use of the labor force. Data are needed concerning natural resources—the extent, location, and availability of oil, minerals, land, water, and forests. Data must be collected about economic activity—savings and investment, transport, water and power and communications, prices and trade, agricultural and industrial production, and consumption. Data systems must extend to social welfare and its indicators—education, health, employment, and income distribution.

The work involved in recording, collecting, and publishing these data is very great. It involves the taking of periodic censuses of population, agriculture, and industry. Sample surveys or other special studies and analyses are often needed. The systematic recording of a great deal of social and economic activity and of natural events is involved, including vital statistics, savings, investments, agricultural production, industrial output, imports and exports, weather, and water flow. Regular annual and other reports of central and local agencies, public and private, are included in comprehensive national data systems.

These several data and information systems are usually the immediate responsibility of the relevant agencies, such as the ministry of agriculture for crop information, the ministry of health for vital statistics, and the ministry of education for school enrollments. These operating organizations are usually in the best situation to collect the data relevant to their activities, and they are the primary users of the data in the discharge of their program and administrative responsibilities. In addition, however, every country should have a highly competent central statistics office because of the overall national need to collect, compile, and publish such data series as those involved in national income accounts and the ten-year census. The need to use expensive modern data processing equipment efficiently and to assemble and use an often short supply of statisticians and other experts effectively are other reasons for organizing a central statistical service. A professional office can also coordinate and give assistance to the many agencies which operate data systems to support their own work but which tend to duplicate or overlap with other agencies and their systems. The central statistics office itself might even collect and analyze certain data as a service to operating organizations when there are economies of scale to be gained, especially when more than one agency is involved.

The dependence of the planning systems and the national planning agency on a competent and reliable statistical system of this kind is clear. The product in the form of data is the raw material for development analysis, assessment, and planning. In the 1950s, when planning agencies were being created in many countries, such statistical systems and services hardly existed, and the data available for planning were sparse and incomplete. It was more usual than not for the planning agency in such circumstances to set up its own statistics office, often as the country's statistics center. The statistics center, once located in the planning agency, tended to become established there because of the concern of planning staff that it have reliable access to information considered necessary to its work and because of the lethargy which often inhibits changes in organization.

This organizational arrangement has serious disadvantages, however, disadvantages so great as to suggest the separation of the statistics office from the planning office. In the first place, the relationship of the statistics office to other agencies is not the same as that of the planning office. The statistics office has functions of supervision, regulation, and control, with respect to data systems, which are inconsistent with the cooperation that should be fostered in the planning process. Second, the operation of the central statistics office and system is a very large operation—a heavy and repetitive administrative load. This kind of responsibility is not natural to the staff functions of planning. It tends to be a distraction and even, in its size, to overwhelm a desirably small planning group. On the whole the planning agency would be well advised to divorce the statistics office. The responsibility of the planning agency for making arrangements to assure the flow and the availability of needed data would remain, of course, but others should be induced to do the work.

The second correlative function, and one which is inseparably related to planning, is the coordination by the recipient country of foreign economic aid and technical assistance. Unlike the operation of statistical services, the coordination of foreign aid is usually handled outside the national planning agency, and yet there is very good reason for assigning that function to the planning office. Although foreign aid usually represents a comparatively small proportion of a country's development program and budget, it often has a disproportionately large influence. Most foreign aid is received in support of a country's development program, although there are occasionally other aspects, such as military aid, or food or other commodity aid to help meet some emergency situation, or financial assistance in support of a country's current monetary or budgetary position. But the great bulk of foreign aid is specifically and directly in support of development programs and projects.

Foreign aid, characteristically, is not given for general support or even for the broad support of some sector. Rather, economic aid in the form of loans or grants and technical assistance for institution-building or program development is almost always provided on a project basis, with matching or other conditions. These conditions often commit the host country to an involvement along the lines of some development route of longer distance and duration than that supported by the amount and length of assistance. In this way foreign intercession becomes a major factor in the planning and budgeting of the development program.

Also, foreign donors are heavily represented in developing countries by specialists who have the function of negotiating aid projects and of monitoring those finally agreed to. This personnel is in addition to the large numbers of foreign advisers and experts who accompany individual projects. These donors include the United Nations and its specialized agencies and frequently the World Bank. They also include bilateral country contributors, often in some numbers, and private agencies and foundations. This community of foreign development specialists, with its several agency or country or individual views of what priorities and projects should prevail, has in itself a very strong influence on the planning process. Yet the responsibility for coordinating these relationships is usually assigned to a ministry or office of economic affairs created for the purpose, as in Pakistan, or to the ministry of finance, as in India, rather than to the national planning agency. The consequence of this organizational arrangement is to create a dual system of planning and project approval—two offices requiring coordination to avoid confusion, where one would do better.

Several reasons might be ascribed to this seemingly mistaken division of responsibility for development planning. Foreign aid programs were initiated and evolved even sooner and more rapidly than planning systems. In those first years, the national planning agencies were weak not only in capability but in status and influence in the bureaucracy. Their formulations did not have weight comparable to that of other offices, such as the treasury, in the existing establishment and its patterns of decision-making. The plans were not related in any binding way to budgets as early as they might and should have been. Foreign agencies, even the multinational donors, were not inclined to respect plans or planning agencies when there was a conflict of judgment or opinion about a project not recognized in the plan. Also, foreign aid representatives were often more familiar with the established and prestigious patterns of relationship with foreign ministries and finance ministries than the uncertain channels of new planning organizations.

As national planning agencies grow in strength, and as plans and the planning processes become effectively imbedded in the bureaucracy, ways are being found to involve the agencies in the coordination of foreign aid. Probably they should assume the whole responsibility for development aid. This move will appear even more reasonable as development activities become more completely integrated into the regular life and work of the bureaucracy and are not considered to be some rather strange and perhaps ad hoc set of projects to be treated separately. As the ministries and the field agencies of government assume fuller responsibility for development, they can assume more of the responsibility and the burden for relationships with foreign donors in their own sectors and spheres, at least within the limits and provisions of the development plan.

Perhaps another reason for handling foreign aid outside the planning agency, at least at the outset, was the large and onerous logistics operation which was entailed. A mountain of detailed and not very pleasant work is involved in arranging for the housing, transport, imports, educational facilities, and other amenities of foreign experts and their families. Negotiations are involved over petty problems that never cease. This operation is certainly not natural to a planning agency. Neither, however, is it sufficient reason to separate the planning of foreign aid for development from the planning of development as a whole. It should be possible to meet the logistics needs of foreign aid not only adequately but even better through an experienced ministry of supply or its equivalent.

Organizing the Planning Agency

Having identified the nature of the several functions involved in planning, we find it possible to arrange for their accommodation in the internal organization of the planning agency. For this purpose there are two underlying considerations to bear in mind. The first of these, already emphasized, is that the planning agency is as heavily involved in coordinating and guiding the preparation of development plans as it is in making them. The second is that there should be as much organizational connection as possible of the several specialized components of plan preparation so as to avoid the scattered duplication of staff specialization. The purpose of this focus is to assure that specialized staffs are in command of the resources of knowledge and skill that they need to reach sound judgments, which will permit them in turn to make their optimum contribution to processes relating to planning.

This second consideration, involving the interrelationship of specialized components of planning, suggests that the planning agency be organized primarily according to its basic purposes—that is, first, research concerning policies and measures regarding the mobilization of resources to support the economy and society overall, including fiscal, monetary, tax, credit, and trade policy; and second, the synthesis of policies and plans and aid for each of the several sectors of development, such as physical resources (agriculture, water and power, fuel and minerals), industry (transport, communication, and shipping), and human resources (population, education and manpower, health, social services, and housing). These two major organizational divisions, which might be called "social and economic research staff" and "sectoral planning staff," could be divided into a larger or smaller number of branches depending upon considerations involving the extent of economic management on the part of the government and the degree and adequacy of participation of other parts of the bureaucracy.

Each of these divisions and its respective branches should be provided with the specialized capabilities needed and involved in its own area of planning, from goal-setting through planning and implementation to monitoring, evaluating, and reporting. These capabilities include the competence to analyze the financial, technical, and administrative feasibility of and requirements for viable projects and programs and to coordinate foreign economic aid and technical assistance. Separate advisory and coordinating units might be justified in such areas as foreign aid, monitoring, evaluation, and reporting; but it would be an error to separate the performance of these functions from the divisions that have the basic overall responsibility for the work of the national planning agency in their own respective spheres. This principle of organization gives greater assurance that the several specialized considerations of development can be brought to focus on the sector of concern and its proposed programs and projects.

If these pieces of the planning responsibility were compartmentalized in separate divisions, the planning agency's two primary units would be weakened and limited in capacity, and the costs and complexities of administering the agency would be increased. The integration of foreign aid with the planning process would not be accomplished, for example, by merely transferring the unit to the planning agency and maintaining its parallel system of project and program review. On the other hand, if other major responsibilities are assigned to the planning agency, such as those of the central statistics office and the office for administrative planning, they ought to be placed in separate operating divisions. The national planning agency should have, of course, its own staff units of budget and personnel.

Under this form of organization each major operating unit of the planning agency would be the focal point in that agency for the expression of all functions related to plan preparation and progressing at that level. That unit, the agricultural branch for example, would be concerned not only with goals, plans, and policies for agriculture, and progressing and reporting, but also, to the extent of the planning agency's need and responsibility, for foreign aid and for project feasibility analysis as related to agriculture. The unit would be staffed with the specialized personnel qualified to perform these supporting functions as well as with those needed for its plan preparation and progressing.

The other underlying consideration in organizing the planning agency is that its responsibility consists predominantly of soliciting project and plan ideas from others—the bureaucracy and the public—and synthesizing them into a consistent and viable overall development plan for the consideration of the appropriate political institutions and the executive. This responsibility, for its effective discharge, depends on establishing and maintaining a system—indeed several systems—of working relationships with the ministries, with a multitude of public organizations, with the regions and provinces, with the legislatures and other political institutions, and with the chief executive and his staff. For this reason, units in the planning agency might well be called "planning relations" branches, rather than merely "planning" branches. Their essential duty is to facilitate a process of reaching governmental decisions on plans and projects which are not only feasible and appropriate to the accomplishment of broadly stated purposes but which are understood by and acceptable to the implementers—the bureaucracy and the public—and therefore susceptible to implementation.

On the whole it is desirable that the national planning agency and its essential processes be given statutory recognition in the same way that recognition is given to other major organs and processes of government. The alternative is the establishment of the agency by executive order or other equivalent act of the chief executive. This kind of action by a chief executive in setting up a planning organization, usually in his own office, often has the effect of creating a powerful instrument in achieving the political and administrative goals of a particular president or prime minister. Such an agency is, however, ad hoc in nature and its effectiveness depends almost entirely upon the prestige, effectiveness, and tenure of an individual. A statutory body, on the other hand, has the advantage of being a continuing organization designated to carry out functions understood and endorsed by the legislature and incorporated into the bureaucratic system as an integral component. The statute regularizes and systematizes the planning process.

The status and style of the planning agency's staff is influenced directly by the decision to make it a statutory organization. An ad hoc organization might have the advantage at the outset because it is comparatively easy for a chief executive to persuade competent professionals to join for a time in an exciting and prestigious exercise and to enjoy comparatively generous remuneration. As time goes on, however, as the glow of new adventure dims and as tenure considerations influence recruitment and retention, it is necessary to the assurance of continued staff competence to establish a personnel system that will attract and hold good people over the long run. Such a system almost always depends upon the regularization of the agency by its recognition in statute.

The question of personnel quality in the planning agency remains even after a decision is made to embody the agency in law. Will it be staffed by generalist civil servants, or by professionals from the specialized services, or both? If staffed through the regular civil service system, will economics and other professional specialties be recognized and position rotations lengthened, as in some countries? Or will the agency be authorized to select and set salaries for its staff outside the civil service, as in the case of the state or national banks, public corporations, and universities, in most countries? The requirement of the planning agency for superior staff as measured by professional qualification and interpersonal skills is paramount if the planning function is taken seriously and if it is expected to be at the center of a government's decision-making process.

More than one personnel system is capable of fulfilling this requirement. A preferred system is one which represents progressive modifications in the civil service system as a whole and which meets the needs of new agencies and processes for development. Such modifications, by recognizing changing and growing needs for professional specialists of a number of kinds, and the advantages of long tenure rather than rapid rotation for some positions, are more likely to meet the overall needs of a country, including for example the planning units of ministries and states and public enterprises, than is a system that gives special treatment, as an exception, only to the central planning agency. The career opportunities for the economists and other professional specialists are better in a broader system of this nature, and that circumstance would also contribute to the increased quality of planning personnel in ministries and provinces. In these ways also, as it influences personnel practice, does the planning agency establish its productive relationships with the bureaucracy as a whole.

A remaining issue of organization in connection with the central planning agency is whether it should be headed by a board or by a single executive. The logic of the relationships and methods of work outlined in this chapter suggest that the agency is best headed by a single executive. The planning agency is in its best environment when it is an integral unit in the chief executive's management staff organization rather than a semi-autonomous body with its own separate political identity—a status which would be implied and even intended if the agency were set up as a board or as a commission. Political and regional participation in the planning process is better achieved in the network of councils, committees, and task forces through which the sophisticated agency gives leadership to the planning process. The economic council of the cabinet or other equivalent group representing the political relationship is more soundly based and more clear-cut in its function than a political or semi-political board which also attempts to administer the planning agency.

Coordination for Planning

It is desirable that social and economic plans for development programs and projects be prepared and carried out at a number of places in the overall government establishment. It is conceivable that as many as six different plans or sets of divergent plans could be prepared in as many as six disparate systems. These different sets of plans would include those prepared by the several central functional ministries, especially the ministries charged with the nationwide development of such sectors as agriculture, industry, communications, commerce, education, and health. Another set of plans might be those prepared by the ministry or ministries responsible for the country's field units of government and administration, especially the provinces and districts into which the country is divided for the purposes of development on a more or less integrated geographic, as distinguished from a functional, basis. Or, in the third place, the plans for the several geographical areas could be prepared by instruments of state and local self-government with varying degrees of autonomy and financial independence, including the complex systems of metropolitan planning. It is not unusual now to find identifiable regional planning systems, such as those for selected river basins, outside the normal and traditional divisions of government's functional and geographical organization.

Also outside the traditional organization of public administration, forming the fifth group of development plans, are those of the public enterprise sector, the several public corporations especially charged with a variety of important responsibilities in the conduct of development programs. The sixth kind of plan, of course, is the national plan itself, usually prepared by the central planning agency of the government. These several sets of plans—functional and geographical, horizontal and vertical, central and local, administrative and political—need to be brought into a reasonable degree of harmony if they are not to be competitive and self-defeating in their relationship with one another as efforts are made to put them into effect.

There is no particular virtue in consistency as such, or in uniformity. On the contrary, the very purpose of a variety of diverse plans is to recognize and act upon differences in circumstances, needs, preferences, goals, and methods as they vary from place to place and from functional field to functional field. It is when these differences are in conflict with each other and thus impede the satisfactory accomplishment of local or national plans, or regional or functional plans, that reconciliation, and to that extent consistency, becomes desirable and necessary. There are several different kinds of coordination which are required when several sets of plans are under consideration for comparative viability and implementation. One kind of consideration which should be obvious but which is too often overlooked or underemphasized is the financial and managerial feasibility of the plans when they are considered in relationship to each other and in their totality. Questions of feasibility involve not only those of the sufficiency of money and personnel and organization for plan implementation, but also the timing of projects in relationship to one another and the scheduling of resources for them.

Still another kind of divergency requiring the reconciliation of diverse plans and their coordination for purposes of implementation is the conflict between competing goals of development. One of the issues here is whether development activities will be located in an area exclusively in the interest of the success of economic enterprise, or located also with consideration for the growth of backward regions, or rural as distinct from metropolitan areas. Related issues are whether labor-intensive projects or methods to provide jobs should be selected in preference to more economically efficient capital-intensive systems, and whether the future returns of development should be postponed for longer or shorter periods of time in order to share some of the benefits of development sooner. Other conflicts between separately prepared plans at a variety of localities and in a number of sectors can be thought of, such as the competition between two cities for a steel mill or some other industrial enterprise, or such as the dispute between irrigation and power agencies over the utilization of water resources. The point is that the feasibility of one set of plans often depends upon its coordination with other plans to the extent that, and at the points at which, they touch each other either in some form of conflict or some form of dependency or mutual support.

The multiplicity of plans raises the question of whether planning in a country should be from the top down or from the bottom up. The issue is whether there is to be a predominantly national plan checked with greater or lesser care against local and special interests, as in India and Indonesia; whether there is to be a system of state or regional and functional plans brought together and packaged in a reasonably homogeneous country plan and program, as in Tanzania; or whether there is to be a system which attempts a compromise between these two extremes. There is a variety of systems by which the plans and planning interests of the several levels and sectors of government are attempted to be accommodated. Certainly there are diverse interests at these levels and in those sectors which are involved—the interests of the planning experts and the government officers, and also the interests of the residents in the localities and of the clients of the agricultural, industrial, and other sectors. Projects and programs should be planned at and according to the geographical level of their application, and the whole package of such programs and projects should be tested not only for the technical, financial, and management practicability of each of these but for the feasibility of their relationships with one another and the several levels of government and administration which are involved. These relationships include public understanding, support, and participation.

A composite system would seem to account for most of the many considerations which complicate the planning process. To begin with, the central planning agency, with suitable instruction from the central political and executive authorities, might prepare and circulate to other planning units throughout the country—both the area and the functional units—a statement of goals or targets for the ensuing plan period, the dimension and nature of the resources available to the development effort, and general guidelines for the preparation of local and sectoral plans. Within this framework, as a second step, the localities, states, ministries, regions, public enterprises, and any others appropriately concerned would prepare draft plans. These draft plans would then be molded into a consistent and feasible whole by the central agency for renewed debate in the public forums of the country and for further negotiation among planning authorities—debates and negotiations which would follow the public discussions and the expert consultations which would have taken place in the process of draft plan preparation.

A revised national plan containing references to modified local and sectoral plans would, following this process, be transmitted for consideration and approval to the chief executive and subsequently to the parliament or other national legislative body. Such approval would be signified most appropriately by incorporation in the national budget with provisions for grants and other aids to the budgets of those state and local governments whose plans are brought into consistency with the coordinated planning effort. Budget allocations to branches of the national bureaucracy, both central ministry and field office, would of course be more easily administered and controlled than those to state and local governments and even those to public corporations. State and local agencies and public corporations have some degree of autonomy and certain independent sources of funds and would therefore be in a position to adjust their local plans to their local priorities within the limits of the budget sacrifices they would be willing to make by giving up central government subsidies. The national planning process thus involves the systematic adjustment and integration of local, regional, and sectoral plans offering the prospect of implementation by programs of management which are at least reasonably coordinated for the purpose.

Coordination for Development

The acceptance by governments of responsibility in greater and greater degree for social and economic development has resulted in the creation of many new agencies and institutions and in the assignment of additional and varied functions to existing agencies. The large increase in public functions and agencies and in their widespread geographical extensions has intensified the need to assure the establishment of effective working relationships among them and in their several levels of expression to avoid overlapping and duplication on the one hand, and to achieve the correlation of complementary functions on the other.

To organize is to divide work and to arrange it by bureaus for the purpose of sharing the load, but primarily to assure the application of specialized skills to specialized purposes and tasks. This dividing of functions among compartments is the essence of bureaucracy. As soon as an organization's specialized competencies are put into compartments, however, it immediately becomes necessary to reunite them—to reunite them in an effective relationship to accomplish that organization's overall purpose. This process is called coordination. It is the function of combining the several units of an organization in harmonious action for the purpose of achieving an integrated or unified result. Coordination means that the various parts of an organization work together, without friction, overlapping, or duplication in the accomplishment of a common, overall goal. Coordination has its negative side, that is, to keep competition within bounds and ease tensions; and it has its even more important positive side, which is to integrate the essential contributions from two or more organizational units in the effective accomplishment of a common purpose. Coordination is therefore the very essence of administration.

The purposes of coordination can be served in several ways, and usually more than one of these ways must be used to achieve the desired result. If a statute or ordinance is used to establish an agency or to assign a function, a clear and complete description of duties and responsibilities will help to avoid misunderstanding and, if drafted carefully, to avoid duplication and overlapping of functions and therefore competition among agencies. Similarly, skillful organization will delineate the duties and responsibilities of the several parts of an agency. Organization of course emphasizes compartmentalization; it establishes jurisdictions. In this sense, organization helps to avoid the conflict and tensions among bureaus and parts of bureaus that arise frequently in the administrative process. The organizational function can be much more constructive and complete, however, if it recognizes the inevitability and desirability of cooperative and joint efforts of bureaus whose mutual efforts are required in the achievement of a common objective.

Organization charts and manuals should show not merely the differences and distinctions among agencies and their boxes in the structure, but also their interrelationships with other agencies and boxes as they are expected to work together. These interrelationships can be delineated still further in production and delivery systems which show the role of each contributing agency, in procedural and work-flow manuals which specify interagency methods of participation in a cooperative task, and by administrative policies and choices of methods of work which emphasize cooperative endeavor. Organization should therefore show how each bureau or unit shares in and contributes to the larger tasks of the organization as a whole. Above all, each bureau and unit in the organization should be charged with the function and responsibility of self-coordination—that is, for initiating and participating in cooperative associations with sister bureaus and units to accomplish a task that requires the contribution of each and that without the contributions of all would thwart the purposes of each.

A powerful force in support of coordination is the staff's understanding of and agreement with an agency's purpose and conception. The difference in effective coordination and therefore accomplishment achieved by staffs which believe in and have enthusiasm for the goals of the agency as contrasted with staffs which do not understand the goals, or who oppose them, is enormous. The strength and influence of employee devotion to a cause, plus loyalty and enthusiasm, cannot be overemphasized. Coordination by common purpose and understanding can be made specific in day-to-day administration by assuring the recognition of the mutuality of interest among units that should be related and by securing the acceptance of responsibility for self-coordination as a matter of self-interest and standard operating procedure. Personnel and agency performance appraisals, for purposes of evaluation and rating, should include the relative effectiveness of self-coordination efforts. The benefits of coordination which comes from staff acceptance of agency purpose depend upon effective management arrangements of at least three kinds: (1) systematic programs of employee orientation and indoctrination of high quality; (2) organized systems of employee participation in program formulation and the methods of its execution, so that their contributions can be made and so that they belong and feel that they belong to the enterprise; and (3) specific processes and procedures for expressing interagency contributions and interests under particular circumstances.

Budgeting helps coordination in many of the same ways as, and through processes similar to, those of planning. In addition, the budget carries with it the power and influence of money. Budget allocations determine which agencies are able to perform which functions. Such allocations could be made even stronger instruments of coordination if they were to recognize areas of interrelated activity and to specify the agencies involved—particularly at the functional level of ministerial activity. Grants-in-aid can be used in much the same way as budgetary allocations to achieve coordination of relationships at the state and local level and between that level and the center. The degree and pattern of delegations of spending authority can thwart the coordinating process or can strongly facilitate it. If authority to commit funds is given to the responsible operating agents, and given without the inhibition of a pre-audit system, those agents then have the capability as well as the responsibility to work out the cooperation needed with each other. If funds are not allocated in this way but held back for second approval, and are made subject to pre-audit approval as well, the process of coordination is hampered seriously.

Coordination is a principal function of executive management; it is at the center of really first-class administration. It is the responsibility of the executive-administrators and managers at all levels to see to it not only that there is clarity in assignments but also that such assignments carry with them the charge of self-coordination. The good executive will provide for participatory methods of supervision for the purpose of achieving agreement on and acceptance of work programs and methods, as well as cooperative relationships and methods of improving them, for the purpose of reconciling the differences and easing the tensions which are bound to occur. He must be sure that a sound and reliable system of evaluative reporting underlies the whole process. Thus a reliable reporting and communications system is basic to the process of coordination. It is needed to identify and to illuminate the problems and opportunities of interagency cooperation and coordination. Reports, and their distribution and discussion, facilitate understanding and acceptance of the phenomenon of coordination and provide the occasion to enlist the participation and appropriate staff in the process.

On occasion, special agencies or mechanisms are created to assist or to supplement the single executive, particularly at the level of prime minister or president, where the administrative or coordinating load is particularly heavy. These additional arrangements are hazardous because coordination is an integral part of the executive function and should not be separated out for distinct handling without recognition of the risks. The chief executive himself might set up a deputy or assistant, or several of them, in a designated secretariat to help him in a staff capacity. Sometimes a separate agency is set up at that same level, parallel in status to the budget and planning agencies. It is not uncommon for governments to set up special bodies to coordinate the activities of several ministries in a broad and particularly important area, such as energy or environment. Holding companies for a number of government corporations operating in one field, such as fertilizer, perform a coordinating function, as do cabinet and interministerial committees on such subjects as the economy and security. Still another form of governmental coordination is often found in the responsibility of a home ministry or its equivalent to administer and coordinate the field establishment of the central government and its relationships with evolving local governments. Whenever these special and extraordinary arrangements for coordination are made, unless on an ad hoc and temporary basis, they create their own new and additional problems of coordination and integration, problems which inevitably return for resolution to the executive at the appropriate level.

It is always necessary at the operating level to establish patterns and mechanisms for interagency collaboration, particularly when neither of the cooperating agencies has administrative precedence over the other. These are frequently the circumstances of development administration and its programs and projects. New patterns of association and collaboration must be found and established, ranging from informal and unstructured relationships to structured and formal systems. Informal patterns include regular or irregular meetings and conferences and the regular exchange of reports and information. Somewhat more stylized forms of relationship are found in cross-representation or participation in each other's meetings. More formal patterns might be joint task forces or committees with specified and recognized functions, or even jointly sponsored councils working under contractual agreements. These devices are available to public agencies at the same level—national, state, or local—or between levels, as between a national and a state agency. But at whatever level and whether interagency or intra-agency, the process of coordination is essential to administration for development. The several ministries become nation-building departments not only because of their several individual capabilities and contributions, but because of their synchronization in a single and integrated program of development in association with local instruments of government and administration.

Note on Sources

The best single reference on the organization of planning agencies is that by Albert Waterston, *Development Planning: Lessons of Experience* (Baltimore: Johns Hopkins University Press, 1969). Of direct relevance also are the United Nations publications listed below:

Administration of Development Programmes and Projects: Some Major Issues, Sales No. E. 71. II. H. 4 (New York: United Nations, 1971).

Proceedings of the Interregional Seminar on Organization and Administration of Development Planning Agencies, Sales No. E. 74. II. H. 2 (New York: United Nations, 1974).

Appraising Administrative Capability for Development, Sales No. E. 69. II. H. 2 (New York: United Nations, 1969).

C. Y. Wu, *Development Administration: Current Approaches and Trends in Public Administration for National Development,* Sales No. E. 76, II. H. 1 (New York: United Nations, 1976).

Other references which contain useful insights include the following:

Gerhard Colm, ed., *Organization, Planning and Programming for Economic Development* (Washington, D.C.: U.S. Government Printing Office, 1963).

Keith B. Griffin and John L. Enos, *Planning Development* (London: Addison-Wesley, 1970).

Bertram M. Gross, ed., *Action under Planning: The Guidance of Economic Development* (New York: McGraw-Hill, 1967).

Everett Hagen, ed., *Planning Economic Development* (Homewood, Ill.: Richard D. Irwin, 1963).

A. H. Hanson, *The Process of Planning: A Study of India's Five Year Plans, 1950–1964* (London: Oxford University Press, 1966).

W. Arthur Lewis, *Development Planning: The Essentials of Economic Policy* (New York: Harper and Row, 1966).

Jan Tinbergen, *Development Planning* (New York: McGraw-Hill, 1967).

Louis J. Walinsky, *The Planning and Execution of Economic Development* (New York: McGraw-Hill, 1963).

Among the case studies of my students concerning aspects of planning organization are those by Mon-Hsiu Chang, "Division of Responsibility for Sectoral Planning: Transportation in Taiwan as a Case," Occasional Paper, Center for Development, University of Wisconsin–Madison, November 1976; and Nikubuka N. P. Shimwela, "Organization for Planning in Tanzania," Occasional Paper, Center for Development, University of Wisconsin–Madison, October 1977.

The five-year plans of many countries describe the organization and relationship of the central planning agency. Several references in the notes on sources in other chapters are relevant to organization for planning, including those in chapter 1, "The Concept of Development Administration"; chapter 7, "Regional and Local Organization for Development"; chapter 8, "Budgeting for Development"; and chapter 11, "The Impact of Foreign Aid on Development Administration."

For administrative reform, see Gerald Caiden, *Administrative Reform* (Chicago: Aldine, 1969), and A. F. Leemans, ed., *The Management of Change in Government* (The Hague: Martinus Nijhoff, 1976). A paper by one of my students is on the same subject; see Chung Kie-ok, "Korea's Administrative Reform Commission," Occasional Paper, Center for Development, University of Wisconsin–Madison, February 1978.

Coordination is the subject of three essays:

George F. Gant, "Unity and Specialization in Administration," in *Public Administration: Readings and Documents,* ed. Felix A. Nigro (New York: Rinehart, 1951).

Luther Gulick, "Notes on the Theory of Organization," *Papers on the Science of Administration,* ed. Luther Gulick and L. Urwick (New York: Institute of Public Administration, Columbia University, 1957).

C. Y. Wu, "Coordination and Harmonization in Development Planning," in *Proceedings of the Interregional Seminar on Organization and Administration of Development Planning Agencies,* Vol. 1, Sales No. E. 74. II. H. 2 (New York: United Nations, 1974).

7

Regional and Local Organization for Development

The Role of the Region in Development

The extension and expression of a government's plan and program for development throughout a country are heavily dependent upon strong public organizations with the personnel and financial capabilities needed to perform their share of the planning and executing functions involved. A government's support of social and economic development requires the reorientation of agencies and administrative systems, and the creation of new agencies and systems, in the regions, states, provinces, and districts throughout the country as well as at the center. Stronger forms of local government and district administration are needed to encourage and provide for the participation of the people in the processes of planning and development. Development administration therefore includes prominently in its area of interest regional and local organizations for planning and development.

A region is a designated place. It is the location of peoples' homes and employment and lives. A region is where development takes place; it is the site of projects and programs. Regional planning is therefore concerned with development in specified areas. It is distinguished from country planning, which is concerned with national economic growth and the major overall influences on that growth, such as investment, trade and foreign exchange, and major industrial and agricultural projects. National plans, at least historically, have given too little at-

163

tention to the comparative advantages and disadvantages of geo-graphical dispersion and the choice of location of development ac-tivities. Regional planning is also distinguished from sectoral planning, which is concerned with a field of development, such as agriculture, industry, health, or education, on an overall national basis. This areal or regional aspect of planning and development can be denoted as spatial organization for planning and development.

This spatial organization—that is, the arrangements to accommodate regions in plans—can be for political advantage, for administrative advantage, or for economic or geographical advantage. Spatial organization for political advantage means the involvement of state and local governments in the planning and development process. These state and local governments, in the sense used here, are those which represent the people, those which are the instruments of representative self-government. Spatial organization for administrative advantage means the deployment from the central bureaucracy of competent agents and agencies to the countryside and the delegation to them of the resources and the authorities to operate expeditiously and efficiently in the provincial or district offices of central governments and their ministries or departments.

Spatial organization for economic advantage has the purpose of focusing upon and dealing with the unique characteristics of a defined geographical area, either the characteristics of population or of nat-ural resources or both, when the boundaries of that area are not coinci-dental with those of the administrative or the self-governing hierarchies of field organization. The term "regional" as applied to planning and development is sometimes used to mean all aspects of areal ar-rangements, including administrative and political organization as well as special arrangements for economic purpose and advantage. The term "regional" is also used to refer more narrowly to areas selected for special planning and development attention when they do not lend themselves naturally and easily to treatment through the existing ad-ministrative and government organizations in the field. This use of "regional" in two senses is often confusing. The second and narrow use of "regional" as related to planning and development is perhaps somewhat more common and more useful, even though many of the principles which apply to the consideration of spatial aspects of development apply as well to projects and programs in states and districts as they do to separately defined areas, or "regions."

Even in this narrower sense of regional planning and development for geographic purpose and advantage, at least six different kinds of regions can be identified. The term "regional planning" was first applied systematically to metropolitan or urban planning to emphasize the importance of planning for an urban area as a whole rather than for only that area within the statutory city limits, or for only some and not all of the political and administrative units of the area and population of concern. Metropolitan areas are faced, for the purpose of planning, with the confusion as well as profusion of government jurisdictions, such as towns and counties and sometimes even states over which they extend, and also with numbers of autonomous special-purpose bodies in the form of such agencies as school boards and water districts. Most metropolises these days have succeeded in creating regional planning bodies to deal with the urban area as a whole, at the same time attempting to represent the special interests of the several governmental units which are involved in whole or in part. The Calcutta Metropolitan Planning Organization is one illustration. Moreover, in Calcutta there has also been created the Metropolitan Development Authority, with special powers and resources granted by the state to implement major projects in the plan formulated by the planning organization. The City of Calcutta proper, or any other single jurisdictional unit, would not have the authority or capacity to plan effectively for the metropolitan area in its entirety.

River valleys are a second kind of region for purposes of planning and development. In history, rivers have been selected frequently as the boundaries between states and countries. More recently the recognition of their potential contributions for development in the form of flood protection, irrigation, electric power, navigation, fish propagation, and recreation, as well as the inseparable relationship of these rivers to the forest and agricultural lands in their basins, has produced a number of notable efforts to plan and develop river basins in terms of their optimum multipurpose benefits. These efforts require the creation of planning and development mechanisms which both cut across and go beyond the boundaries and jurisdictions of states and countries whose political borders and programs did not foresee or provide for development in geographical terms. Well-known examples are the Tennessee Valley Authority in the United States, the Cauca Valley Authority in Colombia, the Mekong Committee in Southeast Asia, and the Damodar Valley Project in India.

A third basis for regional planning is the location of strategic natural resources, such as mineral deposits or forests, in a prescribed area. The exploitation of such resources and their utilization in desired ways for industrial growth and development often requires, or would at least benefit from, selective planning and development attention. Sometimes, unfortunately, the unwise exploitation of mineral or forest resources threatens to produce undesirable and even dangerous environmental or ecological results. Regional planning has sometimes been introduced to deal with these unfortunate side effects of development and to guide the use of resources into safer and more beneficial channels.

A fourth and somewhat different kind of region for planning purposes is a production and marketing network. This kind of region takes two forms, one of which is based upon the product, as is illustrated by the coconut and rubber "communities" in Southeast Asia. The second kind of marketing region is more geographical, as represented by hierarchies of market cities and towns with interlocking networks of financial and commercial and other supporting systems, and also as represented by market communities, such as the European Common Market in the international sphere.

It is not uncommon now to find regions which are selected for special planning and development attention because of the lagging and disadvantaged condition of their populations, which the concerned countries as a matter of policy wish to remedy. Regions of this kind are illustrated by Appalachia in the United States, by northeastern Thailand, and by the Sahel of Africa, which involves several countries. This fifth kind of region, the underdeveloped area, might attract special attention either for political or humanitarian reasons on the one hand or, on the other, because a country finds that its overall development depends upon the relative prosperity of all its several parts, or regions. In either case the disadvantaged region is selected primarily because of its need rather than because of its advantage in resources.

The sixth kind of region which needs mention here because it often influences processes for planning and development is that based upon cultural identity. Such identity can be racial or tribal or religious, and can reflect itself in programs and policies to give favorable opportunity to specified groups. Or such identity can be more nearly cultural and historical, not marked clearly by racial or religious ties, but more tangibly by attitudes toward life which are shaped by climate and geography with distinguishing and characteristic economic forms. The "South" and "West" are in this sense identifiable regions in the United States. The "plains" people and the "mountain" people recognize their differences in many countries, as do "desert" people and "jungle" people.

There are, then, several kinds of regions. They can be smaller than a country, or larger. One region might overlap and include some states or countries, or parts of states or countries, for one purpose, such as the rubber community, while another region might be composed of some, although not all, of the same countries or states, or their parts, together with others for another purpose, such as the development of the Mekong River. There can be regions within regions, such as the five-country Association of South East Asian Nations (ASEAN), which is a part of the even larger region of the Economic and Social Commission for Asia and the Pacific, which is a part of the major region of the world called Asia.

Any particular region, however, for the purposes of planning and development must be identified and selected for attention, and must be so chosen because of its homogeneity in some respect or respects relevant to development. A region could be selected for special development attention because it has the greatest advantages for productive results in terms of efficiency, economy, and speed. The location of an industrial complex, for example, in the interests of the fastest national growth would be determined by the comparative availability and quality of the needed minerals, water, energy, transportation, and manpower. Conversely, a region could be selected for preferred development attention because of a country's decision to achieve thereby some desired political or social purpose, such as to raise the per capita income of an area lagging economically or to benefit a racial or cultural segment of the population which commands preferential treatment, even though this kind of spatial treatment of development would not contribute as immediately to overall national economic growth as a region selected because of its economic advantages. The first criterion for selecting a region for development is its homogeneity for the purpose of development.

The second criterion of a region's qualification for planning and development is the availability of a viable capacity to make the analyses, prepare the plans and projects, make the development decisions, and implement the projects and programs of the approved plan. Unless there is an administrative structure or system with a sound legal base and sufficient resources of personnel and money to make sound analyses, recommend viable projects, and carry out authorized programs, regional planning and development of any validity or effect can hardly take place. This administrative capacity for the planning and development of a region is sometimes created at the national center and sometimes takes the form of a new agency in the field, such as a river valley authority or a regional development commission.

At the center, the national planning agency might include in its recommended plans, subsequently approved and financed in the regular way, provisions that components of industrial development programs or food production programs be located in specified areas because of the natural advantages of those areas for rapid and efficient increases in growth and production. Or, the planning agency might organize units within itself to draft and subsequently to monitor the execution of plans for regions selected for attention because of their need or because of a major project, such as an extensive irrigation scheme. Other regional foci can be mentioned, such as extensive land resettlement programs and public forest and grassland management areas. These are usually the recognized responsibility of a central ministry, such as home or interior, agriculture, or rural development. They must frequently set up offices in the region to carry out the relevant projects.

Even when outlying regions are selected for planning and development from the center, the opinions and attitudes and specialized information of the residents are important factors. The acceptability to the local people of national plans for regions is almost always a major condition of the success in realizing such plans. Central planning and development for regions is therefore usually accompanied by informational or advisory committees of residents who can express the views and channel the ideas of the regional population about alternative projects for regional development. Sometimes those committees are given substantial responsibility in connection with regional plan preparation. Essentially, however, this form of regional planning and development from the center is from the top down and is a component of national planning.

Decentralization for Development

It is more common to find agencies and processes for planning and development in the traditional political and administrative divisions of government than in special regional agencies which cut across those divisions. When public functions are assigned to subdivisions of a national government, either local governments or field offices, the process of deployment is called "decentralization." More precisely, when functions are decentralized by assignment to state and local governments, the process is called "devolution," and when they are delegated to field offices of the central government the process is known as "deconcentration." Because planning and the implementation of plans are closely related to the functions for which subdivisions of government have been given responsibility, the nature of decentralization—the reasons for it and the conditions for its success— determines the conditions for successful planning and development at the local level.

A basic principle in selecting functions for decentralization—for the delegation of responsibility for planning and action to a local agency—is the nature and location of those functions. Functions which have only or predominantly local significance, along with functions which depend substantially for their performance upon information and resources available locally, are those normally and naturally assigned to local agencies. Some functions, such as the development and operation of energy and communications systems, are clearly functions to be performed by central or by large regional organizations. Other functions are better suited to local than to central administration, such as community roads, markets, local water supply, dikes, and schools. The best practice is to make centralized or decentralized assignments of functions according to the nature and requirements of the functions under consideration.

A second reason for decentralization, considering the issue from the point of view of administrative efficiency, is to divide up and disperse the work load, in this case to organizations in the field, to avoid congestion at the center on the one hand and to benefit from local knowledge of local conditions on the other. Central approval of local works projects, for example, is time-consuming and depends in any case upon information most reliably available in the local community. Decentralization of functions to achieve decongestion in administration gives dividends in terms of speed and efficiency in service and performance. In the same way, by permitting and enabling decisions to be made at the local level, coordination of related functions assigned to a variety of local officers is more readily achieved—and achieved on a better basis of information and also much more quickly—than if multiple views are transmitted for resolution to multiple ministries in the capital city.

A third reason for the decentralization of public functions—for their deployment throughout the countryside—is to extend their benefits to people in the localities in which they live, localities with distinguishable characteristics and localities with residents who have information and opinions about the development and expression of those characteristics. The purposes of decentralization are derived therefore not only from the nature of the functions and from considerations of administrative efficiency, but also from the need for a system of interconnection between the people where they live and the national government in its central seat. This interrelationship, a two-way process, can and does vary from country to country and from system to system, but provision for it, whether by administrative deconcentration or by governmental devolution, is a conscious and important element in decentralization.

The effective and responsible exercise of decentralized authority in the performance of assigned functions depends upon the assurance of several indispensable conditions. One of these conditions is of course an environment of stability assured by the preservation of law and order.

Another is the availability of a reliable information and reporting system which permits the local officer to act with assurance of the facts and which also assures the central government that delegated functions are being performed credibly. Such information systems are essential to the coordination of local and central programs and to the development of whatever national guidelines for local performance as may be required for such coordination and for assistance to the local organization. Of overriding importance, however, is the local organization's capacity to do the job, to deliver results in the performance of assigned functions. Decentralization means the delegation of specified responsibilities. Such action is impotent without administrative capacity in the form of adequate money and qualified personnel and an operating organization structure. In the absence of this capacity, decentralization is meaningless and fruitless.

Most countries have or aspire to have a decentralized system of public administration in the form of devolution to state and local governments, which are autonomous to the extent of their delegated functions and which are self-determining. The essential difference between local self-government as a form of decentralization and the delegation of powers to field offices of the central government is that the control in the former is in the charge of elected representatives of the people. Programs of social and economic development which have the primary purpose of serving the interests of the people in the community and which recognize the large part the people play in carrying out such development will benefit from systems of state and local self-government.

A few countries, among them India, Malaysia, and Nigeria, have well-developed state governments whose powers and functions are enumerated for them in their national constitutions. Other countries which are smaller or younger or for other reasons have not yet matured their local political institutions continue to rely upon their administrative offices in the provinces or districts for the performance of decentralized functions. In both cases there is a general tendency to adopt the three-tiered system of local organization—the three levels of village, block or circle, and district organization. These levels of local government seldom derive their powers from their country's constitution but, rather, are given specified duties and authorities—and rights of participation and voting—by the national or state governments; these are duties, authorities, and privileges which are subject to withdrawal or modification.

State and local governments, more frequently than not, lack adequate capacity to act with full effectiveness even on those limited functions delegated to them. This inadequacy is almost always in the area of financial resources and frequently exists with respect to personnel resources, not to mention operational competence. In such cases it is a common practice for the central government to come back into the picture, at least with financial assistance but often with personnel assistance as well. This assistance is mostly to the good, but it usually has strings; it is conditioned on the willingness of the state or local authority to modify its program or projects to meet the standards of the central government or even to adjust its development plan to meet central ideas. This central influence may have the merit of improving technical standards and achieving desirable coordination, but it also negates to that extent the local government's capacity for final decision, a criterion of local self-determination, unless of course it decides to forgo the aid and therefore the project.

The problem of relationship of the district or provincial or other area administrative office with the central government is just the reverse of that of the state or local government. The administrative office may have the funds and the personnel and the organization to carry out its functions, but it does not have the mandate of the people in that district through their elected representatives. An effort to fill this gap in the system is often made by creating advisory councils of citizens, usually appointed, although at times some members might be elected. In some cases these councils are seen as a step preparatory to local self-government.

Another problem the central government has with deconcentration to its field organization, particularly for purposes of social and economic development, is the correlation of the work of the several ministries through their representatives in the field. A part of this problem is due to the primacy of the responsibility of the field representative to his ministry rather than to any authority in the district. The other part of the problem is that the senior district administrator, although often deputed to preside over a development committee of ministerial representatives, is often not able to spare the time from his traditional administrative duties. Also, the district head may not be qualified by disposition or training to meet the demands of development administration regardless of how well he is suited to the functions of law and order.

The environment for the establishment of the planning and development function at the state and particularly at the local level is therefore not very favorable in these circumstances, which consist of the immaturity of political institutions, the shortage of trained personnel, the paucity of financial resources, and the prevalence of antiquated administrative systems. These are not the only constraints to decentralized planning, administration, and development. The very process of modernization, consisting heavily of new technologies and industrialization, tends to centralization rather than decentralization because it calls for economies of scale in the application of science to development. Powerful selfish and vested interests too often gain control of local political systems and thwart rather than advance and support those policies and projects which would advance the well-being of the community as a whole. In other cases, where training and experience and public expectation are as yet weak, inefficiency and corruption might taint local administration, leading to disaffection with decentralization and the reinstitution of centralized control and operation. It is too often the case, in these and other circumstances, that the central authorities are happy enough to retake or retain control because of their reluctance to disperse the power of government, fearing, perhaps, the divisive threats to unified purpose of tribal or other special group ambitions.

It is not surprising, for these several reasons, that there is seldom found a rational and theoretically correct division of powers and functions between a central government and the state and local governments, or even between a central government and its own field offices. Rather, most systems are mixed, made up of compromises which attempt to accommodate at particular places and for particular periods the competing demands of centralization versus decentralization and central authority versus local self-determination. A country might have a government divided nicely between the center and the state and local government units, or it might have a single bureaucracy with district and division offices dispersed throughout the countryside. Most countries, however, have some aspects of both arrangements, a kind of dual system, in a pattern of shifting relationship which is marked by elements of tension and conflict and competition. The centralization versus decentralization issue is never quiet, can never be silenced, and the balance persists in shifting back and forth, from center to field to center again, at irregular intervals.

Under these circumstances the task of organizing the function of planning and development at the local level and for the local community becomes difficult. There are, however, a few guidelines which are useful in focusing attention on the feasibilities and guarding against the impracticalities of planning and development efforts. One of these guidelines is that planning and development energies should be expended on the functions over which the jurisdiction involved, state or local, has been given charge. The primary role of the state or local planning agency is to plan well and to strengthen the functions for which it is accountable. A corollary function is to inform the central agency of the development needs and opportunities peculiar to its geographical area and the interests of the residents of that area. For its part, a national planning agency should solicit the views of the planning agencies and the people at the state and local level both about the national plan as a whole—its targets, policies, programs, and methodologies—and particular projects in the states and localities to be immediately effected.

A second guideline is that the planning and development efforts should be organized in the context of the governmental and administrative system which prevails. The planning process in a large state government, for example, is in most respects much the same in its structure and methodology as the planning process at the national level. It is typical of state governments, in most countries where they have been established, that they are given responsibility for development activities in agriculture, education, industry, and health. State governments are usually assigned sources of development revenue, even though they are insufficient in most cases. When planning and development are organized as a function in a district office of a national bureaucracy, however, it is quite different from the planning of a state government. Planning at the district administrative level usually consists of contributing to, or at least reacting to, plans drafted by or for the central planning agency; coordinating the development plans and activities of central ministry representatives; engaging in one way or another the participation of the populace in understanding and supporting the national development effort; and making suggestions about the plan, especially with respect to projects and programs to be carried out in the district.

Planning and development at lower levels of local organization and administration are more difficult to characterize because it is here that the planning function shifts from the experts to the people. Expert planning, project planning by experts, is not often found to be organized effectively at the district or local level, except in some major urban centers, even in more highly developed countries. Project planning requiring expert professional attention is almost always focused on projects and programs considered to be within the state or national jurisdiction. The role of people in planning at the local and even district level is often expressed in the form of a citizen committee, which gives some kind of assurance that local priorities for local projects are established and, with the help of higher governmental or administrative bodies, carried out. Another role of people in the planning process is to debate and react to state and national planning proposals, as well as to take the initiative with respect to local efforts.

The third guideline with respect to state and local planning efforts is that they be consonant with the hard realities of what is feasible and what is not. If money for development projects is in large supply, and if well-qualified expert personnel is amply available, the planning and development process can be relatively expansive. If these resources are not to be had, at least adequately, planning must be proportionately limited or colored heavily by the predilections of the higher government agency which provides the money and the experts.

Systems for Rural Development

Seventy-five to eighty percent of the population of developing countries is rural, people who live and work in the countryside. Moreover, increases in agricultural production for trade and farmer savings for investment are basic to economic growth and national development. For these reasons most countries are now giving special attention to the rural sector. The purposes of this attention are to enlist the interest and support of the people in the national regime, particularly in a newly independent country, by helping them to improve their lot in life and to encourage and assist them to improve their farming efficiency and output. If strong and reliable systems of decentralization for government and administration were in operation, which they are usually not, these regular institutions and processes of government could be strengthened and utilized to conduct programs and projects of political, social, and economic development. Their existence would provide the instruments of linkage and communication between the people where they live and the government at its central capital seat.

In almost all newly independent countries, however, and many others as well, the agencies of local government are non-existent or weak, and systems of decentralized administration are also frail. This circumstance has prompted experimentation with a variety of alternate systems for rural development, systems that in many respects are intended to substitute for or to supplement local government and administrative agencies and programs. These experiments illustrate the application of development administration in an area involving particularly complex interassociations of central and local agencies and systems.

Historically, an early step to strengthen administration for rural development was to charge the district administrator or provincial governor with the responsibility for engaging the interest and support of the people in the area in government programs to increase their agricultural productivity and to improve other patterns of village life. This new charge to the field organization of the central bureaucracy was often accompanied by provisions for advisory councils and special citizen bodies of a variety of kinds in an effort to achieve better-informed program decisions and popular understanding and acceptance of such decisions. These consultative bodies, sometimes elected in part but usually appointed, have a spotted record of success depending upon the degree of their use by the administrator and the extent of the acceptance of their recommendations by the government. These expanded functions of district and provincial administration were often accompanied by larger numbers of better-qualified specialist officers deputed by the several ministries, such as for agriculture and small industries. These officers were expected to work in constructive and coordinated relationship with the district administrator or his counterpart and the advisory committees of citizens as they were set up, which took a variety of forms.

Another prominent form of government effort in rural development is that of agricultural extension—that is, field agents of the ministry of agriculture increasingly equipped to advise about and facilitate improved farming methods. Not infrequently these extension services foster the organization of farmer associations to serve as vehicles of communication and as agencies for education and for the dissemination of information and to promote the program being fostered by the extension service. This extension-farmer organization system is sometimes used as a mechanism to provide supply, credit, marketing, and other services to farmers. It is more typical, however, for the government to foster the organization of rural cooperative societies to provide these services, which are so badly needed in modernized agriculture. Not always, but almost always, such systems of cooperatives are dominated by extension or government officers or are so weak as to provide merely a cover for a government operation.

One of the best-known and most elaborate of the systems devised for rural development in many developing countries, prominently in India and Pakistan, was called Community Development, with a capital *C* and a capital *D*. In the 1950s and 1960s especially, Community Development was nurtured by the Ford Foundation and the United Nations and was supported heavily by other aid-giving agencies and countries as well as sponsoring governments. It was considered to be the ultimate instrument for innovation and change in the countryside, a movement of rural modernization which would dramatically and quickly improve the lives of members of the rural populace. The purpose of Community Development was to assist villages to identify and meet their "felt needs," whether in farming, water supply and sanitation, education and community activity, roads and dikes or other local public works, in handicrafts, or even in small industry. It should be emphasized that Community Development did not have as its target—at least at the outset or primarily—increased agricultural productivity. Rather, the focus was on the organization of villages to act on their needs and desires as they themselves defined them, in the belief that if they were to do so they would, with a little help from the government, quickly and measurably improve their productivity and their standards of living. Emphasis was put on organization; comparatively little provision was made for the introduction of new technology or the provision of better services of supply.

Each village as it came into the orbit of Community Development was encouraged and assisted to establish its planning committee. The government provided a village-level worker, usually one worker for every five villages, to advise and assist the village committee. The village-level workers were directed and supervised by a development officer at the block level of about one hundred villages. They were supported from the district, at least in theory and on paper, by specialists in such fields as agriculture, health, education, public works, and small industries, who were supposed to be assigned by their respective ministries to assist and advise the villages with their specialized projects. These representatives of the ministries sat on district development committees presided over by the senior civil servant in the district.

The village-level worker was expected to be the link and the liaison between these specialized and administrative resources and the villages. Limited amounts of funds were available to support village projects, which had to be approved at least at the district but all too often at the state level. States also, where they existed in such countries as India, established separate departments of community development with their interdepartmental development committees, which were expected to co-ordinate the total rural development effort. At the center, the national level, a common practice was to create a separate strong and well-financed ministry or other strong organization for Community Development with its own bureaucracy of offices, officers, and systems.

This Community Development program failed in its purpose as initially conceived. One fundamental error was the belief that villages could improve the productivity of their farming and the quality of their lives without massive injections of technology, supply, and assistance. This belief has proved for the most part to be false. The village-level workers were, at the most, secondary-school graduates with six months or so training in a village-level worker training center. Each was expected to work effectively in five villages as political organizer, administrative operator, and something of a specialist in agriculture, education, health, public works and services, and small industries. This burden was just too great. The support of technical services at the block and district levels was almost as weak, both in quantity and especially in quality; the nation-building departments had not as yet evolved their technologies or personnel expertise to the levels presumed by the theoreticians of Community Development. The administrative and specialist burden of Community Development was just too heavy to be borne. The mechanism was simply too frail to accomplish its noble mission.

The third reason for the failure of Community Development as a movement and as a special program was that it was set up, in most countries where it was undertaken, outside of the regular and traditional bureaucracy. That separation proved to be a fatal error. Not only the several ministries but the many field agents of those ministries resented the removal from their jurisdiction of many of their functions in relation to the villages and their subordination to the new Community Development bureaucracy for the remainder of their development interests. They cooperated in giving support and assistance only reluctantly, and even opposed the new system openly. This attitude impeded the performance of an already weak system. In the end, the traditional bureaucracy prevailed and the new Community Development mechanisms for the most part did not. Very often, interestingly enough, the Community Development apparatus collapsed when the foreign aid to support it withered away.

Nevertheless there were some important successes in the Community Development movement and some remnants which in the long run might be as important, or nearly as important, as the original conception and mechanism. For one thing, in countries like India and Pakistan, the villagers were exposed to an expression of their government's interest in their welfare, perhaps for the first time. Although difficult to measure, this expression, this first evidence of a development interest on the part of the government of a newly independent nation, was a favorable indication of better things to come. It no doubt had the effect of attracting support to the government in its task of unifying and developing a new country. Administratively the Community Development exercise loosened up the bureaucracy and prompted the civil service elite to consider whether the mechanisms of the colonial period were adequate to satisfy the requirements of independence and development.

Politically there is no doubt that Community Development paved the way to further steps toward local self-government—the Panchayati Raj movement in India and the Basic Democracies program in Pakistan, into which the Community Development program was converted. The Panchayati Raj and Basic Democracies conceptions are to encourage and assist elections of limited-power councils at the village level, sometimes supplemented by government-appointed members. Those councils elect selected ones of their members for the second-tier councils, which in turn select members of district and even state bodies. With respect to agriculture, it is probable that the Community Development activities of the 1950s and 1960s prepared many farmers for the Green Revolution, which did depend upon the introduction of new technologies and new services of supply. In India the Community Development hierarchy was turned over to the Ministry of Agriculture and, especially at the block level, it is now an integral part of India's new and expanded agricultural extension system. The Community Development system as originally conceived, however, with its own separate bureaucracy, has not generally survived.

The decline of the Community Development movement and programs similar to it did not mean that the problem of administration for rural development had been solved. The focus of attention tended to shift for a time toward efforts to build institutions for local self-government and to strengthen systems of district and local administration, on the one hand, and toward programs to increase agricultural productivity, on the other. But efforts to create viable systems of self-government have been disappointingly slow, and the modest increases in administrative capacity in the field along the traditional lines of functional jurisdictions by sectors does not meet the needs of an overall coordinated program of rural development.

Rural development depends upon an increased agricultural production which will support higher incomes and higher living standards. If, however, increased production and income benefit only some and not all of the target population, the purposes of rural development are not served. The poor and unemployed must be benefited too. Perhaps a larger proportion of the disadvantaged might share in greater agricultural prosperity by their employment in more labor-intensive systems of farming, which are reasonably consistent with the economies of a desirable technology. Others in the rural population could be employed in public works, which focus first on a supporting infrastructure for agriculture, such as roads, dikes, and irrigation works, and second on such socially beneficial facilities as schools, hospitals, and clinics. Other employment opportunities would be created by expansion of agrobusiness enterprises, particularly those which are related to production, as are those for fertilizers, pesticides, and grain processing. In some countries, landless labor can be provided with opportunities in new areas opened for settlement as well as in the cities. Rural development means higher incomes for the poor as well as for the rich, and from several forms of economic activity, although predominantly from farming.

Rural development thus involves not only the agricultural sector but other sectors as well, including commerce, industry, public works, and transportation. Rural development is usually interpreted to mean not only higher incomes for all parts of the population but also higher standards of welfare in the form of health, nutrition, education, and social security. Because rural development in this way involves not only the ministry of agriculture and its local counterpart agencies for agriculture but also the government institutions in support of industries, public works, education, health, local government, and perhaps others, its central administrative requirement is that of effective coordination. Hence, programs which are currently being designed and tested are often collectively called "Integrated Rural Development."

There are other requirements of Integrated Rural Development. One is that the people whose welfare is the target be systematically involved in planning the projects and programs expected to benefit them and whose successful implementation depends upon their support and participation. Another requirement of rural development administration is that it be decentralized, not only to accommodate local participation more fully, but also to encourage and support expeditious, relevant, and coordinated technological and management support to local projects. All of these elements of a successful program of Integrated Rural Development depend upon the availability of trained specialists and the institutions needed to produce them and to undertake the related research.

There is no single pattern of coordinated, decentralized, and participatory central and local systems in the bureaucracy to produce Integrated Rural Development. Quite a few countries have underway experimental projects—model projects or pilot projects—to try out patterns which might work in their particular situation. Some of these projects feature "development centers," rural market towns linking villages to larger metropolises. Some are autonomous projects with separate administrative structures parallel to the existing bureaucracy, which threaten to repeat the errors of the earlier Community Development program. Still other efforts emphasize new policies, such as those designed to assure that the benefits of rural development accrue in a fair share to the poor, to be implemented by special systems of central coordination and a greater degree of overall decentralization. In all cases the question remains whether the methodology that is successful in a single pilot project can also succeed in a national program. These are issues in development administration.

The Comilla Project

Integrated Rural Development continues to be expressed primarily on a project and therefore experimental basis in developing countries, taking a number of forms and shapes. The Comilla Project is one of the most successful and best known of the efforts to identify and to deal with the several factors involved in rural development. It is a conscious exercise in development administration. Comilla is a town in Bangladesh, formerly East Pakistan. Comilla is also a district, which is the focal point of government administration in the field. The district comprises twenty subdivisions called "thanas," each one of which includes about three hundred villages containing a population of about 200,000 in an average area of one hundred square miles. It was in this district that the Comilla "project" evolved in the late 1950s and 1960s, although in fact there was no single project as such but rather an interrelated series of governmental, administrative, educational, and economic projects and programs which in their sum were intended to deal effectively with the problems and opportunities of the district and to demonstrate the kinds of institutions, systems, and programs which lend themselves to those purposes, at least in Bangladesh.

The Comilla Project has become well known because it has had much success in achieving its objects and because it is well documented and well reported. It is noteworthy also, and perhaps especially, because its institutions, systems, and programs were deliberately designed to operate within the established administrative structure of the government, albeit a structure much affected by the project, and not outside that structure and in conflict with it. The Comilla Project stands in contrast, in this respect, to the Community Development program which preceded it. Other rural development projects in other countries have also provided demonstrations of and lessons in the difficult dilemmas of rural development. The Comilla Project has been selected for attention here because of its multifaceted, comprehensive coverage in a defined area and because of its contrast to Community Development.

The Comilla Project developed from the interaction of the Academy for Rural Development and Akhter Hameed Khan, its first director. The academy, together with its counterpart for West Pakistan in Peshawar, was established in 1958 with the corporate autonomy, the resources, the authority, and the status to perform its unique function. That function was to reorient and train government officers in development administration, officers who until Pakistan's independence had been engaged primarily in maintaining law and order, administering justice, collecting taxes, and exercising regulatory functions of a variety of kinds. The academy was expected to provide special short courses and experiences, especially tailored to the needs of various groups of civil servants, which would advance their conception of and capability for development administration in the area of their responsibilities. The Comilla academy was distinguished among other such academies by its emphasis upon research and analysis and by the size and quality of its especially recruited research staff.

Akhter Hameed Khan was the leader who directed the academy at the outset and for a decade thereafter. His insightful leadership inspired the staff, the populace, and the government to contribute their designated and respective shares to the project and to benefit from its lessons. Akhter Hameed Khan, who had been a member of the Indian Civil Service before independence, became East Bengal's Director of Community Development in 1950. He resigned from that post in 1955 out of frustration with its inherent deficiencies and particularly because of its disharmony with the government's administrative system. In the academy he recognized the opportunity and the challenge to accomplish the purposes of Community Development by relating the talents of the villages to the reoriented capabilities of the bureaucracy.

Akhter Hameed Khan convinced his academy board, the government, and his staff that retraining government officers for rural development could be done well only if the problems and processes of that development were really understood from research and study and, even more, if the academy and its trainees actually had the task of carrying out a rural development program in a defined area and, in performing it, of learning how to do it. Akhter Hameed Khan persuaded the government to put the academy in charge of rural development in one of Comilla's thanas as a development laboratory.

The fascinating story of how studies were undertaken and analyses made, how contacts were made with villages, how government agencies were persuaded and pressured to cooperate, and how programs were designed and conducted and evaluated is too long to repeat here; it has been well told elsewhere (see Note on Sources, below). The lesson of the Comilla Project to be learned for the purposes of development administration lies in the institutions which were built or strengthened as part of the central methodology of rural development in that area, and in the linkages between those institutions and their counterparts at the thana level, on the one hand, and at the provincial (now national) level on the other. The first of these institutions was of course the academy itself, with its staff training and research capabilities, its relationship with the civil service in its capacity as a staff training arm of the bureaucracy, and its at least temporary operating responsibility for rural development programs in the district of Comilla. The significance of these research-and-education institutional resources should by no means be overlooked in assessing the components of successful rural development. The academy's first concern was and is the improvement of the quality and scale of rural administration.

Perhaps the set of institutions closest to the center of the structure for rural development in Comilla, organized through the initiative of Akhter Hameed Khan and the academy, was the cooperative village societies.

These village societies were virtually single purpose in their function, at least at the beginning, devoting their entire energies to almost compulsory periodic savings on the part of their farmer members. They had such success that in a very short time the farmers and the villagers were able to free themselves of their debts and their bondage to private moneylenders and to save money for village development projects. Having gained money and success, the societies undertook with more assurance and competence their second function, that is, as a channel of information and communication with authorities in the thana and as a network of relationships with each other for the introduction of improved farming practices.

The village societies were individually too small to perform other needed functions, such as those of supply and marketing, so the next step was to establish, again under the aegis of the academy, the Central Cooperative Association, a federation of the village cooperative societies. The central association used the pooled funds of the village societies to provide many central services, including the purchase and rental of tractors, pumps, and other equipment; cold storage and food processing; and the operation of a machine shop. The capacity and performance of the Central Cooperative Association made it a natural and effective vehicle for relations with other development agencies at Comilla and at the capital at Dacca and for foreign aid. The government located a bank for cooperatives in the district and accepted the hospitality of the academy by situating there its Cooperative Staff College for co-op management training.

The academy is located at Kotwali, not many miles from the town of Comilla, in fine new academic and residential quarters especially designed to meet its needs. During the construction period the academy inaugurated its program in a small but pleasant place called Abhoy Ashram, which was to become the center of the laboratory thana, also located outside Comilla town and some distance from Kotwali. It became the practice at Abhoy Ashram, in connection with the rural development program as distinguished from the academy's own classes at Kotwali, to bring groups of people from the villages for special meetings and training and educational activities of a variety of kinds. One of the first of these training groups was in bookkeeping for the accountants of the village cooperative societies. Great emphasis was put on accuracy and reliability in the management of these societies, an oversight in the development of cooperatives in many other places. Other groups also were encouraged to come to Abhoy Ashram, including the mullahs and imams, religious leaders whose views were sought by the academy and whose influence with the villagers in their response to rural development programs and projects is great; women who were given instruction in nutrition, family planning, child care, and sewing; and model farmers who had been selected by the village societies to learn about, practice, and pass on information about improved agricultural practices.

Not only the cooperative bank but other government and private agencies found it useful to locate their service facilities at Abhoy Ashram, where people found it convenient and practicable to visit. This arrangement evolved, almost without plan, into another institution called the "Thana Training and Development Center." The activities at Abhoy Ashram continued even after the academy moved to its new quarters at Kotwali and were sustained by the government when the academy finally withdrew from its program-operating responsibilities.

In many ways the most remarkable results of the academy's work and experience in rural development in Comilla were reflected in institutional changes in government administration at the thana and district levels. Previously, the thana representatives of government departments, including agriculture, education, and health as well as police and other organizations, lived and worked in comparative isolation in a variety of places in the thana and often lacked adequate transport even in the form of bicycles. Their contacts with their clients and constituents under such circumstance were thus very limited, and to that extent ineffective. Learning from the experience at Abhoy Ashram that villagers in a thana can easily come to a central place, and are willing to do so, government personnel and the agencies they represented were readily persuaded to come to live and work in that central place, in this case Abhoy Ashram. This focus of thana activity immediately improved the impact of individual programs; it also improved their coordinated effectiveness in relationship with each other.

A somewhat similar process of administrative reform took place in Comilla District. The Department of Agriculture stationed in Comilla an Additional Director of Agriculture to direct what came to be known as the Integrated Rural Development Program as that program grew out of the respective efforts of the academy and the Central Cooperative Association. The Department of Education deputed an Assistant Director of Public Instruction for Adult Education. The Water and Power Development Authority enlisted the support of the Comilla Project in the local conduct of its electricity and irrigation projects, as did the Agricultural Development Corporation in providing equipment and supply services to the farmers. The capstone of this new system of intergovernmental relationships at district and central levels was the posting to Comilla of an Additional Deputy Commissioner for

Development to preside over the District Technical Coordination Committee, composed of the field representatives of the several specialized ministries, and to assist the overburdened deputy commissioner in the administration of development.

This review of the Comilla Project has emphasized the institutional and administrative aspects of its innovative contributions. The project's contributions to the substance of rural development were also important, particularly as a kind of laboratory to try out and to demonstrate the efficacy of new kinds of projects and programs. These introductory and experimental activities included birth control and family planning campaigns and systems to introduce the new seeds and other novelties of the Green Revolution. An especially significant pilot operation was in the area of public works, where the Comilla Project demonstrated the speed, effectiveness, and reliability of locally planned and executed projects to build and repair and improve roads, dikes, tube wells, and other local works. The public works project paid off well not only in terms of wages for the labor but in economic returns to agriculture from improved transport and irrigation. This pilot project of public works laid the basis for a program of nationwide application. That larger program did not go as well as at Comilla, partly because the local institutional capacity developed at Comilla was not generally available and partly because the supply of projects which can be handled at the local level is limited by the absence of the engineering and other technical skills required by larger or more sophisticated works.

It is the institutions and systems which support the small man and the small farmer that are basic to rural development, the supporting agencies, and the delivery systems. This was demonstrated at Comilla so persuasively that Bangladesh is now seeking to extend its lessons to all 410 thanas as the base for the country's program of Integrated Rural Development. This process of extension and expansion is not easy, for a number of diverse reasons. For one, almost every pilot project, anywhere, is successful; there is little excuse for an unsuccessful pilot project because its sponsors are so determined that it succeed that they pour in any amount of resources to guarantee a happy result. For another, most pilot projects are given the most talented leadership and highly qualified staff available for an experiment or demonstration which is considered to be important and innovative and prestigious. Both of these typical circumstances are true in the case of Comilla. The distinguishing mark of Comilla's success, therefore, is its institutional development of organizations and systems and networks of relationships which serve their development purposes and which survive.

The extension of these organizations and systems to other thanas and districts is inevitably slow because the resources are not as plentiful, the leadership and staff are thinner, opposing vested interests are stronger, and, most important of all as a restraint, the inevitable central barriers to decentralization are erected once more, especially the inhibitions to decentralization which cut across the jurisdictional domains of the functional departments at the capital. The same general situation inhibited the duplication of the Tennessee Valley Authority pattern, successful as it was, in other river basins in the United States. Although it is doubtful, for these reasons, that the Comilla format will be applied unchanged throughout Bangladesh or elsewhere, the lessons and examples of the Comilla Project will certainly influence for the better the systems of rural development which are designed for the future. These influences will no doubt include a role for the research and training function, for networks of cooperatives, for more realistic location and expression of government services in the field and provision for the association of local abilities with central agencies for the accomplishment of their purposes. These are illustrations of institution-building and of development administration so well exemplified at Comilla.

Planning for Urban Development

There is a direct and positive relationship between the process of urbanization and the process of change and development. From the point of view of the national interest, this relationship directs special attention to the planning and administration of urbanization. At the same time, the rapid increase in the number and size of cities and their changing role creates a special and unique problem of planning and administration in and for each metropolitan area. Planning for urban development embraces both of these aspects of the urban phenomenon— national policy and practice with respect to a country's cities and their role in development, and the problems of planning and administration in individual metropolitan regions.

Cities are dynamic and vital factors in the process of industrialization, modernization, and development. Basically unlike their historical predecessors, which were comparatively placid and tranquil centers of court or cathedral or university or limited market and port services, the comparatively recent industrial city is a vigorous center of production and service, of change and progress. The city attracts migrants from the countryside to new employment opportunities. It encourages and supports the mobility of restless and energetic young people prepared to break with tradition and contribute to the changes without which development is not possible. The city thus becomes the center for trade and commerce, a reservoir of talent and manpower, and a new focus of political and economic power. The city represents the concentration of the essential functions of production and trade.

Because of this inseparable relationship of urbanization and development, urban development must be a tangible and integral consideration in a country's planning and policy formulation with respect to the national development program. This consideration should be comprehensive in that it treats cities and metropolitan centers in the aggregate, as a system in their relation to each other and in their relationship to the rural sector and to the several regions of the country. Plans and policies must be concerned with the capability of cities to absorb additional investment for needed industrial expansion, capability which depends upon adequate supplies of energy and water and reliable transport, communication, and delivery systems. The provision of these components of an infrastructure of support for industrial development requires national as well as local planning and development of networks of such facilities and services.

Comprehensive urban planning involves not only considerations of industrial development but of rural development, which should be served by more efficient market towns that, in this sense, can become centers of growth, focal points for development programs and change. The national interest in cities and metropolitan areas must extend also to migration policies which might restrain excessive movement to the cities. And this interest should extend to the best accommodation and adjustment and utilization of millions of immigrants to the urban centers so that they become assets and beneficiaries in the development process and not its victims. The national interest requires other kinds of considerations, too, prominent among them being questions of whether industry should be dispersed rather than concentrated in a few centers and whether existing cities should be supplemented with new and satellite towns. These are questions both of economic efficiency and of regional and social equity in national development. Their answers depend upon a country's objectives and policies, which provide a basis for choice when there are issues of economies of scale versus social justice versus fastest growth versus regional priorities. Urban planning, a large part of spatial planning, is thus inevitably a major ingredient in national planning.

The industrial cities of the world, the metropolitan areas of both the developed and the developing countries, are replete with enormously complex and difficult problems. These problems arise because of the rapid growth of such cities to often gigantic size and because of the drastic changes brought by the process of industrialization and the creation of the intricate infrastructure required to support and to sustain industrial development. Migrations to these cities are frequently too great to be absorbed and outstrip all efforts to enlarge facilities to accommodate them, thus creating serious problems of unemployment, housing, health, education, and transportation. These problems of growth and change and adjustment, faced by each individual city, cry out for planning and action at the local level. They also require attention from the national authorities in these terms of local adjustment as well as in terms of national development.

Consider first the physical problems of a large and rapidly growing metropolitan area. Streets, utilities, transport and communications systems, and sanitation and waste disposal organizations need to be planned, financed, constructed, maintained, and operated in a rational and effective relationship with one another and in reliable support of the city, its residents, and its industrial, commercial, and service enterprises and activities. Housing must be found or provided for the immigrants. Land, controlled by private interests, becomes a scarce and costly resource in the history of every fast-growing metropolitan area.

It is no wonder that the first expressions of town and city planning, sometimes called "regional" planning, were in the form of blueprints and master plans for physical development. Solutions were recommended in the form of land planning and zoning ordinances, which reserved specified areas for designated purposes of residence, trade, industry, etc., and ways were found through condemnation procedures to procure privately held property for public purposes. These and other methods of achieving physical plan objectives involve metropolitan governments in development activities more and more directly and extensively. An early and still prominent illustration of government intervention in the handling of a city's physical problems is in efforts to solve the seemingly perpetual housing shortage with low-cost public housing schemes of a variety of kinds. Another and common example of early government intervention is municipal operation or close regulation of public utilities and mass transit systems.

The human problems of burgeoning metropolitan areas are especially acute. Most urban growth is the product of mass migrations from the countryside. These migrants are for the most part poor, not qualified for industrial employment, and not prepared for urban life. Having left an extended family or other cultural system with its own sort of security, they enter a society where a substitute social welfare system has not yet evolved. Without money or remunerative employment and in the face of often severe housing shortages, crowded into inadequate living quarters of frequently slum-like quality, the migrants experience severe and difficult problems of family disruption, delinquency and crime, poverty and bad health.

It is incumbent upon the city to plan well for the solution of these problems so that its new residents can be assisted to make the difficult cultural adjustments needed to convert their potential abilities to productive resources in the city's growth and in the country's development. This aspect of urban planning involves not only housing but health services, vocational training, and social welfare services. Migrants must be made employable and jobs for them found or created in productive enterprise.

The enormous and rapid growth of industries and the enormous and rapid growth of populations in comparatively small and restricted areas produces other kinds of difficulties often unanticipated in the drive to expand and develop—difficulties concerning the quality and even the safety of the environment. These include the tendencies to pollute the air and the water. They also include the tendencies to overlook or postpone the provisions of parks, greenbelts, and other open spaces which contribute to a more satisfying quality of life. A related consequence of rapid and large growth is to increase the density of the population in the city to uncomfortable levels on the one hand or, on the other, to encourage a kind of urban sprawl on the outskirts, which is not only inefficient and uneconomic in itself but which inhibits the kind of guided growth that more nearly provides the quality of city life to which most of its residents aspire. Concern with the environment—concern both with its safety and its aesthetic qualities—is a concern which is too frequently in conflict with the speed and cost of industrial expansion upon which the population also depends for employment and for the comforts of life. Metropolitan planning finds many of its most difficult technical and political problems in this environmental arena.

In spite of the great need to act rationally and responsively to solve or even to avert and avoid the enormous problems of physical and human accommodation in cities and large metropolitan areas, and to protect the environment reasonably, most cities are singularly ill-equipped to do so. Even though in most countries the cities and towns have been given the rights and powers of self-government, sometimes as corporations, to improve their planning and administrative capabilities, their government structures remain inadequate to the task. Cities are characterized by a multiplicity of subordinate but relatively autonomous districts and units charged with limited but important functions, such as school districts, and this practice magnifies problems of coordinated planning and action. Not only functionally but geographically, most cities in their metropolitan outreach overlap with county or other local units of government so that here, also, there are jurisdictional issues which complicate the processes of agreeing to solutions to problems, finding opportunities for action, and then acting upon them.

The city, as a form of local organization for purposes of government and administration, is subject also to supervision and intervention of one kind or another from higher levels, such as the state or province or national government. These interventions become especially tangible when financial and technical assistance is required in the city's management and development and when aid is needed to coordinate the interests of overlapping jurisdictional units—and such assistance and aid are invariably required. The whole situation is exacerbated by explosive political conditions fomented by the energies and demands of development, fermented by the restlessness and drive of young immigrants on the move, and ignited by the frictions of poverty and crime and maladjustment in the slums.

It is no wonder that urban planning is difficult both to define and to practice, and there are all too few examples of its effective and successful expression. It would be easier to prescribe a planning system if governmental and administrative reforms could be instituted first, so that a single, homogeneous, political-managerial organization of the size, authority, and financial and organizational capability appropriate to the task could emerge. Although some such reforms are always going on, they are never complete enough to deal with all problems of intergovernmental relations; therefore compromise arrangements are required to assure the participation in the planning process of all of the several local, intermediate, and national units involved in acting on plans if they are to be implemented. It has already been emphasized that the interest of the national planning authorities is involved because of the role of the city in national development. In a similar way, the city's economic life and development are inextricably linked with and dependent upon the surrounding or adjacent region, and therefore these associations must be related to a viable planning effort. The several governmental units which are involved in an urban area must be able to participate.

The criteria of sound city or metropolitan planning are that it include the human aspects of health, education, social welfare, and employment opportunity; the economic aspects of industrial and commercial development; and the physical aspects of housing, the environment, and such municipal services as transport, utilities, and sanitation. Traditionally and even now, there has been a tendency for physical planning to dominate the field, with separate and too often unrelated but influential initiatives in housing especially, and in education, transportation, and industrial promotion. Finally, the planning exercise, in its methodology, must find a way to blend technical rationality with political consensus in the solutions it produces if such solutions are to be both feasible and acceptable.

The "metropolitan planning agency," such as that in Calcutta, is the form of planning organization found increasingly to be the kind of instrument which satisfies these several diverse but inseparable components of planning for a large urban area. Such an agency is typically governed and directed by a commission or a board composed of political representatives of the several governmental jurisdictions involved and staffed by technical and professional specialists. The influence of the metropolitan planning agency depends upon the quality of its work as it appeals to each separate operating organization and upon the persuasiveness of its politically composed board, the success of the staff's educational efforts, through public hearings and otherwise during plan formulation, and the financial commitment of the state and national governments. Because of this complexity, this distance between plan and the multiple acceptances required for its implementation, some cities, with the assistance of their state and national governments, have formed metropolitan authorities, also as in the case of Calcutta, which are public corporations with multiple or limited purpose charters that provide for action on the developmental phases of the metropolitan plans.

By using the public enterprise device, usually with a state or federal charter, the city avoids the inhibitions not only of competing governmental jurisdictions but of the financial and personnel controls of the established bureaucracies. Such authorities of course tend to do capital projects and are not in a position to operate continuing programs, such as for education or health, although some of them maintain and operate infrastructure systems, such as those for ports, bridges, and transport and utility systems. Much progress in urban planning and development is being made along these lines. There is room for much more innovation in metropolitan control and development. There is also much need.

To deal effectively with metropolitan regions, river valleys, and the other kinds of regions for which special attention is needed for planning and development, governments are obligated to strengthen old instruments of administration and to find new ones. This need and process extends to state and local governments and administrative offices, particularly in the area of rural development. These regional and rural dimensions of development administration are of particular importance and special difficulty.

Note on Sources

Several United Nations documents are relevant to regional and urban development:

Administrative Aspects of Urbanization, Sales No. E. 71. II. H. 1 (New York: United Nations, 1970).

Planning of Metropolitan Areas and New Towns (New York: United Nations, 1967).

Migration, Urbanization, Economic Development, Vol. 4 of *Proceedings of the World Population Conference, 1965* (New York: United Nations, 1967).

Selected Experiences in Regional Development, Sales No. E. 70. IV. 14 (New York: United Nations, 1970).

Urbanization in the Second United Nations Development Decade, Sales No. E. 70. IV. 15 (New York: United Nations, 1970).

"Urbanization: Development Policies and Planning," *International Social Development Review,* No. 1 (1968): entire issue.

Among other useful references are the following:

Avrom Bendavid, *Regional Economic Analysis for Practitioners* (New York: Praeger, 1972).

Avrom Bendavid and Peter P. Waller, *Action-Oriented Approaches to Regional Development Planning* (New York: Praeger, 1975).

Gerald W. Breese, ed., *Urbanization in Newly Developing Countries* (Englewood Cliffs, N.J.: Prentice-Hall, 1966).

Gerald W. Breese, ed., *The City in Newly Developing Countries* (Englewood Cliffs, N.J.: Prentice-Hall, 1969).

I. J. Dwyer, ed., *The City as a Center of Change in Asia* (Hong Kong: University of Hong Kong Press, 1972).

John Friedmann, *Urbanization, Planning and National Development* (Beverly Hills, Calif.: Sage, 1973).

James J. Heaphey, ed., *Spatial Dimensions of Development Administration* (Durham, N.C.: Duke University Press, 1971).

John D. Herbert and Alfred P. Van Huyck, eds., *Urban Planning in the Developing Countries* (New York: Praeger, 1968).

E. A. J. Johnson, *The Organizing of Space in Developing Countries* (Cambridge, Mass.: Harvard University Press, 1970).

Salak El-Shakhs and Robert Obudho, *Urbanization, National Development and Regional Planning in Africa* (New York: Praeger, 1974).

Raanan Weitz, ed., *Urbanization and the Developing Countries* (New York: Praeger, 1973).

Local government is treated in these United Nations documents:

Decentralization for National and Local Government, Sales No. E. 62. II. H. 2 (New York: United Nations, 1962).

Local Government Reform: Analysis of Experience in Selected Countries, Sales No. E. 75. II. H. 1 (New York: United Nations, 1975).

Popular Participation in Decision Making for Development, Sales No. E. 75. IV. 10 (New York: United Nations, 1975).

Other references for local government are the following:

Harold F. Alderfer, *Local Government in Developing Countries* (New York: McGraw-Hill, 1964).

Ursula K. Hicks, *Development from Below: Local Government and Finance in Developing Countries of the Commonwealth* (London: Oxford University Press, 1961).

Samuel Humes and Eileen Martin, *The Structure of Local Governments throughout the World* (The Hague: Martinus Nijhoff, 1961).

Hugh Tinker, *The Foundations of Local Self-Government in India, Pakistan and Burma* (London: Athlone, 1954).

C. A. G. Wallis, *Urgent Local Government Problems in Africa* (Addis Ababa: United Nations Economic Commission for Africa, 1962).

Edward W. Weidner, ed., *Development Administration in Asia* (Durham, N.C.: Duke University Press, 1970).

Ronald Wraith, *Local Administration in West Africa* (New York: Africana, 1972).

Relevant papers of my students are those by Yip Seong Chee, "The Restructuring of Local Authorities in West Malaysia," Occasional Paper, Center for Development, University of Wisconsin–Madison, January 1977; James J. K. Kyondo, "The Role of the District Officer in Kenya," Occasional Paper, Center for Development, University of Wisconsin–Madison, December 1977; and Young-Key Lieu, "Economic Development and Central-Local Fiscal Relations in Korea, 1962–1971," Occasional Paper, Center for Development, University of Wisconsin–Madison, February 1977.

The literature on rural development is voluminous, centered first on the community development movement of the 1950s and early 1960s and more recently on "integrated" or "extended" rural development in the context of concern for poverty. A United Nations document is illustrative of this first period: *Community Development and National Development,* Sales No. 64. IV. 2 (New York: United Nations, 1963). A World Bank analysis is typical of the second period: *The Assault on World Poverty: Problems of Rural Development, Education and Health* (Baltimore: Johns Hopkins University Press, 1975). Other good references are listed below:

William W. Biddle and Loureido J. Biddle, *The Community Development Process: The Rediscovery of Local Initiatives* (New York: Holt, Rinehart and Winston, 1965).

Lee J. Cary, ed., *Community Development as a Process* (Columbia: University of Missouri Press, 1970).

Guy Hunter, *Modernizing Peasant Societies: A Comparative Study in Asia and Africa* (New York: Oxford University Press, 1969).

Guy Hunter, A. H. Binting, and Anthony Bottral, *Policy and Practice in Rural Development* (Montclair, N.J.: Allanheld Osmun, 1976).

Uma Lele, *The Design of Rural Development: Lessons from Africa* (Baltimore: Johns Hopkins University Press, 1975).

Henry Maddick, *Democracy, Decentralization and Development* (London: Asia Publishing House, 1963).

Henry Maddick, *Panchayati Raj: A Study of Rural Local Government in India* (Harlow, Eng.: Longmans, 1970).

Jack D. Mezirow, *The Dynamics of Community Development* (New York: Scarecrow Press, 1963).

Gayle D. Ness, *Bureaucracy and Rural Development in Malaysia* (Berkeley: University of California Press, 1967).

Raanan Weitz, *Rural Development in a Changing World* (Cambridge, Mass.: MIT Press, 1971).

Concerning rural development, among the best current material is that being produced, much of it in mimeographed form, by a few universities, notably Cornell, Michigan State, and Wisconsin. Cornell University's Rural Development Committee, an interdisciplinary group in Cornell's Center for International Studies, has made a sixteen-country comparative analysis of the role of local institutions in rural development. The countries are Bangladesh, China, Egypt, India, Indonesia, Israel, Japan, Korea, Malaysia, Pakistan, the Philippines, Sri Lanka, Taiwan, Thailand, Turkey, and Yugoslavia. Its summary and concluding analyses are contained in two works: Norman T. Uphoff and Milton J. Esman, "Local Organization for Rural Development: Analysis of Asian Experience," mimeographed (Ithaca, N.Y.: Rural Development Committee, Center for International Studies, Cornell University, 1974); and Norman T. Uphoff et al., "Training and Research for Extended Rural Development in Asia," mimeographed (Ithaca, N.Y.: Rural Development Committee, Center for International Studies, Cornell University, 1974).

Michigan State University's Department of Agricultural Economics is at the center of a "Rural Development Network" which expresses the first emphasis of the Overseas Liaison Committee of the American Council on Education. The committee is a specialized organization of twenty-one scholars and administrators to promote communication between the American academic community and higher education in Asia, Africa, and Latin America.

At the University of Wisconsin, the Land Tenure Center and the Center for Development have a deep interest in rural development. The Land Tenure Center is an institute established primarily for research, but also for education, concerning rural institutions, particularly in Latin America but also in Asia and Africa. Its *Newsletter* contains signed articles on issues related to land tenure and agricultural development. The Center for Development sponsors a program of teaching, research, and overseas service which focuses on synthesis of the planning and the administrative aspects of development. The Center's "Occasional Papers" are made up of selected research papers prepared by its students and by staff and visiting contributors. Of these, one concerning rural development is that by Jagadish K. Chitrakar, "The Role of Panchayats in Nepal's Development," Occasional Paper, Center for Development, University of Wisconson–Madison, April 1977.

The following references on Comilla give a good overall picture of the projects there:

Harry W. Blair, "The Elusiveness of Equity: Institutional Approaches to Rural Development in Bangladesh," mimeographed (Ithaca, N.Y.: Rural Development Committee, Center for International Studies, Cornell University, 1974).

Akhter Hameed Khan, "Reflections on the Comilla Rural Development Projects," mimeographed (Washington, D.C.: Overseas Liaison Committee, No. 3, American Council on Education, 1974).

Akhter Hameed Khan, "Rural Development in East Pakistan," mimeographed (East Lansing: Asian Studies Center, Michigan State University, 1964).

Arthur F. Raper, *Rural Development in Action: The Comprehensive Experiment at Comilla* (Ithaca, N.Y.: Cornell University Press, 1970).

8

Budgeting for Development

Traditional Government Budgeting

The purpose of government budgeting is to allocate public funds for the conduct of the public business. Traditional budgeting, before the advent of social and economic development as a major government activity, was designed to serve the financial needs of government agencies engaged in maintaining law and order, in administering justice, and in providing essential public services. The concern of governments at that time was to preserve stability, and this concern was reflected in the budgets. Sudden changes in program and money needs were not expected. The requirements of the administering agencies were comparatively static and not difficult to anticipate. The activities of the several agencies of government were not relatively diverse or complex. The function of the budget was to allocate funds to the agencies on as frugal a basis as possible and to supervise closely and to control the use of those funds so as to conserve the resources of the public treasury to the maximum extent possible.

Traditional budgeting systems served their purpose reasonably well. They showed income estimates which were almost exclusively from taxes and levies. Estimates of expenditure were categorized by organizations— that is, by ministry, department, bureau, and section—and, in the field, by province, district, and circle, or the equivalent of that hierarchical organization. Anticipated expenditures for each of these administrative units was shown by objects—that is, by items of expenditure such as individual personnel compensation for each approved position, and the detail of personnel support such as leave, travel, and any benefits, which might include pension, medical assistance, housing, and education allowances. Other objects might be for office space, supplies and materials, equipment and communications. Traditional budgets, when approved, gave authority for expenditure on a line-item basis—that is, each line authorized an expenditure without granting discretion, unless additional approval was received, to make adjustments within or among items, even within the total budget and even under changing circumstances.

Thus the traditional budget was expressed in minute and explicit detail and in the form of financial support to the administrative structure of the bureaucracy. The traditional budgeting system was accompanied by complementary systems of accounting and auditing. These systems have the purpose of assuring that expenditures are made in compliance with law and in accordance with budgetary authorization. They are the instruments by which officials are held accountable for their expenditures. Accounts are set up to coincide with budget categories, and in traditional systems they reflect detailed objects of expenditure line-by-line. Accounting was on a simple cash basis, that is, transactions were recorded only when monies were received or expended.

Audits enforce and support the accounting systems to assure accountability. The post-audit is an examination, usually on an annual or other periodic basis, of expenditures after they have been made to check their legal and budgetary validity. The pre-audit, a common practice in the traditional system, is a review by the auditors before a proposed expenditure is actually made. The requirement of the pre-audit shifts the responsibility for the exercise of judgment from the administrator concerned with his agency's performance to the auditor who is concerned that unquestionable authority exists for the expenditure in financial as distinct from administrative or program terms. The pre-audit process is thus ponderous and cautious.

Both the detailed form of the budget and the accounts and the use of the pre-audit system have the purpose of controlling, and do in fact control tightly, the expenditure of public funds. They have the purposes of preventing waste, overspending, and misuse of government funds and, generally, of saving money. This tight control is assured even further by other features of the traditional system. When a traditional budget is finally approved at the end of the executive and legislative process, that approval does not necessarily carry with it the authorization to the administrative agency to make expenditures under it, particularly when construction or other capital investment, new positions, or program extensions are involved. In these cases, the applicant agency must make and justify its proposal once again, usually to the budget office. This requirement slows and tightens the budget process to such an extent that annual allocations are almost never used, or expected to be used, in their full amount. Similarly, if an agency needs an adjustment among the objects and line items in its budget to meet a new situation during the year, even within its budget total, it must return to the budget office for approval—which is uncertain at best, and always slow.

The process of preparing the annual budget of the traditional type was comparatively simple. The ministries solicited estimates from their departments, bureaus, and divisions and combined them in a request to the treasury or the finance ministry, where the central budget office was usually located. There might then be a conference on the estimates, but this step would be almost a formality unless some major expansion of program or physical plant was proposed. The process was treated as a routine, almost clerical-level, operation. The rule-of-thumb criterion was whether an increase was proposed and, if so, on what grounds. There were few criteria of other kinds. The budget officers kept and applied their own measures, such as ratios of teachers to pupils, extension agents to farmers, and policemen to population. These, too, were based upon past experience and precedent; changes were difficult to justify and achieve.

The budget offices of the ministries and major bureaus, even when they existed as distinct administrative units, were staffed chiefly with clerical personnel supervised by a few middle-level civil servants. Their specialized professional and analytical capacities were limited. This staff pattern prevailed, generally, in the central budget office and even in the treasury itself because the budget work was conceived as being primarily one of compiling and adding. Budget officers and budget offices for this reason did not have any especially high professional esteem or official status. The decisions were made by senior civil servants in the treasury or finance ministry, which for a long time had been the dominant force in matters of finance and administration, in consultation with the ministers and senior civil servants in the administrative ministries.

Thus traditional budgeting was focused on organizations in the administrative establishment and it was designed to keep expenditures to a minimum by detailed line-item authorizations and controls. Its processes of repetitive approvals and pre-audits even of approved expenditures were tedious—deliberately so. Budget-making was highly centralized and largely subjective and arbitrary in its methodology. This budget process and the elementary accounting systems which accompanied it served the executive not too badly as an instrument of organizational orientation and control. It was this form of traditional government budgeting which prevailed at the time countries in increasing numbers sought budgetary support for their development plans and programs.

Budget Needs of the Development Program

Development plans cannot be carried out unless they are financed, and therefore unless provision for them is made in the central government budget, which is by far the largest although not the only source of funds for development programs and projects. Other sources of development funds, in addition to the private sector, are state and local government budgets and foreign grants, loans, and investments. The linkage of development planning to budgeting and other systems in the bureaucracy is thus imperative.

The planning budget and the central government budget overlap but they do not coincide. A budget to support a development plan would include the development programs and projects in state and local as well as central government budgets. It would include the relevant budget programs of the public enterprise sector and of foreign aid and investment, and it would take into account the private sector's role in the development plan and program. The planning budget should comprehend the allocation of natural and manpower resources as well as fiscal resources. None of these components is customarily included in the central government budget. On the other hand, the government budget provides for the support of all government operations and activities, and not only those for social and economic development. Through its budget the government assures financial support for legislative, judicial, diplomatic, military, and police services and all of the basic organs of governance and public administration. Nevertheless, the development component of the central government budget is always a large and influential part of the planning budget, for purposes of plan implementation, and it is the nature of that budget which is of special concern to the planners and the planning agency.

The interest of the planning agency, and of other agencies and groups concerned with the implementation of the approved development program, is that the central government budget and the whole budget process support that program and its policies, programs, and projects. That kind of budget would be as large as possible, rather than as small as possible, to encourage investment for growth rather than to emphasize the stability of the existing situation. Development means to invest and spend, rather than to save. The interest of planning and development is not only in the money, the fiscal support, but in converting the plan and its programs and projects into programs of action and operation. This conversion process is accomplished by incorporating provision for the desired development components in the regular budget of the bureaucracy and its operating administrative organizations. The needed linkage of development goals and plans with action and execution in the government establishment is achieved in this way. The hope and desire of the planning agency, therefore, is that the central government budget will be a growth budget for development and that in its process it will help to activate and speed up the administration and implementation of the development program through the appropriate channels of the bureaucracy.

For development purposes the classifications of the budget should be primarily in terms of programs and projects rather than being exclusively in terms of organizations and objects. The interest of development is expressed through the several functions—fields or sectors—in which approved programs and projects are carried out and expressed, such as agriculture, industry, education, and health. To put it another way, the budget focus for development purposes is on the hoped-for product, result, or output of the proposed expenditure and only secondarily on the organizational objects which might be involved. The planning agency desires to know that the specific programs and projects of the approved development plan are identified and provided for and are in a system of classification which permits the measurement and evaluation of the results—the expected output.

It is imperative, after that, for the public accounts to be reclassified to match the new program heads of the budget. Too frequently administrators are prone to mold their systems to accord to already established bookkeeping systems, although in theory the accounts and the accounting profession should assist in order to effect and support improvements in administration methodology. Accounts should reflect and not determine good administrative practice. Changing the classification headings in the accounting system is not the only adjustment needed for development budgeting and administration, however. Simple cash accounting is not sufficient because it does not adequately record or report the allocation of accumulated costs among the several project headings and subheadings, the obligations of income and expenditure, and charges for overheads, depreciation, and amortization when appropriate. Records of the several costs of programs and projects and the components of programs and projects are necessary to make possible more accurate allocations of funds and estimates for them, to provide information for evaluation, and to help management to identify and correct weaknesses in performance. The system should make it possible to measure and evaluate the unit costs of an agency's production—its outputs, such as miles of highway or tons of fertilizer. This kind of accounting is called, variously, "cost accounting," "accrual accounting," and "management accounting."

Even these important charges in budget classification, accounts, and accounting are not enough to satisfy all of the management requirements of development and development projects. The extent to which a government engages directly in commercial and economic activity determines the extent to which the accounting systems applied to them need to be adjusted to those of the accepted systems used in comparable commercial practice in the private sector. The standard government accounts would normally not be applicable, and it would be an error to force this kind of public enterprise into a mold which was cast for a different administrative purpose. Audits, similarly, should be made in the same terms as the accounts which are authorized, and therefore in terms of the approved administrative practices which they reflect, according to the unique circumstances of the program and agency concerned—usually a government corporation or a public company.

A direct concern of the planning agency is that development programs and projects which do not fall within the approved plan do not slip into the budget either inadvertently or by circumvention. An even more important concern is that projects and programs which are comprehended in the development program will be included in the budget in the proper sequence and for the number of years needed for their completion. These concerns can be satisfied for the most part by procedural arrangements for coordination and review. A more difficult question is how to make the judgments necessary to reject or select programs and projects for both the development plan and the budget. Clearly, incremental budgeting—that is, budgeting focused on changes from the previous year—is not sufficient in itself as a basis to judge the merit, and especially the comparative merit, of alternative projects, particularly when based solely upon rule-of-thumb criteria which are largely subjective. Planners, and budget officers as well, when the government becomes heavily involved in the selection and support of programs and projects for development, are faced with questions of feasibility and justification and choices among alternative projects. The answers to these questions can be found more easily when the tools of rational and objective judgment are applied, tools such as cost-benefit and cost-effectiveness analysis. The need for this kind of procedure in budgeting was not so apparent when the questions asked were primarily those of size of staff for organizations and the support for that staff.

Prompt and effective implementation of development plans depends not only upon the inclusion of the funds for their programs and projects in the budget, but also for the expeditious release of the allocated funds to the administrative agencies once the budget is approved and the funds are appropriated. The traditional budget systems were designed to inhibit expenditures from the budget even when those expenditures were approved. They measured their success by the amount of money saved. For development, the measure of effective budget procedures is the amount of money spent on relevant and approved programs and projects. Lump-sum budgeting, for example, instead of line-item budgeting, would increase the flexibility of the budget at the discretion of the responsible executive officer. He would not have to take the time and trouble to return to the budget office or the treasury for approval to make readjustments among the allocations for minor objects within his total allocation; work on a project would not be held up pending the completion of that procedure.

Similarly, the pre-audit system of advance approvals of novel expenditures would be dispensed with for the purposes of effective development administration. The pre-audit procedures are not only time-consuming, holding up work progress and increasing project costs, but they transfer the judgment for expenditures from those responsible for work and program results to those concerned with accounting rules and fiscal safeguards. The accountable program manager should be authorized to decide the validity of an expenditure under this approved budget, with the advice of his own accounting personnel, without the intervention of an external fiscal officer. The post-audit is the appropriate device to assure responsible adherence to the intent of the law and the budget.

This kind of budgeting for development would underpin a decentralized rather than a tightly controlled and centralized pattern of administration. By making funds from the approved budget speedily available to the program administrator and the project manager, the budget process would support delegations of authority with the provision of the financial capacity to make real the activation of that authority. Program budgeting, cost accounting, lump-sum budgeting, and abandonment of the pre-audit would help to do this.

Decentralization needs to be carried even further in the interest of providing funds for development expeditiously and effectively. When the budget is approved and funds are appropriated, they should be made available immediately and directly to the ministries and major administration departments and, further, to program and project officials rather than to the budget office or treasury for reappropriation, as it were, upon reapplication on the part of the concerned administrative agency. This straightforward procedure would speed up greatly the administrative process and the monitoring of development projects. It would also put a burden on the ministries and departments on the one hand, and the planning and budget officers on the other, to include in the budget only those programs and projects which clearly meet the tests of desirability, feasibility, and economic justification.

Additional aspects of decentralization for development and its effects upon budgeting are the increase in the number of new development agencies, such as government corporations and other public enterprises, and the increasing involvement and participation of state and local governments. Public enterprises, set up to strengthen a government's capacity to carry out its development program, are freed from the traditional restrictions of budgetary and fiscal control. Nevertheless, the revenue and the expenditure practices of public enterprises have an impact upon both the budget and upon the development program. New provisions in the government's budget system must be drafted to accommodate these new public instruments for development. Similarly, the participation of state and local governments in development activities usually depends upon financial contributions from the central government. This necessity puts a responsibility upon the budget process to formulate new systems, such as those for grants-in-aid and for revenue sharing, to implement the new and decentralized engagement of local governments in development.

Still another part of the budget process needs to be adjusted to accommodate good development planning and execution—that is, the synchronization of the budget year and the longer periods contemplated by the plan, the synchronization of the cycles of budget preparation at the central, state, and local levels, and the synchronization of the cycles of budget preparation with the cycles of development project preparation and review. Plans for development are frequently prepared for five-year periods—and the so-called perspective plans for twenty years or more. Individual development programs and projects more often than not require several years for their completion. The interests of development require that the budget anticipate and provide for these longer periods of project execution and that the development plan anticipate and accommodate the shorter periods of budgeted fund availability. Similarly it is desirable, even necessary, both for good budgeting and for good planning, to harmonize the annual cycles of budget and plan preparation and review so that central, state, and local governments, ministries, and agencies can relate their work according to the same calendar.

The development program of a country for its effective implementation depends heavily upon a budget and budget system which support it. It also depends heavily upon the support of the other institutions engaged in that country's financial planning and management, including the treasury or ministry of finance and the central bank. Almost all aspects of public finance policy and practice have an impact upon development policy and planning. These aspects include taxes—whether income, property, or consumption—both in their support of the revenue budget and in their use to encourage or discourage economic activity which bears upon development. They include policies pertaining to foreign trade, foreign exchange, and foreign debt, such as those on import substitution, export promotion, and foreign investment. And they include measures to encourage and mobilize savings and credit through commercial and development banks and to influence domestic purchasing power through wages and prices. Public sector borrowing and deficit financing for development is a major policy issue, and intersectoral flows and foreign resource transfers are of concern. The honesty and effectiveness of tax and fiscal administration are major factors in the consideration of alternative policies and measures.

It is necessary, in the interest both of viable development planning and responsible public financial management, that financial plans and policies be consistent with and support a government's development program and that the development program be realistic in terms of such financial plans. Interagency committees are frequently set up to achieve this consistency and realism—committees composed of officials from such agencies as treasury, central bank, budget, and planning. Such committees should serve the needs of treasury and bank agencies to participate in financial planning. Financial planning thus involves not only estimating financial requirements and deciding on measures for mobilizing the needed resources, but also arranging for the participation of planning officials as well as treasury, budget, and bank officials to assure full consideration of the interrelationships of development policy and financial policy and to achieve agreement on the realistic harmonization of these two interests.

In countries embarking upon development programs, as pressures are brought to bear upon those in charge of the budget and the budget systems to make the rather substantial adjustments needed to accommodate new and novel government programs and activities, it is inevitable that strains will appear. In addition to the lethargy with which significant administrative changes are almost always faced, there are major and honest differences of opinion over policy and the principles of administration. Is it good policy, for example, to facilitate the expenditure of public funds, or is it preferable to conserve such funds and to inhibit their expenditure? Is it good administration to relax fiscal controls and to delegate large spending powers in a more decentralized system, where officials of uncertain competence and honesty are likely to waste more money, than in a centralized system?

The budget agencies and offices faced with these pressures and questions are by tradition and by background inclined to resist drastic changes in policy and in administrative practice. In addition, the changes in the budget system, even if they were to be made, involve technical innovations in classifying expenditures and accounting for them and in the criteria for judging the comparative worth of programs and projects to include in the budget. This new methodology and the personnel trained to apply it are not readily at hand in a majority of the developing countries. And even if they were available, there would be concern lest these new people displace the existing budget officers. These are the fears.

Another and perhaps a major factor in the resistance of budget and finance agencies and officers to decentralization is the tension created by the friction between them and the planning agencies and the planners. Not only are the conceptions of the planners contrary to those of the budget officers, but their backgrounds are different in many cases, making communication and understanding difficult. Budget officers in the traditional systems tend to have legal and accounting backgrounds plus training at home and experience in the tenured civil service. Planning staffs tend to be composed of economists and other highly trained professional specialists, many of whom were trained abroad, and who have had little experience in the civil service. Even if these differences did not exist, the problem of institutional rivalry would persist in a struggle for predominant influence in policy and in program determination.

Reform of the Budget Process

Because of the budget needs of development programs, it is not surprising to find that the five-year development plans of many countries refer to the changes which should be made in their budget systems and processes. These countries, to name a few, include India, Pakistan, Malaysia, Indonesia, the Philippines, Kenya, Zambia, Nigeria, and Ghana. Typical among these references to changes are that budget provision be made for, but only for, those development programs and projects specifically identified in the plan and that provision be made for the future recurring, operating costs of such programs and projects, as well as for their initial capital expenditures. Recommendations in these development plans include those to support the decentralization of decisions to authorize expenditures from approved budgets by abolishing systems of additional expenditure authorizations on the part of the ministry of finance, and systems calling for the pre-audit of proposed expenditures. Other measures recommended would strengthen the budget and finance capacities of ministries and bureaus and their field divisions and would establish working parties, committees, and other coordinating devices to relate the interests of planning, budget, and administrative agencies in securing approval and funding for programs and projects in the development program.

Budget reform was prompted not only by the needs of development and the espousal of planning agencies, however. Even before development planning became prevalent there were pressures to improve and to modernize budgeting in newly independent and other developing countries. Evidence of the movement toward budgetary reform is to be found in the reports and recommendations of administrative reform commissions, representative of which are those of Ghana, Nigeria, Kenya, India, and the Philippines. These recommendations are consistent with and similar to those found in five-year development plans, although they were not necessarily made merely or even primarily to satisfy the budget needs of development. They generally advocate performance budgeting by programs and projects, and the delegation of financial and administrative powers to the operating and executing agencies of government to "the maximum possible," rather than to "the minimum necessary," extent.

A number of powerful influences account for the strong trend to reform governmental budget processes. The governments of newly independent countries had the tasks not only of gaining control of the civil service which formerly served the predecessor colonial governments and of making the civil service responsive to indigenous sovereignty, but similarly of gaining control of the financial resources available to them and allocating and applying them in such a way as to express and support the new and different needs and purposes of independence. The budget is not merely an accounting tool. Even more, it and the process by which it is formulated are a major, and perhaps the major, method of deciding what the government's policies and programs are to be and reflecting them in an implementing framework. For this purpose the budget must be made responsive to the intent of government and it must express the means by which the government's capability to carry out its intent can be built and strengthened. Changes in the traditional systems of budgeting need to be made to achieve this responsiveness of purpose and this effectiveness in deciding and supporting the execution of government policy and program.

This concern that the budget be responsive to and support government purpose is closely associated with the movement to make the budget and the budgeting process an effective instrument of management and administration in the implementation of government program and activity. Previously, in traditional budgeting, the budget was dominated by the treasury or the finance ministry in its orientation, preparation, and content. It was an instrument for financial control. Governments are now impelled to use the budget and its process of preparation as an instrument for positive and effective program implementation. This change often means the transfer of the budget functions from the finance ministry to the office of the chief executive, or at least to change the relationship of the budget office so that it serves the prime minister or president more directly and responsibly. This change in the orientation of budgeting also requires the professionalization of budget offices so that the tools of economic and management analysis can be applied to the evaluation of agency performance in relation to the budget provided for specified policies, programs, and projects.

The purpose of good administration in this context is not only effective performance but also performance which is economical and efficient. The costs of project and program activities, therefore, need to be related to the accomplishment—the output—of those activities. Headings for accounts must be adapted to this management use of the budget, and accounting must be modernized to provide the unit costs appropriate to the several budgeted activities. Both budget officers and accounting officers have to be newly trained or retrained to perform these more sophisticated duties of budget preparation and management.

Economists and other professional specialists, as they have been engaged increasingly in budget operations, have themselves become a force in support of budget reform. Their focus has been the application of objective, scientific, and largely quantitative measures as a basis for budget judgments. This interest and competence is relevant, although not necessarily coincidental, to the government's desire and need for better systems for the allocation of limited funds among competing projects and programs. This desire and need of government itself constitutes pressure for improvement in budgeting. The attraction of professional economists and budget officers to econometric methods adds to this pressure, although not always successfully, because of political reservations about the infallibility of such methods.

A strong motivation for budget reform is to make the budget an instrument for decentralization rather than centralization by facilitating the delegation of expenditure authority to responsible administrative and program agencies and officials. The greater and still growing size, complexity, and diversity of the government establishment and its multitudinous activities make such decentralization necessary and inevitable. Moreover, most countries now are seeking for ways to extend the capacity for action to both central and field organizations, the agencies of federal but also state and local government, not only to facilitate performance but to encourage and support initiative in all of the several sectors and regions of the country. Changes in the traditional budget system to accomplish this move toward decentralization include lump-sum budgeting to give flexibility to the responsible official, combining expenditure approval with budget approval to make additional budget office approvals unnecessary, and abandoning the requirement of the pre-audit, which is not only a tedious process but emphasizes the accounting rather than the management function of the budget.

These changes to support and facilitate heavier delegations of administrative capability assume and depend upon stronger and more professional budget and finance capacities in the ministries, bureaus, and districts to support the executive at the appropriate level. If, however, finance officers are deputed from the treasury in such a way that they are merely relocated, while retaining their veto powers of pre-audit and of item transfers within approved budgets, not much will have been accomplished. The next step, often taken, is to make those finance officers responsible to the head of the agency in which they are located but to continue their countersignature, and therefore joint approval, function on a par with the agency head. The correct solution is to give the agency head or other official with program responsibility the authority to certify expenditure for accounting accuracy as well as program necessity without reference to the finance officers unless he needs their advice.

The World Bank, the United Nations and its specialized agencies, and bilateral donors of development assistance, as well as private foreign investors and contractors, constitute another and major source of pressure for budgetary reform. The target of these several agencies and interests is almost always a particular project or program. The concern of the external partner is that such project or program is demonstrably feasible, that it is carried out efficiently as planned, and that its product or result or output is profitable or otherwise successful as anticipated. They insist, therefore, that the budget process and its relevant accounting support be reliably adequate to assure that the desired justification and subsequent measurement and evaluation performance and accomplishment are sufficient for responsible judgment. Unfortunately, in too many cases, these individual and narrow external interests are devoted to the success of specialized projects out of the context of the broader concerns of the host government, and therefore they insist on specialized provisions which are not necessarily sound in terms of the whole situation. Nevertheless, such external pressures almost always result in modernizing, in some respects at least, traditional forms of budgeting and accounting.

Budget reform, or modernization, is the process now evident in many countries, including Pakistan, India, Malaysia, Indonesia, Kenya, and Nigeria, to respond to these several pressures and influences as well as to accommodate the budget needs of development programs. The first of the major changes in budget reform is the reclassification of categories in the budget from organizations and objects to programs, projects, and activities and, more than that, to the intended and expected products and results, the outputs, as well as the inputs of the programs, projects, and activities. Most reform proposals are in exclusive terms, that is, the proposal is to replace the organization form of budget classification with the program form. This drastic change does not please many administrators, legislators, and political and public interest groups because they find it easier and more effective to exercise fiscal judgment and budgetary control in specific agency and personnel terms rather than in broader and possibly vaguer program terms, which often involve parts of several operating agencies. As a matter of fact, both classifications, by organization and by program, are needed in a kind of cross-cut pattern so that personnel, organization, and other resources can be assessed in terms of programs, projects, and activities and especially in terms of their outputs of product or service. The solution is not either one or the other, but both.

A second major aspect of budget reform is the introduction of capacity for objective cost-benefit or cost-effectiveness or some other form of econometric analysis. This analytical capability is needed to help decide which of several competing programs and projects should be selected for inclusion in the budget from among those proposed to serve agreed-upon purposes. Scientific analysis can be used to judge subsequently, on the basis of unit costs, the relative performance and the relative success of those programs and projects. This approach to budgeting, in combination with other aspects such as program and zero-base budgeting, is sometimes called "rational" or "scientific" as distinct from "intuitive" or "political" budgeting. Here again, administrators and politicians are not satisfied if these program and budget decisions are made "scientifically," partly because quantitative methods, even if they were infallible in that regard, which they seldom are, cannot deal with questions of non-quantitative value, and partly because the administrators and legislators are not willing to relinquish to professional specialists their functions of formulation. Here also the issue of using a rational system versus a political system is not a matter of either one or the other. Clearly the administrators, legislators, and others involved in a country's decision- and policy-making process should make the choices and judgments. Certainly, however, they should have the benefit, in so doing, of the relevant analyses made by the professional specialists.

There cannot be a difference of opinion about the need for, and the important place of, cost accounting in modern budgeting. Difficulties arise when accounts, and the audits of such accounts, are designed for one kind of agency but are applied to another kind of agency, such as a government corporation, where they do not apply and therefore hamper rather than support good program administration. Difficulties can also arise when accounts, although well designed at the time, become outmoded and remain so rigid that they inhibit clearly desirable innovation. Computerization, as valuable an accounting tool as it is, often contributes to the rigidity and inflexibility of the accounting system because of the added difficulty of correction and change in a large, complex, and centralized system, thus tending to freeze administration in an outdated form.

Finally, although sometimes not included as a component of budget reform, it is essential that budgeting be converted from an instrument of financial control to a major and integral instrument of administration in the management system. This concept of budgeting is that it is a continuous, ongoing process to give meaning to and support for the desired systems of decentralization and delegation of authority and responsibility needed to conduct the public business expeditiously. Some of those who do not share this view consider the budget to be merely a blueprint, a kind of ad hoc document for the present. Others share the views of traditional budgeting—that the budget's purpose is to conserve money rather than to expedite its expenditure and that, in any case, men, generally speaking, are dishonest or incompetent and therefore cannot be trusted to spend money prudently or wisely even for activities for which they are held accountable. It is true that the best way to save money, if that is the purpose, is to centralize tight controls. If the purpose is to make funds available for the expeditious conduct of a development program, however, the best way to proceed is by delegating expenditure authority as extensively as is required by the needs of program management. Another essential condition of effective budget reform, therefore, is highly trained and competent budget officers, on the one hand, and highly trained and competent administrators and program managers, on the other.

Fashions in Budgeting

Budget reform is a slow and uneven process of change and adjustment in the shifting balances between organizational and programmatic emphases, national and political judgments, zero-base and incremental starting points, and centralization and decentralization. Efforts to graft alien systems upon traditional systems often fail. The tendency merely to add some aspects of program budgeting to existing controls often defeats the purpose of budget reform and adds to the cumbersomeness of the process. Too much reliance might be placed upon comparable, but nevertheless dissimilar, budget systems and experience in the private sector. Often insufficient attention is given to the problems of transition and to the careful preparation required in the successful modernization of budgeting.

A review of budgetary reform in the federal government of the United States shows the results of the changing shifts in these several balances. It shows also the influence of new administrations and different leadership upon patterns and styles of budgeting, some of which take on the characteristics of temporary fashions. Such forms are intended to give the appearance of reform and the impression of dynamic leadership, but they frequently do not add much to the effectiveness of the budget process or the validity of its outcome; they merely put a greater burden of paperwork on those involved in it. Also, every new or adjusted system tends to impose additional rigidities and centralized controls, which are themselves the targets of reform.

"Program budgeting" is the general term used to mean budgeting by activities, functions, and projects instead of or in addition to budgeting by organization and object. Program budgeting should be but is often not accompanied by suitable adjustments in the systems of accounts. "Performance budgeting" was the term used by the New Deal and thereafter, until the 1960s, to describe a form of program budgeting providing for the use of work and cost measures in preparing and executing a budget for specifically identified work programs. This kind of budgeting involved both the inputs and the outputs of programs, accurate allocation of costs and benefits, and the application of systems analysis to the process.

The budget style of the New Frontier of the 1960s was entitled

"Planning-Programming-Budgeting System" (PPBS). Its purpose was to relate goals (planning) to work schedules (programming) to financial support (budgeting). Its orientation was to make budgeting as rational and scientific as possible and to reduce to a minimum the application of intuitive, subjective, or political consideration. PPBS relied heavily upon systematic cost-benefit analysis of program and project alternatives and of the outputs of each program in terms of its goals. Its stylized methodology came to the public bureaucracy from private industry via the Department of Defense. It was by nature a highly standardized and centralized system. PPBS collapsed from the overwhelming weight of paperwork and red tape in the system and from the resistance of those favoring legislative and incremental budget decisions to those made by staff specialists. Although PPBS was discarded as a system, many of its components remain to enrich present-day budgeting, notably greater capacity for the use of cost-effectiveness analysis in the assessment of the comparative merit of alternative projects and systems.

The slogan of the 1970s and the primary concern of budgeting was efficiency in performance. The fads of budget reform became "productivity" and "Management by Objective" (MBO) as a new administration sought to distinguish its management style from that of its predecessor. The concept of productivity involves that change in the relationship of inputs to outputs which results in more or better goods or services at the same unit cost, or in the same quantity and quality at less unit cost. Borrowed from industrial practice, it is a way to measure and to stimulate the improvement of performance by better use of manpower, equipment and capital, improved technology, and better organization.

Government activity does not ordinarily have the profit motive of industry, which permits increases in productivity to provide higher wages (although perhaps fewer employees) or lower prices or higher profits, so that there cannot be established easily a relationship between the volume of goods and services per total input and the relevant agency's budget. The concept does, however, provide a basis for making judgments about the adequacy of the performance of an agency or a program over a number of years or in comparison with comparable agencies or programs in other places. Also the measure of productivity, of performance, must be applied to the primary operating units in an organization; productivity thus requires for its success and its usefulness the decentralization of the process and the decentralization to that degree of the related process of budget preparation.

MBO is a stylized procedure of budgeting and management which has the purpose of increasing efficiency by engaging staff in each service or production unit in setting and accomplishing goals for that unit in appropriate synchronization with the overall goals of the organization. The expectation is that staff performance will improve by virtue of staff participation in setting goals and will result in enhanced commitment to the achievement of those goals. In addition, however, it is assumed that budgeting will be more accurate and its estimates more reliable if based upon action plans prepared with the help of staff engaged in their implementation and therefore well informed about the components needed for implementation. Such plans would then serve as the basis for the measurement of performance and employee evaluation.

MBO, like productivity, involves a decentralized process of analysis from the bottom up, in contrast with PPBS, which was inherently centralized in its conception and operation. MBO contemplates, however, comprehensive adherence to the uniform and rigid procedures of its embrace, with all of the enormous amounts of time, effort, and paperwork which the prescribed system entails. It is unlikely that it can survive without adjustments in its requirements to meet numerous and differing conditions and situations, adjustments which would destroy the procedural characteristics that now distinguish it. It is hoped, nonetheless, that it will leave as its contribution to good budgeting and management more widespread participation of staff members in setting program goals for their production units and estimating the budget support needed for their accomplishment.

The current fashion in the United States is "Zero Base Budgeting" (ZBB). ZBB, in the broad sense of the term, would replace incremental budgeting to the maximum extent possible. Thus there would be an objective, comparative, and analytical review of every program, activity, and project proposed for the budget, even though a project might be already underway and in operation, and a fresh determination annually as to its inclusion and at what level of support. What is called "sunset legislation" has much the same purpose. Sunset legislation establishes a timetable, usually of five or six years, for the review of a program or policy or agency and requires either affirmative action by the legislative body for its continuation or automatic termination. ZBB and sunset legislation are concerned with the undue proliferation and perpetuation of agencies and activities in the bureaucracy and are designed to put an end to that multiplication. Those who believe that the incremental approach—that is, to judge the merits of proposed additions, reductions, increases, or other changes as a basis for budget-making—is more realistic than ZBB point to the formidable amount of time and effort involved in the zero-base approach and especially to the undesirable uncertainties imposed on ongoing organizations, their staffs, and the public which they serve. Neither do they like the idea of another heavy intrusion on the part of specialists in programming and administration. The concept of incrementalism gives deference to the thousands of past decisions and compromises made with respect to budgeted programs and organizations and is reluctant to bring them up for review without compelling reason and without adequate time for recognition.

ZBB has recently been defined more precisely, and it has been embodied in procedural systems. The question it raises now is whether current activities should be reduced or stopped entirely, either because they have become redundant or because funds are needed for activities considered to have a higher current priority. The process involves the identification of "decision units," much as in the case of MBO, a cost-benefit analysis of each "decision package," a ranking of these, and the preparation of operating budgets. Thus ZBB is a decentralized system, but within a rigidly structured and centralized frame which entails enormous amounts of paperwork annually. The data systems themselves, dependent as they are upon computers, are instruments of centralization. These characteristics alone will inhibit its success, in spite of its prescriptions of decentralization and staff participation.

The greatest weakness of ZBB, however, is the aura of uncertainty imposed on each and every government function, program, and agency, on the employees involved, and on the members of the public dependent upon those government activities. The creation of such uncertainty is as unnecessary as it is undesirable. No organization or program should continue indefinitely without reexamination and appraisal, but provision for consideration could easily be made at appropriate intervals of ten years, more or less, according to the need. These arrangements would make unnecessary both the formidable time- and effort-consuming exercise now contemplated on an annual basis and the elaborate and standardized procedures designed to carry it out. It should be possible to make better applications of the ZBB system if it were adjusted according to the case and to the time rather than to encompass all varying situations in the same all-enfolding mold.

There have been, and there are, other fashions and fads in budgeting and budget management, such as "Modern Management Technology" (MMT), "Operations Research" (OR), "Management Science" (MS), and "Presidential Management Initiatives" (PMI). There will be other formulations in the future as incoming executives wish to identify their own management instruments or as the balance shifts periodically between scientific and incremental systems or as other circumstances dictate. Budget systems will vary from time to time and from country to country. The measure of their adequacy for development should be not only their financial but also their organizational and administrative support of program and project implementation.

Coordination of Budgeting and Planning

A plan for social and economic development is of little consequence unless its programs and projects are carried out. A first requirement of implementation is that funds for the public sector component of the development program be made available through the government's budget process. The impact of the plan and the development program on the budget is so great, and the influence of the budget on the plan and the development program is so crucial, as to make it imperative that they be harmonized and that the planning and budgeting processes be coordinated. The interests of the country and its government require the responsible and systematic reconciliation of the planning and budgeting systems.

The first requisite of plan-budget coordination and harmonization is that relevant national goals and policies are established and articulated. The enunciation of such goals and policies gives consistent guidance and direction to budgeting and planning alike; both processes are thus obliged to respect the same policies and puruse the same goals. The second requisite of coordination in this respect is that both the budget officers and the planning officers must be well schooled in their government's purposes and policies and indoctrinated in the importance of coordination and the measures to be taken to assure it. The third requisite of coordination is that organizational, systemic, and procedural arrangements be introduced to facilitate the processes of reconciliation and harmonization between plan and budget. Clearly stated goals and policies and well-trained staffs, although necessary to such processes, are not sufficient in themselves to achieve a coordinated result. They need the assistance of stipulated channels of communication to support and expedite agreed-upon systems of coordination.

One organizational solution to the problem of coordinating planning and budgeting is to assign the responsibility for both functions to the same agency and to place both the planning and budgeting office in that agency under a single head. This solution has been attempted in some countries, but not successfully, because the two separate offices and the two distinct processes still exist and the problem of harmonization remains. The common executive might be expected to be relatively more effective in achieving coordinated results, but usually he is inclined to be biased one way or another. Also, other problems of coordination exist with other involved agencies, such as ministries of finance and economic affairs.

An alternative organizational solution is to integrate, rather than merely to combine, the planning and budgeting processes. Such integration is virtually impossible to achieve. In the first place, the budget and the plan do not coincide but merely overlap, as pointed out before. That lack of coincidence means that the two functions, taken as a whole, cannot be performed by the same personnel, even though parts of them might conceivably be joined in the same staff. Disparate functions, however, such as the macro-economic analysis involved in national planning, would continue to require for their performance the establishment of separate staff units, presenting the problem of coordination. In the second place, it would be exceedingly difficult to find and train and orient staff members to the breadth of competence and objectivity which would be required to deal concurrently with issues of program and project feasibility and implementation and with issues of organizational capacity. There would also be a question as to whether individual staff members, and the collective staff of a unit, could in fact be without bias either toward growth and expenditure or toward stability and thrift.

There are those who advocate not a merger of the planning and budgeting functions, but the elimination of formal planning as such, relying instead upon the budget office and the budget systems for the allocation of resources for development purposes. They point out that in practice the budget office is, in any case, frequently the planning authority because of its control of funds and because it takes a very long time to build an effective planning agency and process. Their position is that planning agencies are not only deficient but costly in the use of men and resources while budget offices are institutionally superior in terms of resources, status, and power. The crux of their argument, however, is that planners are oriented to the expenditure of funds because the development process is based on spending, while budget officers are schooled to husband public funds and are thus more reliable custodians of public funds and therefore should be given that charge. It is true that planners are necessarily spenders and that budget officers are savers, but which is to be dominant? Most countries are attempting to create an appropriate role for each.

It is not only spending versus saving which is at issue in considering the role of the budget office. Those who would assign planning functions to it recommend its strengthening, and the strengthening of nation-building departments and ministries, with economists and other analysts to make the budget more effective for development. But they would at the same time bolster central control over the budget office and treasury officials by repetitive budget reviews and the release of funds gradually during the year, rather than at its beginning, in order to increase financial certainty and to protect the surplus. In this system the head of the budget office or his minister would make decisions during the year on which development projects would be financed from funds he considers available and which would not. This position is at the other end of the pole from those who believe that administration for development requires decentralization to permit the expenditure authority to support and expedite rather than restrain and delay the implementation of approved development programs and projects, even though more funds would be spent and some, perhaps, wasted. The granting of foreign aid for general budget support rather than to specified development projects and programs would still further tighten budget office control over the nation-building departments. Each country must decide for itself what balance of bureaucratic function it prefers and what relationship it will arrange to assure the cooperation involved in that balance.

Most countries do not try to combine the processes of planning and budgeting but attempt to solve the problem of relationship through the device of two budgets—one for planning in the form of a development budget, and one for incorporation in the regular budget, sometimes called the "ordinary" budget. This use of a development budget has merit, but it does not solve the problem of coordination. The merit of a development budget is that it serves to convert the longer development program to an annual basis and makes it possible to identify readily the dimension and adequacy of funding for the public sector aspects of the approved development program. But there cannot in fact be two separate budgets and budgeting systems which are managed by separate organizations and without regard to each other. At the very least some third authority would have to decide the limits of the two budgets in total and to arbitrate competing demands of each for a larger share of the total. And to operate two systems of budgeting with their respectively distinctive systems of classification, accounting, and expenditure control would be to create a governmental and administrative monstrosity.

Some countries have made the development budget equivalent to the capital budget, but that practice does not solve the problem either. The capital budget must include items unrelated to development, such as facilities for military and police personnel, and the development budget must include provision for the recurring costs of maintaining and operating new facilities, such as schools, after they are constructed. Indeed, some development programs and projects do not involve capital expenditure at all, but do depend upon increases or changes in the ordinary budget. The problem of providing financial support for the development program remains, as does the problem of coordinating budgeting and planning.

Most countries are now evolving coordinating networks to assure systematic and responsible participation of planning and budget agencies and other fiscal and administrative agencies in joint consideration of proposed development programs and projects. One pattern consists, as in Pakistan, of a system of working parties in the several development sectors. Each party is composed of a representative of the planning agency, usually the chairman, a representative of the budget office, and a representative of the administrative agency initiating the program or proposal. These working parties decide which programs and projects will be included in the development plan, and thus will be eligible for subsequent inclusion in the budget, and which will be rejected.

Programs and projects of major size which would require central financial subsidy are then considered by a central working party, also composed of representatives of planning, budget, and functional agencies, but of other fiscal agencies in addition, such as the ministry of economic affairs and the state bank. They are frequently lacking in systematic provision for the resolution of disputes and differences, however, in which case a powerful agency or a strong personality might dominate a committee or party unfairly. It should be made possible, as a regular part of the system and the process, for an agency to appeal the decision of a working party at one level of government and administration to a working party at a higher level and eventually to the country's National Development Committee or its equivalent, at the cabinet level. Most countries have this kind of structure, but many of them do not provide for an appeal procedure.

This kind of network of working parties is designed to assure coordinated decisions on programs and projects eligible for inclusion in the development plan and in the budget when funds are available. The system also serves to make other programs and projects ineligible for inclusion in the budget and thus ineligible for financing, a condition which the budget office is obliged to honor if some agency nevertheless proposes such a program or project. This network of working parties serves primarily to engage the budget office in the development planning process, although it serves also to give the planning office assurance that undesirable projects will not be included in the budget.

It remains to provide for the participation of the planning office in the budget process. It is not enough for the implementation of the development program that the planning office merely has assurance that unapproved projects will not appear in the budget. The planning office desires to participate in the processes by which it is decided what development programs and projects will be included in the budget and by which the total size of the budget will be determined and particularly what proportions will support the development plan and effort. One way to arrange for this participation is to provide for planning office involvement in the annual consultations of the budget office with the several ministries and agencies on their estimates, as is done in Malaysia. An interagency committee or other mechanism can systematize processes by which the planning and budget agencies, and the other major finance agencies as well, can jointly decide on the development budget and its components. In this process, also, there should be a regular and readily available procedure by which disagreements can be resolved, possibly by the National Development Committee or its counterpart. This coordinating system can also be used to resolve policy issues of mutual concern to planning and budgeting, such as measures of taxation which affect development and the disposition and utilization of foreign economic aid and foreign exchange.

These coordinating networks should extend to the several central ministries and departments and also to a country's states and provinces, as well as to the budget and planning agencies. Development programs of any size and consequence involve substantial investments in programs and projects in states and provinces throughout the country. Such investments almost always depend upon subsidies—loans as well as grants, but mostly grants—from the central government. The growing practice of the grant-in-aid, that is, a grant for a specified purpose, extends the scope and purpose of the budget and to the same extent calls for the participation of the planning office in deciding the size and purposes of such grants. India has a very large and sophisticated program of grants-in-aid to states. Because such grants are customarily made in response to state and provincial initiatives, supported by the commitment of local funds, for the purpose of development, they themselves become instruments of coordination.

In a somewhat similar way the financial policies, practices, experiences, and needs of government corporations and other public enterprises involve the interests of both the planning office and the budget office. In most respects public enterprises are set up and exist as instruments of development under the development plan, and their performance is therefore of legitimate interest to the planning agency. Whether or not such enterprises need additional funds from the public treasury, their financial condition is relevant to the overall responsibility of the budget office. Although public enterprises are relieved from many of the procedural inhibitions of the budgeting process, many countries require them to submit annual reports and budgets to the planning and budget offices for information and review.

Emphasis has already been given to the important relevance of program budgeting and cost accounting and analysis to effective budgeting for development. Program budgeting and cost accounts are of equivalent importance to the coordination of planning and budgeting because they provide the basis in relevant information and analysis for comparative judgments. To these modifications in budget practice there must be added another, and that is the timing of the budget cycle and the adjustment of the plan period. Budgets, traditionally and even now, are prepared annually for periods of one year. Development plans, typically, are prepared for five- or six-year periods. A common practice in the reconciliation of these time differences is to convert the five-year plan into an annual development plan and then to relate that plan to an annual development budget.

These are the major targets of the coordination process. There is, however, a desirable trend to loosen the one-year rigidity of the budget by the use of multi-year budgeting and "roll-over" or "rolling" budgets to anticipate and even provide for future-year support for projects and programs which cannot be completed within the period of a single fiscal year. This trend is of obvious advantage in the improvement of development budgeting. The necessary correlation of the timing of budget-preparation and plan-preparation cycles is made more necessary, but also easier to accomplish, by the coordinating networks for planning and budgeting. To be correlated with these also are the planning and budgeting cycles of state, provincial, and local governments.

The coordination of budgeting and planning is important not only at the stage of plan, program, and project formulation but also during the process of implementation. An overlapping function of both planning and budgeting is to assure reliable reports of program and project progress and of expenditure experience and to evaluate these reports for the purpose of making both current-year and future-year adjustments. Much, perhaps most, of this information is relevant to the respective interests and responsibilities of both the budget and the planning offices. By arranging to share in establishing and monitoring the required information systems, and by arranging also both to divide and to share the evaluative analyses based upon them, the budget and planning offices have the opportunity to coordinate their work to their mutual advantage in still another way.

In development administration, money is considered in a light different from that in traditional administration; it is looked at in a new way. A major function of the budget in a country with an aggressive development policy and program is first to allocate money for expenditure in accordance with the government's decisions on the development program, and second to make the money easily and readily available. These are enormous departures from the traditional budget functions of avoiding and delaying the expenditure of public funds. The mere allocation of funds for development is not sufficient, and traditional budget offices might be reluctant to do even that. Their allocation at a time and in a way that facilitates their use is equally important. Budget reform to support development involves coordination with development planning to accomplish these changes.

Note on Sources

The references for chapter 6, "Organization for Planning," are useful here also, and are not repeated. A good understanding of government budgeting in general can be gained from three works in particular:

Jesse Burkhead, *Government Budgeting* (New York: Wiley, 1962).

R. D. Lee, Jr., and R. W. Johnson, *Public Budgeting Systems* (Baltimore: University Park Press, 1973).

Aaron Wildavsky, *The Politics of the Budgetary Process* (Boston: Little, Brown, 1974).

More specialized treatment of budgeting for development in developing countries is found in the following works:

Naomi Caiden and Aaron Wildavsky, *Planning and Budgeting in Poor Countries* (New York: Wiley, 1974).

Milton J. Esman, *Administration and Development in Malaysia* (Ithaca, N.Y.: Cornell University Press, 1972).

Irving Swerdlow, *The Public Administration of Economic Development* (New York: Praeger, 1975).

The five-year plans and administrative reform commission reports of several countries, including India, Kenya, Malaysia, Nigeria, Pakistan, the Philippines, and Zambia, call attention to the need for budget reform to relate budgeting and planning more effectively to each other and to the development process. Several of my students have written research papers on aspects of budgeting in their countries. Four of these have been made available in mimeographed form:

Saghir Asad Hasan, "Provincial Budget Making in Pakistan," Occasional Paper, Center for Development, University of Wisconsin–Madison, May 1977.

Mohammed Sabo Nanono, "Advantages and Disadvantages of Program Budgeting in Nigeria," Occasional Paper, Center for Development, University of Wisconsin–Madison, March 1977.

Kang Hoon Park, "Divergence of Planning and Budgeting in Korea," Occasional Paper, Center for Development, University of Wisconsin–Madison, June 1976.

Nik Mohamed Sidek, "Budgetary Reform for Development in Malaysia," Occasional Paper, Center for Development, University of Wisconsin–Madison, July 1976.

Budgeting for development is the subject of several United Nations documents. Among the most useful are these three:

Budgeting and Planning for Development in Developing Countries, ST/ESA/Ser.E/4 (New York: United Nations, 1976).

David Curzon and Bertram M. Gross, "PPB: Budgetary Review of the Costs and Effects of Government Activities," in *Interregional Seminar on the Use of Modern Management Techniques in the Public Administration of Developing Countries,* Vol. 2, Add. 2, Sales No. E/F/S.71. II. H. 7 (New York: United Nations, 1971).

A Manual for Programme and Performance Budgeting, Sales No. E. 66. XVI. 1 (New York: United Nations, 1965).

9

Personnel Management
for Development Administration

Personnel Needs for Development

Effective systems of planning, budgeting, and fiscal management will activate and make real the delegations of authority to the agencies charged with the execution of specified development programs and projects. Those agencies will fail in the accomplishment of their mission, however, if the personnel, both the officials in charge and the agency staff, are not qualified by training, native competence, integrity, attitude, and public acceptance to perform their assigned duties. To the extent to which the personnel of the agencies in the administration of development do not measure up to the responsibilities of their public trust, to that extent would the bureaucratic forms of the agencies be meaningless and the delegation of fiscal and other authority be fruitless. It is the anticipation of incompetence and dishonesty that spawns centralized and detailed systems of control which inhibit rather than expedite development action and progress. It is therefore incumbent upon a government bent upon effective development administration to gear its personnel system—its civil service—to the novel and unique requirements of that new kind of administration.

The personnel needs for development are great, and they are diverse. Consider first the sheer size of the public establishment. A country like Nigeria, with state as well as central governments, will easily employ five hundred thousand civil servants, not including the military, police, judicial, and legislative systems. A modest monthly turnover rate of severance, new employment, and promotion of only 1 percent would call for five thousand personnel actions a month, sixty thousand in a year. The performance of these personnel functions is a very large operation. This problem of size is compounded by the rapid growth in the diversity and complexity of the public establishment, a growth brought about by the introduction of new agencies and systems to support and encourage economic development and by the adjustment of the bureaucracy's attitudes and loyalties and methods of work to new political institutions throughout the countryside. These burdens of size and novel diversity were thrust upon newly independent countries before outmoded systems of personnel utilization could be revised to accommodate new and rapidly changing situations. At the same time those countries were replacing experienced expatriate personnel with inexperienced national personnel, yet they lacked both reserves of qualified manpower and educational institutions adequate to provide such manpower in the needed quantity and quality.

In broad terms the three categories of personnel needed for development are scientific and technical, entrepreneurial, and managerial. The applications of modern technology and new knowledge to achieve increased agricultural production and to establish profitable industrial enterprises require specialized professional and technical personnel possessing many expert skills. The improvement of health, education, housing, and other social conditions, whose betterment should follow economic growth and also contribute to development, calls for the expert services of specialized personnel. The training and productive utilization of such personnel is the first and perhaps the most distinctive characteristic of the change in the composition of a working force that contributes effectively to the development process.

Two other kinds of personnel are needed for development—managers and entrepreneurs. Management personnel are the central interest of this chapter and will be considered in detail. Entrepreneurs are the risk-takers, those who have the capacity to recognize an opportunity for investment and the will to gamble on the success of the enterprise once it is undertaken. They must also, of course, have access to the resources necessary to make the investment. Some scholars have concluded that development depends more on entrepreneurs than on any other segment of the population. Be that as it may, entrepreneurship is a key factor in the development process. Not only entrepreneurship in the literal sense of risk-taking in the economy, but the entrepreneurial spirit in public administration is a significant aspect of development administration.

Entrepreneurship and management are not the same thing. The entrepreneur needs to be a gambler, and it is desirable that he be a persuasive promoter, one who is successful in selling his enterprise's product, but he is not necessarily an efficient manager. Effective management involves skills in organizing, directing, supervising, and accounting for production and other processes of the enterprise; all of these skills must be available to the entrepreneur and to the development effort, just as specialized scientific and technological skills must be available. A development or investment undertaking would fail, even when imaginatively promoted and well financed, if the technology were badly applied or the executing agency poorly managed.

The development process involves the government both in traditional governmental activities and in public enterprise, and it also involves private enterprise. Regardless of the proportion of government, of public enterprise, and of private enterprise involved in the total economic activity of any particular country, the three categories of personnel—scientific, entrepreneurial, and managerial—are needed in the same degree. From the overall personnel point of view, for the purpose of analysis and planning it is less significant that the requisite personnel be in the public or private sector than that they be present in sufficient quantity and with the required competence. Both "public" and "business" administration in their research and training manifestations are of concern to and within the scope of development administration. Enterprise or business administration in the private sector must accommodate the requirements of government expectation and regulation. Enterprise or business administration in the public sector must respond to the unique requirements of the public service and public expectations of it.

On the other hand, there are categories of government employment and service which are not directly involved, for the most part, in administration for development. Such categories include the military, the police, the judiciary, foreign service, and legislative activity. But all these services are inevitably related to the success of the development effort in some degree. The police and military services are relied upon for the preservation of the security of persons and property. The judicial service is expected to assure equity in treatment before the law. The foreign service has the responsibility for achieving friendly relations conducive to trade. And the legislative service should support effective political expression of development purpose and methodology. Indeed, there are times and places when one or more of these services has engaged directly and in a major way in a country's development program, such as in the conduct of public works by the army or the negotiation of trade or investment agreements by the diplomats. By and large, however, the great burden of administration for development is borne by the public, civil administration of the executive branch.

It is not only the adequacy of the supply of specialized personnel in both quantity and quality which is required by development; also required is the quality of work environment that encourages and supports the most productive efforts of such personnel. Before the days when economic development became a major concern of governments, and especially before the days when countries intervened in and actually engaged in economic activities, the need for specialized technological and other personnel in government service was not perceived as very great; indeed, the numbers of such personnel were small. The status of specialized personnel was even more diminished than their numbers, in many countries. They were not prominent in policy-making or even decisive in program formulation. The salaries and prerequisites of such specialized personnel, actually called "subordinate" services in former British colonies like India and Pakistan, were less than those of other, "superior," services such as police, revenue, foreign, and administrative. The generalist, as distinguished from the specialist, was the elite civil servant in both role and public esteem. A function of development administration therefore is to provide the specialist services with the facility for program and policy formulation and execution commensurate with the specialist content of such programs and policies. The role and prestige which capability for effective participation in development administration necessarily involves should be accompanied by equivalent recognition in compensation and prerequisites relative to the generalist and administrative classes.

A similar point might be made concerning the entrepreneurs—the promoters, risk-takers, and agents of change. In an earlier day, status and prestige in society accrued for the most part to the civil service and to the military—to government officials. The operator in the marketplace was definitely second class. Also, stability of the society was the desideratum, certainly not change in any disturbing degree. Development, however, does involve, and more than that depends upon, economic promotion and management and the changes in society which such activity entails. A development responsibility of the government therefore includes support, recognition, and encouragement for business managers. The significance of this point becomes even more clear when it is remembered that the government's intervention in the economy frequently involves the use of public officers in business activity. These specialized officers in economic affairs, like the specialists in science and technology, should receive the status and recognition and compensation due the importance of their functions in comparison with the administrative class in the civil service.

An increase in the number and an elevation in the role and status of specialists and entrepreneurs in government service in relation to the generalists is involved in improving personnel in the public service for development. Involved also is the creation of an environment conducive to change and growth and development in government's administrative methodology. These are the changes which give meaning and effectiveness to the specialists and entrepreneurs in their newly acquired status and role in the conduct of their challenging and respective functions of applying knowledge and technology to opportunity and of assessing the probable outcome of such application. The unique function of public management, of development administration, is to create and support this environment.

Categories of Public Management Personnel

The rapid and large increase in the size of the governments of most countries has itself been responsible for the increase in the numbers of public officials, the civil servants engaged in the performance of management and administrative functions. Other trends in public service have been even more influential in changing the nature of public administration and increasing its importance. The first of these trends is the expansion of government's role in new and growing fields, including not only economic development but also the several aspects of social welfare and the wise use of natural resources from the ecological and the environmental points of view. The extension of the public establishment into these areas has called for the creation of new kinds of agencies, such as government corporations, and it has called for new systems of administration, such as planning and budgeting, to permit and facilitate program decentralization and the effective and responsible exercise of delegated authority.

A second trend in public administration is a substantial improvement in many technical aspects of management, including data, fiscal, and personnel systems. A third trend is a deeper understanding of the obligations of administration to act responsibly in relationship both to its employees and to its public clientele. The trend toward expertness and specialization in administration is prompted by the growing realization that management must be related to the project or program being conducted. The traditional generalist administrators were not, unless by accident, equipped to perform well in this rapidly changing milieu of administrative service. They were oriented in their loyalty to their elite, upper-class, "superior" administrative services rather than to their agency staffs or the public they were serving; and they were not, for the most part, trained either in administration or in the program sector that their management support was expected to serve. More and better qualified personnel are needed to perform the management and administrative functions upon which successful development program implementation and policy execution depend for their success. These functions are the essence of development administration.

Several different kinds of skills and personal qualifications are required to perform the several different kinds of functions and tasks involved in the effective performance of the administrative function as a whole. An identification of these several classes of public management personnel will help to clarify the relationship of duties in certain kinds of positions to the qualifications needed by the incumbents of those positions, and will thus help to determine the training and recruitment systems needed to get the required personnel result. Administration and management are frequently but erroneously addressed as functions to be performed by one class of personnel with a single and common system of professional training. It is important to recognize that several different kinds of professional skills are involved in the broad field of management—skills which require different kinds of professional training and preparation. These different kinds or categories of management personnel are (1) experts in special aspects of administration, (2) staff analysts, (3) managers, and (4) development administrators.

Several, and a growing number of, administrative processes and functions rely for their best performance on the application of highly specialized techniques. Among such processes and functions are accounting and cost accounting, data management, reporting and information systems, personnel evaluation and testing, personnel classification and compensation, employee relations, manpower planning, materials procurement, and office management. These specialized functions should be performed by experts—experts with professional training that qualifies them to perform the functions competently and reliably. Such expert personnel, having received the appropriate university degree, should be qualified to apply their specialized professional management skill immediately upon employment, under appropriate supervision at the outset, of course. Such experts in special aspects of administration are comparable in this regard to engineers or doctors or teachers or other professional personnel prepared educationally to undertake prescribed types of duties immediately upon graduation and employment.

A major component of administration for development is staff analysis. Competent and reliable staff work at every level—departmental, ministerial, provincial, and central—is necessary to provide the relevant administrators with the expert information and analyses they need as a basis for arriving at sound decisions or for formulating responsible recommendations to their superiors or to policymakers. Such staffs of analysts include those for social and economic planning, budgeting, personnel administration, operations and systems research, and organization and management. The appropriate incumbents of these staff agencies are economists, organization and management analysts, systems engineers, fiscal experts, and personnel and manpower planners. As in the case of experts in special aspects of administration, staff analysts are best prepared and qualified by relevant professional training in a university, and they are capable of relatively fast and easy orientation to their staff work, although there is need for supervision in the beginning positions.

The third category of public management personnel is composed of the heads of departments, bureaus, or agencies or services where the primary objective of management is the internal effectiveness and efficiency of the organization and its operations. These agency heads can for convenience be called "managers." It is not easy or usually important or necessary to distinguish between the terms "manager" and "management" on the one hand and "administrator" and "administration" on the other. For convenience here, however, the manager can be considered as focusing on the direction or management of an agency or organization—internal administration—and the administrator as directing or executing or administering a program—external administration. The manager is responsible for synthesizing the several specialized skills of management in their best application to the operation of the agency and, more than that, he is responsible for providing effective leadership in decisions acceptable to the staff of the organization so as to maximize its effectiveness.

This kind of agency management is often, even usually, characterized by the repetitive and standardized character of the operations, processes which can be and are codified and systematized. Water and utility systems, railroads, communications networks, and even hospitals and agricultural and industrial research centers involve this kind of management, which is internal in its focus and orientation. Other agencies, although of a somewhat different character, are also headed by managers concerned with internal efficiency and effectiveness. These would include, for example, tax collection and regulatory agencies and law enforcement agencies. These kinds of agencies deal in special and restrictive ways with the public to assure adherence to laws and regulations and prescribed codes of more or less routinized behavior.

These managers, concerned primarily with the internal workings of their agencies, in most countries were traditionally, and are even now, professional or technical specialists in the agency or in related government service. Over the years they rise in the ranks and are promoted to ever more responsible positions, which gradually involve more supervisory and managerial duties and fewer professional or technical functions. Thus the turbine operator might eventually become the power plant manager and the agronomist might become the research institute director. Police privates become captains and chiefs; lawyers of the staffs of regulatory bodies are appointed to the governing board. Expertness in the specialized functions and processes of the agency, as distinct from skills and experience in specialized or general management, is generally the test passed by such managers at the time of their initial selection. They learn the comparatively routinized management systems of their agencies by experience.

This general tendency of a specialist in the area of the agency's program function to attain the managerial position is not universal, however. There are cases when an expert in some aspect of management, or a management staff analyst, is selected for the top management post in the agency because of his comparative merit in the eyes of the selecting authority. Or a manager from some other agency might be selected because of his outstanding qualifications, or because of a paucity of qualified persons or a plethora of management problems in the situation, either of which may seem to call for an external appointment.

Another exception to the common practice of promoting professional specialists to managerial roles—and an exception which is becoming the rule in certain areas—occurs when, in a given field such as hospital administration, both the medical and nursing professions and the government or private establishment recognize that the management aspects of the operation not only outweigh the professional aspects but have certain unique features of their own which are deserving of separate systems analysis and application. It is also thought, in some such cases, that the long and expensive professional training of a doctor or other specialized professional person should not be wasted or diluted by diversion to management preoccupations. It is not uncommon, therefore, to find management specialists in certain areas of institutional administration, such as hospital administration, community development, and educational administration, including, even, the sub-specialty of university administration. When these specialized areas of management evolve, they are often and quite appropriately reflected in the professional education offerings of supporting higher education institutions. The graduates of such programs find employment readily in the field of their management interest, usually as assistants or junior management personnel, working their way up to the senior management posts through the years.

Whatever their source, agency managers are obliged to know or to learn something about both the management and the substantive professional or technical program of the agency to be directed. The professional program specialist would have to be indoctrinated in the management systems of the agency and the management specialist would need to learn and understand the unique operating requirements of his agency's program. As specialized professional personnel are given more recognition and opportunity in government service, they receive more recognition in consideration for management posts. This trend is consistent with and supportive of the increased status of professional specialists in government service.

Another and badly needed class of managerial personnel is at the level of rural cooperative and small industry management. It has been pointed out that entrepreneurial genius, even when combined with investment resources and technical feasibility, fails unless supported by competent management. Such management consists of reliable accounting—cost accounting if feasible—prudent procurement and marketing, and effective staff supervision and direction. The same can be said of cooperatives, particularly at the local and rural level where the enthusiastic fervor and good will of the cooperative movement is too frequently expected to produce the financial and service results which only good management can assure. Managers for rural cooperatives and local small industries can and should be trained in large numbers. That training can probably be accomplished quite satisfactorily at the technical level and in technical institutes. Small industry and cooperative managers thus trained could engage in useful management activity immediately upon graduation and could aspire to senior management responsibility in time.

The fourth identifiable category of public management personnel is made up of development administrators. The development administrator is distinguished from the agency manager chiefly because he is concerned with the administration of a program which depends heavily upon effective and productive interactions with people and agencies external to his own organization. The development administrator is concerned primarily with external administration to achieve such changes in social and economic and institutional behavior as are necessary to accommodate the desired program and to achieve its results. Clearly the manager is in varying, though lesser, degrees concerned with external factors in agency direction, and the development administrator for his part must be concerned with the internal aspects of agency management. No sharp line separates the two categories, and certainly all categories of management personnel are important to the development process and to development administration as a whole. Somewhat sharper distinctions than actually exist are often made in the differentiation of managers and development administrators in order to highlight considerations which need to be given weight in policy and practice.

The Development Administrator

The function of development administration is to carry out and to facilitate specified programs to achieve social and economic progress. Agencies directly involved with development programs include nation-building departments (such as agriculture, education, health, and industries), regional or river basin authorities, agricultural development corporations, industrial promotion agencies, and rural development programs. The common and distinguishing characteristic of these agencies is the enlistment in their programs of the people and the agencies and institutions, private and public, central and local, whose participation is essential to the progress and success of such programs. This is external administration. For development programs, internal agency efficiency is not enough. The individual development administrator typically heads an agency charged with the responsibility for advancing a development program or providing support and services to facilitate development in a sector or in a region. He might head an operating branch of the agency, or play a key management staff role in planning delivery systems.

The success of this external function of development administration requires that the program, both in its purposes and its methods, be made attractive and also possible to the farmers, or the businessmen, or the communities who are expected to be served or affected by it. Existing agencies whose interests are involved or who can help or hinder in the prosecution of program objectives, and new agencies and institutions needed to act upon program opportunities or to serve their needs, as well as updated networks of effective relationships among these, must all be enlisted in the effort. The responsibility as central agency for providing motivation to these communities and agencies and for forging effective operating arrangements with them is the distinctive role of development administration.

In a program of rural electrification, for example, development administration requires that local cooperatives or private systems be engaged in the arrangements for building rural lines and handling the local distribution of centrally generated energy. Cooperative, private sector, or local government stores and banks need to be established or encouraged to finance and to guide the use of home, farm, and business machines and appliances. When agricultural or other production changes as a result of electrification, other institutional services such as those of banking and marketing, which are essential to development at any particular place, also need to be invited, or induced if necessary, to play their part. Similar illustrations could be given with respect to irrigation and fertilizer in agricultural development, credit and infrastructure support for industrial development, and loans, grants, and technical assistance to communities for social welfare services of a number of kinds. There are many examples.

The development administrator, the man who heads or plays a prominent managerial role in an agency conducting a development program, must therefore have the competence—the qualifications—to perform well in external as well as internal administration. This added and major responsibility distinguishes the development administrator from the manager, whose chief concern is agency operating efficiency even though he often has some concern for his agency's relations with the client public it serves or upon whose support it depends. This responsibility of the development administrator for close working relationships with cooperating communities and agencies distinguishes him also from the administrator who deals extensively and even primarily with the public or some part of it in a restraining or regulatory way, as in the case of police service, tax collection, and rules of trade. The development administrator must appeal to the self-interest of his agency's public clientele and must gain its confidence in the conduct of a program of mutual benefit and reward. His relationship must therefore be close and even warm and intimate. Managers of other public agencies, particularly those involving restraint and regulation, are obliged to be distant and aloof rather than close and warm in community relationships. Their sanctions are not those of economic gain and social reward but of punishment and reprisal. Their methods are those of command and compliance rather than of persuasion and cooperation.

The development administrator may also be distinguished from the government administrator—the senior civil servant or chief secretary—in the traditional bureaucratic system of the past. That officer of a former time was inclined to consider himself a kind of governor and to use authoritarian methods to assure compliance with his orders. Civil servants in many countries were members of an elite upper class and had few ties with the masses of the people under their management aegis. Their loyalties were to that elite class and to the ruling power rather than to the people of the country. The traditional administrators were commissioned to maintain the status quo, the stability of life as it was, rather than to promote or facilitate fundamental social and economic and, least of all, political change. The development administrator is the antithesis of the traditional government officer in almost every respect. He is not an authoritarian ruler representing an elite class intent on the stability of the existing order. On the contrary, his commitment is to the people involved in a program that they have undertaken in cooperation with him and his agency. His hope and expectation are for social and economic change in systems in which the people participate.

The well-qualified manager, for the purposes of efficient internal administration, should have sufficient command of the specialized tools of management to use them well and in concert for the best overall result—tools of planning, organizing, budgeting, personnel administration, cost accounting, and information systems. He should have an understanding of the technical and professional aspects of the substantive elements of his agency's program interest in order to coordinate them with each other and to synthesize them with the economic and administrative considerations conducive to the optimum result. In performing these functions it is incumbent upon the manager to gain the confidence and respect of his staff and colleagues not only by his integrity and competence but also by enlisting their participation in achieving coordination of policy decisions and operations, and by dealing with them openly and fairly. He should have the ability to communicate.

Thus, the development administrator must have the traits and the capabilities of the manager. In addition, for the purposes of effective external administration, he should understand the dynamics of the development process, especially the nature of motivation and innovation for change, and the cultural, economic, and political traditions and systems which regulate development in any particular place. The development administrator should have a grasp of and a belief in the indispensable role of people in development program formulation and conduct. He must also understand the ways in which their participation can be effectively and responsibly engaged, ways which especially include the processes of institution-building and institutionalization to regularize such participation.

Finally, the development administrator should have the entrepreneurial spirit—that is, the vision and the capacity to take advantage of program opportunities and to use his delegated authority responsibly and accountably in doing so. Both the manager and the development administrator should be leaders, however that difficult word is defined. High intelligence, integrity, charisma, expressiveness, and warmth, as well as inherent ability for analysis and organization and self-confident willingness to make tough decisions, are qualities of leadership beyond the mere possession of an office of authority.

It should be clear that managers and especially development administrators are born and not made. Unlike experts in specialized aspects of administration, such as accounting or data management or personnel testing, and unlike professional specialists in fields such as law, engineering, teaching, medicine, and agronomy, administrators are not produced by systems of pre-service training. One reason that administrators are not produced in school is that the incumbent of a senior administrative post, such as the head of an agency or a major subdivision of an agency, is usually and understandably a senior man in both age and experience who has demonstrated to all concerned his capacities for management and his qualities of leadership. A college degree does not suffice as evidence in these circumstances. The other, and perhaps the overriding, reason that managers and administrators cannot be produced by training systems is because qualifications essential to the exercises of administrative responsibility are inbred and cannot be acquired. These are primarily the personal qualities of character and leadership, but they also include such skills as analysis and communication and such values as equity and participation in human relations. There is no question that those with the potential and aptitude for administration can benefit from systematic study and from a variety of administrative experiences. No amount of such study and such experience, however, will produce a top-flight administrator who does not have the innate qualities and abilities for that kind of work.

As for managers, then, and particularly for development administrators, the need in public personnel administration is first to devise a method to identify persons with the potential for administration, persons with the character, ability, and flair which give promise of success in agency management and program execution. Second, the need is to provide such persons with the opportunity for the supplementary study and experience that they need to occupy successfully management or development administration posts. Such study and experience would vary widely in length and emphasis according to the individual and also according to the nature of the program and agency to be administered. In the case of management posts in well-routinized agencies, the selection is often made by promotion of those specialists in the agency's function who demonstrate ability to discharge competently supervisory and management as well as professional functions. In the case of development administration posts, systems for selection are not so comparatively simple. For one thing, the programs to be carried out often involve the application of several professional and technical specialties, and their focus and synthesis for an integrated purpose can be complex and difficult. In the second place, the talent and experience required for external administration is even scarcer than for internal management. The search for such talent must therefore range over a wide area and must include personnel in several agencies.

The qualities which indicate probable success in development administration might be found in either a professional specialist in one of the substantive areas of program interest, an expert in some specialized field of administration, or a generalist administrator who was previously responsible, for example, for the administration of a district or a province or for a regulatory function, but who also displays evidence of capability for development administration. All such sources should be tapped for administrative talent, thus not only broadening the base of recruitment but also giving opportunity for promotion to larger numbers of public servants, particularly the specialists who in the past have been too frequently excluded from consideration for administrative posts. Once found, the potential managers and development administrators would need, and should be given, the opportunity to supplement their knowledge and to increase their skills in areas not required of them previously. The agronomist or other agriculturist, for example, would give attention to the processes of internal management and the art of external administration. The management experts selected to administer the conduct of a technical function or functions would also need to learn the policy and methodological characteristics of the technological or professional program to be carried out as well as the components of external administration.

Issues in Selecting and Assigning Personnel
in the Public Service

The quality of specialist and administrative personnel services for development depends not only upon the concepts and expectations of the government but even more specifically upon the personnel policies and systems for attracting, retaining, and efficiently utilizing well-qualified civil servants. The function of the public personnel administration process is to do just that, to recruit competent staff and to assign it in terms of effective and efficient performance and accomplishment. In the public service, however, it is not enough that the objective of recruiting competent personnel is achieved. It is also important that the general public as well as the government have assurance that civil servants are selected and assigned on the basis of qualification and that it has confidence in the public service and its personnel process for this reason.

This appropriate and desirable concern of the public for the quality of the processes of personnel administration extends beyond mere confidence that civil servants are competent. The public also desires access to opportunities for public employment and public service, not only for the widening of economic opportunity but also to be given assurance that the public service, the civil service, is not the possession of any special elite governing class, with the selective loyalties of such a closed system, but that it is a system open to public access whose members have loyalties to and are responsive to that public. The first and most important condition of merit and efficiency, therefore, although a condition not inconsistent with the principle of competence, is that the recruitment processes for the public service provide for the ready and easy accessibility to it of candidates from the public and provide sufficient advertising of job opportunities to inform potential candidates of vacancies and openings.

The processes of recruitment will of course have small success in attracting well-qualified candidates for public service unless the terms and conditions of such service are clearly favorable in comparison with employment benefits in the private sector. Even in countries where the private sector is small and employment opportunities few, so that comparisons are relatively meaningless, the conditions of the public service are significant because they have a direct bearing on the morale and the performance of the civil servants. The inducements to public employment are therefore basic and of first consideration in establishing government recruitment policy. The extent to which government recognizes and acts upon this key aspect of its personnel policy is an indication of the relative role it and the public as a whole expect the bureaucracy to play in development.

The inducements which attract the best-qualified persons to the public service include attractive pay and medical and retirement benefits; they also include opportunities for promotion and reasonable assurance of job security and tenure. Of importance also, and perhaps of equal weight in attraction to the public service, is the status it has in the public view; if esteem for the bureaucracy and its staff is high and civil servants stand well in the community, they occupy positions that are desired and are easily recruited for. Of measurable importance in recruiting and especially in retaining good staff is the quality of administrative and supervisory systems, and their reputation, which condition the environment for efficient and productive job performance. These systems include those for delegating authority and responsibility and providing for participation in program planning appropriate to the requirements of the function. They also include assurance of equity in treatment with respect to job assignment, promotion, and tenure, and a grievance procedure which assures fair consideration of complaints. In other words, the quality of the administration depends upon the quality of the staff, and the quality of the staff depends upon the quality of the administration.

The first object of public personnel administration is to fill positions in the government service with competent, well-qualified people. Rightly or wrongly, however, merit and efficiency alone are not always the only criteria for employment. It is not difficult to find countries like Malaysia which give preference to citizens of a particular race or religion or tribe or caste as a matter of public policy. Many countries, like Nigeria, consider the place of national or regional origin or residence as a factor in selection for employment. It is not uncommon to find preference for government jobs given to those who have served in the military, particularly in time of war.

These dilutions of the principle of relative merit in the consideration of qualifications certainly do not increase the quality of the public service. On the other hand, personnel preferences of one kind or another may not do serious harm provided that those selected, even with the advantage of such preference, are required to be clearly and well qualified, although perhaps not the best qualified. The differences among well-qualified candidates are often comparatively slight and difficult to identify and measure, in any case, and even if found do not always make a difference of any great significance in job performance. The country itself has to decide, as a matter of public policy, whether the political, social, or even economic advantages of preferential systems in public employment offset the disadvantages of dilution in the quality of the service.

When, on the other hand, preference is given to members of special groups because of vested class influence and interest rather than for reasons of public policy, the quality of the public service clearly suffers. The integrity and objective application of public personnel policy is violated by such class preference, and those selected by virtue of that special influence are obliged to give their loyalty to that external influence rather than to the agency they have been employed to serve. Intervention of this kind in public personnel selections is to be deplored, whether its motivation and influence is personal, family, economic, or political interest. There is a legitimate place for political appointments to support elected officials, but there can be a debate about how deep in the bureaucracy such political appointments should be made. Political influence in appointments to the administrative bureaucracy has the same adverse consequences for administrative integrity and efficiency as those appointments made for other reasons of vested interest external to the purposes of the system.

After candidates have been sorted out according to applicable public policies, the task is to separate those who are well qualified from those who are not, and then to select the best qualified for the job opening or openings. Presumably no one would advocate the appointment of an unqualified candidate even though from a preferred group. It is easier to identify and describe the several qualifications for a given position than it is to evaluate them, particularly on a comparative basis. First there are personal characteristics, those of native intelligence and capacity, integrity and reliability, and of compatability. Second, there are the qualifications derived from training and education. And third, there are the qualifications based upon work experience. A well-trained personnel man can readily, in most cases, identify the well-qualified candidates on the basis of their records, which are supplemented by evaluative references prepared by persons who know the candidate well from a relevant association and who are also known, if possible, to the examiner. Written and oral examinations are often useful, in addition, in weeding out those candidates who are clearly not qualified.

The so-called objective examinations are not, however, a satisfactory way to select the best candidate from among several well-qualified candidates, which is the final step in the personnel recruitment and selection process. Such examinations are good sieves, but they cannot sift so finely as to assure perfection in choosing exactly the right person for the subject job—unfortunately. The personnel process would be much simpler if such were not the case. On the one hand, examination techniques are not yet developed to the point of such refined use. On the other hand, the intangibles of success and of predicting success for a position in a particular agency or in a type of agency in a series of locations are not easily measured. Their consideration is best taken into account by the agency or the service in which the candidate is being considered for employment, and which is responsible for program results. If the personnel agency and the public are both assured that the candidate selected is well qualified, they should not feel obliged to debate whether he was the best or next best or third best; the distinctions are difficult to judge and relatively unimportant. When the personnel agency or the public does not trust the responsible administrator or operating supervisor even to this extent, the "objective" written examination has proved a convenient public relations device in the selection of the successful condidate. But the examination is less reliable than the administrator on the scene for choosing the candidate most likely to succeed.

Different countries have different methods of entrance into the public service, and not a few have more than one method. One kind of entrance system, that inherited from the British colonial civil service, provides for entry at the beginning or lower end of the scale of a government-wide specialized service, such as revenue, education, or administration. In this system assignment and promotion are customarily the functions of a central personnel agency, and promotion is within the relevant service. This system is sometimes called "closed," because the ever-higher positions in the subject service are not open to competition from outsiders. A somewhat comparable entrance system also involves appointment in a broad or generalized service immediately upon graduation and examination, or after completion of other suitable educational qualification, but assignment is made to an agency, rather than to a service, with non-competitive promotions permitted only in the agency rather than in an interagency service. This is another type of closed system; it is used in Thailand.

The kind of system that is sometimes called "open" involves, essentially, comparatively open competition for each position as it is created or becomes vacant no matter what its level: this is the "American" system. Even in open systems, the advantages of tenure and of career services are sought to be achieved by giving first choice in consideration for such openings to qualified employees who are already on the payroll and by recruiting from outside only when well-qualified persons already in the service are not available. Some countries use a combination of both systems, with some types of positions—usually in one profession in one major agency—incorporated in a closed service, as, for example, the Forest Service in the U.S. Department of Interior; and other types of positions follow the pattern of open systems.

By and large the incumbents of closed services are classified by rank which they carry with them, along with its accompanying pay and benefits, regardless of job and agency assignment. This system provides a certain amount of desirable flexibility, which is sometimes enhanced by recognizing specialties, such as economists within the administrative service, as in India and Malaysia. The incumbents of positions in the open systems, on the other hand, perform their functions in positions which are classified; they are paid according to the position classification. This open system provides a broader range of job opportunities for civil servants and a better basis for meeting the specialized requirements of any particular position or agency.

The classification process, whether applied to ranks or positions but particularly when applied to positions, is a valuable tool of personnel administration and of management. Because it describes the functions and duties of the position, and its relationships with other positions, the job description is an excellent tool for personnel assignment and organization. Because the job description indicates the qualifications and skills requisite to the performance of the duties and the discharge of the functions, it helps to assure the matching of persons with jobs. A major purpose and accomplishment of a position-classification system is to assure equal pay for equal work, an important characteristic of a personnel policy which is concerned with equity and morale. Classification by rank also provides a basis for equity in pay, assignment, and promotion related to comparative seniority and service experience.

Insofar as the job descriptions in a well-ordered classification system provide a basis for and also reflect good working relationships and organization as well as providing an equitable foundation for compensation scales, they are very useful. By attempting, however, to make minute refinements in differentiating positions for the purpose of pay, classifications can disrupt good organizational harmony by emphasizing those distinctions rather than by focusing on the teamwork and interrelations of staff. Also, by rigidity and detail in their formalization, job descriptions can calcify administration. Classification should serve, and not be served by, good management and sound personnel practice.

In view of the unique requirements of administration for development, the greater the opportunity to match, on the one hand, the specialized professional and technical functions involved in a program with, on the other hand, the experts best qualified to perform them, the better the system. It has been emphasized that both the internal and, especially, the external functions of development administrators require selection and assignment of those who have demonstrated special aptitude well after their entrance into government service or who have equivalent records in private service. Systems which permit lateral and upward mobility on the part of both administrative and specialized personnel are therefore to be desired for the administration of development.

The closed career service system is often characterized by job rotation for periods of fairly short duration. For the conduct of development programs this is a disadvantage. Assignment to a series of positions, even in the same service, often requires a breadth of knowledge and expertise rather than the competence in depth that is involved in the introduction of a new technology as part of the development effort. The non-competitive closed service system provides automatic promotion, based upon seniority, unless there is some gross fault in the performance of duty. This is not a disadvantage; seniority has been too much maligned as a factor in tenure and promotion. In a large number—perhaps a majority—of cases of choice between persons for retention or promotion, the difference in the qualifications and performance of the individuals concerned is so narrow as to make substantially no difference in job efficiency or effectiveness. In these cases seniority provides an understandable and reasonable basis for making the needed distinction.

The fact remains, however, that in the closed system it is assumed that the existing cadre can and will do the jobs needed to be done, whereas in the open system the expectation is that people will be sought out according to their specific qualifications for performing those jobs. The open system, which has the clear purpose of finding the right person— the specifically qualified person—to do the job in hand, aspires to meet the requirements of the program; this emphasis puts the job first and the man second. Even rules such as promotion from within do not in this respect protect the tenure and promotion interests of personnel as well as the closed, tenure, service system, which puts the man first and the job second. Each system has to be compromised in some degree in an effort to overcome its inherent deficiencies.

Issues in Organization for Public Personnel Management

There is nothing more important in administration, whether in the successful execution of a program or a project or in the conduct of the public business as a whole, than the quality of the personnel as judged in terms of the job to be done and the excellence of the leadership and direction given to that personnel. Provisions for effective personnel administration are therefore of the highest priority in public administration and in development administration. There are few countries which could not improve the quality of the conduct of development and the entirety of the government's affairs by devoting more attention and more resources to organization for personnel management. That organization involves both the provision of professional staff services and the conduct of the personnel aspects of line operations. Most of the issues of organization for personnel management arise in the relationships between these staff, or specialist, and line, or executive, components of personnel management.

The staff functions required in first-rate personnel administration are performed for the most part by trained personnel specialists and technicians. These functions consist in the first instance of advice to the chief executive concerning the policies, standards, and rules which are expected to guide and regulate the conduct of personnel management, no matter who performs the functions covered by such policies, standards, and rules. This advice covers such aspects as job qualification and classification specifications; compensation levels and medical, retirement, and other welfare benefits; employee relations and grievance procedures; training; and assignment and promotion, including performance appraisals. In the second instance the personnel staff function often includes the exercise of certain personnel controls on behalf of the executive, or advice to him on his application of those controls. Such controls are illustrated by approvals required for the creation of new positions or the establishment of manning tables often used in connection with annual budget and program reviews. This function frequently leads the personnel staff into organization analysis and advice.

The third aspect of the professional personnel staff function concerns its service tasks: that is, recruitment of personnel and testing for their qualifications, classifying persons and jobs, administering performance rating systems, providing training services, monitoring grievance procedures, and managing compensation, retirement, and benefit schemes. An essential part of this service aspect of personnel management is personnel planning—manpower planning for the public service—in order to anticipate the needs for relevant categories of professional and technical personnel and to advise the concerned government agencies and educational institutions.

The line functions in responsible personnel administration are to select, assign, and promote personnel within the applicable policies and rules laid down by the government. Personnel administration is an integral and indispensable part of management, and that management is seriously weakened in its capacity to act if it cannot control its personnel with the power to hire and fire. A management which cannot hire and fire cannot be held fully accountable for its program performance. Hiring and firing are by no means the total personnel function of line management; they are only the beginning. Agency and program and system administration depend crucially upon an environment—created by good supervision—which permits and encourages the expression of the full abilities of the personnel in the organization. That environment must be coordinated and harmonious. Such administration involves the development of personnel, its deployment to the best possible advantage of the organization, and its supervision.

It is at the point of hiring and firing—selecting, assigning, promoting, and terminating—that the issues of control become critical and most difficult. Under the closed service system, civil servants are selected by the public or civil service commission and are assigned and promoted either by that commission or by another central personnel or establishment office. The "responsible" executing agency is expected to do its best with personnel but is not required to be essentially interested in it, or loyal to it, or actually accountable to it except for the purpose of more or less routine performance reports. When the selection process, an executive function, is delegated instead to the personnel staff, the civil service commission, to assure the public that the "best" qualified candidate is selected from an open competition, a result somewhat similar to that of the closed service is produced, diluting the executive capability of the operating agency. The basic issue is whether the program—the job, the agency, and the process to be administered—is the first objective, or whether the personnel cadre is first. Which exists for which—the employees for the job, or the job for the employees?

As pointed out in another context, development administration depends largely for its effectiveness upon specialized technological and administrative personnel who are selected for the particular task in hand, and upon management which has the requisite operating capabilities to conduct the program for which it is accountable. Development administration therefore would put as much as possible of the authority for personnel management at the level of program or project operating responsibility. This delegation should be exercised within appropriate overall policies, of course, in accordance with prescribed standards and with the assistance of competent professional personnel management staff. Adherence to well-conceived policies and standards can go a long way to protect the tenure and career interests of personnel, to give assurance to the public that there is open and competitive access to government jobs, and to prevent personnel abuses on the part of unwise or inept or dishonest administrators. Thus it is possible to make the job the first concern, and the personal interest the second, of personnel administrators.

There are other methods of selection and promotion which give additional assurance of objectivity and honesty and which at the same time preserve the integrity of management decision and accountability. One such arrangement is for the central personnel examining agency to certify candidates who are well qualified for a position, or a category of related positions, and then place their names on an open register. This is a valuable service for the administrator who makes the individual selection from the register; it assures an external finding of competence, thus avoiding the selection of an appointee in abrogation of the managerial prerogative. The open register should be continuously available both to new candidates and to the appointing officer, unlike the closed register, which is of use for only a limited term of specified length. Another system provides for selection of civil servants by the central personnel agency at the entrance level, but provides that position assignment and promotion thereafter must have the authorization of the operating line.

Since personnel administration is a crucial and inseparable part of management, of program execution, the professional staff for personnel management should be in the immediate office and in direct contact with the chief executive—that is, in the office of the president or prime minister. An autonomous personnel agency which is not responsible to the executive cannot serve him reliably for his purposes, nor can an agency lodged elsewhere in the bureaucracy. Autonomy in a civil service commission has the purpose of avoiding political or other undue influence in appointments, but this purpose can be assured as well by law and policy and by limiting the degree of autonomy to the comparatively narrow function of certification of qualified applicants. The other objective of autonomy is to give the personnel establishment and its services a degree of freedom from executive control; but that separation defeats the very purpose of making personnel management an integral, effective, and responsible arm of administration. That kind of autonomy would in effect transfer executive responsibility from the agency and its managers to the personnel cadre and its elite leadership.

The central personnel agency is well advised to limit its work as much as possible to overall personnel planning and formulation of policies, standards, and guidelines, and to conduct the minimum possible number of control functions. Considering that personnel management should be closely wedded to agency and program administration, the service and operating aspects of the personnel function should be decentralized to the department and agency level. These aspects include selection and classification as well as payroll, performance evaluation, training, and employee relations. At this location and level the personnel office is also in a position to assist the departmental and agency planning process by making analyses of project feasibility and by advising on the solution of problems in plan implementation. Another important reason for making the department or agency the focus of personnel administration is that the personnel—the employees and staff—of such departments and agencies are then attracted to the specific and tangible programs and purposes which are of concern to those departments and agencies, rather than to the broad and vague generalities of the public services as a whole. Personnel loyalties and enthusiasm are thereby encouraged to be more particular and direct and are therefore more productive in their result.

It follows that states and provinces or other units of local governments should have their own independent personnel systems to the extent that their jurisdictions are in truth independent and are sustained, at least in large measure, by their own revenues. The same rationale as for the central government applies, namely that effective and accountable administration depends upon personnel management and control. Systems in which the central government participates in personnel management by combining state with central cadres or services are systems which not only dilute local agency administrative capability and accountability but also weaken the integrity of local government by extending the influence and control of the center. Avoidance of these kinds of participation should not preclude arrangements by which experienced central officers can be seconded to local jurisdictions and by which state officers can be given experience in central agencies.

Another problem of organizing personnel management for development administration is in the area of public enterprise. Public enterprises are for the most part agencies established outside the regular public administration bureaucracy so that they can be granted the management capabilities they need to perform their unique functions of commercial operations to accomplish the government's purpose, which in this case is to intervene in the economy. Public enterprises are thus typically exempted from the regular civil service or other public personnel management systems. The basic object of this exclusion is to enable the government corporation or other public enterprise to hire and fire its personnel so as to have the personnel capability necessary for its assigned function and thus to be appropriately accountable for its success or failure. Other reasons for granting autonomy in personnel management are to set salary scales and other considerations of remuneration at levels competitive with private industry in order to attract the specialized professional and technical personnel needed and to employ highly qualified and successful managers.

The purpose of this autonomy in personnel matters for public enterprises has too frequently failed to be accomplished. The failure is due chiefly to the fact that in many countries public enterprises have neglected to evolve distinctive personnel systems which would serve their needs and at the same time satisfy the government and the public that they were not abusing their powers. In many cases there has been abuse. In other cases timid managers have failed to support innovations which deviated in any effective degree from traditional government personnel practice. In the absence of viable new systems, it is not surprising that several countries, among them Nigeria, have permitted or encouraged their public service commissions to intervene and to reestablish some measure of central control once again, negating to that degree the originally intended autonomy of public enterprise in personnel matters. In most such cases the public service commissions were not loath to intervene, and the supremacy of the civil service was asserted once again. In these and other cases refuge was taken in the fallacious principle that uniformity of personnel policies and practices in traditional public sector agencies and public enterprise sector agencies was of higher importance than the unique personnel requirements of either.

For development, whether in the regular civil service or the public enterprise sector, personnel administration needs to be reoriented from cadre-centered systems and controls to program-based processes and services designed specifically to meet the needs of the agencies conducting those programs. It is this orientation of public personnel administration which assures that the loyalty of civil servants will be to the public, rather than to the state, and to the programs which serve the public. Civil servants who are selected for their positions (1) by accountable program agencies, (2) on the basis of their specialized qualifications, and (3) in competition which is open to the public are obliged to be more responsive to the public than civil servants who are selected by an autonomous commission to be permanent members of a cadre on the basis of their generalist qualifications and who are assigned and promoted, without public competition, by that commission rather than by responsible program agencies. The open personnel system, which puts first the work to be done, produces a more responsive civil service than the closed system, which gives first place to individual status and tenure. The administrators of development are obliged to be responsive to the public because of their need to involve that public in the successful accomplishment of the program purposes of their agencies. When political leadership and processes are strong, they quite rightly take precedence over the bureaucracy in fixing civil service loyalties. The nature of the public personnel system itself, however, whether open or closed and whether agency or service controlled, can determine the focus of loyalty of the civil service.

Note on Sources

The following United Nations documents are directly relevant to problems of personnel administration in developing countries:

The Central Organs of the Civil Service in the Developing Countries, Sales No. E. 68. II. H. 3 (New York: United Nations, 1969).

Handbook of Civil Service Laws and Practices, Sales No. 66. II. H. 2 (New York: United Nations, 1966).

Local Government Personnel Systems, Sales No. 67. II. H. 1 (New York: United Nations, 1966).

Lucian W. Pye, *New Approaches to Personnel Policy for Development,* Sales No. E. 74. II. H. 1 (New York: United Nations, 1974).

Report of the United Nations Interregional Seminar on the Employment, Development and Role of Scientists and Technical Personnel in the Public Service of Developing Countries, 3 vols., Sales No. E. 70. II. H. 6 (New York: United Nations, 1971).

The following reform commission reports are illustrative of the focus of government reviews concerning the status, compensation, and amenities granted to civil servants:

Commission on the Reorganization of the Executive Branch of the National Government of the Philippines, "Integrated Reorganization Plan," mimeographed, Manila, 1972.

Federal Republic of Nigeria, *Public Service Review Commission: Main Report and Government Views on the Report* (Lagos: Ministry of Information, 1974).

Republic of Ghana, *Report of the Commission of the Structure and Remuneration of the Public Services* (Accra: Ministry of Information, 1967).

India Administrative Reforms Commission, *Report on Personnel Administration* (Delhi: Government of India Press, 1969).

Republic of Kenya, *Report of the Commission of Inquiry* (Nairobi: Government Printer, 1971).

There are many studies of civil service systems and associated topics in developing countries, among which the following are representative:

A. L. Adu, *The Civil Service in New African States* (New York: Praeger, 1965).

Ralph J. Braibanti, ed., *Asian Bureaucratic Systems Emergent from the British Imperial Tradition* (Durham, N.C.: Duke University Press, 1966).

Louis Fougère, ed., *Civil Service Systems* (Brussels: International Institute for Administrative Sciences, 1967).

Henry F. Goodnow, *The Civil Service of Pakistan: Bureaucracy in a New Nation* (New Haven, Conn.: Yale University Press, 1964).

Lawrence S. Graham, *Civil Service Reform in Brazil: Principles versus Practices* (Austin: University of Texas Press, 1968).

Martin Kriesberg, ed., *Public Administration in Developing Countries* (Washington, D.C.: Brookings Institution, 1965).

V. A. Pai Panandiker, *A Personnel System for Development Administration* (Bombay: Bombay Popular Press, 1966).

F. F. Ridley, ed., *Specialists and Generalists* (London: Allen and Unwin, 1968).

Kenneth Younger, *The Public Service in New States* (London: Oxford University Press, 1960).

10

Institutions for Management Training and Research

The Nature and Magnitude of the Training Problem

The concept of development administration involves not only the conduct of planned programs of growth and change but also the development of an administrative capacity to do so. The development of this administrative capacity depends in turn upon the adequacy—the vigor and competence—of the institutions and mechanisms upon which the bureaucracy must depend and from which it must draw the personnel, the technology, and the systems that are needed to inaugurate the effectively innovative methods necessary to achieve social and economic development. The most immediate and most directly associated category of supporting institutions needed in this connection consists of the specialized systems and associated staff services of the administrative establishment itself.

These staff services include a public personnel office capable of recruiting and assigning civil servants who are able to discharge competently and honestly the many and varied tasks demanded of modern government; the personnel office must also be capable of retraining those civil servants for their evolving duties. The services include staff units to give attention to the kinds of management accounting and methods of effective procurement which should be introduced to serve development administration. They include staff capacity to analyze and devise development delivery systems. And they include the facility for

248

evaluating and introducing new technology as an aid to management effectiveness and efficiency. A strong budget office should be among the first of these staff units in order to make possible, as well as to assure the feasibility of, delegation of authority for expenditures. Unfortunately these institutional resources for the strengthening of development administration in the bureaucracies of most nations newly embarked on ambitious development programs are not themselves strong and are not, generally speaking, receiving the recognition and attention they require if they are to play their part.

The lack of strong bureaucratic staff offices and systems for development administration becomes even more serious in light of the fact that in almost none of the developing countries, with a few possible exceptions such as India and the Philippines, is there a pool of qualified manpower adequate to meet the enormous needs of a bureaucracy expanding in size and increasing in diversity and complexity. The new governments of the 1940s, 1950s, and 1960s replaced expatriates with indigenous personnel and at the same time increased precipitously the number and kinds of new development agencies at the center; they also increased the size of the administrative establishment in the states, provinces, and districts. Nor did the educational systems at that time have the capacity to produce the kinds and numbers of persons needed for development administration.

The first and most obvious obligation of these educational systems, particularly the universities, was to produce the specialized manpower—the scientists, engineers, lawyers, doctors, and other professional personnel—needed to perform the specialized tasks of development. A second and less understood responsibility of the educational system was to produce managers and administrators, not only civil servants for both the traditional bureaucracy and for the new public enterprises, but the managers of the hundreds and thousands of private and cooperative enterprises by which a major and even a predominant proportion of any country's development effort is pursued. It is a function of development administration to plan for and to help bring into being the educational institutions to meet these personnel needs, both for professional and for managerial personnel.

It is not only the personnel requirements for public administration that need to be met, but also the need for research concerning management methods and systems and the need for consulting services. The management centers should be centers of research and consultation as well as training institutes, whether autonomous bodies or attached to the universities or to the government. Supporting institutions of quality to perform these multiple services are needed to staff and support new and expanded systems of administration for the achievement of ambitious development goals. It is discouraging to see country after country plan bold new programs for progress and then falter in devising administrative vehicles to carry the programs, and falter again in creating the institutions to provide the personnel and the supporting technology and research.

The sheer size of the public establishment is staggering when considered from the point of view of finding well-qualified persons to staff it adequately. The volume of personnel recruitment and selection is very large in terms of mere numbers alone. The personnel load is even heavier in view of the marked increase in the diverse kinds of functions assumed by government in the last two or three decades. These new and additional functions include those for public enterprise and rural development and they have entailed the renovation of management and delivery systems such as those for budgeting, personnel, accounting, and procurement. These new and growing demands on public administration were aggravated when countries which gained their independence after World War II launched campaigns to replace expatriate civil servants with nationals.

The question was, and still is, where these thousands of civil servants are to come from—where they are to be produced. In most countries, including many developed countries, existing educational and training institutions are inadequate in the number and quality of their programs of professional and technical instruction to graduate a supply of trained personnel sufficient to meet the needs of government and of the economy as a whole. They were certainly inadequate to this purpose in colonial pre-independence days, the period before the expectations of development were translated into organizations and programs of public administration, and there were therefore no reserve pools of trained manpower to supply the demand. These inadequacies were perhaps most evident in those professional and technical fields involved in specialized technological development; commendable and effective progress to remedy them has been made in most countries. The paucity of institutions for public management training and research, on the other hand, has not been generally recognized as a serious problem, and efforts to overcome the deficiency are not equal for the most part to the task of rectifying the situation.

While it is true that most countries, upon achieving independence, did create and support programs to train civil servants in administration, the number and the quality of those programs have not been sufficient to the need. One reason for the insufficiency is no doubt the persistence of outmoded concepts of management and the belief that generalists can perform administrative functions reliably after an orientation period, of the type given in an academy in the civil service. These concepts did not take account of the rapid technical and technological revolution in management technique represented by the computer and other machines and by advances in specialist aspects of management, such as cost accounting and personnel testing and classification. These outdated concepts did not anticipate or provide for the enormous growth of staff analysis units and positions at all levels of government—planning, personnel, budget, procurement, operations research, and organization analysis staffs—which ought to be manned by professionally trained personnel. Similarly, the needs and demands for managers of public enterprise, both large and small, were not foreseen. Perhaps the largest blind spot of all was the failure to perceive the different qualities of administration and of administrators required in the development process as contrasted with traditional law and order systems.

It is useful to identify the types of training and educational institutions needed in a country to produce each of these several types of management personnel—the experts in specialized aspects, the analysts, the managers, and the administrators. First, of course, are the universities. They are the appropriate institutions for training the professional and specialist personnel in management just as they train professional and specialist personnel in science, engineering, medicine, education, and agriculture. In this same category of specialized education it is appropriate to include the diploma-level institutions, technological institutes where subprofessional management personnel can be trained very well to the desired level of performance—bookkeepers, for example, and store managers and computer programmers. The second category of institutions for the development of management personnel includes those serving as the training branch of the public establishment's personnel arm. The strategic role of in-service and post-entry training is too often underestimated, especially in the public service. It should serve the very specific job and task requirements of an agency's systems, and programs, in contrast to the more generalized professional and technical preparation of pre-service education and training. Post-entry, in-service training recognizes and draws upon the value of continuing education both for the advantage of the individual employee and for the benefit of agency performance.

The third kind of institution for management training and research is the specialized institute, or center for public administration—the "IPA." There is great variation from country to country and even within countries with respect to the functions, the students, the autonomy, the status, and the relationship of the IPA. The categorization of public

management personnel by types and the identification of the different
kinds of training and educational institutions which ought to be available
to produce those types will help to isolate and identify the unique role,
the distinguishing functions, of the IPA, particularly in its relationships
with universities on the one hand and the public personnel establishment
on the other.

The University's Role in
Management Training and Research

The university is the natural and appropriate place to train
professional experts in special aspects of administration, staff analysts in
a variety of managerial areas, and management personnel for specified
types of agencies. These categories of personnel include specialists in
such fields as accounting, statistics, personnel testing and classification,
manpower planning, management and systems analysis, economic
planning, records and office management, hospital management, and
educational administration. Other management specialties might be
thought of. These fields are characterized by bodies of knowledge and
collections of skills appropriate to instruction and study at the university
level. The specialized personnel produced by mastering the relevant
knowledge and skills are considered to be qualified to practice their
specialties in the public service immediately upon successful completion
of the specified course of study. In these two regards, management
specialists of the kind indicated are similar to professional specialists in
other fields such as engineering, law, medicine, agriculture, and science.
They can be trained at a university and they can practice their profession
upon the completion of their university training.

This review of the normal and natural role of the university in
producing designated types of management personnel makes it possible
to sort out the kinds of training for management which do not fit easily
into the university framework. One of these kinds is that which is more
appropriately handled at the diploma or technical-institute level. This
level of training includes bookkeeping, office management, and
procurement and stores. These are the management services badly
needed but often missing in rural cooperatives and in small industries
and family enterprises. Most countries would be well advised to include
competent instruction in these areas in their technical and rural institutes
as a standard component of their offerings. Those countries which now
do give some attention to the management personnel needs of
cooperatives, as is true of Pakistan and Egypt, are inclined to do so
through separate cooperative management institutes, and they are
similarly inclined to deal with personnel needs of small enterprises

through small-industries institutes or centers. Such specialized centers may have their place, but because they are outside the regular streams of diploma-level education, they are expensive to operate and they are limited in their enrollment.

A second kind of training for administration that is mistakenly undertaken from time to time by some universities is the effort to produce full-fledged administrators, or at least personnel whom it is hoped, after a period of apprenticeship and experience, will become agency managers and program administrators. As pointed out previously, administrators are rarely selected and developed in this way, except for the managers of such discrete and specialized institutions as hospitals or schools or prisons or hotels. The production of administrators as such does not lend itself to the same university treatment as the production of professional specialists, such as engineers and doctors and scientists and even specialists in aspects of the management field. Too many personal attributes of character, personality, and aptitude must combine with acquired knowledge and skill as recorded in the evidence of performance to permit formal selection and training at the early age typical of the regular university pattern. Many universities would make life easier for themselves by abandoning the attempt to offer courses designed to train administrators in this broad professional sense.

Neither are universities always the best kind of institution to provide the specialized kinds of educational courses and experiences needed by older men and women who, after demonstrated aptitude, are selected for special preparation to qualify them for highly responsible administrative posts. Such special programs should be tailor-made in content, method, and length to meet the particular needs of the individuals involved. Occasionally a university's extension service is equipped to arrange such special courses and activities. Usually, however, the IPA is better equipped to perform this post-entry training function.

This identification of a university's role in the field of training for administrative work is by no means the entirety of the university's function in this field. The university has the added obligation and opportunity to increase through research the general understanding of the nature and processes of organization and administration in their several manifestations, chiefly in the environment and in the circumstances of the host country's system and needs. Acceptance of responsibility in this research area involves postgraduate research and teaching in various aspects of organization and management, decision-making theory, and comparative practice. This kind of university graduate program in administration could be expected to advance specifically applicable knowledge of value to practitioners and to specialized management institutions not only in the form of reports and articles and books but also in the form of case studies and other teaching materials based upon local situations. A program of this nature might also produce teachers of administrative subjects for specialized programs and highly skilled analysts in aspects of public administration. Research and teaching in administration at this level can and should be enriched by contributions from several disciplines including political science, economics, sociology, psychology, law, and engineering (systems). The growing popularity of university centers of public policy and administration which are interdisciplinary is evidence of the breadth of the academic knowledge and expertness that is involved in management studies.

There is still another dimension to the university's role in management training and research, namely the introduction of relevant aspects of management analysis and the administrative process in the training of professional personnel in substantive fields such as agriculture, engineering, and health. It has been emphasized in earlier chapters that the realization of professional and technological opportunities in development, and even the fulfillment of the individual professional's potential contribution, depends upon the expression of such contribution in administrative terms which are managerially feasible. The full accomplishment of a profession depends upon this administrative factor and therefore should be a part of the working knowledge of the professional, acquired at least in part through his university training.

This addition to the professional's development would make him more productive, personally, and it would strengthen the competence of the agency of his employment, public or private, in the accomplishment of its substantive goals. The interaction of management with substantive fields, the sectoral areas, should be productive not only for the sector professionsls, but also for professionals in administration. Administration does not exist for itself but rather as the process by which some substantive program is effectively carried out. Students of the administrative process may and must, therefore, learn from analyses of that process how it is involved in interaction with tangible sectoral and substantive activities and programs.

The universities of developing countries have generally been slow to act upon their several and unique opportunities and obligations in the field of management training and research. This tardiness in their effective performance in this field is partly, even largely perhaps, due to the failure of many colonial regimes and their immediate successors to understand the new dimensions in scope and technique of public and development administration and its new requirements in terms of research and university teaching. Even today, in many countries, including India, Pakistan, Malaysia, Kenya, and Nigeria, generalists are sought for the opening posts in the administrative service, generalists with good records in history and the classics. Let it be emphasized that a good liberal education is an exceedingly important part of the preparation of the civil servant, whether technological or managerial, and the provision of such education is one of the essential services to be performed by the university. It might be added that such liberal education ought to include a somewhat fuller exposure to the nature and process of political and administrative and economic systems as well as to the contributions of philosophy and literature. Nevertheless, because of their preoccupation with liberal education, the universities emerging from the period of colonial dependence were not generally conscious of their training obligations in the management field.

The government manpower planners of most countries were similarly blind to the enormous and specialized requirements of public administration in those countries. The catalogs of professional manpower needs given to the universities as guides listed prominently doctors, engineers, scientists, and agriculturalists. The catalogs also included economists, accountants, statisticians, and systems engineers who are involved in aspects of management and the administrative process, but the need for these specialists was not perceived in those terms by the government or university planners. It must be remembered, too, that in many educational systems of colonial and newly independent countries, such as India, Pakistan, Nigeria, and Indonesia, the universities were only nominally in charge of professional training. The engineering, medical, agricultural, and education colleges tended to be controlled in terms of curriculum, student selection, and teachers by the government ministries or departments of public works, health, agriculture, and education. These ministries considered such colleges to be integral parts of their own personnel establishments rather than as autonomous complements of higher education. The universities were mostly collections of undergraduate arts and sciences colleges. The conversion to full-fledged university status of institutions having responsibility for planning and conducting professional and postgraduate teaching and research as well as undergraduate instruction has been difficult and understandably slow in evolving. It is not surprising that the somewhat obscure personnel demands of development administration are slow to be recognized and acted upon.

In spite of these reasons for delay and the traditional inhibitions to the creation of university programs specifically designated as dealing with "administration," universities are now quite rapidly extending their offerings in that field. This recent trend is due in part to the overall logic and requirements of the situation. More direct influences are those of the new schools of business administration and the applicability of much of their expertness to both the public and private enterprise sectors; the glamor of computers and the use of data systems in public administration; and the growing recognition on the part of economists and planners that plan implementation involves the attention of professional administration. As these and other influences are felt, and particularly as university planners analyze their professional training responsibilities in the light of government requirements, universities will increase their role in management training and research.

In-Service Training

In-service training—post-entry training—is distinguished from pre-entry training in that it consists of training and learning experiences of individuals after their employment in an agency and also after completion of the appropriate level of pre-entry training in the formal educational system. This pre-entry training is sometimes distinguished from post-entry training by calling it "education," because the vocational purposes of education are to prepare a person for technical or professional work in comparatively broad terms. Post-entry or in-service training, on the other hand, has the purpose of instructing the individual in the performance of a specific job or series of jobs in the environment of a particular and established agency with its distinctive objectives and methodology. It would be a mistake for educational systems to attempt to train individuals only for specific jobs because there is too great a variety of such jobs in too many agencies to make it practicable to do so. The educational system should provide the graduate with a broad enough complement of knowledge and skills in the relevant occupational field to qualify him basically in a type of work, after which a comparatively brief period of orientation and training will prepare him for the specific duties of a particular job. Otherwise the individual would have too limited a choice of job opportunities and, with the passage of time and changes in technology and job specifications, his narrow training would not suffice.

The employee-training function is too often underrated and undersupported as an instrument of management and a component of personnel administration in view of the inescapable fact that the first and probably the major duty of management is to maximize the work effectiveness of the staff. From this point of view, employee training is an indispensable and integral part of good management. Employee training in these terms becomes a major instrument of management, a major vehicle for the management process. This concept assumes the recognition and the expression of a teaching-learning relationship at every level of management, from the first line of employee supervision to the operation of the bureau, the direction of the department, and the administration of the government as a whole.

In-service training is also a major component of personnel administration on a level with other key functions such as recruitment and selection, assignment and promotion, and classification and pay. Assignments and promotion, particularly, cannot be made without the assumption that employees learn on the job and in connection with their employment, that learning can be accelerated and improved by systematic programs of training, and that such learning is reflected in job performance and in qualifications for other and higher positions. If this assumption of personnel growth after employment did not exist, other foundations of a successful and reliable personnel system, such as reasonable tenure in a career and such as promotion from within, would not be very firm. Both personnel efficiency and growth for the future can be advanced by appropriate programs of in-service training.

The several types of employee training can be identified by purpose. The first of these purposes includes the induction of new employees into the public service as a whole, orientation to the agency and unit of assignment, and indoctrination in the philosophy, purposes, and methodology of the program of concern. This induction-orientation-indoctrination process is best handled by the personnel office of the operating agency of assignment, although it should include contributions from the civil service agency of the system and particularly from the line management of the agency and unit involved. If the responsible managers do not participate prominently and sincerely in the indoctrination process, it is often not taken seriously either by the external indoctrinators or by the new employees. A similar arrangement for orientation should also exist, of course, on the occasion of personnel reassignment, depending for its nature and intensity upon the distance in geography and agency relationship from the previous assignment.

A second purpose of employee training is to achieve agency morale and efficiency, that is, the esprit de corps and the work effectiveness of employees in relationship with each other in a unit or a group—on a team. This purpose should be the primary concern of the first level of supervision, where the responsibility lies for securing an understanding of and belief in the work to be done by the unit and also an understanding of the interrelationships and interdependencies of each position and each employee in the unit. This is at the heart of the supervisory function. Agency morale and efficiency must be achieved in addition by assuring understanding, harmonious, and effective relationships among the several units of an agency. This requirement involves the participation of managers at the bureau and department levels not only in informational and instructional activities to achieve the understanding important to good morale but, even more important, it involves the establishment of workable systems of position interrelationships and employee participation to assure job and unit effectiveness and therefore satisfaction.

A third and much more specific purpose of in-service training is to assure and to improve the efficiency of the individual employee in his job. This purpose is usually the responsibility of the immediate supervisor and is accomplished right on the job. There are situations, however, and kinds of jobs, usually highly technical and special, where the supervisor is not a technical specialist, at least not in the fields of all of the employees he supervises, and where therefore assistance from a staff unit or service should be available, although in a functional and training capacity. Generally speaking, the employee would be expected to be broadly qualified to perform well in the job assigned, but he might need not only orientation but also instruction to do his work in the context of the specific policies, systems, and methodologies which have been prescribed. Even after that the experienced and skilled supervisor can often instruct his less-experienced staff in techniques to improve performance, or can arrange for staff members to learn from each other, or to bring experts from outside to advise and instruct—all to achieve individual efficiency on the job.

The fourth purpose of employee training is to prepare the employee for promotion or to give him the opportunity to secure the additional qualifications necessary for promotion. This purpose is important to the agency and the service because, if achieved, it helps in a major way to assure the availability of competent and qualified persons for future vacancies. The purpose of providing opportunities for individual development is important to the employee because it offers him not only opportunities to qualify for advancement but also greater assurance of tenure in his government career. The very existence of such opportunities contributes to good morale. Policies and programs for individual personnel development are appropriately the concern of the service as a whole and of the operating agency; they are usually not the responsibility of the immediate supervisor.

Because in-service personnel training is a significant and integral part of management, it follows that such training should be the responsibility and the function of each operating level of program execution. As in the case of personnel administration as a whole, the focal point for employee training is appropriately the department or the large agency. The central personnel agency, the public or civil service commission, has the important duty of recommending policies; evaluating and coordinating agency programs of training; giving encouragement, assistance, and counsel to them; and recording employee training participation for consideration in connection with retention, assignment, and promotion. When there are government-wide services or cadres which cut across agency lines, the central establishment also has the important duty of arranging for the appropriate sequence of training and work experiences, although most of the specific training would of course have to be done by the agencies of assignment. The use of these service-wide personnel systems or cadres dilutes and weakens the management capabilities and accountability of the individual operating agencies.

The greater the capability and responsibility, and therefore the accountability, for management on the part of an agency, the greater its motivation and obligation for mounting a full-fledged program of employee training to serve the several purposes outlined above. That program would appropriately be the function of the agency's central personnel office. It would properly include making serveys of training needs and opportunities and making plans for realizing them; recommending agency-wide policies and conducting agency-wide activities; and encouraging, assisting, and coordinating the training activities of individual units. The full and effective performance of this training function at the agency level should by no means dilute, but on the contrary support and strengthen, the direct management use of training as an administrative tool, particularly at the first level of supervision.

A wide range of methods is available to the several needs of employee training—a range which is as wide as, and which might even be greater than, the range in a formal educational institution. Instruction can be provided off the job, often within paid hours of work, in longer or shorter courses or seminars over a period of time or in the form of whole-time "institutes" for an intensive period. Individual instruction can be offered in the form of correspondence or supervised reading courses. Individual instruction on the job might involve supervised practice and even rotated assignments. Formal plans involving periods of apprenticeship or internship, alternating periods of work and study, and systematic assignment and promotion through a series of jobs, sometimes also involving classroom or related study, are increasingly being found to be productive in a variety of kinds of public employment. Industrial apprenticeships and graduated on-the-job training systems have long been standard practice in programs involving high levels of technology. The elitist, career civil service systems traditionally and even today are based on this same principle of progressive rotation. It is when the rotated assignment is timed with less regard for the requirements of the job or the responsibility of the management than for the individual's training experience that the system is flawed. Nevertheless, the concept of systematically progressive assignments is uniquely adapted to the training of managers and development administrators.

Not to be overlooked as tools and methods of employee training are leaves of absence for travel and observation and also for advanced study at a university either in the home country or abroad. Such leaves of absence for personal development might be for refresher training or retraining at the initiative either of the agency or of the individual. The study might have the purpose of qualifying the employee in a new methodology in the interest of the agency as well as of the employee, or it might have the purpose of qualifying the employee for promotion primarily in his own interest. The progressively managed agency would be well advised in its own interest to facilitate opportunities for employees to increase their qualifications for advancement through outside study and even to finance such outside study or travel when there will be a direct return in the form of agency competence and effectiveness.

For the purposes of in-service training, it is often appropriate and sensible for those in charge to arrange, by contract or otherwise, for a university or institute of public administration or other institution to provide educational and training services for specified employees and purposes. Such arrangements typically meet the requirements and specifications of the agency and are best understood in this perspective as contract services. These contract programs, often ad hoc and transitory in character, are clearly a part of the in-service training system even though they are conducted by an external agency. The employee training agency might also set up and operate training centers or institutes of specialized kinds, such as community development, or cooperative management or police administration, which are nevertheless a part of the in-service training system.

Institutes of Public Administration

Even if the universities were to perform well their functions of producing management and staff specialists of the quantity and quality needed, and even if in-service employee training programs were well conceived and executed, a vitally important training function would remain—namely, the training of agency managers and development administrators at senior levels. The performance of this function is the unique and special duty of an institution here called the Institute of Public Administration, the IPA. To discharge the responsibility, at this senior level, for training personnel in the problems and processes which distinguish agency management and development program administration, the IPA must clearly be an agency of first quality with the status and prestige and influence needed to gain the respect of its clients—its students—and to produce results in administrative methodology to meet the needs of the government's development administration.

Dozens of institutes of public administration were set up in countries all over the world in the 1940s and 1950s and 1960s, when many countries had recently gained their independence and were gradually formulating their own systems of administration. A major motivation for the creation of many such institutions was to train large numbers of civil servants for a burgeoning bureaucracy. A second but laggard objective of the typical IPA was to serve the management personnel needs unique to new and rapidly growing social and economic objectives and programs. Unfortunately, the typical country loaded upon its institute, or institutes, responsibilities and functions which would have been better and more appropriately assigned to universities and technical institutes in the educational systems or, on the other hand, performed in vigorous and imaginative programs of in-service training. In most cases, had more time been taken and more thought given to the total problem of manpower planning and personnel administration, particularly for management in the public service, the unique and special function of IPAs would have been recognized and provided for. The other requirements of management training would have been met or sought to be met by the universities and through programs of in-service training. As it was, there was often lack of clarity about the specific mission of the IPA, and a miscellany of management-training duties at a variety of levels was frequently imposed or undertaken, many of which would have been better performed elsewhere.

If universities had been expected to expand their offerings to meet government's needs for specialized personnel and yet had refused or failed to do so in sufficient measure, the government could not be blamed for setting up other institutions to meet that need or for asking the IPA to do so. Certainly, that second alternative would be better than nothing, although not quite correct systemically. Many governments have created special training centers to meet highly specialized preservice and particularly in-service needs. Academies to orient new civil servants come to mind as an illustration. Police academies, small industries, and cooperative management institutes and academies for rural development are other examples. Some governments have lumped some or several such training programs with other functions and have put the whole package in the hands of the IPA.

It would be a better solution for the government to strengthen its in-service system, including the creation of such additional training units as may be necessary, than to turn the whole over to the IPA. In the first place, under such circumstances the IPA's distinguishing function becomes blurred, if it was ever sharp at all, and in the second place, and more forcefully, the immediate demands in terms of numbers are bound to relegate the special problems of a few select administrators to second place in the schedule, to be taken up at a later time. In the meantime the staff and program and interests of the IPA will tend to become crystallized. The proper course, therefore, is for the IPA to resist as long as possible the assumption of interests and duties which do not center in senior agency management and in development administration and to divest itself of such extraneous, although perhaps temporarily necessary, functions as soon as feasible.

Once the central mission of the IPA has been agreed upon—namely, training for agency management and development administration and the overall improvement of governmental administrative performance—certain other issues which frequently plague such institutes are more easily resolved. Students, for example, would not be those chosen by the IPA; they would instead be selected by the government as having the potential for holding senior administrative posts. The IPA can render a valuable service by advising the government on the guidelines for selection and even by giving consultation on the selections themselves. Thereafter, the courses and other learning experiences would be arranged to meet the needs of the students—the participants—including the subject matter and also whether such courses and experiences should be long or short, extensive or intensive. It is unlikely under such circumstances that questions would arise as to undergraduate or graduate credits, or degrees. If degrees are desired, arrangements should be made for the candidate to go to a suitable university.

The teachers and staff of the IPA would by necessity be required to be outstandingly and specifically competent in the subject under study. This requirement means that much of the staff for any particular training exercise would necessarily be selected and employed for the occasion and would not be limited to the staff members of the IPA. Such resource personnel would most commonly be found among scholars at the university or among thoughtful and skillful administrators or management staff experts in public or private administration. Borrowing short-time staff from other countries and international agencies should not be forgone. The IPA should, however, have a small number, a core, of exceptionally able staff with scholarly and practical credentials to assure the continuity of an instructional program of quality to support and supplement the visiting teachers and to assure the maintenance of the IPA's esteem in the academic and administrative community.

Another kind of issue is the relative autonomy of the IPA in relation to the university and the government. Many variations of IPA location and status are to be found. Some IPAs are in universities, as is Ghana's Institute of Management and Public Administration; some are in the chief executive's office or are attached to the public service commission, as is the Kenya Institute of Administration; and some are independent, as is Thailand's National Institute of Development Administration. Several very good reasons can be advanced for the establishment of the IPA as a semi-autonomous center in a university. The university's environment and facilities are hospitable, and the interdisciplinary support which strengthens research and teaching in administration should be available. Many of the scholars and specialists who would be desirable as teachers in the institute would normally be found in a good university. The relative autonomy which most universities enjoy would also protect and serve the IPA. On the other hand, any expectation that the institute would be bound by the traditional rules of academia, such as those relating to selection of staff according to scholarly publication and the approval of course offerings according to departmental requirements, would inhibit and frustrate a vigorous IPA.

Similarly, a good case can be made for making the IPA a more or less integral part of the chief executive's establishment or, as a somewhat less desirable alternative, a branch of the public service commission or central personnel agency. After all, personnel training, even for management, is a function of administration as well as a tool of good administration and from that point of view should be an instrument at the immediate disposal of the chief executive. Also, the prestige and weight of a program sponsored and conducted from that high place in the hierarchy has effective influence on the attitude toward it of the establishment and therefore its effective utilization for the purposes of executive development. The drawbacks to this location of the IPA are consequential, however. One of them is that the IPA would most likely be staffed by civil servants who are senior and therefore more likely to be of the old school rather than the change-agent variety of administrator, who are subject to comparatively frequent rotation, and who are often nearing retirement. Another drawback is the tendency of such establishment IPAs to be burdened with the kinds of extraneous duties more appropriately assigned to others. But perhaps the greatest drawback is the inhibition in such a setting to criticism and innovation, which ought to be freely expressed in an institute dedicated to development administration.

All things considered, therefore, the IPA is probably best situated as an independent, autonomous body, the kind that in some countries like India would be called a "chartered body," which has the powers of a public corporation although it is dependent upon the government for funding. Such a body would at least have the prospect of an eminent and qualified governing board, the freedom of personnel action, and the management flexibility to formulate and conduct a program as a peer both of the university and of the establishment office. This position seems best for the IPA. The government can protect its interest in this relationship not only because of its indirect control of the chartered body through its board but also by the very nature of the situation, which requires negotiated agreement on the several individual training exercises for selected management candidates.

The Training Function of the IPA

The specialized function of institutes of public administration, their first and most important function, is to supplement the training and experience of agency managers and development administrators, and especially prospective agency managers and development administrators. The content and the method of IPA training activities is thus influenced and determined by the characteristics of the students, or participants, on the one hand, and by the nature of the subject matter on the other. The participants, ideally, are comparatively mature men and women who have been identified as prospective agency heads or directors of development programs, or those who have already been selected for and appointed to such posts. These participants are older than typical university students and they are not ordinarily seeking an additional university degree. They would have become qualified earlier as professional specialists in some such substantive field as engineering or agronomy or as experts in some area of management such as personnel or planning or fiscal or district management. If they or their government desired the acquisition of an additional degree related to agency or program administration, the natural and best course of action would be to give them leave to enroll in the relevant course in a university.

The training activities of IPAs are consequently offered on a part-time basis over a period of time or on a whole-time, intensive basis over a relatively short period of a few weeks or two or three months. Some countries have established the IPA type of institutions at two or more levels in order to specialize in aspects of administration at progressive stages of complexity and responsibility and at progressive stages of the participants' advancement to more responsible positions. Pakistan has done so, for example, with its national institutes of public administration at the deputy secretary level and its Administrative Staff College at the secretary and joint secretary level. Some countries even go so far as to relate promotion directly to successful participation in the prescribed course in the designated IPA as well as to good performance on the job.

The type of institution called "staff college" is a form of IPA, modeled after the successful and prestigious mother institution at Henley-on-Thames, in England. The staff college is typically concerned with senior officers already posted to highly responsible positions but selected for a refresher course, which consists of the examination of a special and currently important topic or topics. The method which distinguishes the staff college is called the "syndicate" method, which is best understood as a committee or a number of committees that study and discuss an assigned subject in some detail and often prepare a report on it. Staff colleges are now to be found in quite a few countries, including India, Pakistan, Nigeria, the Philippines, and in Addis Ababa to serve East Africa.

The subject matter unique to the IPA is agency management and the administration of development. It should include the management requirements peculiar to public corporations and other public enterprises. The good agency manager need not be an expert in all of the several aspects of technical management, but he should know enough about them, their purposes and processes, to utilize them well in his coordinating and synthesizing task. These specialized phases of management, often represented in staff units, include planning, budget, personnel, accounting and auditing, organization and systems analysis, and data information and reporting systems. The good manager will understand the processes of arriving at and making decisions, and he will understand the concept of delegating authority commensurate with responsibility in arranging for the execution of decisions. This last principle of administration—that of authority, responsibility, and accountability—is of special significance in the accomplishment of a coordinated agency effort. Above all, the successful manager must understand human motivation and behavior and their relevance to his systems and methods of making decisions and of resolving differences in so doing, and their relevance to employment and work incentives and morale. These are among the more important aspects of internal administration. Quite often the IPA will treat them by organizing a seminar or other learning exercise centering on the introduction of a new management system, such as one for planning or budgeting, or the treatment of a difficult problem, such as a demand for collective bargaining.

External administration, which characterizes the conduct of development programs, depends first of all upon reliable and efficient internal administration—agency management. Program execution without an effective operation instrument for internal agency management would be difficult or impossible. Also, development administration shares with agency management many of the same considerations and conceptions of relationship and process. These include, notably, an understanding of human motivation and behavior and the fundamentals of communication, conflict resolution, and decision-making. The processes for reaching viable agreements on relationships effective in conducting programs dependent on more than one agency are infinitely more complex and subtle than those of internal management, but the principles of the methodology are the same.

In addition, the development administrator ought to have a comprehension of the components and dynamics of the development process and the environment of resources, cultural values, and social, economic, and political systems which determines its nature. He should understand the complexities and methods of building new institutions in the form of organizations and systems and networks to accommodate new functions and changed ways of doing things. The development administrator must know the methodology of innovation and how to anticipate and accommodate its consequences. As in cases involving agency management, the IPA can find many opportunities to approach these broad conceptual topics by organizing sessions around immediate and practical problems of plan implementation, such as the operation of tertiary irrigation systems or the establishment of delivery systems for seeds, fertilizers, pesticides, and spare parts for a program in agricultural production.

Agency managers and especially development administrators almost always assume responsibility for directing an operation which is composed of several parts, both administrative and substantive, in only one or two of which they can claim to have intimate expert knowledge. The head of a river development authority might be an engineer but have only a peripheral knowledge of irrigation and power distribution and of labor relations and program budgeting. The director of an agricultural development agency might know a great deal about plants but comparatively little about soils or farmers or employee welfare systems. A unique and very special function of IPAs is to supplement the qualification of managers and administrators, or prospective ones, in the areas of their comparative ignorance.

A promising way to meet this obligation is to give particular and intensive attention to the special systems and problems involved in administering programs of sectoral development—such as programs in agriculture, industry, health, education, and communications. The Indian Institute of Management at Ahmedabad has achieved this integration in agriculture with singular success. The challenge is to identify and analyze the way in which administration is effectively applied to each of these fields for the purposes of program planning, budgeting, and project preparation and execution, and each in accordance with its distinctive characteristics and requirements. The prospective administrator need not and cannot be a specialist in all of the fields required in his agency and program, but it is incumbent upon him to understand the overall processes of the sectoral program he is concerned with and the contributions to it of those several fields. The IPA, in helping participants learn to apply administration to selected sectoral programs, can also help distinguish the unique and special requirements of each, and in this way can give impetus to the desirable trend to tailor administration to programs rather than attempt to shape programs to an external administrative machine.

Finally, IPAs have a special and unique opportunity, even an obligation, to give attention to the problems of management which are especially characteristic of public enterprise. It is not appropriate for an IPA to give instruction in all of the aspects of business and related public administration which are common to business management, whether in the public or the private sector. Existing university and business management centers can or should do that kind of training very well. What distinguishes public enterprise management is the need to clarify the points and the ways in which, in administrative terms, a viable balance is obtained between government controls to assure adherence to public policy on the one hand, and enterprise management autonomy to provide program-executing capability on the other. The issues here include relations with budgeting and financing agencies, planning and programming offices, and with the ministries and staff agencies involved with these central systems. The management systems that are related to the resolution of those issues are primarily the financing, personnel, cost accounting, and reporting systems. As in the case of sectoral administration, IPAs can render a distinctive service by focusing on public enterprise management in these terms. These fields of sectoral ad-

ministration and public enterprise management, together with agency
management in general and with development administration in particular, are the appropriate and special domain of institutes of public
administration.

Research, Consultation, and Other IPA Functions

Training is the first and central function of an institute of public
administration, but research is a close second. Training would before
long become sterile without the understanding and insights which are the
product of research and analysis. In the case of IPAs, the subject of this
research attention is of course the institutions and processes and systems
which even today are not well enough understood. Further comprehension of them is a requisite for instruction of high quality about
them. This study, to be even more specific, is immediately necessary to
the preparation of case studies and other analyses and teaching materials
which are relevant to the indigenous situation in which the teaching takes
place. There has been an unfortunate tendency to teach public administration from the textbooks and experiences of other countries and
systems; these are sometimes not pertinent or useful.

Universities also should conduct research on development administration, as should organization and systems analysts in government. Although there is naturally some overlap, not harmful at all, there
are nevertheless distinctions among the research emphases appropriate to
universities, to government, and to institutes of public administration.
Universities are primarily interested in research, sometimes called
theoretical, which it is hoped will lead to fuller and more complete and
more lasting understanding of cause and effect relationships in, in this
case, administration and administrative behavior. Government, at the
other extreme, is most often concerned that its research and analysis, or
the studies done on its behalf, will provide the basis for some immediate
or early action to correct or improve an organizational setup or the
operation of an agency or its systems.

Research of both types, university and government, is grist for the IPA
teaching mill, but it cannot be counted upon fully because it may not be
adequate or timely for the purposes of satisfactory preparation for an
upcoming seminar or other instructional activity. Conversely, if an IPA
were to be required to do all or most of its research to satisfy the
government's operating requirements, and at the government's bidding,
it would not be able to undergird its teaching adequately. The word
"analysis" should be paired with the word "research" in this discussion
to emphasize that analysis, although perhaps comprehended under the

term "research," is peculiarly important as a tool not only to understand organizational and administrative phenomena but also to devise solutions to the administrative treatment of sectoral and other development programs.

The consulting function grows naturally out of the knowledge and understanding gained through research and analysis. Consulting is advice given by an individual or a group or an agency based upon a professional analysis of the problem. Management consulting is not a new phenomenon in private business, nor is it very new in government and public administration in developed countries. Consulting on problems of public management is a comparatively new experience in developing countries, but it is now evolving very rapidly. The Indian institutes of management at Calcutta and Ahmedabad and the Administrative Staff College at Hyderabad are excellent examples. There are indications that, at least in several countries like India and the Philippines, skillful consultation and government action on such consultation may be having a more rapid and beneficial effect on the quality of public administration than any other kind of effort, including that of training itself. It must be remembered, however, that knowledge based upon research, consultation concerning the application of that knowledge, and the readiness of trained personnel to effect the recommended changes are actually inseparable components of the whole process. The growing popularity of management consulting seems to have progressed from the private sector, and specifically from large industry in that sector, to public corporations in the same or related fields, and then to regular government operations.

How to handle the consulting function often poses a difficult policy question to the IPA. Should it go into the consulting business—employ staff for the purpose, and take responsibility for the consulting advice? If so, to what extent will it compete with private management firms for the consulting business of private and public enterprise and old-line government agencies? Should it organize a special and discrete consulting staff for such work, or should it use a kind of multipurpose staff, each member of which also teaches and does research and perhaps performs other duties? There is such a paucity of management consulting talent and capability that the entrance of IPAs in the field has not so far distressed the private firms very much. Most of the IPA business is in public enterprises; not much of it is in the private sector. There is still not enough consulting on the administrative inadequacies of the older government agencies and systems; the danger is that the government will come to overburden the IPAs beyond their talent and strength and to that extent cut too deeply into their resources for research and teaching.

Most IPAs have found it better to share both consulting and research duties and opportunities with teaching staff in order to enrich the professional capabilities of all and at the same time to be able to assign the staff appropriately qualified to each research or consulting job as it comes in.

Even when IPAs do not identify consultation as an institutional function and take steps to organize for it, its role comes up for consideration because staff members are often called upon to take consulting assignments on a personal basis. This activity is usually welcomed by the IPA as a needed service to the community and to the country, but the question arises as to the time and the compensation to be allowed the individual for such consulting activity. Most IPAs now, unless consulting is a regular and paid function of staff, allow and even encourage staff members to consult up to a closely supervised limit of both time and additional income.

The other functions and supporting services of institutes of public administration grow naturally out of the primary functions of teaching, research, and consultation. The staff and participants should, for example, have access to a good reference library. Even more important, the IPA should, unless one already exists in a convenient location nearby, set up and operate a document center. A management document center would store the major reports of and to governments about public administration and about the planning and conduct of development. Most such reports are often not published or made easily and readily available, yet they are the real meat of the research and training diet in administration. The key to the successful operation of a document center is to keep it current and to make it a reliable and accessible depository for such material. Once established, the center is of great value and service to students and scholars from other institutions and other countries as well as to those in the home country. It should, as a matter of fact, include in its files representative and comparative documents from other countries. In these ways the IPA can serve as a clearinghouse in the service of the public administration profession in the home country and also as a point of contact with sister institutes in other countries. Regional professional organizations, such as the Eastern Regional Organization for Public Administration and Management, are effective vehicles to facilitate these beneficial associations.

It is an easy step from research and analysis and consultation, supported by library and document centers, and careful preparation for training seminars on important topics of administration, to the sponsorship of special conferences on policy issues that are of pressing concern to a country's development program and its administration. The participants of such conferences would not necessarily be the regular clientele of the IPA, but would for the most part consist of the administrators and legislators involved in the formulation of the policy under consideration, buttressed by such scholars as had studied the subject. Conferences of this kind, which have been held in Nigeria and several other countries, have been an exceedingly effective method not only of assuring carefully prepared and informed consideration of difficult issues but of achieving wide public discussion of them by virtue of news media reporting and the publication and distribution of conference reports.

The effective and satisfying performance of one or a series of activities and functions leads naturally, if not always easily, to another. The publication of key conference reports, for example, can stimulate the organization of a publications program which might consist of IPA "papers" and even a journal of public or development administration, such as *The Indian Journal of Public Administration* and *Philippine Journal of Public Administration*. Publication opportunities, particularly those in professional journals, are a tangible inducement to scholarship, analysis, and reporting in administration—scholarship, analysis, and reporting which are of importance to the country and region of origin as distinct from writing designed to meet the publication interests of a foreign journal. The encouragement that publication gives to the professionalization of public and development administration is often accompanied by—or preceded or followed by—the formation of a professional organization which, through its meetings and representations, can be a powerful force in support of good public administration.

A somewhat less obvious and less known function which might well be cultivated by IPAs, and one in full harmony with the kinds of functions already presented, is that of serving legislators and legislative bodies with reference services and briefing papers. In many developing countries where representational systems of government are just now emerging, the elected legislators, from up-country and elsewhere, have in many cases not had an opportunity to learn the facts or to understand the issues pertinent to measures upon which they are expected to vote. Neither the legislature as an agency nor the political parties as institutions have as yet evolved a reliable system for briefing their members on these matters. The sponsor of the measures at issue, often one of the government's ministries, is not always as forthcoming as it might be in describing the demerits as well as the merits of proposals advanced, or at least some legislators might fear as much. A non-partisan, disinterested, scholarly briefing and informational service for legislators, badly needed in many countries, is a natural and exceptionally useful function for an IPA to undertake. Such an activity would be a natural outgrowth of the policy conferences.

There is, then, a clear and important role for institutes of public administration, one that parallels the role of universities and government employee training programs, in support of agency management and development program administration. The opportunities for service— training, research, consulting, conference, documentation, publication, and legislative service—are separately, but especially in combination, directly supportive of improvements in administrative performance. As time goes on and the need for such support becomes clearer to more people, and as the potential of IPAs to give that support is better illustrated, more opportunity and scope will be given to them to demonstrate their full place in the public administration establishment.

Note on Sources

The source references listed for chapter 1, particularly those for institution building, and for chapter 9 are pertinent to this chapter. The descriptive brochures, catalogs, and annual reports of institutes of public administration and equivalent institutions are informative. Directly relevant is *The United Nations Handbook of Training in the Public Service,* Sales No. 66. II. H. 1 (New York: United Nations, 1966).

Other United Nations documents on training for the public service include the following:

M. B. Brodie and E. A. Life, eds., *Education for General Management: The Staff College Approach,* UNITAR/74/St/12 (New York: United Nations, 1974).

Report of the Interregional Seminar on the Development of Senior Administrators in the Public Service of Developing Countries, 2 vols., St/TAO/M/45 (New York: United Nations, 1969–70).

Training in Public Administration, Sales No. 58. II. H. 1 (New York: United Nations, 1958).

Other references are listed below:

Adebayo Adedeji and Colin Baker, *Education and Research in Public Administration in Africa* (London: Hutchinson, 1974).

George F. Gant, "A Note on Applications of Development Administration," *Public Policy* 15 (1966): 199–211.

Bertram M. Gross, *The Managing of Organizations,* Vol. 2, chap. 32, "The Expansion of Administrative Education" (New York: Free Press, 1964).

Inayatullah, ed., *Management Training for Development: The Asian Experience* (Kuala Lumpur: Asian Center for Development Administration, 1975).

Hahn-Been Lee, *A Handbook of Development Administration Curriculum* (Brussels: International Institute of Administrative Sciences, 1970).

Sidney Mailick, *The Making of the Manager: A World View* (Garden City, N.J.: Doubleday, 1974).

Mary E. Robinson, *Education for Social Change: Establishing Institutes of Public and Business Administration* (Washington: Brookings Institution, 1961).

Kenneth J. Rothwell, *Administrative Issues in Developing Economies* (Lexington, Mass.: Heath, 1972).

Bernard Schaffer, ed., *Administrative Training and Development: A Comparative Study of East Africa, Zambia, Pakistan and India* (New York: Praeger, 1974).

Donald C. Stone, ed., *Education in Public Administration: A Symposium on Teaching Methods and Materials* (Brussels: International Institute of Administrative Sciences, 1963).

Clarence E. Thurber, "Mobilizing Human Resources for the Administration of Development Programs," part 2 in *Development Administration in Latin America,* ed. Clarence E. Thurber and Lawrence S. Graham (Durham, N.C.: Duke University Press, 1973).

F. J. Tickner, *Modern Staff Training: A Survey of Training Needs and Methods of Today* (London: University of London Press, 1952).

Yip Yat Hoong, ed., *Role of Universities in Management Education for Development in Southeast Asia* (Singapore: Regional Institute of Higher Education and Development, 1972).

11

The Impact of Foreign Aid
on Development Administration

International Organization for
Economic Aid and Technical Assistance

Social and economic development is clearly the concern and the responsibility of each developing country. Economic growth and progress in alleviating social inequities depend upon the programs and policies supported and sustained by each country and upon the national planning and administrative capabilities to assure their implementation. This national initiative and leadership is, however, exercised in an environment of international interest, assistance, and well-intentioned intervention. Development administration, and its application to each sector, must therefore take account of and accommodate the organizations and systems which express the international concern. One such system is that for extending economic aid and technical assistance to developing countries.

Generally speaking, economic aid for development, as distinguished from disaster relief and military assistance, is given in the form of capital or credit on concessional terms, such as lower rates or longer periods, by a wealthier country or organization, multinational or private, to a country or an institution in need. Technical assistance is provided, in the form of advice and personnel training by a country or an organization which has the desired technological or specialized competence, to a country or an institution which lacks but needs such competence. The definitions of these processes are not exclusive in practice because

274

economic aid very often depends upon and therefore includes technical advice and assistance—for the construction and operation of an irrigation system, for example, or for a fertilizer plant, or for the expansion of power supply.

Technical assistance for its part often involves and provides for financial assistance for the buildings and equipment required to make the relevant project complete and fully effective, which would be true, for example, of a project to strengthen indigenous competence in engineering training or in economics research. The basic difference, however, between economic aid and technical assistance is useful in diagnosing them as distinctive and separable types of operations, even though on occasion they overlap and even duplicate one another. Aid-giving agencies are usually devoted to one or to the other; if their work involves both, they organize that work to accommodate the unique characteristics of each. Economic aid and technical assistance together constitute foreign development aid.

Development aid from multinational aid agencies and wealthier countries to less developed countries approximates twenty-five billion dollars a year. (Dollar figures are discussed below, at the end of the next section.) This concessional aid almost certainly does not exclude all of the transactions of the normal market process because the countries reporting their aid do not use a standard formula for distinguishing concessional aid from normal trade. Presumably, economic aid is in the form of grants, gifts, or loans on terms which are superior to those available on the capital market in rate or time or repayment currency. Arrangements for trade and investments which help the economy of a host or recipient country might concurrently be beneficial to the contributing country. It is not easy to determine what degree or amount of concession differentiates an aid arrangement from a normal commercial transaction. In any case some countries prefer and some economists advocate increases in trade and investments of the marketplace to systems of economic aid which are often influenced by political rather than by strictly economic considerations.

Technical assistance, similarly, is not precisely and uniformly defined in inter-country practice. There are thousands of "advisers" reported (to the Organization for Economic Cooperation and Development) to be engaged in technical assistance around the world. Some countries, however, include in their reports teachers and other specialized personnel who occupy regular jobs in the developing country of residence. As many as 40 percent of the total number of experts who are reported under technical assistance may be in this category. Even though their salaries may be paid by a contributing aid agency and even though they may be meeting a shortage of teachers or other personnel in the host country, it is questionable that these persons are involved very actively or effectively in developing indigenous competence or transferring technological capabilities, the contributions usually expected of technical assistance.

In spite of these ambiguities of definition of which planners and administrators of development should be aware, the volume of the foreign aid business in the world is enormous, and the international and national organization to process it is formidable. Because of its size, because of the conditions under which it is given, and because of the ways in which it is planned and made available, not to mention the political factors involved, foreign aid has a substantial impact on planning and administration in every developing country. Even though the motives and methods of foreign aid may be of the purest intent—that is, to help all of the countries of the world become self-supporting members of a harmonious community of poverty-free nations—the impact of that aid must be accommodated by the recipient country if it is to remain in charge of its own destiny and if it is to make the best use of those external resources. Even though exceedingly important, foreign economic aid constitutes only 10 percent or less of the annual development investment of most countries, and this percentage should not dominate the domestic 90 percent.

Since World War II a very large world-wide organization, or, rather, several international organizations, have evolved to administer economic aid and technical assistance. Interestingly enough, these organizations, for the most part, were not established for the purposes of conducting foreign aid, although that is the predominant preoccupation of many of them today. The United Nations, for example, did not include economic development or foreign aid prominently or specifically among its objectives or prospective activities when it was established in 1945, even though Article One of its charter, in stating purposes, contains these words: "to achieve international cooperation in solving international problems of an economic, social, cultural or humanitarian character." It was not until 1947 that technical assistance was identified as a program activity, and another two years passed before the Expanded Program of Technical Assistance (EPTA) was organized under the aegis of the United Nations Technical Assistance Board (UNTAB), composed of representatives of the several specialized agencies of the United Nations. These agencies, including most prominently the United Nations Educational, Scientific, and Cultural Organization (UNESCO), the Food and Agriculture Organization (FAO), the International Labor Organization (ILO), and the World Health Organization (WHO), were the institutions which actually planned and provided the meager technical assistance made possible by the small voluntary contributions of the few donor countries which had the interest and felt that they could afford it. The UNTAB was merely a coordinating body; it had no executive authority.

Similarly, in the field, although there were UNTAB representatives in most developing countries, they were coordinators and not directors of the miscellaneous technical assistance programs of the specialized agencies. The programs had a small beginning, too, consisting usually only of a few "seats for training abroad" and a few foreign experts to serve as advisers, both provisions usually for only one year at a time. The largest of the country programs in those early years of technical assistance amounted to a million dollars a year or less. Perhaps the best results at that time, through the EPTA, were those accomplished by highly qualified short-time consultants, who made reports and recommendations about pressing development problems.

The specialized agencies were not organized for technical assistance, nor did they have the capacity for it, because that function had not been anticipated at their creation. Their systems for selecting personnel, for example, requiring as they did the use of national quotas and systems of government clearance, were clearly designed to serve political purposes as well as the objectives of effective professional advice. At the same time the specialized agencies were not institutions controlled by the United Nations. Rather, they were autonomous, each having its own governing board and field offices, and each intent upon pursuing its particularized and unarticulated path.

The first major step in correcting this rather ineffective capability of the United Nations for technical assistance was the establishment of the United Nations Special Fund in 1958. The fund represented considerably larger amounts of money than were available to the UNTAB, and more than that, these amounts were required to be matched by countries in which mutually agreed upon projects were located. The projects, too, consisted of much more than the comparatively haphazard provision of a miscellany of advisers and scholarships. They focused on pre-investment activities, represented chiefly by surveys and feasibility studies, and they focused most prominently on the building of institutions to provide a developing country or region with the capacity to administer effectively investment funds for development. The Special Fund used the facilities of the UNTAB representatives and the specialized agencies to assess project proposals and to monitor approved projects; it did not set up a field organization of its own. It succeeded, however, by the excellence of its policies and their administration and by the weight of its resources in improving vastly the quality and impact of the United Nations presence in the technical assistance field. A further major improvement in the United Nations Special Fund in 1958. The Fund represented considerably in 1966 by merging the UNTAB and the Special Fund into the United Nations Development Program (UNDP).

In 1969 there appeared another and significant milestone in the progressive improvement of the United Nations program of technical assistance—namely, the completion of *A Study of the Capacity of the United Nations Development System* (see the Note on Sources at the end of this chapter). The achievement of the study lay not merely in the completion of the report but in the implementation of many of its recommendations. The report is also called the "Jackson Capacity Study," after Sir Robert Jackson, who presided over the study commission, composed of knowledgeable and competent as well as prestigious members.

The commission found a deplorable condition of ponderous yet faulty programming by thirty separate, autonomous, and uncoordinated United Nations agencies working in unsatisfactory relation with the subject countries as well as with each other, hampered seriously by inadequate personnel, financial, and reporting systems. The study recommended a system of country programming rather than agency functional planning, under the direction of the UNDP representative, in a decentralized system of decision-making which subordinated the specialized agencies and their representatives to the United Nations program as a whole. The UNDP in New York was strengthened with the addition of qualified technical and program policy and administrative staff with modernized finance and reporting systems. In spite of vigorous opposition from the specialized agencies, many of the commission's recommendations have been put into effect.

A failure has been the United Nations' inability to establish viable generalist and expert personnel systems which would assure the availability of more prompt and more reliable technical assistance, which is, after all, the commodity of concern. The Jackson Capacity Study did not extend to the role of the regional economic commissions of the United Nations, although perhaps these bodies also have a function in an evolving system which provides for further decentralization and coordination on a regional basis. Certainly the desired emphasis on programming of United Nations contributions to strengthen the development programs of the countries themselves might be achieved even more certainly by harmonization with the study and conference activities of these important regional bodies.

The total numbers of fellowships for study abroad and foreign assistance experts provided in 1975 by the several members of the United

Nations family were, respectively, about 17,000 and 15,000; about half of the fellowships and 80 percent of the experts were UNDP-financed, for a total of about five hundred million dollars. This brief review of the United Nations' activities in technical assistance should make clear a particularly important point, namely, that the United Nations' focus and almost exclusive attention in the world of foreign aid has been and is technical assistance and not economic aid. A moribund and for the most part inoperative United Nations agency exists, largely on paper, under the name of the United Nations Capital Development Fund. It was brought into being through the initiative of the developing countries, but has practically no support or, crucially, contributions from the countries of wealth. This action, or lack of it, has left the economic aid function pretty much to the World Bank family and to the more recently established regional banks, and also of course to the bilateral programs.

The International Banks and Bilateral Aid

The World Bank group consists of the International Bank for Reconstruction and Development (IBRD or World Bank), the International Monetary Fund (IMF), the International Finance Corporation (IFC), and the International Development Association (IDA). The World Bank and IMF resulted from the Bretton Woods Conference of 1944, which sorted out financial and economic problems as they appeared at the conclusion of World War II. The IMF is concerned with monetary systems and their stability. For a full decade after its creation, the World Bank was concerned exclusively with the economic revitalization of Europe, but since then it has devoted its energies and its resources to the developing countries. It spurred the creation of the International Finance Corporation (IFC) in 1956 to encourage and support private investment in poorer countries and the International Development Association (IDA) in 1960 to provide credit to the poorest countries on very concessional terms indeed, including low interest rates, long-deferred payments, and payments on occasion in "soft" currencies.

The World Bank and its close collaborator, the IDA, are the giants of economic aid. Their loan programs totaled seven billion dollars in 1977, a very substantial amount although less than half the development aid available from national sources. The World Bank's quality of performance, however, and its prestige is such as to make it the premier influence in the world with respect to economic aid policies and issues. Its investment program has evolved, slowly but surely, from the more traditionally solid loans for utility, communications, and industrial enterprises to the much more difficult financing of education, agriculture, and even population control programs. The Bank proclaims the importance of helping the poorest people in the poorest countries, yet the ways of giving this help are obscure and not easily come by.

There is now a full complement of regional development banks, also, including the Inter-American Development Bank, the Asian Development Bank, and the African Development Bank. These are international banks with the same general purposes as the World Bank but whose focus of interest is in their respective regions. They are members neither of the United Nations nor of the World Bank families, although they are not vigorously opposed by the World Bank and are encouraged by the United Nations and its regional commissions, which would be happy to have a sponsoring relationship. These regional banks are compiling impressively helpful records and, although there has been occasional competition with the World Bank for choice projects and even less occasional disagreement about the viability and priority of certain others, the bankers seem to have a way of seeing development projects which make the projects look alike. The banks are finding ways now to share and divide projects and to exchange information about regional economic trends and prospects. Their lending programs now total about two billion dollars a year.

It is important to understand that the World Bank group especially, but also the regional banks, have the authority, and have exercised the authority, to employ outstandingly competent staffs without the political complications of national ratios and clearances which plague the United Nations and its specialized agencies. They also have installed modern financial and reporting systems and have avoided, so far, most if not all of the insidious evils of political interference in policies or actions on loan applications. Wider representation and more frequent public conferences on development bank programs and policies have contributed to the preservation of this relative autonomy. The World Bank and regional banks appear to have the administrative capabilities they need to perform their essential function, which is economic aid for development.

In spite of the elaborate and quite comprehensive worldwide machinery to support international development through economic aid and technical assistance, most of such aid and assistance is provided through bilateral programs in a country-to-country arrangement. Not to be forgotten in this context are the aid programs of private philanthropies, foundations such as Ford and Rockefeller, which have had not insubstantial activities of some notable significance in key areas including rice, wheat, and maize breeding, economic planning, and university development. These private foundations often have the advantage of being apolitical, bent only on being of assistance rather than accomplishing other and external policy objectives. The overwhelming volume of foreign aid, however, both economic and technical, is on a bilateral, government-to-government basis.

Many developing countries that are recipients of aid would prefer that it come from and through multilateral rather than bilateral channels. Their views are shared by many, although not all, specialists in the development process, who are more concerned with equitable modernization than with the international political game. Multilaterally provided aid is considered to be comparatively neutral in its effect upon domestic politics, and to have relatively fewer strings or conditions of use than bilateral aid. Also, its availability in volume is thought to be more equitably allocated through the international organizations. The donor countries continue to prefer programs of direct aid, however, as evidenced by the proportion channeled in this way, and for reasons which are just opposite to those of the multilateral school. They often do wish to influence the political and economic policies of the recipient countries, at least indirectly. They desire, not unnaturally, that credits be applied against purchases of advantage to them, and they are inclined to allocate funds to countries where there is a special interest, political or economic. The wealthy donor nations have other reasons, too, for conducting their aid programs directly, one being that the international organizations and particularly the United Nations are relatively inefficient in the conduct of their aid activities, and another being that their allocations of funds and their policies of administration are too subject to the influence of international politics.

This distrust of the United Nations and of the other components of the international system as a reliable coordinating and directing instrument for the totalities of the world's aid effort does not negate the feeling of the major donor countries that their bilateral efforts ought to be harmonized in some way. Regional organizations have sprung up to perform this function, such as, for Asia, the purely consultative Colombo Plan for Cooperation and Economic Development, which has the purpose of facilitating cooperation and coordinating assistance. By all odds the most prestigious and effective of these international bodies is the Organization for Economic Cooperation and Development (OECD) and its Development Assistance Committee (DAC). OECD, completely outside the United Nations and the World Bank systems, had its origins in the Organization for European Economic Cooperation (OEEC), which was created in 1948 to coordinate the Marshall and other plans for Europe's economic recovery after World War II.

Composed of the nations of western Europe plus Canada, the United

States, Japan, Australia, and New Zealand, OEEC was converted in 1960 to OECD and assumed, as a major function, harmonizing and maximizing, through its Development Assistance Committee, the aid efforts of the member countries insofar as those happy results can be achieved by staff analyses and member conferences. In spite of its restriction of methods to study and discussion, OECD's work, which is of high quality, does have the influence of forceful analysis and the persuasion of confrontation and the desire to reach consensus. This non-United Nations international bureaucracy can be considered to include the administrative establishments and their new breeds of professional development specialists that have grown up in almost all of the contributing countries. Their purpose is to recommend aid policy to their governments and to manage the several bilateral aid programs. The bureaucracy for handling foreign aid, or rather the several overlapping bureaucracies, are formidable and their impact on the planning conduct of the development programs of the various countries is substantial.

Membership in OECD and its Development Assistance Committee now includes seventeen countries. Their combined "Official Development Assistance," that is, aid given on concessional terms for the purpose of assisting development, totaled almost fifteen billion dollars in 1977 (World Bank, *Annual Report, 1978,* p. 35). Of this program, about one half is in the form of bilateral grants; about one quarter is in bilateral loans; and one quarter represents multilateral flows, chiefly to the World Bank family and regional banks and to the United Nations and its associated agencies. The technical cooperation component provides about 100,000 fellowships for training abroad, and about the same number of experts and volunteers. Bilateral aid in addition to that of OECD members is principally from members of the Organization of Petroleum Exporting Countries—about nine billion dollars in 1977 (World Bank, *Annual Report, 1978,* p. 36)—and from centrally planned economies.

The Impact of Foreign Economic Aid

Considering the fact that foreign economic aid represents only a fraction, as little as 10 percent, of the current capital formation for investment in most developing countries, it might be concluded that such external aid is not very important. The record shows, however, that there is a reliably direct correlation between the availability of foreign economic aid to a country and the growth of its gross national product. This relationship is what might be expected, not only because of the fundamental importance of capital for investment in the development process but also because most poor and underdeveloped countries would not be able to generate and sustain a satisfactory or satisfying rate of growth without the increment of external economic aid, particularly in the form of hard currencies which can serve the purposes of foreign exchange.

The first impact of foreign economic aid is that of its volume, which determines the overall size of the development program as well as its nature. The total amount of the foreign aid and therefore the dimension of the development program is influenced directly by the external judgments of the donors about the capacity of the recipient country to use the desired amounts effectively in economic and management terms, and also by the donors' purely political attitudes and intentions. These considerations that influence the size of economic aid also affect the size and nature of technical assistance, because development projects for their success frequently require the acquisition of the requisite technological competence, and technical assistance might even be stipulated in the terms of the relevant development loan.

Grants or gifts for capital purposes are declining in number and volume, and in any case they have been made and are still being given primarily for enterprises which are non-productive in the economic sense—usually to meet the physical requirements of some technical assistance or institution-building project, such as a hospital, or for some disaster relief or social welfare purpose, such as flood or famine. Capital for investment, whether in the form of credit or loan, is money that must be paid back. The terms of repayment therefore become of great importance as they affect the volume and foreign exchange value of future-year capital for investment. Such terms are chiefly those of the length of time given for repayment, the rate of interest to be paid, and whether repayment can be made in hard or soft currency or in some product of the country. Even with concessional loan terms that are favorable, the more loans there are, and the larger they are, the larger the burden of debt service and of repayment when the due dates finally arrive.

It is not a rare phenomenon now, but rather a common experience, for developing countries to be faced with the necessity of renegotiating a debt for some advantage in size or time, or of reducing drastically and even tragically the continuing programs of investment upon which the sustaining of their growth and development depends. More than one country borrowed too much too soon on terms which proved too difficult and is now faced with bankruptcy unless foreign economic aid comes to the rescue. This combined debt of developing countries, about two hundred and thirty billion dollars in 1977 (World Bank, *Annual Report, 1978,* p. 22), requires for its servicing almost one half of the new

assistance which is available. The diversion of such aid from development to debt service is not the most satisfying use of money.

Because loans have to be repaid, the investors not unnaturally go to
great lengths both to satisfy themselves of the feasibility of individual
projects before advancing the money and to select or adjust projects for
the purpose of assuring as far as possible that their successful completion
will pay off in terms of money. This banker's point of view is usually
held more strongly by the external lender than the internal development
agency, which should and ordinarily does have in mind a broader result
than the limited and isolated monetary success of an individual investment. Illustrations of the conflict between financial profit as the sole
or major criterion of viability and a broader standard in both social and
economic terms are easily, although unhappily, found. The investor
might tend to insist upon the use of a capital-intensive technology, for
example, even one not suited to local conditions, whereas the developer
might prefer a labor-intensive methodology in the project to accommodate such factors in the situation as unemployment and foreign
exchange, even when the rate of financial return might be reduced.

The investor would tend to select a site for the project in terms of its
financial efficiency, whereas the developer might have in mind a location
which, while perhaps somewhat more costly, would serve to even out
disparities in welfare among regions. The investor would no doubt hope
that the price of a project's product, electric power or fertilizer for
example, would be sold at the highest possible market price, or at least
one which would return a comfortable profit. The developer, on the
other hand, might see more advantages in a low or even subsidized price
to motivate and support greater investment and enterprise on the part of
industrialists and farmers and thus to gain an even greater return on the
investment as well as a faster pace in national development.

Clearly, loans must be repaid. The insistence of foreign economic aid
givers, however, that project provisions assure maximum profit for the
individual project often succeeds and, even when it does not, puts the
burden of proof on the domestic developers. The terms finally agreed
upon—and delay is one of the least of the inevitable consequences—
represent an impact on development policy and plan and also on the
terms and conditions of execution and management. Even when
governments guarantee project loans, the impact of the tension between
the disparate points of view of the external investor-banker and the
domestic planner-developer is a major influence on a country's program
of planning and on its development administration.

Aid-giving countries customarily, although not always, attach conditions to their loans in addition to the usual understanding of purposes

and terms. Such conditional loans are called "tied"; they have strings attached to them. A typical and very common condition is that the equipment for a project be procured in the lender's country, even though the price may be higher and even though the costs and problems of maintenance be greater. Or the lending country may insist that the project be designed and even constructed by one of that country's firms, although the costs and even the suitability might be less desirable to the recipient country than otherwise available alternatives. Another form of tied aid, frequently prevalent when the loan is in the form of a line of credit, is to require that it be used to finance trade with the lending country or others it designates. Almost all economic aid in the form of loans and credits is tied, and to that extent cannot be considered to be wholly altruistic. And the more tied it is the more difficult it is to make the distinction between concessional economic aid and the normal investments of the open market.

The fact that most economic aid is in the form of tied loans and credits does not make such aid totally undesirable, even though untied aid would theoretically be preferred by the recipient country. For one thing, since practically all aid is tied, one set of strings would merely have to be exchanged for another if credit is to be secured or money borrowed. For another, far more concessional capital than would otherwise be forthcoming is certainly available to developing countries because of the protection given by the terms and conditions to the lending countries. These lending countries, although perhaps in some respects wealthy, frequently have their own problems, and severe ones, of trade balance and of foreign exchange flows. If they can be protected at these points, their capital-lending propensities are to that extent encouraged and made more feasible. Nevertheless, the selection and execution of projects in developing countries, and their economic planning and administration, is directly affected by conditions of these kinds which are attached to economic aid, as well as by the magnitude and the terms of such aid.

Economic aid is ordinarily in the form of money or money credit, but occasionally it is in the form of a commodity. One of the better known of these and perhaps the one creating the most serious impact problems is known as the United States "P.L. 480" program. P.L. 480 is a public law, numbered 480, which provides among other things for the supply of enormous quantities of food grains and other commodities, formerly surplus in the United States, to selected developing countries having serious food deficits in return for payments which are deferred until such time as the payment funds can be used for mutually agreed upon development projects. This scheme, which appeared to be so sensible and practicable when it was conceived, was devised to solve simultaneously the problems of food needs, capital needs, and grain surpluses and concurrently to provide exceedingly welcome flexibility and resources to the development programs of countries with enormous burdens and barriers to growth, countries like India and Pakistan and Indonesia.

Two unforeseen and unfortunate consequences flowed, however, from this commodity form of economic aid, even though some good was done as well. One consequence was that, assured of generous supplies of food for a number of years, countries receiving P.L. 480 assistance were inclined to give lower priority to the strengthening of their own capacity for food production and to devote their major efforts to other sectors of the economy. The second consequence was that enormous amounts of local currency representing the reserve to pay for the food grains was accumulated on the books of the receiving-owing countries, to the point that the reserve offered a major threat of runaway inflation and even bankruptcy. This P.L. 480 "debt" became a thorn in the relationship of the lending and borrowing countries, a thorn that grew sharper through the years. Large proportions of the P.L. 480 loans to India and other countries have now been canceled, and other parts have been assigned to more viable uses and settlements. India has also increasingly focused efforts on its agricultural program, but still without the success of self-sufficiency which might have been more nearly approached if the external supply of food had not blunted India's perception of its danger and its problem.

Foreign aid is not infrequently dependent upon other and different kinds of conditions imposed by the national or international donor. The World Bank, for example, pushes to the point of insistence its advocacy of projects and project modification which reflect its own judgment about propriety and priority in a government's development policy— about population and family planning, for example, and about orientation for development in the interests of disadvantaged and poor people in poor regions. No matter how justifiable, these conditions are strings. The United States denies assistance to certain countries which are in gross violation of human rights as found by suitable international bodies. Many countries are more inclined to give development aid to those who follow consistently acceptable economic and political policies than those who do not, and to those adhering to previous colonial groupings. One way or another, practically all foreign economic aid has strings.

Foreign economic aid is an exceedingly important and in many cases an indispensable element in a poor country's development effort. The nature of this aid, however, in the form of loans or credits from lending agencies or from wealthy countries, is such as to have a tangible impact on the developing country's program of projects, its planning activities, and its development administration policies and systems. This impact is represented not only by the volume of money or commodities made available through the aid program but also by the terms and conditions attached to its availability, the inevitable repayment burden, and the intrusion of the resulting external judgments and interests which color and influence decisions in development planning and administration.

The Impact of Technical Assistance

The volume and quality of technical assistance as well as the amount and forms of economic aid have an immediate and direct bearing on a poor country's progress in development and, therefore, on its planning and administrative considerations. Technical assistance is needed in the planning and conduct of development programs and projects when a country does not have the requisite technology or expertise or a sufficient supply of personnel to apply that technology or expertise. Technical assistance can therefore be provided in the form of expert personnel to fill the gaps in the host country's complement of trained manpower, or in the form of training of such staff to make up the deficiency, or in the form of institution building to create the agency and system capacity of a country to meet its requirements for technology, expertise, and specialized personnel.

Most developing countries receive technical assistance of all three types at the same time, often through the same project or projects. The extent to which such technical assistance is available to them inevitably influences the priorities of development programming. Projects which can be supported well by technical assistance can proceed, whereas those which are not so supported, in the absence of indigenous talent, must falter or be deferred, regardless of the importance of or the need for the project as measured in other terms.

Technical assistance which is effectively and directly related to a country's development program has a desirable impact, whereas technical assistance activities not so related have a distracting effect and can even impede, at least for the time being, the pace and effectiveness of the program. The achievement of this effective relationship depends first of all upon its consistency with the methodology required to make and carry out a development plan which has government and public approval and support. The aid-giving agency which proposes to provide the technical assistance must also accept and respect at least that portion of the plan, that project or program, to which the assistance is to be supplied. If this coincidence of interest and understanding is not achieved, the project either will not be undertaken or it will be launched on a shaky and unreliable course. The comparative impact of the two circumstances of technical assistance is readily seen. A very particular aspect of this dimension of technical assistance is the importance of relating it to economic aid. The projects or programs to be financed from foreign loan sources often depend upon technical assistance, or at least can be advanced in time or improved in quality if good technical assistance for them is forthcoming. Conversely, technical assistance projects can themselves, for their own purposes of developing indigenous competence and capacity, benefit from their application to a well-financed development project.

The very number of foreign experts in a country, their sheer volume, produces an impact of consequence upon both the character and quality of the assisted agency or system and the operational capacity and patience of the host country. When they are found in quantity in a single agency or system, the foreigners will obviously color the pattern of institutional behavior with their own cultural inclinations, even when not by deliberate design, and thus will influence its style and methods of performance and will complicate the long process of institutionalization. Quantities of foreigners in several agencies in a community can have a similar impact upon that community. Moreover, the dependence of such agencies, systems, and communities upon sizable proportions of foreigners in their key staffs increases the severity of problems of timing when there are delays in filling posts and the severity of problems of orientation when new experts are assigned.

In addition to these problems of the volume of foreigners in the work environment are those of accommodating all of the guest experts and their families and support personnel with special housing and with arrangements to import or procure the transport, furnishings, and consumable commodities, and the problem of accommodating supporting establishments of foreign schools, medical services, and even stores. Some host countries, notably Thailand, have gone so far as to provide some of these special facilities, housing in particular, at their own expense. In any case most countries must set up operations offices to serve these foreign groups and to facilitate the procurement of their special privileges of import and consumption. This burden increases geometrically if the indigenous staff, and the native residents of the community in addition, are repelled by ostentatious standards of living achieved in part through their own country's support and yet which seem deliberately to differentiate the foreign expert from his national counterpart.

Foreign experts are not infrequently employed in regularly established positions because there is not a sufficient supply of adequately trained persons in the host country. This form of employment is often included as a component of what is known as technical assistance. More narrowly defined, however, and more appropriately, technical assistance involves giving advice or training indigenous personnel in the application of some new technology or other expertness. These technical experts are engaged either in giving advice about the solution of some policy or project or program problem, which might take a short time or a long time, or in assisting in the development of indigenous capacity by helping to set up or modernize an agency or system and helping to train the personnel to man the agency or system—institution building. Whether of the problem-solving or the institution-building kind, a large part of the successful viability of the foreign expert's advice depends upon its applicability to and in the indigenous situation.

The foreigner's advice is bound to have some impact, if it is followed to any extent, because his advice would not be needed if customary ways of doing things would suffice. Foreign ways of doing things, however, even when they involve a new technology, are not often transferred for adoption and application without change. On the contrary, most new systems that are successful in their establishment are not those which represent an automatic transfer from one country with one set of cultural systems to another country with a quite different culture. Rather, new systems and agencies which are successful in their establishment and operation are those which are adapted and adjusted to the environment—political and social—while accommodating the requirements of new technology and new competence. The astuteness of the foreign expert advising on this transfer of an institution and its adaptation to the local situation, as well as his technical expertness, is therefore a factor in the softening of the inevitable impact of the new institution. Technical assistance cannot be separated from the impact of change.

The foreign experts themselves, as individuals, but also including their families, constitute a large portion of the total impact of foreign assistance in and on a country. It is required only to consider their qualifications as professional specialists to understand their relative capacity for acceptance and effectiveness. This qualification of expertness is not the only measure of effectiveness, however. It can be diluted to a substantial degree of ineffectuality or increased to a very high rate of accomplishment according to the expert's attitude toward his assignment and his ability to work with his hosts in making the necessary and desirable adjustments in the project to reflect the environment, and according to his skill at organization and implementation. Experts carefully selected according to these several considerations of suitability are far more likely to achieve the productive technical assistance result desired than those whose qualifications are defective or deficient in one or more of these areas of relevance.

It is not only the individual expert and his qualifications which count toward the success of his project but also the relationship of the expert to his fellow experts, to his sponsoring aid agency, and to the counterpart personnel of the host country. The relationships of the sponsoring aid agency with the host country, whether the agency is national or multinational, public or private, are also directly relevant to the quality of the environment for the best delivery of technical assistance. These relationships depend in the first instance upon full understanding and agreement concerning the purpose and nature of the project itself. Of equal importance is the same degree of understanding and agreement on the points of responsibility—who is actually in charge, the agent or the host country or the representative of the aid agency? Does the aid agency assume the accountability for the quality and nature of the advice and assistance which is given, or only for the competence of the foreign expert or experts it provides? Is the technical assistance effort in connection with a particular project expected to be a coordinated effort of the several experts working as a team or of individual advisers working directly with assigned counterparts?

The first rule is that there must be clarity on these points, and not confusion, to achieve the maximum benefit of the assistance effort. The second consideration is that some systems of technical assistance relationships are better than others, depending in part upon the particular situation but depending also on underlying concepts of the technical assistance process. By and large it is the host country and its representatives which should be in administrative charge of the aided project in order to achieve realism in the steps of building the institution; the aid-giving agency, or even its subcontractor, is well advised to recognize the responsibility of the experts themselves, selected usually by agreement with the host country, for the advice they give. Other systems diffuse and confuse the exercise of authority and responsibility in a complex situation already compounded by international and interagency complications.

Perhaps the greatest impact of technical assistance is derived not from the advice of foreign experts or from their employment to fill personnel gaps, but from the training of indigenous staff. It is the availability of fully qualified personnel and the creation of an institutional environment that supports their work which make possible the introduction of a new technological or other system or the establishment or creation of a new agency competent to achieve its purpose. The overriding importance of this personnel factor in institution building cannot be emphasized too much. The training of only a few local experts as a one-time effort almost never suffices because, first, their minority position in potentially hostile association with untrained but senior colleagues muffles their voice and influence and because, second, there is no assured source for their replacement.

The greatest technical assistance impact is quite frequently derived from projects to establish and strengthen training and research institutions so that there may be a sufficient and continuing supply of trained personnel. Even for these projects, however, and for other types of technical assistance, a major component is the training of staff or potential staff in suitable educational institutions in other countries. The major considerations in making such arrangements are that the training be relevant to the staff needs of the project and that the number trained be large enough to assure the effective manning of the project. If a bare minimum of trainees is provided, then loss through accident and failure, and even more by hiring away by other agencies, will threaten the project. Even more significant, perhaps, the returning specialists will not have enough weight in the planning and conduct of the new program as against the larger number of staff members, who are often older and, perhaps, jealous of persons trained abroad.

The impact of numbers is a very important factor in staffing new institutions. This impact can have unforeseen aspects, too, although some of those aspects could, with the exercise of some imagination, be anticipated. One such aspect is often the manifestation of a desire on the part of foreign-trained staff, even junior staff, to participate in the making of program and administrative decisions in the agency and to press for new systems of employee representation in management. Adjustments to these several impacts of technical assistance are a part of the process of establishing new agencies and systems for development and consequently become in themselves components of the technical assistance field. Certainly these impacts and adjustments to them are important in planning and administering development programs.

The Impact of Foreign Aid Methodology

It is not only economic aid and the provision of technical assistance which have a substantial impact on planning and administering development by individual countries and for selected regions; it is also and equally the methodology of foreign aid—the ways in which external assistance is planned and given and monitored by national and multinational agencies. These methods of external agencies are designed in part to achieve objectives which may or may not be consistent with the objectives and especially the priorities of the host countries. Such objectives range from narrow and selfish ones, such as preference for a project because of its prestige value as a highly visible structure—a football stadium or hospital, for example—or the imposition of designated social policies and reforms, such as those for population control and regional distribution of income. These externally derived objectives, whether national and political or international and idealistic, together with the conditions attached to loans and technical assistance, motivate aid-giving agencies to adopt aid-giving practices which are consciously designed to influence a recipient country's development plan and the execution of that plan. Additional and perhaps more legitimate, or at least more easily understood, objectives of external intervention are to assure the effective and efficient use of aid both in terms of the country's overall capacity to absorb it and in terms of the economic, technical, and management feasibility of any particular aid project under consideration.

In both bilateral and multilateral systems of giving aid the donor agencies tend to retain, by the use of three devices, a substantial degree of influence over the development program they are assisting. One of these devices is the requirement of matching funds as a condition of aid—matching funds to be put up by the host country for a project as evidence of its interest and its intention to support the project fully in the long run. This matching condition may be, and probably is, a justifiable basis for assessing the value of a project to a country, but it also represents an external influence of major impact on the country's plans, priorities, and budget. A second way in which a donor sustains its leverage in the development program being assisted is to give its aid for short periods of a year or a small number of years rather than to assure it for a long time. And the third way is to give aid for specifically defined projects rather than for broad program purposes. It is true that some donors might wish to give assistance in more flexible terms of time and purpose but are unable to do so because of uncertainties about their own financial resources in future years or because of legislative or other political restraints. In general, however, the inhibiting effects of these externally generated practices upon development plans and their administration are manifest and, in truth, the external agencies do have the intention of intervening in and influencing those programs.

Bilateral programs—programs of aid given by one country to another—are now characterized by comparatively large aid missions, related closely to or embodied in the embassy, and by a supporting bureau in the home capital, which is often quite sophisticated in its analytical and aid methodology and is often well staffed with professionally trained personnel. These agencies of the wealthy aid-giving countries have the function of finding and acting upon aid projects that are consistent with their own country's policies and objectives in relation to the host country's development program. Many such agencies, particularly the less affluent ones, limit the fields of their interest and expression of aid in order to enlarge that aid's comparative impact. They consider project ideas which are suggested to them by the host country in the fields of their interest and in accordance with the terms prescribed by their country's policy. Typically, however, they advocate particular projects of their own fancy because of their preference for such projects, or their known expertise to support them, or because professional specialists on their staff advocate them. The capital cities of many developing countries are well populated with members of aid missions from other countries, each mission advancing its own ideas of development and not infrequently contradicting or competing with one or more of the other missions.

The effect of this multiplicity of resources for assistance is heartwarming and exciting but also confusing and disrupting in its impact on development planning and administration. OECD has had some effect in harmonizing its members' aid policies and programs overall, but its limited efforts to achieve coordination at the country level have been rather feeble and ineffective—and indeed possibly inappropriate, considering the coordinating interests of other international bodies and, particularly, of the host countries themselves. Nevertheless, "coordinating groups" of OECD members were set up and used in the past for such countries as Thailand and Turkey to share and discuss information about the environment for aid and about the possibility of greater articulation of the aid projects of the several donor countries. These efforts did not amount to much.

Having acted with surprising and welcome effectiveness on many of the recommendations of the Jackson Capacity Study, UNDP has placed emphasis on country programming, which has been a boon to the planning and programming agencies and processes of aided countries. The stated focus of UNDP's programming is the country, and its perspective is that country's own development plan. The delegation of more program authority to the local UNDP representative and the dilution of the project authority of the specialized agencies has contributed further to the strengthening of country programming.

It should be remembered, however, that United Nations foreign aid is in the form of technical assistance and not in the far weightier area of economic aid. And it should be noted that the representatives of the specialized agencies are still not timid about advocating and even pressing for projects inspired by their home offices in Paris, Rome, Geneva, or elsewhere. Sometimes these special interests are represented by and buttressed by especially appropriated and allocated funds, such as world-wide campaigns to restrict population growth, to protect the environment, to grow more food, and to eradicate illiteracy. These functional approaches to development, no matter how worthy, do have an immediate and distinctive impact on the development programs of individual countries.

Another kind of impact that the United Nations has on country development programming is that expressed through the efforts and activities of the United Nations regional economic commissions established to "harmonize" the development plans of the several countries in each region and to encourage selection and location of development projects on the basis of international and regional as well as purely domestic considerations. The coordination of trade and monetary and shipping policies and programs, and the encouragement of cooperation in these areas among the countries within a region, are stated objectives of the regional organizations. The accomplishment of these regional goals, although they would presumably produce country benefits, certainly requires for its success the cooperative participation of the countries involved as reflected in their development plans and programs. Regionalism is having a growing, and it could have an overriding, impact on the planning for development by individual countries.

In spite of the sound purpose and orientation of the country programming system of UNDP, it is the influence of the methodology of the World Bank group and particularly of the World Bank itself which has greatest effect upon development planning and administration in the several poor countries. This impact derives from the weight of the resources available through the Bank for economic aid and equally from the enormous influence of the Bank on the policies and projects of bilateral donors: the World Bank tends to set the patterns and the styles—the norms and standards—of economic aid. But also of great impact are the methods by which the World Bank studies, analyzes, and reacts to the environment and opportunities for development in poor countries, countries of the Third World.

The basic surveys made by the Bank consist of periodic country economic reports and sector studies. The country economic reports are the product of comprehensive survey missions composed of Bank staff and selected consultants. Sector studies are analyses made in some depth by Bank staff in cooperation with professional personnel from the relevant specialized agency of the United Nations, such as UNESCO for education and FAO for agriculture. Although both the comprehensive economic surveys and the individual sector studies had their origin in the Bank's need for a reliable basis for its loans—investment programs and operations—they very soon became, in addition, the basis for the Bank's uninhibited advice to a country about its development program as a whole and about its priority needs and project opportunities in the several sectors. The Bank points with pride to changes in educational policy and agricultural strategy and even organization for development which have been suggested in its studies and pressed for by its officials, often with the implication that further external investment depends upon positive response to the Bank's initiatives. These comprehensive surveys and sectoral studies are undertaken by the Bank at its initiative, not at the request of the subject country, although with its consent, no matter how reluctant. This methodology has major impact, obviously, on a country's planning and development system.

This impact of World Bank methodology is multiplied by the weight carried by the Bank's findings in the councils of other dispensers of economic aid. The Bank's formal reports and the Bank's formal and informal advice set the tone for attitudes toward needy countries. The consortium, or "club," is the most formidable of these expressions of the Bank's influence. A consortium, usually for a country like India or Pakistan, is a forum composed of supporting countries and international contributors presided over by the Bank and attended also by the recipient country. There, usually once a year, the plans, projects, and programs of the developing country are debated on the basis of the Bank's analysis as well as on the basis of the country's own development program and its presentation. Effort is made to reach a consensus on the dimension of the program and the approximate portions which will be financed by each donor and in what form. The consortium device, which has been typified as bilateral aid in a multilateral framework, is considered by some to be the next best system to a single international-agency conduit of aid. It has obvious advantages for the developing country that is dependent upon enormous injections of foreign economic aid to finance its plan and to sustain its development. The device—and especially the Bank's leadership in it—does have, however, an enormous impact on a recipient country's planning and on its development administration.

Both the United Nations and the World Bank, therefore, exert influence directly on the processes of development planning and administration, and these two prestigious international bodies are not altogether comfortable with each other as they play their roles. As pointed out earlier, the two organizations are distinguished by their functions—the United Nations providing pre-investment technical assistance and the World Bank giving loans for investment purposes. Actually, the Bank is also a source of technical assistance. It is not at all uncommon for the Bank to give technical advice and assistance in connection with pre-investment studies of loan prospects or as a part of the process of perfecting a specific loan application. Technical assistance is a normal part of the Bank's process of monitoring loans. Advice is involved in follow-up action on comprehensive economic surveys and on sector surveys for project identification and preparation. From time to time the Bank has gone so far as to provide technical assistance missions to help establish or strengthen country planning systems and organizations to sustain those systems. The Bank feels somewhat uncomfortable in this planning role because of the prospective conflict of interest between a Bank-advised country proposal and a Bank-analyzed loan decision.

Thus the powerful World Bank group and the prestigious United Nations system conduct inevitably overlapping functions for the purpose of influencing as well as assisting countries to make and carry out their development plans. It is true that UNDP and the Bank try to keep each other informed and that they invite mutual participation in key conferences. They are beginning to share sponsorship of and membership in ad hoc functional bodies, such as special commissions on agricultural development or population control, to develop mutually acceptable positions and to share appropriate portions of the responsibility for program support in those fields.

The World Bank uses UNESCO and FAO as its preferred contractual advisers and partners in the country sectoral surveys and in assessing and even conducting development projects financed by the Bank. In many loan arrangements now, particularly those involved in building institutions in the fields of education or agriculture, the Bank insists on a component of technical assistance which might be donated by one of these specialized agencies or by some other agency, or which might be paid for out of loan funds. Thus the very system of tension and cooperation emerging from the United Nations–World Bank confrontation has its own impact on systems and methods of a country's planning and administration for development.

It cannot be said that these several impacts and influences of economic aid and technical assistance, along with the policies and operational methods of the bilateral and multilateral donors, are wrong or that they are bad. On the contrary, the overall result of the foreign aid effort is undoubtedly favorable in very satisfactory measure. Even the specific policy and program interventions of the powerful World Bank are considered to have improved the general performance of the affected countries in connection with their development efforts. The fact remains that the several and often diverse impacts of external agencies and forces, no matter how well meant, require coordination and accommodation by the host country if it is to retain even a modicum of control over its own plan and over its own development priorities and programs.

No one doubts the need to coordinate the economic aid and technical assistance available to a country from a plethora of national and international bodies. And there is no dearth of aspirants to the coordinating role, among them UNDP and World Bank representatives in the field and even in New York and Washington. The logical and appropriate place for such coordination, however, is the planning agency of the affected country, because the several impacts have such a powerful bearing on the nature and feasibility of the plan within which they must be accommodated in connection with the plan's preparation and subsequently in the plan's execution. Efforts to coordinate foreign aid in an agency separate from the planning organization only beg the question and leave the coordination still to be achieved. Complaints, on the other hand, heard often from representatives of external agencies to the effect that indigenous arrangements for coordination are not adequate or efficient are not always soundly based because that country agency might deliberately, although uncomfortably for the participants, be playing one donor against another and avoiding sharp clarity in an attempt to retain some measure of flexibility and self-determination. Too often, however, such charges may be true, and under those circumstances it is hoped that the pressure and the efforts will be to apply the proper remedy and not to succumb to further loss of self-determination to external although "efficient" coordination.

Technical Assistance for Planning and Administration

Technical assistance itself, even for planning and administration, has its own special impact on planning and administration for development. OECD members currently provide about 4500 experts in various aspects of administration and 1700 experts in the field of economic planning. Five to six thousand seats for training outside the developing country are financed each year for study in administration and economic planning. Comparable figures representing the magnitude of United Nations assistance in these areas are 450 experts and 500 scholarships. These experts and trainees are in addition to those categories in other fields, such as education and agricultural economics, but who are engaged more or less directly in projects to improve and strengthen planning and administrative processes in either the central or in sectoral or state or local systems. The weight of these numbers of foreigners is in itself substantial. It is not surprising that this emphasis exists, because the several impacts of economic aid and technical assistance already reviewed, in addition to the fundamental importance of development planning and administration, require and demand as much attention as can be given in order to improve the quality and to increase the strength of the indigenous agencies which plan, coordinate, and administer development.

The fields of planning and administration readily attract offers of technical assistance because they are at the center of a nation's decision-making about its vital social and economic policies and activities. These are the prestige areas for technical assistance, and they are also the points at which external agencies may most readily influence decisions friendly to those external interests, whether that influence be selfish or philanthropic in purpose. They therefore attract foreign interest and attention. At the same time, and conversely, many governments consider technical assistance for planning and administration to be especially sensitive and are inclined with respect to projects in these fields to be more cautious about the role and methods of the foreign experts than in projects of a technological or sectoral kind.

This unique sensitivity of planning and administration as subjects for technical assistance is due not only to the opportunity for the exercise of external influence on policies and systems. It is due also to the predilection of foreign aid-giving agencies and their experts, sometimes consciously and deliberately but at most times subconsciously, to reflect in their advice their own largely Western ideologies and values. A large majority of the technical assistance experts in planning and administration are from Europe and North America—the "West" and the "North." They are inclined to advocate systems which emphasize particular forms of law and order and stability as well as program operation and which are designed to perform with a high degree of efficiency and economy. These systems and forms might or might not be consonant with indigenous conceptions of public administration and, more significantly, they might or might not be necessary to accomplish the desired purpose of operating effectiveness in planning and administration in a particular cultural setting.

There is even a tendency on the part of aid-giving agencies, both national and international, to oblige their experts to press for certain systems whose values are held high by the donors but which are not considered so immediately relevant by the recipients, especially in the form advocated. One such focus is the desire of some external agencies to persuade the host country to set up particular kinds of arrangements for public participation in certain fields of public policy and program, a focus which comes close to interference with that country's political systems and therefore with its very form of government. There is no reason to bar the receiving or giving of aid for political development, when mutually and specifically agreed to, but there is much reason to question the validity of ideological pressures not relevant to the project in hand.

Another such focus is the desire of some external agencies and experts to deal with what they perceive to be the problem of corruption. While all might agree on some forms and expressions of action which can be identified as corrupt and therefore not only evil but disruptive to administrative efficiency or effectiveness, there are many more such forms and expressions which might be considered corrupt in one country and its culture but which in another are not only considered not corrupt but which actually facilitate agency performance and the effectiveness of systems operations. For these several kinds of reasons, technical assistance for planning and administration is sensitive and is difficult.

Nevertheless, the volume of such assistance is large and the international establishment to give it is substantial. There is an understandable tendency on the part of host countries to prefer assistance for planning and administration from international, multilateral agencies than from other countries so as to avoid undesirable influence on key policies or systems, or the appearance of such influence. The volume of such bilateral assistance remains high, however, particularly for institutions or processes somewhat removed from immediate involvement with sensitive decision-making, such as an economics faculty or a public administration center on the one hand, or a computer center or an accounting system on the other. Private consulting firms and universities with special competence in planning and administration, such as Harvard University's development advisory service, appear to be more welcome as technical assistance contractors than government agencies, particularly when the host country is able to be the second party to the contract. A major—perhaps the major—contribution by individual nations is their support of leading educational institutions and training centers in development administration and in economic and other aspects of planning and in their provision of fellowships to attend those institutions and centers. The Institute of Social Studies at the Hague, the Institute of Development Studies at the University of Sussex, and the special programs offered by United States educational institutions, including Harvard, Williams, and Wisconsin, illustrate the special attention given to development planning and administration as a field of analysis and study.

International organization to support the strengthening of development planning and administration is even more imposing than the special arrangements of national donors. The specialized agencies have gone heavily into technical assistance projects for planning in the sectors of their interest, such as, in particular, UNESCO in education, FAO in agriculture, and ILO in manpower. The record of these agencies in providing assistance to strengthen sectoral administration is not nearly as good, however, and their record in considering and accommodating management feasibility in their technical assistance projects generally is unimpressive. The United Nations' performance in giving overall assistance to central planning agencies and systems is relatively poor. It has no central office fully equipped to do this work and therefore has relied for the comparatively small number of its undertakings of this kind upon the rather loosely coordinated contributions of the specialized agencies. This somewhat awkward arrangement is diluted still further in its effectiveness by the compulsion to assemble advisory teams from a number of different countries whose specialist personnel might or might not be compatible and consistent in their advice.

The United Nations is better organized for assistance in public and development administration than for assistance in planning. It offers assistance through its Central Division of Public Administration and Finance and counterpart offices for public administration in each of the regional commissions for Asia, Africa, and Latin America, and now, in addition, through the regional office in Beirut. Asia, Africa, and Latin America have their own institutes for economic development and planning—institutes nurtured first by the Special Fund and now by UNDP, and supported by matching contributions from the member countries in the region. These institutes give short courses, for the most part, and have sponsored special conferences and seminars on special aspects of economic development for middle-level and senior personnel who are sent by member countries.

Each region is also evolving its own institutional arrangement to encourage and support development administration. The results of these efforts are the African Training and Research Center in Administration for Development (Centre Africain de Formation et de Recherche Administrative pour le Développement, CAFRAD) and the more recent Asian and Pacific Center for Development Administration. The support of these institutions is also given in the form of short courses and seminars, special studies and conferences, and consultation. Their programs are supplemented by other organizations of a more professional membership character, such as the Eastern Regional Organization for Public Administration, and the African Association for Public Administration and Management. The World Bank is no longer inclined to give technical assistance in a project sense for either planning or administration, although its Economic Development Institute is a major influence in planning methodology and provides outstanding training resources for middle- and senior-level planners. OECD is not an operating or a technical assistance agency, but its Development Center does some of the best research and produces some of the best reports available on various aspects of the development process. It does not, however, focus on planning or administration as such.

Arrangements for the successful provision of technical assistance for planning involve the resolution of interesting and difficult issues of purpose and methodology. Specialized consultation with respect to a specific project being considered in the plan, or even aid with respect to planning the development of a sector or an institution for that purpose, does not involve processes or methods of technical assistance which are markedly different from those of the general run of technical assistance projects. The sensitivities associated with national planning, however, the sensitivities of both the policies of trade and development and the cultural environment for the growth of the system, present serious dilemmas concerning the appropriate role of the external expert. The first question raised is whether the expert or experts, and the technical assistance project as a whole, has the purpose of helping to create an agency, a system, and a methodology of planning, or of helping to draft or even actually drafting the plan. That question is usually answered quickly these days, in order to make it clear that the staff of the host country will prepare the plan, as indeed it should, although not so many years ago the experts were expected to do some or even most of the plan preparation. The primary purpose of the project should be to help to establish a viable and effective institution of central planning.

By limiting advice to the organization, the processes, the inter-institutional relationships, and the other aspects of institution building for planning, it might appear that the sensitive areas of policy are for the most part avoided. This is not the case, for the training of staff often involves close relations between that staff and the experts right on the job. It is difficult in this kind of situation for the national staff and its leadership to refrain from urging the foreign experts to help do the work and even to prepare the plan, even though that process of preparing the plan could be used to train the local personnel for the purpose. Too frequently the foreign experts do not resist the temptation to do this plan-drafting, even to the point of giving that work first attention and neglecting the learning experience of the counterparts. Even when the local staff does the drafting and other work of the planning agency under the tutelage of the foreign expert, and thus increases its competence to do so, it is difficult for the expert to avoid a strongly held position about the rightness or wrongness of policies and projects proposed to be included. Such strong feeling is all the more difficult to avoid when the expert is initiating and therefore advocating the policies and projects in the first instance. Faulty relations and methods in giving advice and assistance can thus cause as much difficulty as misguided purpose in efforts to establish a sound basis for technical assistance in planning.

The other major issue in technical assistance for planning, especially in creating an effective institution for planning, is the training of staff and the assurance of a continuous flow of replacement staff. An important part of staff training for planning should be done in close connection with the agency's daily and regular work. Almost always, however, most members of a new staff have not had the basic professional education necessary to qualify them to perform at the requisite level. Nor are such fully qualified persons usually available on the domestic market. This kind of situation needs to be dealt with both by the provision and financing of study leaves for current staff and by arranging for the establishment of the relevant training courses in the university or other appropriate domestic institution to provide a continuing flow of economists, statisticians, management analysts, and others needed to staff the organization. Even these arrangements may not suffice.

The painful experience of many planning projects is that good staff, after having been trained, is in such demand for high-paying positions in other agencies, such as state and development banks and the universities themselves, that the personnel turnover rate cannot be satisfied. Or, as is also too often the case, the planning agency staff is composed of civil servants who are subject to rotational transfer at the direction of the public service commission or other external personnel agency, and indeed must be transferred under that older system to gain promotion. The training of a large number of professionals, therefore, and the support of a good professional training course or courses are obliged to be indispensable elements of a soundly conceived technical assistance project for planning, together with such adjustments in the civil service system as will allow and encourage professional specialization and promotion in the system or agency of that specialization.

Technical assistance in administration faces many of the same problems of sensitivity which influence the purpose and the methodology of assistance for planning. To be reminded of this sensitivity it is only necessary to recall the intense campaigns for "localization," or "indigenization," to replace foreign expatriate civil servants with home nationals as an additional expression of independence and self-government. As in the case of planning, however, it is possible to differentiate types of administration which are essentially technical in character and which for that reason do not have an undue measure of delicacy in the relationships of technical assistance. These types of administration are illustrated by computer-based systems of data collection and analysis and by cost accounting systems.

These technical kinds of management specialization are distinguished from such areas as budgeting, personnel, and public enterprise management, which involve processes very close to a country's intimate methods of making and implementing national policy. The nature of this latter kind of administration suggests strongly that it can be best improved and strengthened by external assistance which is applied to the undergirding institutions of research and training. These supporting institutions are the universities and technical institutes and especially the institutes of public administration which can produce the knowledge of management systems, the personnel to man them, and the consulting advice to improve them. These strengthened institutions of training and research can be the channels of foreign advice as well as centers of local consultation on public administration problems and institutions. This emphasis upon management research and training institutions by no means forecloses foreign consultation on specified problems of administration or on the design and installation of specialized management delivery systems, such as those for farm supplies or for raw materials, or for power and water for industry. Business management consulting firms or similar agencies are readily and appropriately available for such operational assistance.

It is incumbent upon a developing country to accommodate these several external influences of foreign aid if it is to retain the initiative and preserve its priorities in planning and administering its program for social and economic development. It must be able to cushion the impact of economic aid and technical assistance, and it must be able to blunt the pressures of external bureaucracies and to adapt the advice and recommendations of foreign advisers and consultants. These capacities require personnel and organizational strength not only to carry the administrative load on project, loan, fellowship, and consultant clearance and coordination and on logistical treatment but also to deal as professional equals with foreign representatives in matters of foreign economic and administrative policy and judgment. These are the capacities which will destroy the aura of neo-colonialism which persists in tainting the relationships between donor and recipient countries and which inhibits indigenous predominance in development policy and program.

Note on Sources

There is extensive literature on economic aid and technical assistance to developing countries, including the informative annual reports and yearbooks of the donor countries and international organizations. The references given here are highly selective. Those published by the United Nations are listed below:

Economic and Social Progress in the Second Development Decade: Report of the Secretary General, Sales No. E. 77. II. A. 11 (New York: United Nations, 1977).

R. G. A. Jackson [committee chairman], *A Study of the Capacity of the United Nations Development System,* 2 vols., Sales No. E. 70. I. 10 (Geneva: United Nations, 1969).

The Joint Inspection Unit, UNDP, "Report of the Role of Experts in Development Cooperation," mimeographed, Geneva, 1978.

Colin Legum, ed., *The First United Nations Development Decade and Its Lessons for the 1970s* (New York: Praeger, 1970).

Public Administration and Finance for Development: Strategy for the Second United Nations Development Decade, Sales No. E. 75. II. H. 2 (New York: United Nations, 1975).

Public Administration in the Second United Nations Development Decade, Sales No. E. 71. II. H. 3 (New York: United Nations, 1971).

Jan. Tinbergen [committee chairman], *Report of the Committee for Development Planning: U.N. Second Development Decade* (New York: United Nations, 1970).

"United Nations Development Programme, Report of the Administrator for 1977," mimeographed, DP/321, April 19, 1978, and Statistical Annex, DP/321/Annex I, April 12, 1978.

Key references to the World Bank and other financial aid institutions include the following:

John P. Lewis and Ishan Kapur, eds., *The World Bank Group, Multi-Lateral Aid, and the 1970s* (Lexington, Mass.: Lexington Books, 1973).

Edward S. Mason and Robert E. Asher, *The World Bank since Bretton Woods* (Washington, D.C.: Brookings Institution, 1973).

Lester B. Pearson, *Partners in Development: Report of the World Bank Commission on International Development* (New York: Praeger, 1969).

Policies and Operations: The World Bank Group (Washington, D.C.: World Bank, 1974).

John Syz, *International Development Banks* (Dobbs Ferry, N.Y.: Oceana, 1974).

John White, *Regional Development Banks: The Asian, African and Inter-American Development Banks* (New York: Praeger, 1972).

World Bank, *World Development Report, 1978* (New York: Oxford University Press, 1978).

Two key sources concerning the Development Assistance Committee of the Organization for Economic Cooperation and Development are Milton J. Esman and David Cheever, *The Common Aid Effort* (Columbus: Ohio State University Press, 1967), and Maurice J. Williams, *Development Cooperation: Efforts and Policies of the Members of DAC* (Paris: OECD, 1977).

The literature on technical assistance includes these references:

Yonah Alexander, *International Technical Assistance Experts* (New York: Praeger, 1966).

Ralph Braibanti, ed., *Political and Administrative Development* (Durham, N.C.: Duke University Press, 1969).

Maurice Domergue, *Technical Assistance: Theory, Practice, and Policies* (New York: Praeger, 1968).

Denyse Harari, *The Role of the Technical Assistance Expert* (Paris: OECD, 1975).

Edward P. Hawthorne, *The Transfer of Technology* (Paris: OECD, 1971).

Kenneth J. Rothwell, "Technical Assistance and Training for Administrative Development," Part 2 in *Administrative Issues in Developing Economies* (Lexington, Mass.: Heath, 1972).

Edward W. Weidner, *Technical Assistance in Public Administration Overseas: The Case for Development Administration* (Chicago, Ill.: Public Administration Service, 1964).

Edward W. Weidner, ed., *Development Administration in Asia,* Part 3, "Technical Assistance and Development Administration" (Durham, N.C.: Duke University Press, 1970).

More general treatments of foreign aid in relevant aspects are contained in the following works:

Jagdish Bhagwati and Richard S. Echaus, eds., *Foreign Aid* (Baltimore: Penguin, 1971).

Bruce Dinwiddy, *Aid Performance and Development Policies of Western Countries* (New York: Praeger, 1973).

Charles R. Frank, Jr., et al., *Assisting Developing Countries* (New York: Praeger, 1973).

Leon Gordenker, *International Aid and National Decisions: Development Programs in Malawi, Tanzania, and Zambia* (Princeton: Princeton University Press, 1976).

Denis Goulet, *The Cruel Choice: A New Concept in the Theory of Development* (New York: Atheneum, 1971).

Gerald M. Meier, *Problems of Cooperation for Development* (New York: Oxford University Press, 1974).

Judith Tendler, *Inside Foreign Aid* (Baltimore: Johns Hopkins University Press, 1975).

12

The Growing Global Bureaucracy

The International Bureaucracy for Foreign Aid

By the end of the United Nations' First Development Decade, which covered the 1960s, the multinational administrative establishment to provide economic aid and to deliver technical assistance to developing countries had become very large. Administration at this international level is another level and dimension of development administration. It takes its place along with national government organizations and systems, and their provincial and local expressions, to make up the bureaucratic environment for the planning and administration of development.

The review in chapter 11 of the international agencies dealing directly and importantly with foreign aid emphasizes their number and the complexities of their relationships with each other and with the developed and developing countries. The bank group numbers seven— the four organizations in Washington (the World Bank, the International Monetary Fund [IMF], the International Finance Corporation [IFC], and the International Development Association [IDA]) and the three regional banks (the Inter-American Development Bank, the Asian Development Bank, and the African Development Bank). The four United Nations agencies involved in technical assistance and foreign aid in a major way are the Economic and Social Council (ECOSOC), the United Nations Development Program (UNDP), the United Nations

Division of Public Administration and Finance, and the United Nations Children's Fund (UNICEF). Because of the close relationship of trade and industrial development to foreign aid for development, three other United Nations agencies are involved: the United Nations Conference on Trade and Development (UNCTAD), the United Nations Industrial Development Organization (UNIDO), and the General Agreement on Tariffs and Trade (GATT). Four specialized agencies in the United Nations family—autonomous agencies which have their own membership, governing boards, staffs, and budgets—are prominently engaged in technical assistance: the Food and Agriculture Organization (FAO), the United Nations Educational, Scientific, and Cultural Organization (UNESCO), the International Labor Organization (ILO), and the World Health Organization (WHO).

Six of these United Nations organizations have their own regional and country offices: UNDP, UNICEF, FAO, UNESCO, ILO, and WHO. The United Nations itself is represented regionally by four economic commissions which, although not involved primarily in technical assistance, are involved in research, conference, and consultative activities which are related directly to development strategy in each of the several regions. They are the Economic Commission for Africa (ECA), the Economic and Social Commission for Asia and the Pacific (ESCAP), the Economic Commission for Latin America (ECLA), and the Economic and Social Office in Beirut (UNESOB). Finally, although not a multinational organization in the same sense as those listed above, the Organization for Economic Cooperation and Development (OECD) should be listed because of the impact of its work through its Development Assistance Committee (DAC) in influencing and coordinating the aid policies of the industrialized countries of the West and Japan. These United Nations and bank agencies, including the regional commissions, total twenty-three. This is a formidable bureaucratic array of establishments which must deal with and be dealt with by developing countries.

The United Nations Fund for Population Activities (UNFPA) became well supported after the United Nations Budapest Conference on Population in 1974. Population growth rates and their consequences did not receive widespread programmatic attention until the last part of the decade of the 1960s, in spite of their comparative and great significance, in contrast to other areas of development given priority attention fifteen to twenty years earlier, such as economic planning, rural and community development, industrial growth and trade expansion, education, and health. The development programs of health focused on the mortality and longevity aspects of human well-being. Their enormous success actually increased the population growth rate and produced many of the problems of population balance with which the development process as a whole should be concerned. It was essentially the energetic efforts of private agencies such as the International Planned Parenthood Federation (IPPF), the Ford Foundation, the Population Council, and the Rockefeller Foundation which recognized and acted upon the significance of population and the regulation of its size as a major factor in development on the world scene in the 1950s.

It was not until 1962 that the United Nations General Assembly formally recognized the close relationship between population growth and economic development. It resolved in that year to help interested governments obtain data on, and to conduct studies of, the demographic aspects of development programs. It should be noted, however, that as early as 1946 the Population Commission was set up in the Economic and Social Council, with a competently staffed Population Division. Since that time the division, in close cooperation with the United Nations' Statistical Commission, has made a series of exceedingly significant and useful projections and studies of the population size and structure of the world, its regions and countries; it has analyzed the world's phenomenal population growth and the reasons therefor.

The United Nations is governed by its member countries, of course, and the reluctance of many countries to permit external intervention in a matter of policy and practice as intimate as birth control and population control was very great. Even now the United Nations is careful to emphasize the right of each country and the right of each family to make its own free and voluntary decision in matters of family planning policy and practice. By 1966, however, the General Assembly had advanced to the point at which it passed a resolution to assist those countries which made the request to develop and strengthen their facilities for training, research, information, and advisory services in the field of population. This resolution marked a departure from the previous restrictions on technical assistance in this area.

At about the same time, from 1964 to 1968, the several specialized agencies of the United Nations extended their technical assistance programs to population and family planning. The World Health Organization, which might have been expected to exert earlier leadership in birth control programs, gradually accepted responsibility for advisory services to governments, if they requested such services, on the health aspects of fertility, sterility, and fertility regulation methods and on the organization of family planning services in the health establishment, especially if these were components of the organization for maternal and child health. The United Nations Children's Fund was authorized by its executive board to give help to family planning as a part of its maternal and child health services. UNESCO undertook to improve knowledge about and to increase awareness of the causes and consequences of population change. The International Labor Organization began to emphasize the demographic aspects of employment and social security policies and programs.

Much larger amounts in support of United Nations technical assistance to family planning and population control became available in 1968 with the creation of the United Nations Trust Fund, made up of voluntary contributions, to supplement the resources of the United Nations Development Program. In 1972 UNDP's governing council was made the governing council of the fund, which was renamed the United Nations Fund for Population Activities. Five million dollars were pledged to the fund by the end of 1969; 15.4 million dollars more were pledged in 1970. Pledges at the end of 1975 totaled almost 240 million dollars.

The World Population Conference held in Bucharest in 1974, through its formally adopted Plan of Action, reaffirmed the traditional position of the United Nations and its members that population policy is the sovereign right of each government to determine for itself and that the number and spacing of children in the family is an individual right. On the other hand, the Plan of Action stated it to be the responsibility of each government to adopt a population policy which recognizes the right of each family to obtain information about family planning and to practice birth control if it chooses to do so. Such policies, in the view of this conference, should be based on the realization of the need for a planned balance of natural resources, food, and environment.

In the field of agriculture there are three new international agencies in the food bureaucracy to add to FAO, UNDP, and the World Bank—the Consultative Group on International Agricultural Research, the World Food Council, and the International Fund for Agricultural Development. The development of these agencies is discussed below.

The interest of the United Nations in increased agricultural production is expressed chiefly through one of its specialized agencies, the Food and Agriculture Organization, in close association with the United Nations Development Program. The FAO, which dates from 1943, was established, in large part at least, because of widespread concern with the consequences of disruption of food production and distribution caused by World War II. According to its preamble, FAO's purposes are to raise the levels of nutrition and of standards of living, to improve the efficiency of the production and distribution of food and agricultural products, to better the conditions of rural populations, and thus to contribute to an expanding world economy and to assure freedom from hunger. For the first decade of its existence, FAO, both because of the limits of its budget and the narrow perception of its responsibilities and opportunities, was chiefly engaged in the collection and analysis of information about agriculture and with studies and conferences based upon that information. Its funds for and ideas of technical assistance to developing countries were limited, consisting chiefly of occasional consultants and a relatively small number of fellowships for the training abroad of specialized manpower for agriculture.

The advent and growth of the United Nations' program of technical assistance provided FAO with both the financial resources and the encouragement to expand its research and assistance activities very substantially. Its technical assistance projects are now subject to the active initiative and guidance of the United Nations Development Program through UNDP's decentralized organization of country representatives and systems of country planning. Also, FAO's technical assistance has evolved from a miscellany of consultantships and fellowships to a series of longer-term and more substantial institution-building projects supplemented by shorter-term consultancies and research reports. These projects are found in all the several functional areas of agricultural productivity, including research and extension, the production of needed inputs, and the economic aspects of marketing and production incentives as well as better methods of storage, preservation, and processing.

Another international body came into being in 1971; it has the potential of exerting significant influence on the world's systems of food production. This is the "Consultative Group on International Agricultural Research," composed of representatives of the World Bank—under whose aegis it was formed—UNDP, and FAO. The Ford and Rockefeller foundations are associated with the group, as are bilateral aid programs of supporting countries such as Canada, Japan, and the United States. The occasion for the organization of the Consultative Group was the desire to increase and coordinate support for the international regional agricultural research centers and to consult on their research priorities. These regional research centers include the International Maize and Wheat Improvement Center in Mexico, the International Rice Research Institute in the Philippines, the International Center for Tropical Agriculture in Colombia, the International Potato Center in Peru, the Institute for the Semi-Arid Tropics in India, the International Laboratory for Research on Animal Diseases in Kenya, the International Livestock Center for Africa in Ethiopia (contemplated), the International Institute of Tropical Agriculture in Nigeria, the International Center for Agricultural

Research in Dry Areas (contemplated), and the International Plant Genetics Resources Board in Rome.

Still other international organizations for agriculture have come into being since the 1974 World Food Conference in Rome. The occasion for that conference was the famine of 1972–73, which so severely affected the Sahel and the subcontinent of India. Also before the conference were issues of food supply, price, and distribution, with which the current systems of production and delivery seemed inadequate to cope. The major problems considered at Rome included food production and distribution, the organization of a world food reserve, the availability of fertilizers and other needed inputs, oil and energy issues, and international organization to implement programs of action. The World Food Council was set up under the United Nations Economic and Social Council and the General Assembly to monitor the world food situation on a continuing basis, to coordinate the activities of the other international food agencies both new and old, and to make recommendations to the General Assembly on the implementation of the resolutions of the World Food Conference, particularly those dealing with the security of world food supplies. The World Food Council consists of thirty-six member states elected by the General Assembly upon nomination by ECOSOC.

The International Fund for Agricultural Development was also planned at Rome. It came into being when one billion dollars was subscribed to its capital fund, of which 50 percent is from the Organization of Petroleum Exporting Countries (OPEC) and 50 percent from the industrialized nations; the agreement establishing the fund has been ratified by six developed donor countries (members of OECD), six developing donor countries (members of OPEC), and twenty-four other developing countries. One-third of the fund's board is composed by OPEC members, one-third by the developing countries, and one-third by OECD members. The fund is set up to make grants and concessionary loans both to other international agencies and directly to developing countries to support measures to increase food production in the poorest food-deficit nations. In December 1978 it was given the status of a specialized agency.

These additions bring the total number of agencies in the development assistance category of the global bureaucracy up to twenty-seven. Still to be counted and assessed are those proposed because of a keener awareness of the mutual interdependence of nations compelled by limited resources, and those proposed to correct inequities and inefficiencies in the international economic system. The countries of the world have expressed increasingly great concern for the critical balances of people and food and of people and environment, energy, and mineral resources. They are expressing similarly great concern about the equity and viability of international economic and other institutional systems.

Major United Nations conferences that have been held to discuss these crucial international issues since 1970—and there were others before and since—reached understandings which provided for, or anticipated, one or more additions to or changes in the global bureaucratic system. They included the International Development Strategy for the Second United Nations Development Decade (1970), the Lima Declaration and Program of Action (1971), the Declaration on the Human Environment (1972), the Conference on the Law of the Sea (1973 and subsequently), the World Population Plan of Action (1974), the Universal Declaration on the Eradication of Hunger and Malnutrition (1974), the Declaration on the Establishment of a New International Economic Order (1974), the Charter of Economic Rights and Duties of States (1974), and the Resolution on the New International Economic Order (1975). The full scale and scope of the global bureaucracy for development can be seen in its possible and even probable dimension from the deliberations of these several conferences and the preparatory reports produced for them, which are the subject of the following sections.

Mutual Dependence upon Limited Resources

In 1972 a book was published under the title *The Limits to Growth*. It reported the results of a study at the Massachusetts Institute of Technology commissioned by the Club of Rome as a part of its Project on the Predicament of Mankind. (The Club of Rome is a non-profit association of prominent scientists, economists, industrialists, educators, and civil servants in thirty-five countries. Its purpose is to foster an understanding of the interdependent components of the global system.) The frightening conclusion was that if the present exponential trends in population growth and industrialization continue unchanged, the limits to growth on this planet will be reached within one hundred years, and a sudden and uncontrollable decline in population and industrial capacity will follow. The basic assumptions of the study were that (1) the world's physical resources are fixed in amount; (2) food production per acre is static and new land is limited; (3) pollution increases exponentially with increase in agricultural and industrial production, whereas the earth's capacity to absorb such pollution is finite; (4) yet the birth rate and exponential population growth will decline only if there is more industrialization; (5) there are not enough resources to allow such industrial expansion to continue unhindered; (6) if, however, growth trends can be altered, a condition of ecological stability might be achieved so as to satisfy the needs of all human beings, but at a different level.

In its *Report on the Limits to Growth* the World Bank, and other analysts in their own reviews, pointed out that *Limits to Growth* was too gloomy in its predictions because (1) the reserves of non-renewable resources are almost certainly in larger supply than is now known and will last longer than anticipated; (2) developments in science and technology will produce more efficient uses of resources, such as improvement of mining and processing methods and recycling, and will therefore produce greater yields in agricultural and industrial production; (3) damage attributed to pollution, although great, is exaggerated, and much of its adverse effect is scientifically questionable; (4) it appears now that population growth will soon start to decline; (5) in any case, economic growth need not continue indefinitely in the same patterns as in the past.

The *Limits to Growth* debate both reflected and intensified national and international concern about the availability of resources in amount and in location because of the mutual dependence of all nations upon those resources for growth and development. This great and universal need for resources creates enormous pressures to search for reserves of exhaustible, non-renewable resources, such as minerals and fossil fuels, and even greater pressure for equity and assurance in the distribution and sharing of such resources as are available. This same need also creates pressures to use renewable resources more efficiently and intensively. However, these renewable and reproductive resources, such as land, water, plants, and animals, must be developed and used according to immutable laws of nature. The ecological principles which govern their use must be understood and respected.

There is a web of intricate, interrelated, interdependent systems which makes life possible on earth. To intervene or intrude upon any one of these systems of interrelationships is to modify and even threaten the integrity of the whole. For example, there are five major recycling systems in nature which serve mankind and all life—those of sun, water, carbon dioxide, nitrogen, and phosphorus. We are everlastingly dependent upon these systems, and the world's well-being depends upon man's respect for their integrity as well as upon the best use of their benefits. Within these global recycling systems there are ecological (eco) systems, each of which is formed by the interaction of a community of organisms with its environment. A natural ecosystem is dynamic and in constant evolution, but it is characterized by a tendency to preserve its equilibrium and stability through natural checks and balances. Man's interventions in an ecosystem might damage or destroy it as a constantly renewable resource for his support, but this result is not inevitable if a viable balance is maintained in the change so that reproductive capacity is preserved. Man's intervention in an ecosystem is justifiable in these terms; it can even establish a new and better balance. Protection of the environment does not necessarily mean the protection of the wilderness.

Minerals have been and continue to be central to the processes of industrialization, communication, and energy production and transmission, and are therefore central to the process of development itself. Because mineral supplies are finite and because they are uneven in their scattered distribution around the world, their exploitation for development in equitable behalf of all nations and peoples depends upon the recognition of international interdependence and systems to express and accomplish that interdependence. In the same way, energy is essential to the process of development as we know it, both to support industrial and agricultural growth and production, on the one hand, and to support higher standards of living on the other.

It is unthinkable that ceilings on the availability of energy would be imposed on the processes of growth and development that are required to eradicate poverty in all countries of the world and to increase standards of living and the ranges of human opportunity and choice. Fortunately such energy ceilings are not inevitable, except perhaps for temporary periods in certain areas, because both the promise of technology and the availability of almost unlimited or renewable fuels provide assurance for the future, even though the discomforts of changing energy systems and of paying inevitably higher costs will have to be borne. But the sharing of technology and of energy systems is required to extend the opportunities for development to the advantaged and disadvantaged alike.

In 1971, even before the publication of *Limits to Growth,* the United Nations Committee on Natural Resources identified many of the problems created by limited and unequally distributed natural resources, by shortages and costs of energy, and by environmental pollution. It pointed out in particular the increases in demand for water which, in fixed quantity, is unevenly distributed and in a growing number of cases is fouled with salt because of improper use. On the whole, however, the committee was optimistic, concluding that mineral and fossil resources, with the applications of new technology, are more plentiful than expected and that environmental tolerance for pollution provides another reason to extend mineral processing to the developing countries, where the mines are.

Even more recently, Wassily Leontief's 1976 study for the United Nations, *The Future of the World Economy,* and Jan Tinbergen's study in the same year for the Club of Rome, *Reshaping the International Order,* report conclusions which are optimistic. Land under cultivation can be increased by as much as 30 percent and yields threefold. Reserves of minerals and petroleum are vastly greater than they were formerly thought to be, and their use will be extended by technological improvements, although substitutions will have to be found for some. Pollution can be reduced to acceptable levels, although at great cost. In recognition of the inescapable interdependence of nations on mineral and energy resources and the benefits of international cooperation, the possibility of two new international organizations has been discussed: a World Agency for Mineral Resources, and a World Energy Research Authority.

Of great and direct relevance to the question of the adequacy of resources for world development are the enormous and largely untapped resources of the oceans. These resources are the fish and fisheries upon which more and more countries are depending for a substantial portion of their food supply; oil and gas deposits which probably exceed the volume of reserves under land; and vast quantities of phosphate, diamonds, magnesium, potassium, tin, copper, and other minerals in the form of "hot brines" and manganese nodules on the ocean floor. Use of this heritage of mankind and other aspects of ocean management have been the concern of a United Nations Conference on the Law of the Sea, which held its first session in Caracas in 1974 and has had several since, with more to come. No new conventions have as yet been agreed to, but differences are being narrowed and the outlines of a pattern of ocean management and resource development can be drawn:

A territorial sea, extending twelve miles from shore, will be under the jurisdiction of the bordering nation. Certain rights of passage will be assured in international straits and certain rights of access will be assured to landlocked nations.

An economic zone extending two hundred miles from shore, generally the extent of the continental shelf, will be a zone of national jurisdiction, especially with respect to fish and petroleum resources. It is expected that concessions will be made to international rights to navigation, overflight, cables, and other such uses of the seas.

The seabed area itself, where lie substantially all of the non-petroleum resources, will be managed in the interest of mankind as a whole and in such a way that the revenues and other benefits of development will accrue to all.

Other issues require resolution, including rights to conduct research within the two-hundred-mile economic zone as well as on the high seas, provisions for the regulation and control of pollution of the oceans, special provision for landlocked and other geographically disadvantaged countries, and the sharing and transfer of relevent technology.

At least two new international agencies will emerge from the Conference on the Law of the Sea when it concludes its deliberations: a Law of the Sea Tribunal to resolve disputes, and an International Seabed Authority to have jurisdiction over the exploitation of seabed resources in the interests of the world as a whole. Although there appears to be general agreement that such an authority is needed, there are many as yet unresolved differences concerning its composition and decision-making mechanisms; its right and capacity to mine and process minerals itself; the extent of its licensing, chartering, and monitoring authority and capacity; and formulas by which the products of the operations and the revenues of such operations would be distributed. In addition, the impact and relationship of the distribution and use of minerals from the sea and of minerals from existing land sources must be assessed and accommodated.

Sharing the Environment

As man intrudes in the environment to extract its agricultural, mineral, and other resources, he also modifies its ecological systems in ways which might or might not be damaging to them and to him, depending upon his care. More than that, man excretes into the air, land, and water the wastes of his personal, agricultural, and industrial activities, wastes which are more likely than not to pollute the environment in such a way as to impair the efficient performance of its functions and thus to reduce its contributions to man's development as well as to harm men individually and directly.

Even the fundamental process of farming has an immediate and directly perceptible impact upon the environment and the ecological systems involved. First of all, the virgin cover of forest or prairie is torn, thus threatening soil erosion, soil leaching, and the modification of the natural watershed. Large artificial water systems to supply irrigation water by use of storage reservoirs and canals can and do, if not well planned, create problems of waterlogging and salinity and can support water-borne diseases such as schistosomiasis. Pesticides which protect valuable crop production may also have a seriously deleterious effect on birds, animals, and human beings in their non-discriminatory effect.

Even fertilizers, which are essential to substantially increased food production, are flushed from the fields to streams, lakes, and reservoirs in such volume of excess plant nutrients as to stimulate lush aquatic plant growth which, as it decays, reduces oxygen supply and kills fish.

Domestic and industrial pollution of the environment is even more direct and more harmful. Enormous quantities of carbon dioxide are released into the air from electric generating plants, industries, and automobiles. These large quantities of carbon dioxide are accompanied by huge amounts of waste heat, both industrial and household. Heat and carbon dioxide, which screens outgoing radiation, could conceivably raise the temperature of the global climate, although the emission of dust particles may be an offsetting factor. Not only carbon dioxide but other airborne emissions of energy and industrial production, such as sulphur dioxide, nitrogen oxide, and compounds of lead, mercury, arsenic, and cadmium, are proven causes of hazards to health in the form of cancer and heart and respiratory disease. These same emissions can also damage plants, animals, and buildings—an economic loss. The possibility of airborne leaks of radioactivity from nuclear energy plants and from the storage of their wastes deserve special attention. Leaks from stored wastes can also contaminate the seas and caves of storage on land. The length and degree of risk they pose are being debated. The threat is considered to be from both direct and indirect genetic damage to human beings, plants, and animals.

The air has only limited capacity to absorb and to accommodate these pollutants. Air currents can carry the pollution to many places and for a long time before the pollutants rain out on an unpredictable location. Smog and other concentrations can occur in densely settled industrial areas due to air inversion, sometimes producing "killer smogs." A traditional repository of wastes is streams, lakes, and oceans. Such wastes include treated or untreated sewage, human waste, and the wastes of industry. Some of these effluents are just as toxic as those which go into the air, effluents such as non-degradable salts in the form of both solids and liquids. Much damage is done by the heat of wastes and of hot water from cooling systems. The adverse effects upon the capacity of streams and lakes to serve downstream needs for drinking water, fish production, and industrial use are evident. The ultimate consequence is the death of streams and lakes when they are unable to absorb such enormous quantities of wastes. The threats of major pollution in the oceans are also very real. Mercury and other poisons are decimating fish populations and are making other fish unsafe to eat. These pollutants, and others such as oil spills and petroleum leakage, threaten phy-

toplankton upon which fish populations depend and which perform
the photosynthesis function in the seas.

It is clear that the ecological and environmental consequences of
agricultural, industrial, and other enterprises undertaken in pursuit of
development activities must be taken into account. The choices and the
questions are not easy ones because the world cannot go back to or
restore the wilderness conditions of some romantically remembered past,
nor can it foresake the agricultural, manufacturing, and energy-
producing activities essential to the improvement of the human lot, even
though they entail pollution in some degree. On the one hand, complete
purity of air and water may be out of the question, but on the other hand
more costly technology might well improve the quality of air and water
to acceptable levels. The answer is neither the absence of growth on the
one hand, or all-out unimpeded growth on the other.

These and other issues were analyzed and debated at the United
Nations Conference on the Human Environment held in Stockholm in
1972. One of the best of the preparatory exercises produced what is
informally known as the "Founex Report," named after a town in
Switzerland where a United Nations panel of twenty-seven experts met in
1971 to prepare the document *Development and Environment*. This
report opened with emphasis on the inseparability of man's relationship
with the natural environment, the process of man's own development,
and the probability of inconsistency and conflict. After reviewing the
environmental pollution consequences of the development process, the
report pointed up sharply the dilemma faced by developing countries in
choosing between growth and quality of life. The report concluded with
sections on pollution of world-wide significance—carbon dioxide's effect
on climate, mercury and lead poisoning, oil spills, nuclear radioactivity—requiring national and international measures. The panel noted
the possible effects of control measures on the international economy—
measures such as substituting non-polluting substances for mercury and
lead, banning trade in fruits and vegetables carrying traces of DDT,
barring mercury-poisoned fish from the market, and recycling raw
materials.

The Stockholm Conference itself, in its Declaration on the Human
Environment, recognized man's responsibility for protecting and improving the environment for present and future generations. It also
emphasized that the environmental problems of underdeveloped
countries are due to the very poverty of their underdevelopment and the
consequent low quality of life. For them, development has a higher
priority than higher standards of pollution control. It recommended the

establishment of an intergovernmental body for environmental affairs, subsequently set up by the General Assembly in the form of the United Nations Environment Programme (UNEP), which has a governing council of fifty-eight country members and an executive director. The major functions of UNEP are to promote international policies and cooperation among members; to provide policy guidance and coordination within the United Nations system; and to keep the world environmental situation under surveillance, especially with respect to its impact upon national and international policies and programs. Hence still another agency has been added to the global bureaucracy for development, bringing the total number of existing and proposed agencies to thirty-two. The agency's work focuses on those aspects of environmental pollution which require international cooperation for their control, such as establishing and monitoring protection, discharge, and technological standards of discharges into the oceans and into the international atmosphere. UNEP provides advice and technical assistance to individual countries on ecological and environmental policies and programs.

Toward a New International Economic Order

In 1970 the United Nations General Assembly proclaimed the second development decade, beginning in 1971, and adopted the declaration titled "International Development Strategy for the Second United Nations Development Decade." The declaration stated:

The ultimate objective of development must be to bring about sustained improvement in the well-being of the individual and bestow benefits on all. If undue privileges, extremes of wealth and social injustices persist, then development fails in its essential purpose. This calls for a global development strategy based on joint and concentrated action by developing and developed countries in all spheres of economic and social life: in industry and agriculture, in trade and finance, in employment and education, in health and housing, in science and technology. (para. A [7])

The strategy set as a target an average annual rate of growth of 6 percent for the gross national product of the developing countries. It fixed 0.7 percent of the gross national product of economically advanced countries as the desired level of development assistance to developing countries. The strategy called for strong efforts to strengthen the trade position of those countries through such measures as pricing policy, buffer stocks, elimination of trade barriers, preferential treatment of exports, and diversification of export trade. Other goals were stated with respect to shipping, science and technology, human development, and the special problems of the most disadvantaged countries.

It was in 1974, however, that the General Assembly, at its sixth special session, adopted its Declaration of the Establishment of a New International Economic Order as well as its Programme of Action for the establishment of that order. In the Assembly declaration the members of the United Nations

Solemnly proclaim our united determination to work urgently for *The Establishment of a New International Economic Order* based on equity, sovereign equality, interdependence, common interest and cooperation among all States, irrespective of their economic and social systems, which shall correct inequalities and redress existing injustices, make it possible to eliminate the widening gap between the developed and the developing countries and ensure steadily accelerating economic and social development and peace and justice for present and future generations. . . .

The declaration found the present international economic order to be in direct conflict with desired developments in international relations and affirmed the reality of interdependence of all the members of the world community in the attainment of prosperity for each of its parts. The Programme of Action identified the corrections and improvements considered to be essential to the attainment of a new international economic order with particular concern for stability and equity between the volume and prices of exports and imports of developing countries, food supply, sharing in technology and industrialization, renegotiation of debts and finance for development, regulation of transnational corporations, greater participation of developing countries in international decision-making, cooperation among developing countries, and strengthening the role of the United Nations system for international economic cooperation.

As was anticipated, this declaration and its Programme of Action were passed only with difficulty and after much acrimonious debate between the developing countries and the industrialized West. Controversial issues included proposed clauses on nationalization, linking export and import costs, producer cartels, and freight and other subsidies. The tone and spirit at the seventh special session were much more harmonious and productive, resulting in a resolution (3362, S-VII), adopted in September 1975 and titled "Development and International Economic Cooperation," which represented a great stride toward the goal of a new order. Its provisions included substantially the same topics as those of the sixth special session, but with more specificity and expression of agreement.

In the meantime, in December 1974 the General Assembly adopted and proclaimed the Charter of Economic Rights and Duties of States, based upon the following principles:

Sovereignty, integrity, independence, and equality of all states.

Non-aggression and non-intervention, peaceful coexistence, and peaceful settlement of disputes.

Equal rights and self-determination of peoples and respect for human rights and fundamental freedoms.

Remedy of injustices brought about by force which deprive a nation of the means for normal development.

Fulfillment of international obligations and peaceful settlement of disputes.

No attempt to seek hegemony and spheres of influence.

International social justice.

International cooperation for development.

Free access to and from the sea by land-locked countries.

The charter has the purpose of promoting collective economic security for development, especially for developing countries, with respect for the sovereign equality of each state and through the cooperation of the entire community. It recognizes the right of each state to choose its own economic system, to control its natural resources, to regulate foreign investment, to supervise the activities of transnational corporations, and to nationalize or expropriate foreign property upon payment of appropriate compensation. Other provisions of the charter spell out rights and obligations in the field of trade and regional and international cooperation for development.

These three actions of the United Nations—the declarations and programs of action of the sixth and seventh special sessions of the General Assembly, and the Charter of Economic Rights and Duties of States—outline in broad terms the concept of a new international economic order and its purposes and dimensions. These documents had their origin in and are supplemented by earlier conferences, such as those of the twenty-fifth session of the General Assembly in 1970, which produced the International Development Strategy for the Second United Nations Development Decade, the United Nations Conference on Trade and Development (UNCTAD), the United Nations Industrial Development Organization (UNIDO), the United Nations Conference on the Law of the Sea, and the World Food Conference.

A prime innovator in these conferences was the Group of Seventy-seven. This group of seventy-seven countries, more or less the number of developing countries at the time, came into being as an informal caucus on the occasion of UNCTAD I, in Geneva in 1964. It has a larger membership now, but continues to be called the Group of Seventy-seven. It meets in advance of, or on the occasion of, key international meetings on international economic issues, notably those of UNCTAD and UNIDO. It does not have a formal organization or secretariat but is served by the secretariats of the United Nations itself in New York and of UNCTAD in Geneva. The Group of Seventy-seven is a powerful and articulate representative of those who wish to move rapidly toward the new order.

The United Nations declarations of 1974 and 1975 are not the final description of the new international economic order and its content. UNCTAD IV, meeting in Nairobi in 1976, and the continuing Law of the Sea Conference, for example, are particularizing in more detail the changes in policies and institutions which are involved and are sharpening the issues of difference which exist, chiefly between the industrialized countries of the West and Japan on one side and the developing countries of the Third World on the other. A dialogue between these rich and poor countries was organized under the name "Conference on International Economic Cooperation" (CIEC). It was set up in 1975 at the initiative of OECD, outside the framework of the United Nations but providing for United Nations observation. CIEC was composed of nineteen developing countries, including seven members of OPEC, and the Common Market countries plus the United States, Japan, Canada, Australia, Switzerland, Sweden, and Spain. Prompted by the motive to establish a forum for the consideration of petroleum issues, the conference extended its interests and set up joint commissions on raw materials, financial affairs, and development as well as a commission on petroleum and energy. CIEC and its commissions were served by an international secretariat provided by OECD. The conference did not reach consensus on major changes in international economic practice in its 1975, 1976, and 1977 meetings. Many hope that it or a comparable forum will continue to explore alternative solutions to the problems which plague its members, chiefly the energy problems of all members and the trade and financial problems of the poor. CIEC was adjourned, however, without provision for resumption.

The Prospect of New and Reoriented Agencies

The creation of a large number of new international agencies is called for to implement the several aspects of the new international order as it evolves. Some of these agencies are recommended explicitly, some are implied, and others have been suggested in debates, staff reports, and in the proposals of individual nations. These new additions to the global bureaucracy would be accompanied by changes in the status, policies, and practice of existing institutions. For example, a major target of the new international economic order is to increase the trade of developing countries not only by lowering barriers but also by extending and increasing preferences given to them. In addition, major efforts are being exerted to create and finance buffer stocks to secure stable and equitable prices for exports in a system of relationship with imports and to finance export revenue fluctuations in order to stabilize the earnings and to guarantee the purchasing power of developing countries. These goals will involve the proposed conversion of UNCTAD into a specialized agency of the United Nations to strengthen its autonomous capacity and the influence in it of developing countries, and they will also involve the reorganization of GATT to increase its effective concern for the Third World. New agencies would be called for, in addition—an International Fund for Buffer Stocks, and an International Development Security Fund to stabilize overall export earnings.

The new international economic order contemplates major changes in the world's monetary system to accomplish an international currency and effective multinational surveillance to prevent the intervention of individual countries. More specifically, with respect to economic development, proposals for the new order involve larger subscriptions to the World Bank, IDA, and UNDP; the linkage of IMF special drawing rights and development assistance; mitigation of the burdens of debt and debt service of developing countries; greater access of developing countries to capital markets; and the accomplishment of assured contributions to development assistance on the part of industrialized countries in the amount of 0.7 percent of their gross national product. The developing countries would like to increase their voting weight in both IMF and the World Bank. They look forward to the time when development assistance without strings might be extended in a kind of international tax system to include not only the guaranteed payments from developed countries but also regular revenues from exploitation of the resources of the sea and other levies, as, for example, on international trade in such international resources as copper and oil. In addition to the substantial changes in existing institutions and systems that these innovations will require, some have suggested the eventual need of a world treasury.

The new international order would rest heavily on increased industrialization and a larger share of participation by the Third World in manufacturing, as well as reform in trade and finance. This emphasis would call for increases not only in technical and economic assistance to support industrialization in developing countries but on greatly improved methods of transferring technology and facilitating the access of developing countries to scientific and technological knowledge relevant to their needs and opportunities. It has been proposed that UNIDO as well as UNCTAD be converted to a specialized agency, and several new international institutions have been recommended by various groups, including an International Center for Technological Development and Information, an International Industrialization Institute, and an International Investment Trust for private investment.

A very special concern of the proponents of the new international order is the transnational corporation, the gigantic private business enterprise which seems to threaten the control of many countries over their natural resources and to threaten their financial autonomy. The total value of international production by these transnational corporations now approximates the value of world trade, exceeding one-half trillion dollars. No one proposes the abolition of these multinational organizations because they are effective and efficient systems for dealing with regional and global economic transactions which transverse political boundaries. But because they do seem to pose a challenge to priorities and values of individual countries, especially the poorer ones, there is widespread feeling that they should be monitored by an international body and even governed by or put under the direction of an international agency. The United Nations has already set up a Commission and a Center on Transnational Corporations to recommend international arrangements to assure the optimum contribution of these gigantic organizations to national and world development. It can be anticipated that an agency, perhaps in the form of an authority, will be established permanently to act upon the United Nations' response to the commission's recommendations.

Other aspects of industrial development on a global scale, particularly with respect to mineral resources, involve the conservation and equitable distribution as well as the exploitation of such resources on behalf of the home country. They also involve the protection and harmonization of those interests with the soon-to-be-realized development of the mineral-rich deposits in the oceans. An agency to perform these functions might take the form of an International Resources Bank.

The documents which sketch the nature of the new international economic order refer to other aspects also, such as the importance of a greater Third World share in transporting, marketing, and distributing their primary commodities; the special measures needed to help the least developed and geographically disadvantaged countries; the basic necessity of assuring adequate food production, security, and distribution;

and the relevance of environmental considerations. The focus of the documents, however, is in the areas of international trade, industry, and finance. The eight new agencies to implement proposed sections of the new international economic order, added to the thirty-two international agencies previously identified as members or probable members of the global bureaucracy for development, make a total of forty agencies. This number, probably a minimum, will require integration and coordination internationally and accommodation nationally if an interaction of significant and productive benefit is to be derived. Reorganizations of major proportions in existing agencies can be expected.

United Nations Organization for Global Economic Cooperation

The United Nations was created in 1945 for the purposes of attaining international peace and security, encouraging friendly relations among nations, and fostering international cooperation to solve economic, social, cultural, and humanitarian problems. The enormous responsibilities and greatly expanding functions for development and economic cooperation which it has been undertaking, however, and which it will assume in even larger measure, were not anticipated in 1945. Consequently the organization of the United Nations family and its coordination, personnel, and other management systems were not designed to serve a system of global economic cooperation.

The social and economic interests of the United Nations are, under the General Assembly, in the hands of the Economic and Social Council (ECOSOC). The United Nations Charter provides that other organs may be set up as needed, and many such have been established in response to the assumptions of larger areas of international social and economic operations, as discussed in the first sections of this chapter and in chapter 11. They include the United Nations Children's Fund (UNICEF), the United Nations Conference on Trade and Development (UNCTAD), the United Nations Industrial Development Organization (UNIDO), the United Nations Environment Program (UNEP), the United Nations Fund for Population Activities (UNFPA), the United Nations Development Program (UNDP) and also IAEA, the International Atomic Energy Agency. There are others. Other independent and autonomous but related members of the United Nations family are the specialized agencies. As already noted, the most prominent for the purposes of social and economic development are the Food and Agriculture Organization (FAO), the United Nations Educational, Scientific, and Cultural Organization (UNESCO), the International

Labor Organization (ILO), and the World Health Organization (WHO). The United Nations itself and the specialized agencies have expanded and strengthened their regional offices and organizations, although not harmoniously. This fragmentation and proliferation of United Nations organizations is being compounded by plans already being drafted for additional international agencies to recognize world-wide dependence upon resources and to implement the new international economic order as it evolves.

The growth in the United Nations structure of agencies reflects the immense range and scope of its new and increasing tasks and the diverse interests of its increasing membership. This growth has intensified the problems of coordination in the effort to achieve cohesive and integrated program results because the dispersed and decentralized distribution of functions of the United Nations system have become even more dispersed and decentralized. Mechanisms have been and are being devised in an effort to achieve systematic and effective coordination, but their number and their overlapping jurisdictions often increase the difficulties of coordination in a structure which was not meant to be coordinated. In addition, two very difficult and unsolved problem areas of coordination remain. There is no effective process for coordinating the international bureaucracy at either the regional or especially at the national level, which puts an enormous burden of synthesis and harmonization upon each individual country. And there is not a complete reconciliation of the policies or methods of the World Bank family and the United Nations family in the global bureaucracy, nor is there an instrument to achieve such reconciliation and coordination.

Although none of the United Nations' management systems, including that of coordination, is adequate to the functions of global economic cooperation, that of personnel may be of the greatest importance. The United Nations Charter provides that the paramount consideration in the selection of United Nations personnel will be the highest standards of competence and integrity, but that the standards will be used, with due regard to recruitment, "on as wide a geographical basis as possible." In practice, this has meant the use of quotas as a basis for employment, with merit measures then applied within quota pools, and it has led to the use of government channels for recruitment and recommendation which encourages the primacy of national over international loyalties. The system has also led to serious "brain drains" in some countries. This personnel policy and practice may be acceptable in a political agency and its systems, but it cannot be relied upon to meet the requirements of professional qualification and integrity called for in the responsible management and guidance of a global system of economic development and cooperation.

The sixth special session of the General Assembly in 1974, which was devoted to development and international economic cooperation, requested the secretary-general to appoint a group of high-level experts to make proposals for structural changes within the United Nations system to make it fully capable of dealing with problems of international economic cooperation. In May 1975 that "Group of Twenty-five" made its report, *A New United Nations Structure for Global Economic ` Cooperation.* In its report the group stated: "It is now widely accepted that the major challenges faced by the human race can only be met through multilateral action, and that a logical place for this action is the United Nations system. Yet it is a paradox that at the very moment when this recognition is becoming widespread there are growing doubts about the capacity of the United Nations system as an instrument to meet these challenges" (p. 2).

The group identified as a major shortcoming the fragmentation of effort, even then, among twelve organizations and operational programs, five regional commissions, fourteen specialized agencies, and the IAEA. It made note of the multiplicity of special funds, of numerous semi-autonomous bodies, and of the several hundred intergovernmental committees, coordination bodies, and ad hoc groups. It also identified as weaknesses the decision-making systems and methods of work, the artificial separation of planning and operations, the levels and types of representation, the quality of staff, and regional organization. The group's proposals were intended to enable the United Nations system to deal effectively with international economic and social problems, to achieve coordination throughout the United Nations system, to harmonize the views of member countries toward economic and social problems, to improve the transfer of real resources and technology to developing countries, to promote economic cooperation between states, and to become a more effective instrument for the establishment of a new, more rational and just, international economic order.

Recommendations of the Group of Twenty-five

The major structural change recommended in the United Nations organization by the Group of Twenty-five is the creation of a new, powerful office directly under the secretary-general, to be called Director-General for Development and International Economic Cooperation. He would be assisted by a Deputy Director-General for

Research and Policy, who would provide staff analysis services on a global, intersectoral basis. The major operational organization would be a United Nations Development Authority (UNDA). That organization would be directed by a second deputy, the UNDA Administrator, and would be governed by an Operations Board, which would replace all existing governing bodies of United Nations operating agencies. UNDA would replace UNDP and all United Nations voluntary programs and funds for technical assistance and pre-investment activities (except UNICEF, for the time being), and it would consolidate all of the operational funds involved.

The Director-General for Development and International Economic Cooperation would chair an Advisory Committee on Economic Cooperation and Development, composed of the heads of IMF, the World Bank, UNCTAD, UNIDO, the specialized agencies, the regional commissions, his two deputies, and others when appropriate. This committee would be expected to serve as an interagency coordinating mechanism and also to maintain surveillance of the world's economic and social situation. A small "joint unit" would be set up in the director-general's office, composed of high-level experts seconded by major involved agencies but responsible to the director-general. That unit's function would be to serve as a global analysis and system-wide planning agency.

This structural change would involve the abolition of the office of Under Secretary-General for Economic and Social Affairs and the divestment of the Department of Economic and Social Affairs of its sectoral technical and operating functions. This department would thereafter focus on policy-making research and advice to the Economic and Social Council. ECOSOC would continue to be the permanent policy-making body for development and economic cooperation, including integrated policy for the new UNDA. The Group of Twenty-five recommended that ECOSOC's performance of its policy formulation and implementation role be strengthened by more frequent sessions, higher-level representation, the participation as appropriate of the heads of the specialized agencies, the use of small negotiating groups, and the discontinuance of most of its permanent committees. In other words, ECOSOC would do most of its work directly. Similarly, it recommended that the General Assembly make more frequent use of special sessions to deal with problems and issues of major world-wide concern rather than resorting to ad hoc world conferences, such as those held in the past on population, food, and environment. A reorganized and strengthened Committee on Development and Economic Cooperation was proposed to assist it in this task.

The Group of Twenty-five made other recommendations, including those that ECOSOC's Committee for Programme and Coordination and the secretary-general's Administrative Committee on Coordination be strengthened; that the budget systems and cycles of the several United Nations agencies be synchronized, harmonized, and related to the country programming systems; that the regional commissions play a more active role in formulating and executing regional programs and projects; and, significantly, that the United Nations resident representative represent, within his country, the whole United Nations system in the economic sphere. The group endorsed earlier United Nations declarations about strengthening GATT, UNCTAD, and UNIDO and improving the voting position of the developing countries in IMF and the World Bank. The group spoke strongly of the need for coordinating World Bank and UNDA policies and programs and for harmonizing them, particularly at the level of each country—organizing joint country missions for that purpose where possible.

In these several ways the Group of Twenty-five indicated its ideas about linking research, policy analysis, planning, and operational activities in a restructured United Nations system. It emphasized that personnel policies and practices need to be improved to make the secretariat staff a top-quality service dedicated to international cooperation. To this end it recommended competitive examinations on a regional, though pooled, quota basis; a program of pre-recruitment training not only to enlarge the recruitment pool but to help developing countries meet their own counterpart needs, including a United Nations Fellow's Programme; an increase in the proportion of women in the professional category; and an in-service training program to upgrade skills, including possibly the creation of a Staff College, provision for sabbaticals, and mobility among agencies for career development. The group also proposed that United Nations agencies move toward a unified personnel system and that the search for talent not be limited to foreign ministries and missions but extended to the academic and scientific communities and even the public and private commercial enterprise sectors.

It is not clear what kind of personnel system would emerge or what quality of international staff would be produced if these recommendations were actually implemented. Perhaps the general level of competence would be raised somewhat by broadening and deepening the recruitment pools and providing pre- and in-service training opportunities, but quota systems would continue and even be extended, and merit would not yet be the first criterion for selection and assignment. At the same time, an internationalized civil service would create an elite cadre of tenured civil servants even more untouchable in terms of responsibility and accountability than is the case now. Perhaps the nations of the world will be somewhat wary of a mushrooming global bureaucracy managed by a new caste of bureaucrats of such status. Much more attention needs to be paid to the requirements of real competence and true responsiveness in the international civil service before full confidence can be had in its performance of functions central to national as well as international economic health.

Similarly, too little attention has as yet been given to the methods by which decisions will be made by these many new agencies which will assume jurisdiction of varying degrees over resources, trade, development, and finance. It is one thing for an agency to have responsibility only for monitoring and reporting functions. It is quite another matter for an agency to have to act, or fail to act, when either action or inaction can have a significantly beneficial or harmful effect. Some acceptable method of making a decision with reasonable dispatch is imperative to avoid stalemate or long and harmful delay. Consensus—that is, unanimous agreement or assent—is not reliable as a method when issues are difficult and views diverse, yet when some action must be taken. Majority vote in reasonable proportion suggests itself, but on what basis—by country regardless of size, or by population, or by size of financial contribution? A particularly difficult aspect of decision-making in the international order is the question of how to distribute the benefits of the processing of common resources, such as those of the seabeds, and the revenues of international taxation, such as assured contributions from industrialized countries. What formulas will be devised and what tests will be applied and what measures of use will be adopted for purposes of evaluation? The growing global bureaucracy will be but a facade unless its personnel management and decision-making capacities are equal to the purposes of its creation.

The General Assembly, at its seventh special session in 1975, at which it adopted its Resolution on the New International Economic Order, established an *Ad Hoc* Committee on the Restructuring of the Economic and Social Sectors of the United Nations System. The committee's charge was to make the United Nations more fully capable of dealing with problems of international cooperation and development and more responsible to the requirements of the new international economic order and the Charter of Economic Rights and Duties of States. It had as a basis for its deliberations the report of the Group of Twenty-five. The recommendations of the committee's first report were approved by the General Assembly in 1977, at its thirty-second session.

The recommendations of the committee and their acceptance by the General Assembly reflect some progress toward the goal of achieving the United Nations' capability to express its role in international cooperation and development. They accept the concepts of the functions and the streamlining of the work of the General Assembly, ECOSOC, and the regional commissions as perceived by the Group of Twenty-five, but they leave it pretty much to those bodies to reorganize themselves for that purpose. ECOSOC is expected to discontinue, redefine, or regroup its subsidiary agencies, its expert and advisory bodies, and its standing intergovernmental committees. Emphasis is placed upon the responsibility of these bodies for forming overall policy and for coordinating the activities of all of the agencies in the United Nations system. UNCTAD, however, was recognized as having the major role in international trade and related areas of international cooperation, and it was recognized that there were other forums as well for the consideration of international economic problems. The autonomy of the specialized agencies was not attacked.

On the other hand it was recommended by the ad hoc committee and agreed by the General Assembly that specific measures be drawn up to accomplish a better articulated system and program for the United Nations family, including a single annual United Nations Pledging Conference, a harmonized budget and program cycle, a unified personnel system with shared recruitment and training programs, a stronger Committee for Programme and Coordination for ECOSOC, and clarified and stronger machinery for coordination at the intersecretariat level through the Administrative Committee on Coordination (ACC), under the leadership of the secretary-general. This last move involves the merging with ACC of the Environment Coordination Board, the Inter-Agency Consultative Board, and UNIDO's Advisory Committee. New units were established under ECOSOC: the Department of Economic Cooperation and Development, and the Department of Technical Cooperation for Development.

The General Assembly invited the secretary-general to appoint an official of his own choice, at a high level of his own determination, who, under the secretary-general's authority, would assist him in carrying out his responsibilities as chief administrative officer in the economic and social fields; he has subsequently done so. Thus the proposal of the Group of Twenty-five, supported strongly by the Group of Seventy-seven, that a semi-autonomous office be established to manage this area of United Nations responsibility was somewhat diluted. Similarly, no action was taken to create a single governing body responsible at the intergovernmental level for all United Nations operational activities, one which would replace all existing governing bodies, although it was recognized that consideration should be given to that change in structure.

The Impact of the Global Bureaucracy on National Administration for Development

The United Nations organization and its management systems will no doubt be adjusted to perform somewhat more adequately the global functions involved in the recognition of intercountry interdependence. It can be anticipated, however, that vested interests in the existing structure and its processes, and also lack of knowledge and experience with new dimensions of international administration, will inhibit the adoption of all necessary measures at this stage and will therefore require even greater adjustments later on if the growing global bureaucracy is to serve the purposes expected of it. Not the least of these areas of adjustment is the relationship of international to national organization and administration. The General Assembly extended the life of the ad hoc committee so that it may continue its work on structural "rationalization" and improved institutional arrangements for program coordination.

As the new international order gradually comes into being, along with international arrangements to protect the environment and to develop the resources of land and sea, it is easy to see that the global bureaucracy will at least double in size. This enormous growth casts some doubt on the adequacy of present proposals to strengthen the United Nations structure and the capacity to manage that bureaucracy, especially because it is probable that many of the new agencies, and some old ones too, will be autonomous and relatively independent of the United Nations' immediate direction. Questions also remain about the viability of decision-making systems and capabilities in multinational programs and agencies and about the availability and reliability of a personnel system to assure a sufficient supply of competent and responsible international civil servants.

It is to be assumed that, one way or another, these large and difficult problems will be solved sufficiently to allow the international establishment to grow in order to implement to a reasonable degree the requirements of national interdependence. Remaining, however, is the imperative that each nation, and especially every developing nation, be able to respond to and interact with the global bureaucracy to its own best interest. The Group of Twenty-five made the point that United Nations member states should make arrangements within their governments for high-level coordination and review of multinational affairs and operations. This interaction of national and global bureaucracies adds a major new dimension to the subject of development administration. International programs must be reflected in national programs which are adjusted to that effort in and by the countries themselves, and in programs which meet the international conditions and restraints of the new order. The advantages of new conditions of trade, industrialization, finance, resource utilization, and regional cooperation are to be attained only by accepting the accompanying restraints of the new international systems and policies.

Ministries of commerce must be expert in new trade opportunities, but also aware of the accompanying limitations. Ministries of resources and of industry must be professionally competent and up-to-date on technological, processing, and environmental developments applicable to their situations and equally up-to-date on the international conditions of exploitation. Ministries of agriculture have to be able to accept and act upon international obligations in order to benefit from international food support. Ministries of finance must be capable of taking full and current advantage of international support of systems that assist and stabilize currency and foreign exchange, and must be equally capable of accepting new restraints on unilateral decisions. As countries enter into regional and commodity arrangements for cooperation, they must be willing to accept the restraining conditions as well as the advantages of such agreements.

In other words, the personnel and research and analysis capacity of every nation-building department of a developing country will have to be strengthened and upgraded to cope with and to take advantage of the activities of the relevant institution of the global bureaucracy. Similarly, the personnel and analytical capabilities of planning agencies and of ministries of economic affairs will have to be extended greatly, not only for these same reasons but in order to perform the synthesizing and coordinating functions at the national level required for the rational harmonization of multiple international interactions. The performance of this task is imperative to the preservation in any self-respecting degree of national autonomy in development policy and implementation. It depends upon reliable data and information systems as well as upon competent personnel and reliable research and analytical capacities.

The new international economic order thus relies not only upon the global bureaucracy but equally upon the success of each developing country in upgrading its professional personnel in number and quality and in strengthening its technical research and analytical organizations and their capacities. To meet these requirements, each country must broaden and intensify its research and educational programs to produce the personnel and the knowledge needed to perform the larger and more complex tasks of planning and administering development in an international context and environment. The urgency and magnitude of this task, and its importance and relative priority, are vastly increased by two other dimensions of the personnel problem: first, the large need of global agencies for well-qualified staff from countries around the world and the concurrent desire of professional personnel from such countries to take such prestigious and well-paid positions (the "brain drain" problem); and second, the need and desire of developing countries to meet the representational requirements of the global system by sending their best people to meetings and appointing them to serve on commissions, committees, and governing boards of many of the agencies involved.

These aspects of involvement in and interaction with the global system entail enormous investment in highly trained and specialized manpower. There can be some alleviation of the burden by sharing representational duties with neighboring countries and through regional arrangements, and by lending personnel for short periods rather than deputing staff indefinitely. But the very large pressure on developing countries for high-level personnel, both for their own service and for international and representational service, remains.

If developing countries are to interact with the global bureaucracy as assumed and expected, and especially if they are to benefit from the new order according to their own priorities and through their own initiatives, it is imperative that they enlarge their relevant professional manpower pool greatly and, especially, that they establish the institutional resources to produce such personnel and to support it with research and analytical competence. Otherwise, and in the meantime, most developing countries, with only one or two exceptions, will be forced once again to rely upon expatriates and foreign advisers to serve and represent them. They will be compelled merely to react to external programs rather than to initiate policies and programs in accord with their own goals and plans. Responsible development administration demands the personnel, analytical, and organizational capacities to accomplish national goals in terms of both the domestic and the international environment.

International administration is directly relevant to the conduct of development administration in developing countries for at least three reasons. In the first place, those countries are participating as voting members in many of the international organizations, and the responsible discharge of this obligation requires staff time for analysis at home and representation abroad. In the second place, these international organizations and expressions of their program administration impinge upon and influence, purposefully, national policy, program, and administration. And in the third place, international administration is increasingly and inevitably involved in handling problems which cut across political borders and boundaries. The interaction of international with national organization and administration for development is central to the comprehension of development administration and to its applications in practice.

Note on Sources

Key documents of the United Nations bearing upon the evolution of the new international economic order are conveniently found in a collection compiled by Alfred G. Moss and Harry N. Winston: *A New International Economic Order: Selected Documents, 1945-1975,* 2 vols. (New York: Unitar, 1976). These documents include declarations of the Group of Seventy-seven, resolutions and programs of action of UNCTAD and UNIDO, plans and programs of action of the World Population Conference and the World Food Conference, and other relevant materials. They also include the most directly pertinent resolutions of the United Nations General Assembly, including the International Development Strategy for the Second United Nations Development Decade (October 24, 1970), Institutional and Financial Arrangements for International Environmental Cooperation (December 15, 1972), First Biennial Overall Review and Appraisal of Progress in the Implementation of the International Development Strategy for the Second United Nations Development Decade (December 17, 1973), the resolutions of the sixth (May 1974) and seventh (September 1975) special sessions of the General Assembly on development and international economic cooperation, and the Charter of Economic Rights and Duties of States (December 12, 1974).

Other pertinent United Nations reports bearing upon resources, environment, the economic order, and the United Nations structure are listed below:

Lynton J. Caldwell, ed., *Organization and Administration of Environmental Programs,* Sales No. E. 74. II. H. 5 (New York: United Nations, 1974).

Development and Environment: Report and Working Papers of a Panel of Experts Convened by the Secretary-General of the United Nations' Conference on the Human Environment at Founex, Switzerland (Paris: Mouton, 1972).

Group of Twenty-five, *A New United Nations Structure for Global Economic Cooperation,* Sales No. E. 75. II. A. 7 (New York: United Nations, 1975).

Martin Hill, *Towards Greater Order, Coherence and Coordination in the United Nations System* (New York: Unitar, 1975).

Human Settlements: The Environmental Challenge: . . . United Nations' Papers Prepared for the Stockholm Conference (New York: United Nations, 1974).

The Impact of Multinational Corporations on Development and on

International Relations, Sales No. E. 74. II. A. 5 (New York: United Nations, 1974).

Wassily Leontief et al., *The Future of the World Economy* (New York: Oxford University Press, 1977).

Multinational Corporations in World Development, Sales No. E. 73. II. A. 11 (New York: United Nations, 1973).

Report of the Ad Hoc Committee on the Restructuring of the Economic and Social Sectors of the United Nations System, A/32/34 (New York: United Nations, 1977).

Daniel Serwer, *International Cooperation for Pollution Control* (New York: Unitar, 1970).

United Nations Committee on Natural Resources, *Natural Resources Development and Policies, Including Environmental Considerations: Note by the Secretary-General,* E/C. 7/2 and Addenda 1–10 (New York: United Nations, 1971).

Recent developments in international organization for agriculture are to be found in the annual reports of the World Bank, the Food and Agriculture Organization, and the World Food Council, as well as in the *Report of the World Food Conference, Rome, 1974,* Sales No. 75. II. A. 3 (New York: United Nations, 1975). For international organization concerning population, see the annual reports of the United Nations Fund for Population Activities and *The Report of the United Nations World Population Conference, Bucharest, 1974,* Sales No. E. 75. XIII. 3 (New York: United Nations, 1975).

Of the many other studies and books on the several aspects of organization for international economic cooperation and resource development, I list only the five most directly useful to me in writing this chapter:

Lester R. Brown, *World without Borders* (New York: Vintage Books, 1973).

Mahbub ul Haq, *The Poverty Curtain: Choices for the Third World* (New York: Columbia University Press, 1976).

Donella H. Meadows et al., *The Limits to Growth—A Report for the Club of Rome's Project on the Predicament of Mankind* (Washington, D.C.: Potomac Associates, 1972).

Jan Tinbergen, *Reshaping the International Order: A Report to the Club of Rome* (New York: Dutton, 1976).

Barbara Ward and René Dubos, *Only One Earth* (Harmondsworth, Eng.: Penguin, 1972).

Index

Abhoy Ashram, Bangladesh: Academy for Rural Development in, 182, 183
Academy for Rural Development: Peshawar, 180; Comilla, 181
Accounting: for public enterprise, 107, 118, 119; cash basis, 196; cost basis, 199–200; and budget reform, 206, 209
Addis Ababa, 265
Administration: traditional, 18–19, 26, 195–98, 250; systems of, 21; district, 21, 27, 170, 171, 173, 174–75, 183–84; external and internal, 22–23, 53, 161, 228–30, business, 223, 224, 225–26
106, 116–17, See also Local
24, 79, 142–44,
5, 116, 123, 124, 24, 32, 144–46,
31–33
71, 174–75
Public Administra-
(AAPAM), 301
ank, 280, 306
l Research Center for Development
centers, international: l Agriculture, 310; In-ni-Arid Tropics, 310; pical Agriculture, 310; for Africa, 310; Maize rovement Center, 310; 310; Rice Research In-enter for Agricultural y Areas, 310–11; Plant rces Board, 311
rch institutes, 310–11
rural development, 35, 40, aditional, 39; functions of

ministry, 44–45; as state subject, 46; and public enterprise, 48–49; international organization, 307–8, 309–11. See also Community Development; Cooperatives; Food; Green Revolution; Land reform; Nutrition; Public works
Ahmedabad: Indian Institute of Management at, 267, 269
Algeria, 57
Appalachia, 8, 166
Asian and Pacific Center for Development Administration, 20, 300
Asian Development Bank (ADB), 280, 306
Association of South East Asian Nations (ASEAN), 167
Auditing, 107, 119, 196, 201
Australia, 282, 322

Bangladesh: and World Food Survey, 34; rural development, 40; land reform, 41; Comilla project, 180, 184–85
Banks. See Development banks
Basic Democracies program, in Pakistan, 177–78
Birth control: methods of, 61, 68–69; motivation for, 61–62; government policy, 62–63; incentives, 63–64; clinics, 64; data systems, 64. See also Family planning; Population
Bolivia, 34
Borlaug, Norman, 36
Brazil, 34
Budapest Conference on Population, United Nations, 307
Budgeting: incremental, 90, 96; traditional, 195–98; expenditure authority, 196–97, 207; in administrative reform, 204–5; for management, 205–6; econometric, 206, 208; for decentralization, 207; types of, in United States, 210–14; effect of foreign aid, 216; in public enterprise, 218; in United Nations, 331

COMPOSED BY FOX VALLEY TYPESETTING, MENASHA, WISCONSIN
MANUFACTURED BY CUSHING MALLOY, INC., ANN ARBOR, MICHIGAN
TEXT AND DISPLAY LINES ARE SET IN TIMES ROMAN

Library of Congress Cataloging in Publication Data
Gant, George F
Development administration.
Bibliography: p.
Includes index.
1. Underdeveloped areas—Politics and government.
2. Underdeveloped areas—Economic policy. 3. Public
administration. 4. Economic development. I. Title.
JF60.G36   350'.0009172'4   79-3966
ISBN 0-299-07980-5